LINKAGE POLITICS

PUBLISHED FOR THE

PRINCETON CENTER OF INTERNATIONAL STUDIES

A list of Center Publications appears at the back of the book

LINKAGE
POLITICS

Essays on the Convergence of National and International Systems

Edited by
James N. Rosenau

The Free Press, New York
Collier-Macmillan Limited, London

ACKNOWLEDGMENTS

THESE essays have passed through several stages of development. They were originally conceived by the authors at a two-day conference in January, 1966, sponsored by the Center of International Studies of Princeton University. The initial drafts resulting from these deliberations were then presented at the Annual Meeting of the American Political Science Association held in New York City in September, 1966.

Subsequently, using the criticisms and suggestions received at the New York Meeting, all the essays were substantially revised and, in several instances, entirely rewritten for publication in this volume.

At each of these stages the Center of International Studies provided facilities and support that helped greatly to sustain the momentum of the project and we are thus pleased to record our gratitude to its Director, Klaus Knorr, and its secretarial staff. In addition, the advice and support of Norah Rosenau eased the editor's task at every stage of the project. Neither she nor the Center, however, are responsible for the contents of the essays or the way in which we have sought to meet the challenge of exploring heretofore unexplored areas of the political universe. The authors and editor happily admit to their adventuresomeness and accept full responsibility for its consequences.

JAMES N. ROSENAU

New Brunswick, New Jersey
November 22, 1967

v

CONTRIBUTORS

R. V. BURKS, born in Duluth, Minnesota, 1913, is Professor of History at Wayne State University and serves as consultant to the RAND Corporation and the Institute for Defense Analyses. From 1961 to 1965 he was Policy Director with Radio Free Europe in Munich. He is the author of *The Dynamics of Communism in Eastern Europe* and editor of *The Future of Communism in Europe*.

DOUGLAS A. CHALMERS, born in Madison, Wisconsin, 1932, is presently Associate Professor of Government at Columbia University in the Department of Public Law and Government and the Institute of Latin American Studies. He taught at Rutgers University before going to Columbia. His writings include *The Social Democratic Party of Germany*, and some papers on Latin American politics.

BERNARD C. COHEN, born in Northampton, Massachusetts, 1926, is Professor of Political Science at the University of Wisconsin, Madison, and Chairman of the Department of Political Science. He has also served as a Research Associate at the Center of International Studies, Princeton University, has been a Fellow at the Center for Advanced Study in the Behavioral Sciences at Stanford, California, and a Visiting Research Scholar at the Carnegie Endowment for International Peace. He is the author of *The Political Process and Foreign Policy* and *The Press and Foreign Policy*, and editor of *Foreign Policy in American Government*.

WILLIAM G. FLEMING, born in San Diego, California, 1936, is an Associate Professor of Comparative Politics at New York University. He has served as an associate of the Institute of Commonwealth Studies in the University of London and at the Institute of Social Research at Makerere College, Kampala, Uganda. While teaching at the University of North Carolina he was a member of the Institute for Research in Social Science and was also director of an African Peace Corps Program. He has contributed to various anthologies and scholarly journals, including the *American Political Science Review* and the *Administrative Science Quarterly.*

OLE R. HOLSTI, born in Geneva, Switzerland, 1933, is Associate Professor of Political Science at the University of British Columbia. He has also taught at Stanford. He is author of *Content Analysis in Social and Humanistic Research;* co-author of *Enemies in Politics* and *Content Analysis: A Handbook with Applications for the Study of International Crisis;* and a contributor to the second edition of *The Handbook of Social Psychology.*

ROBERT T. HOLT, born in Caledonia, Minnesota, 1928, is Professor of Political Science and Director of the Center for Comparative Studies in Technological Development and Social Change at the University of Minnesota. He is co-author of *The Political Basis of Economic Development: An Exploration in Comparative Political Analysis* and *Political Parties in Action: The Battle of Barons Court;* and co-editor of *Soviet Union: Paradox and Change.*

LLOYD JENSEN, born at Blackfoot, Idaho, 1936, is Associate Professor of Political Science at the University of Kentucky. He has previously taught at the universities of Michigan and Illinois and at Northwestern University, where he served as Associate Director of the Simulated International Processes Project. His publications include a number of articles on the subject of disarmament and foreign policy.

RICHARD L. MERRITT, born in Portland, Oregon, 1933, is Associate Professor of Political Science and Research and Associate Professor of Communications at the University of Illinois. He also taught at Yale University. He is author of *Symbols of American Community, 1735–1775;* co-author of *France, Germany and the Western Alliance;* co-author and co-editor of *Comparing Nations* and of *Western European Perspectives on International Affairs;* and has contributed numerous articles to scholarly books and journals.

MICHAEL KENT O'LEARY, born in Fresno, California, 1935, is Assistant Professor in the Department of Political Science, Maxwell School of Citizenship and Public Affairs, Syracuse University. He has also taught at

Princeton University and Dartmouth College. He is the co-author of *Congress in Crisis: Politics and Congressional Reform*, and author of *The Politics of American Foreign Aid*. In addition he has contributed to *International Organization in the Western Hemisphere, Congressional Reorganization: Problems and Prospects*, and *European Views of America: Problems of Communication in the Atlantic World*.

JAMES N. ROSENAU, born in Philadelphia, 1924, is Professor of Political Science and Chairman of the New Brunswick Department of Political Science at Rutgers—The State University. He is also Research Associate at Princeton University's Center of International Studies and has taught at Columbia and New York University. He is author of *Public Opinion and Foreign Policy* and *National Leadership and Foreign Policy;* co-author and editor of *International Aspects of Civil Strife* and *Domestic Sources of Foreign Policy;* and editor of *International Politics and Foreign Policy*.

J. DAVID SINGER, born in 1925, is Professor of Political Science at the University of Michigan and is associated with the Mental Health Research Institute and Center for Research on Conflict Resolution there. Among his books are *Human Behavior and International Politics, Quantitative International Politics*, and *International War, 1815-1966: A Statistical Handbook*.

JOHN D. SULLIVAN, born in San Francisco, 1937, is Assistant Professor of Political Science at Yale University. He is a co-author of a forthcoming work entitled *International Alliances: Unity and Disintegration*.

JOHN E. TURNER, born in Amble, England, 1917, is Professor of Political Science at the University of Minnesota. He is co-author of *The New Japan; The Soviet Dictatorship; The Political Basis of Economic Development: An Exploration in Comparative Political Analysis;* and *Political Parties in Action: The Battle of Barons Court*. He is also co-editor of *Soviet Union: Paradox and Change*.

CONTENTS

LINKAGE POLITICS

CHAPTER ONE

Introduction: Political Science in a Shrinking World

James N. Rosenau

STRANGE things seem to be happening on the political landscape. An American President declares he is a Berliner.[1]   A Soviet Premier sees himself as supplying the crucial 200,000 votes that elected the same American President.[2]   The Parliament of New Zealand engages in a heated debate over the characteristics and aspirations of United States citizens.[3]   While the British Labour Party is fractionated by differences over the policies of the United States as well as those of the United Kingdom, Yugoslavia's only political party, the Communist led Socialist Alliance of Working People, is torn by the role of the CIA in Yugoslavian life.[4]   Soviet authors believe that their freedom to write is highly dependent on the prevailing degree of

---

[1] The declaration was made by John F. Kennedy during his visit to Berlin on June 26, 1963.

[2] In a television interview presented by the National Broadcasting Company on July 12, 1967, former Soviet Premier Nikita Khrushchev reported having told President Kennedy at their Vienna meeting about the strategy the Kremlin followed in order to supply the margin of victory over Richard Nixon in the 1960 election.

[3] *The New York Times*, October 8, 1967.

[4] *The New York Times*, October 5 and November 1, 1967.

international tension.[5] The United States Secretary of State appoints a Special Assistant for Liaison with the Governors and gives him responsibility for "presenting their (the Governors') views in connection with . . . the many problems they have in their states as related to other nations."[6]

Events such as these may seem unusual in a world of sovereign states, but their frequency seems to be mounting. Almost every day incidents are reported that defy the principles of sovereignty. Politics everywhere, it would seem, are related to politics everywhere else. Where the functioning of any political unit was once sustained by structures within its boundaries, now the roots of its political life can be traced to remote corners of the globe. Modern science and technology have collapsed space and time in the physical world and thereby heightened interdependence in the political world.

Political science, however, has yet to accommodate itself to this shrinking world. Even at the level where the changes appear most pronounced— the functioning of national units—events abroad are still regarded as external to, rather than part of, a nation's politics. To be sure, it has long been recognized that national political systems, like all organized human groups, exist in, are conditioned by, and respond to a larger environment. Nor is it denied that international political systems, like all interdependent groups, are shaped by and are responsive to developments that occur within the units of which they are comprised. Yet these national-international linkages have never been subjected to systematic, sustained, and comparative inquiry. The traditional subdivisions of political science are such that most analysts treat linkages as parameters rather than as data. Students of comparative politics tend to take the international environment for granted, as if national systems were immune to external influences and had full control over their own destinies. Similarly, students of international politics tend to make a series of simplifying assumptions about the international behavior of national systems, as if all such systems reacted in the same way to the same stimuli.

Although it may once have been possible to tolerate these gaps in political analysis, today the division of labor that created them no longer seems sufficient. As technology shrinks the world and heightens the interdependence of nations, linkage phenomena are too plentiful and too influential to be ignored. No society is immune from the stresses and strains of the cold war, from the demands of neighbors and the cross-pressures of hemispheric tendencies, from the shifts of trade and the emergence of supranational organizations, from the surge toward development of the new states and the restructuring of their historic relationships. One can no more comprehend the internal political processes of a Latin American country without accounting for the United States presence (or, more accurately, the multiple United States presences) than one can explain the dynamics of political life in Pakistan or India without reference to the Kashmir issue. Recent events

[5] *The New York Times*, July 9, 1967.
[6] *Department of State Newsletter*, No. 74 (June, 1967), p. 3.

in the Congo, Cyprus, Vietnam, and the Dominican Republic are but extreme examples of a worldwide blurring of the boundaries between national and international systems.

For reasons suggested below, however, the study of politics has not kept pace with this growing interdependence in world politics. To repeat, systematic conceptual exploration of the flow of influence across the changing boundaries of national and international systems has yet to be undertaken and is long overdue. Even the important work of the Social Science Research Council Committee on Comparative Politics is conspicuous by the lack of attention to international variables that contribute to the functioning of national institutions and the development of national polities.[7] Almond's pathbreaking outline, "A Functional Approach to Comparative Politics," does not give any consideration to the impact of external variables[8] and while his refined model presented a decade later acknowledges the relevance of such variables, the latter are not actually made part of the model.[9] Likewise, the more empirical work of other Committee members has been subjected to the same criticism. Although praising much of Weiner's work on India and Binder's on Iran, for example, one reviewer notes that "what happens in India or Iran is no longer intelligible in terms of parochial Indian or Iranian events and forces, but must be seen as part of a world transformation in which these particular pockets of semi-autonomy are working out their distinctive yet somehow parallel destinies."[10]

THE NEED FOR LINKAGE THEORY

This is not to say, of course, that national-international linkages have never been probed by researchers. Political scientists do not deny or ignore the existence of complex linkages between national and international systems. Their numerous inquiries into the sources and wisdom of the foreign policies of national systems reflect a widespread sensitivity to such phenomena, as does the vast literature on colonialism and most of the work on

[7] The major works of the Social Science Research Council Committee on Comparative Politics include the following: Gabriel A. Almond and James S. Coleman (eds.), *The Politics of the Developing Areas* (Princeton: Princeton U.P., 1960); Lucian W. Pye (ed.), *Communication and Political Development* (Princeton: Princeton U.P., 1963); Joseph LaPalombara (ed.), *Bureaucracy and Political Development* (Princeton: Princeton U.P., 1963); Robert E. Ward and Dankwart A. Rustow (eds.), *Political Modernization in Japan and Turkey* (Princeton: Princeton U.P., 1964); James S. Coleman (ed.), *Education and Political Development* (Princeton: Princeton U.P., 1965); Lucian W. Pye and Sidney Verba (eds.), *Political Culture and Political Development* (Princeton: Princeton U.P., 1965); and Joseph LaPalombara and Myron Weiner (eds.), *Political Parties and Political Development* (Princeton: Princeton U.P., 1966).

[8] Almond and Coleman, *op. cit.*, pp. 3–64.

[9] Gabriel A. Almond and G. Bingham Powell, Jr., *Comparative Politics: A Developmental Approach* (Boston: Little, Brown, 1966), pp. 9 and 203–5.

[10] Fred W. Riggs, "The Theory of Developing Polities," *World Politics*, XVI (October, 1963), p. 171.

political movements and revolution. Inquiries into the politics of foreign trade and much of the research into the functioning of international organizations are similarly rich with findings and insights bearing on linkage phenomena.

Despite their abundance, however, the relevant data have never been organized and examined *systematically*. To acknowledge the interdependence of national and international systems is not necessarily to make conceptual allowance for it. To probe linkage phenomena intensively is not necessarily to recognize their theoretical implications. It may no longer be possible to ignore such phenomena, but their abundance does not necessarily stimulate intensive investigation of them. On the contrary, virtually all of the findings and insights bearing on linkage phenomena are derivatives of other concerns, and thus their common content has never been probed and compared.[11] Moreover, being only secondarily interested in the linkages they uncover, most researchers tend to see them as results rather than as bases of the functioning of national and international systems. Such phenomena are treated as outcomes of foreign policy, not as sources of it; as necessary consequences of life in a shrinking world, not as mechanisms for absorbing and coping with complexity. In other words, to the extent that they are dealt with at all, national-international linkages are treated as dependent variables, not as independent ones.[12]

Stated in another way, political science as an intellectual discipline has yet to develop theoretical constructs for explaining the relations between the units it investigates and their environments. Students of national and comparative politics have no equivalent of the theory of the firm in economics or the plant in ecology, theories which consist exclusively of propositions about the external relationships of, respectively, basic human and biological organisms. Nor is there a subfield of political science with a history comparable to that of social psychology, which emerged precisely because neither psychology nor sociology was equipped to explain the interaction

---

[11] A possible exception is the set of inquiries stemming from Hartz's interest in and elaborate conceptualization of the "fragment." Concerned with the residues of European civilization "spawned by Europe throughout the world," the fragment could be regarded as a special form of linkage. Cf. Louis Hartz et al., *The Founding of New Societies: Studies in the History of the United States, Latin American, South Africa, Canada, and Australia* (New York: Harcourt, 1964). Other exceptions can be found scattered throughout the essays of three recent symposia: R. Barry Farrell (ed.), *Approaches to Comparative and International Politics* (Evanston: Northwestern U.P., 1966); Herbert C. Kelman (ed.), *International Behavior: A Socio-Psychological Analysis* (New York: Holt, 1965); and James N. Rosenau (ed.), *International Aspects of Civil Strife* (Princeton: Princeton U.P., 1964). Still other commendable efforts to deal with linkage phenomena systematically can be found in Henry A. Kissinger, "Domestic Structure and Foreign Policy," *Daedalus* (Spring, 1966), pp. 503–29, and Kenneth N. Waltz, *Foreign Policy and Democratic Politics: The American and British Experience* (Boston: Little, Brown, 1967).

[12] For a recent study in which an especially wide variety of linkages are uncovered, quantitatively analyzed, and then treated as dependent variables, see Ernst B. Haas, *Beyond the Nation-State: Functionalism and International Organization* (Stanford: Stanford U.P., 1964).

4

between their respective units of analysis.[13] Rather the political unit is simply assumed to have an environment to which it responds and with which it interacts. Students of foreign policy examine the responses and students of international relations investigate the interactions, but neither group considers how the functioning of the unit itself is conditioned and affected by these responses and interactions. In short, the problem with which we are concerned stems from a shortage of theory, not of empirical materials. What may be needed is the advent of an Einstein who, recognizing the underlying order that national boundaries obscure, will break through them and bring about a restructuring of the study of political processes.[14]

Some concrete examples may help to demonstrate the need for unit-environment theory. Consider the processes whereby the top political leadership of a society acquires and maintains its position of authority. To what extent are these processes dependent on events that unfold abroad? Under what conditions will the stability of cabinets and the tenure of presidents be reduced or otherwise affected by trends in the external environment? Are certain leadership structures more vulnerable to developments in the international system than others? Political theory presently offers no guidance as to how questions such as these might be researched and answered. One is hard pressed to uncover even a tentative hypothesis, much less a coherent set of propositions, that links the authority of national leadership to external variables. When the contribution of such variables to the rise or fall of a particular leader is unmistakable, political scientists are forced to fall back on detailed historical accounts to explain what happened.[15] Within a recent six-month period, for instance, international circumstances plainly contributed to the fall of two national regimes, Ben Bella's in Algeria and Kwame Nkrumah's in Ghana. Yet students of comparative politics and government have nothing better to resort to than explanations based on the clash of personalities and other factors unique to Algeria and Ghana at those particular moments in their histories.

The conflict in Vietnam poses equally unanswerable challenges to presently available conceptual equipment. The situation in that distant

[13] For an elaboration of this analogy to social psychology, see my "Compatibility, Consensus, and an Emerging Political Science of Adaptation," *American Political Science Review*, LXI (December, 1967), pp. 983–8.

[14] For useful discussions, though not resolutions, of the unit-environment problem, see David Easton, *A Framework for Political Analysis* (Englewood Cliffs, N.J.: Prentice-Hall, 1965), Chap. V, and Harold and Margaret Sprout, *The Ecological Perspective on Human Affairs: With Special Reference to International Politics* (Princeton: Princeton U.P., 1965).

[15] For an explicit attempt to trace how the internal political processes of a society paralleled developments in the international system over a century-long period, see J. C. Hurewitz, "Lebanese Democracy in Its International Setting," in Leonard Binder (ed.), *Politics in Lebanon* (New York: Wiley, 1966), and especially the table entitled, "The Growth of Lebanese Democracy and Its Interaction with Changing Regional and International Systems," on pp. 236–7. However, even this highly self-conscious analysis of linkage phenomena did not yield any theoretical propositions that might be applied to other societies.

land is manifestly a part of the American electoral process. Unlike other foreign policy questions of recent memory, during 1966 and 1967 events in Southeast Asia became central to the nomination of candidates for *local* offices and to their campaigns for victory on election day. Why should this be so? To say that Vietnam is an important foreign policy issue begs the question. Such an answer tells us nothing about the dynamics of the electoral process whereby external situations are in effect transformed into issues of domestic policy.[16] Yet again one is hard pressed to discover any theoretical propositions that systematically link the course of events abroad to electoral processes and outcomes at home, for either a specific polity or a general class of polities. No dissertations have been written on "elections and foreign policy."[17] Nor do any of the voting behavior models offer guidance in this respect, and the multitudinous writings on political parties and their organization are even more conspicuously inattentive to linkage phenomena. For all practical purposes the political scientist is no better equipped than the journalist to assess when and how international circumstances become woven into the fabric of electoral life.

Another example of the need for linkage theory is provided by the absence of anything but the crudest tools to explain the rash of *coups d'état* that have occurred in various African countries. The similarity of these events, as well as their proximity to each other in time and place, suggests that linkage processes were at work in each instance. But how to account for them? The most that we seem to be able to say is that "a wave of violence presupposes a degree of transnational political community," that one *coup* triggers another through "the power of example," that insurgents in one country are moved to emulate their counterparts in another when these successfully take over the reins of power.[18] Such lines of reasoning, however, can hardly be regarded as theoretical. They do not tell us when the power of example can be expected to operate and when intervening political processes are likely to prevent the establishment of linkages. They say nothing about the range of institutions in a polity that are susceptible to emulation or the conditions under which susceptibility is maximized.[19]

But waves of *coups* and local electoral processes are only among the

[16] For an attempt to identify those types of foreign policy issues that are indistinguishable from domestic issues insofar as the general operation of political systems is concerned, see my "Foreign Policy as an Issue-Area," in James N. Rosenau (ed.), *Domestic Sources of Foreign Policy* (New York: Free Press, 1967), pp. 11–50.

[17] However, although from the somewhat different perspective of "foreign policy and elections," an initial recognition and exploration of some of these linkages can be found in Theodore Paul Wright, Jr., *American Support of Free Elections Abroad* (Washington, D.C.: Public Affairs Press, 1964).

[18] Samuel P. Huntington, "Patterns of Violence in World Politics," in Samuel P. Huntington (ed.), *Changing Patterns of Military Politics* (New York: Free Press, 1962), pp. 44–47.

[19] For an elaborate study of an earlier wave of upheavals in which myriad linkages are explained (p. 7 of Vol. 1) simply "as one big revolutionary agitation," see R. R. Palmer, *The Age of the Democratic Revolution: A Political History of Europe and America, 1760–1800* (Princeton: Princeton U.P., 1959, 1964).

more obvious instances of linkage phenomena.   Viable theory and sustained investigation would undoubtedly yield equally numerous examples of linkages that are no less critical but much less visible.   The reversal in American policy toward Communist China between the 1950s and the 1960s is a case in point.   It is difficult to explain the shift from intense avoidance to purposeful involvement in terms of conventional theories of national and international politics.   To accept the explanation that the reversal was merely a response to a changing international scene is to overlook the subtle operation of latent linkage processes involving interaction between transformations in the legitimacy attached to certain goals and forms of domestic political action on the one hand and realignments in the structure and functioning of certain international systems on the other.

Nor is our capacity to explain manifest and latent linkages that originate in national and culminate in international systems any greater than our ability to identify and account for those which flow in the opposite direction. Again examples abound.   Consider again the fall of Ben Bella.   The very events in the international system that precipitated it—a pending summit conference of non-Western nations to be held in Algeria—were in turn profoundly affected by his political demise: Not only was the conference never convened, but the stability and decision-making capacities of the emergent non-Western international system was substantially reduced by the fall of the ill-fated sponsor and chief organizer of the ill-fated occasion.   Yet international systems theory provides no basis for anticipating such an outcome. No models are available which attempt to assess the dependence of various types of international systems upon various types of leadership structures within the national systems of which they are comprised.   Indeed, since models of foreign policy behavior that estimate the relative potency of the variables underlying purposeful international behavior have yet to be developed,[20] it is hardly surprising that theories which systematically link national processes to their unintended international consequences are also scarce.

In short, the need for linkage theory is multidimensional.   The examples suggest that political analysis would be greatly facilitated if propositions that link the stability, functioning, institutions, and goals of national political systems to variables in their external environments could be systematically developed.   They also indicate that much would be gained if hypotheses linking the stability, functioning, and organizations of international systems to variables within their national subsystems were available. In addition, the Ben Bella example points up the need to trace linkages in which national and international systems function in such a way as to continuously reinforce each other (what are referred to in Chapter 3 as "fused" linkages).

[20] Cf. James N. Rosenau, "Pre-Theories and Theories of Foreign Policy," in R. Barry Farrell (ed.), *Approaches to Comparative and International Politics*, pp. 27–92.

OBSTACLES TO LINKAGE THEORY

Before turning to the question of what research strategy might best facilitate the generation of systematic propositions pertaining to the structure and operation of linkage phenomena, it is instructive to examine briefly some of the reasons for the present shortage of theory. Perhaps the most basic reason is the lack of communication between those who specialize in comparative and national politics on the one hand and those who focus on international politics on the other. Since the discipline of political science has not developed a unit-environment subfield comprised of linkage specialists, linkage theory will obviously have to be generated by a sharing and integration of perspectives on the part of those in the traditional subfields. Yet the record of communication along these lines is not encouraging. A multitude of barriers, most of them conceptual and few of them historical, appear to intervene. There are no long-standing disputes keeping national and international specialists apart, no record of jurisdictional jealousy and righteous bickering over the proper road to political wisdom. Rather the barriers to effective communication and theory building are to be found in the way each group structures political data. Not only do the boundaries that each draws around the phenomena it regards as relevant tend to be mutually exclusive, but each set of boundaries also tends to encompass different kinds of actors who employ different kinds of methods in order to engage in different kinds of behavior. Consequently, far from being jealous of one another, students of national and international politics are essentially disinterested in each other's research and tend to talk past each other when they get together. They are kept apart not by mutual antagonism, but by reciprocal boredom.[21] Each group is trapped, as it were, in its own conceptual jail and, like all prisoners, its members rarely get a glimpse at the life of those incarcerated elsewhere.

While it may be easier to escape from a conceptual jail than to ameliorate an historical antagonism, the obstacles to communication are formidable and the incentives to avoid them considerable. In the first place, there are good reasons why the jails have been built. Some kind of framework is necessary for analysis and research to proceed, and since national and international politics do differ in crucial respects, it is only logical that the practitioners in each field have developed specialized models and concepts suitable to their particular concerns.

Second, there are equally compelling reasons to remain confined within the boundaries of either field. Each field contains more of its own dis-

---

[21] During several recent instances of professional interaction between the two types of specialists, both groups were observed to have been first perplexed, then dismayed, and finally wearied by the commentary of the other. This lack of communication can be readily discerned in the proceedings of one of these occasions that are reproduced in James N. Rosenau, *Of Boundaries and Bridges: A Report on a Conference on the Interdependencies of National and International Political Systems* (Princeton: Center of International Studies, Research Monograph No. 27, 1967), pp. 11–62.

8

tinctive problems than can be studied in a lifetime of research, and there is thus plenty to do without also worrying about the problems that lie in the area of overlap between the fields. The student of foreign policy has enough difficulty estimating the external impact of a nation's foreign policy without also focusing on the internal functions which it serves. Similarly, the student of comparative politics is amply challenged by the dynamics of political change within a society without also having to account for the role external stimuli play as a source of internal changes.

Third, understandable, though not commendable, resistances to a jail-break arise out of the possibility that the attribution of conceptual relevance to variables from the other fields may diminish the elegance of existing models and require substantial revision in their central concepts. One's own jail is comforting as well as confining. For the student of national politics to concede that domestic processes may be significantly conditioned by foreign affairs is to run the risk of introducing a number of seemingly unpredictable factors into matters that he has become accustomed to taking for granted. Likewise, for the student of international politics to treat national phenomena as variables rather than constants is to invite a seemingly endless confounding of that which has otherwise proven manageable.

Fourth, in view of these considerations it is hardly surprising that both the national and international jails are solid structures indeed. The one housing the students of international politics and foreign policy is founded on the bedrock of the national interest. This concept facilitates the boredom of such students with the functioning of national systems by allowing them to view all foreign policies as being similarly motivated. By regarding every national system as acting to enhance or preserve its basic interests, however these may be defined and from wherever they may come, the foreign policy analyst can focus on the international actions themselves and is relieved of having to treat them as responses to variable internal sources as well as to external stimuli. No less sturdy and protective is the conceptual jail that students of comparative and national politics have built for themselves. Its foundations are solidly encased in the prerogatives of sovereign authority. By viewing national systems as ultimate masters of all that transpires within their borders, students of such systems need not be concerned about variations in the international environment and instead can treat it as an un-differentiated condition that operates equally upon the domestic processes and institutions that interest them.

Last, but most important, even if one should overcome boredom with the other field and conclude that the overlap of the fields can no longer be avoided, there remain the tasks of communication and theory building, of learning to use unfamiliar conceptions of what constitute the units, sources, purposes, consequences, and settings of political activity. Such a task is not easily performed: Where students of comparative politics are accustomed to analyzing the behavior of thousands and millions of actors (voters, party officials, interest groups, elites), their counterparts in the international field

9

are used to only a few hundred or so (nations, foreign secretaries, diplomatic representatives, decision-makers); where specialists in national systems are interested in what large groups of people (the citizenry) do either to each other or to the few (officialdom), international specialists concentrate on what the few (nations) do either to each other or to the many (foreign publics); where those who analyze domestic policy actors get used to behavior that is designed to affect wholesale changes, those who focus on foreign policy actors become adjusted to action that is intended to produce slow and relatively marginal alterations; where students of comparative politics tend to perceive grand policies emanating from the clash of actors, foreign policy analysts are inclined to see the emergence of specific decisions; where researchers into national systems can usually afford to lose interest when policies are formally adopted (since compliance by those thereby affected can normally be assumed), their international colleagues cannot take policy outcomes for granted and must instead engage in calculations as to whether the strategy underlying a proposed course of action is likely to produce desirable responses on the part of those toward whom it is directed; where comparative specialists are thus inclined to analyze causes (why parties succeed or why cabinets fall), international specialists tend to focus on effects (what foreign aid accomplished or what the United Nations can do); where students of domestic policy tend to examine the motives of actors, foreign policy analysts concentrate on their capabilities; where those who investigate national systems become used to presuming that action will unfold in an institutionalized context (legislatures, courts, bureaucracies), those who analyze international systems become attuned to dealing with unfamiliar or unexpected settings for behavior (situations, crises, informal contacts); where specialists in national politics are accustomed to looking for stability in the prevailing attitudes toward authority and political activity, international specialists tend to search for it in the prevailing patterns of interaction; and so on through all the many variables that conventionally distinguish the national and international fields from each other.

In sum, the obstacles to theory building require a radical revision of the standard conception of politics that posits a world of national and international actors whose interrelationships look like this:

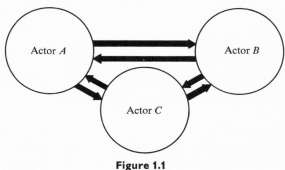

Figure 1.1

Linkage theory requires supplementing this conventional conception with one that looks like this:

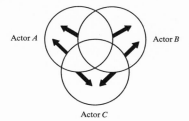

Figure 1.2

or even this:

Figure 1.3

A STEP TOWARD LINKAGE THEORY

Clearly, given their range and depth, the obstacles to linkage theory cannot be easily or quickly surmounted. The development of new conceptual models and a reorientation of long-standing habits of analysis are bound to take a lot of time. Such a lengthy process, moreover, seems unlikely to evolve on its own. It needs to be initiated. The conceptual jails are too solidly built for an unplanned emergence of linkage theory to occur. The problem must be confronted directly and self-consciously. The difficulties inherent in identifying and tracing linkage phenomena need to be experienced and the task of accounting for them theoretically needs to be attempted if new analytic habits are to form and flourish.

The ensuing essays are the consequence of an effort to initiate such a process. They are a first step toward a jailbreak—not an accidental step, but a purposeful one that was taken after two days of discussion among the authors. These deliberations, held in Princeton, New Jersey, in January, 1966, resulted in an agreement that certain aspects of the linkage framework presented in Chapter 3 would serve as the basis for all the subsequent chapters. Each author agreed to compare the linkages sustained by at least two polities that had one major characteristic in common. Thus each essay in Part II contrasts the linkages of polities in the same region, while those in Parts III, IV, and V contrast, respectively, polities that occupy comparable roles in the international system, that exist under similar geographic conditions, and that have transitional structures of authority. Within this context, it was further agreed that the analysis would concentrate on those

11

processes and variables that linked the social background, socialization, techniques, and structure of the "top leadership" in the compared polities to the several aspects of the international system that were explicitly identified in the original linkage framework.[22] Finally, in order to facilitate a common perspective, it seemed appropriate to supplement the original framework with a general analysis of the actors that comprise the international system and the problems that the structure of the system thereby poses for the investigation of national-international linkages. Professor Singer agreed to take on this assignment and his provocative essay on system-subsystem relations is presented in Chapter 2. Beyond these minimal attempts to achieve coherence and comparability, each author was left free to examine any other linkage phenomena that aroused his interest and to do so in any way that seemed consistent with the data available.

In short, the two days of discussion resulted in both a commitment to and an implementation of the assumptions set forth in the original memorandum used to organize the deliberations:

1. that our initial effort to clarify the overlap between national and international systems cannot be the definitive effort and that therefore we should set realistic goals for ourselves, aiming to achieve a volume that is pervaded with selective data, stimulating impressions, and theoretical propositions rather than comprehensive coverage, tested hypotheses, and rigorous models;

2. that it is realistic to aim at essays which will be founded on an analysis of types of polities and will thus be marked by frequent comparisons (even if the result is a frequent notation of differences rather than similarities);

3. that it is realistic to aim at essays that are addressed to at least a few common questions or concerns.

The reader must of course judge for himself whether these initial assumptions proved to be sound. The Editor is satisfied that they did—that the ensuing pages are full of rich insights and intriguing findings that have not been previously available. If, as noted in the ensuing section, our research strategy was not entirely successful, neither did it fail to yield an impressive array of new data and challenging propositions. Some conceptual jails have given way and the collective impact of these essays will make it difficult to return to the comfortable confines of the traditional comparative and international cells. To be sure, one tends to find what one looks for and the reader may thus conclude that we were bound to uncover linkage phenomena and, in so doing, to exaggerate their importance in both national and international processes. A close reading of the essays, however, will reveal that such phenomena are very near the surface of the

---

[22] See the columns in Table 3.2.

political world and that it did not take much digging to uncover them.

Perhaps the most clearcut set of insights and findings concerns the positions of leadership located at the nexus of national and international systems. In virtually every chapter it becomes clear that the occupants of high office in national systems also occupy key roles in the international system and that the way in which these dual responsibilities are balanced serves both to link the polity to its environment and to delineate the boundaries between them. Although a consistent pattern as to how these "linkage elites" or "dual politicians," as they might be called, resolve the conflicts that arise between their systemic and subsystemic roles does not emerge, the fact of such conflicts is unmistakable and so is the fact that their mode of resolution is importantly determined by the nature of the recruitment and socialization of such officials. Stated differently, the essays collectively suggest additional questions about the role of leadership that can fruitfully be subjected to further research: What are the costs linkage elites pay within their national roles for continued attention to and performance of the demands of their international roles? What are the domestic rewards for such behavior? Is there a growing trend toward prior experience in the international system being a prerequisite to elite advancement in the national system? Are increasing numbers of organizations (business, labor, and educational as well as governmental) establishing positions to handle linkages? Does instability in the international system jeopardize dual politicians in the national system? Are linkage elites bound to be more vulnerable than their nonlinkage counterparts? Are the attitudes of the former toward advancement, other elites, system goals, and so on, likely to be significantly different from those of the latter?

Another interesting set of findings concerns the aspects of the international system with which polities become linked. Here the findings are marked by disparity. While Cohen and Merritt, for example, conclude that the contiguous or regional environments of certain kinds of polities are fertile soil for the establishment and maintenance of linkages, Chalmers finds that quite the opposite is the case for Latin American polities, that domestic politics in the various countries of that continent is sustained less by contiguous or regional stimuli and more by those generated by conflicts among the great powers. Jensen comes to still another conclusion when he observes that contiguous and regional linkages are likely to become increasingly relevant as polities that emerge from defeats in war are reconstructed and recover their domestic authority.

That linkage patterns can be highly dynamic and susceptible to rapid, if not radical, change is also evident in several essays. Both Burks and Chalmers uncovered "eras" in the linkage patterns established, respectively, by Communist and Latin American polities. In the former case the transformation from one linkage era to another was stimulated by changes within a single polity (the Soviet Union), whereas in the latter case the transformation arose out of changes that occurred in the international system. The

Holt-Turner chapter carries the analysis of dynamic factors even further by suggesting that linkage elites can and do make conscious choices among various linkage strategies and that these choices can be and are altered in response to long-term trends both at home and abroad. Although placing less emphasis on the role of conscious choice, O'Leary reaches a similar conclusion through his argument that the underdeveloped polities of the world are led by their linkage patterns to seek a radical revision in the structure of international order.

Still another substantive insight worthy of further inquiry is the important role linkages can play as sources of issues within both national and international systems. Their relevance as issue-makers for national systems is especially clear in Chalmers' discussion of the saliency that can attach to linkage problems in Latin American polities. In a like manner O'Leary's analysis of the orientation of underdeveloped polities toward international organizations suggests the considerable extent to which linkages can serve as issue-makers in international systems. In addition, and perhaps of even greater importance, several chapters present some highly suggestive materials that posit linkages as operating differently in different issue areas. The Holsti-Sullivan chapter is particularly impressive in this respect. Their empirical data plainly show how political systems can differ in the degree to which linkage phenomena are narrowly confined within certain issue areas or spread across a wide range of areas.

Nor are substantive insights and findings the only benefits that have derived from our jailbreak. An unexpected degree of methodological innovation can also be discerned throughout the essays. Not only will the reader find both interesting uses of conventional historical materials and unique types of quantitative data, but in several chapters—particularly the one by Holt and Turner—he will also be impressed by the stimulating way in which the two kinds of data have been combined. It is almost as if the experience of examining a fresh subject can free a researcher to come upon fresh combinations of research techniques. For the same reason it is perhaps more than mere coincidence that three of these essays—those by Fleming, Holsti and Sullivan, and Holt and Turner—undertake to test explicit hypotheses and that several others do so in a less formal fashion. Such rigorous procedures are not characteristic of political research and certainly their use was not required by the agreement that emerged from our initial deliberations. Yet a linkage focus somehow appears to have encouraged the predisposition to formulate propositions before examining the data.

This is not to say, of course, that linkage phenomena are particularly easy to research. On the contrary, by definition they involve subtle processes of influence that can be extremely difficult to trace and measure. Even as the essays are methodologically innovative, so are they filled with caveats as to the limits beyond which their data are not applicable. At key points in many of the essays, in fact, the authors were unable to gather reliable data relevant to their concerns and had to rely on unverified impressions about the operation and consequences of linkage processes. Notwithstanding all the substantive and methodological problems posed by linkage phenomena, however, the nine empirical chapters certainly indicate that they can be probed and that further efforts to comprehend them will more than justify the time and energy required.[23]

THE CONTINUING NEED FOR LINKAGE THEORY

Yet it cannot be said that our research strategy was entirely successful. It is a measure of the conceptual challenge posed by linkage phenomena that these essays, taken together, do not achieve the degree of comparability to which we aspired at the outset. Despite the shared commitment to examine certain basic linkages in the same analytic framework, the essays are marked as much by variability as by similarity. The original linkage framework presented in Chapter 3 does infuse the chapters that follow with common dimensions, but comparisons across these nine empirical chapters are difficult to make. They vary in the extent to which they adhere to the original assignment and consider the links between leadership attributes and international system variables. The essays by Burks, Cohen, Holsti and Sullivan, and Holt and Turner closely follow the initial format, whereas the others rely to a much lesser extent upon it. In addition, as previously implied, there are extensive differences in the kinds of data that the authors developed in order to trace and compare linkage phenomena. Most of the authors were able to employ some quantitative materials as a basis for assessing the strength of either the different linkages maintained by one polity or the same linkages maintained by different polities. On the other hand, partly because of the inaccessibility of appropriate quantitative materials and partly because of the kinds of questions to which they address themselves, Burks, Chalmers, Cohen, and Merritt developed their interpretations on the basis of relatively few cases.

But let not the contributors be faulted for the lack of comparability. They were not unwilling to break out of their conceptual jails and their essays plainly reveal that open and creative minds were at work. Rather it seems clear in retrospect that the fault lies with the research strategy followed by the editor. Jailbreaks require more than simply identifying the points at which escape may be possible. To know where the exits are is not to know how to negotiate them. Those who plot successful jailbreaks must outline each of the steps to be taken before the prison walls are cleared and must account for all eventualities. Once the walls are cleared, moreover, the plot must provide instructions as to how to proceed in order to

---

[23] For a similar assessment of the utility of this effort, see Lucian Pye, "The Formation of New States," in Ithiel de Sola Pool (ed.), *Contemporary Political Science: Toward Empirical Theory* (New York: McGraw-Hill, 1967), p. 202.

15

avoid an early reincarceration.   The editor's original linkage framework did not provide this kind of detailed guidance.   A matrix of 144 cells was constructed to indicate the points at which national-international linkages might be found,[24] but only a few vague clues were offered as to the phenomena the investigator could expect to find in each cell and as to how he should proceed upon having uncovered them.   That is, the linkage framework presented in Chapter 3 contains no hypotheses and no theory.   It is merely a typology.   It was reasoned at the time that linkage phenomena were too unfamiliar and too extensive for anything beyond a typological approach to be justified as a first step.   The 144-cell matrix is staggering in its scope and the editor felt that his talents and training were in no way sufficient to the task of rendering it theoretical.   Indeed, it seemed doubtful whether any individual could bring to bear the competence necessary to formulate a coherent theory for all the types of linkages identified in the framework. Accordingly, it appeared preferable to adopt a strategy of identifying a wide range of points at which national and international political systems may be linked.   Accompanying this choice was the hope that not only would each user of the typology find some aspect of it sufficiently intriguing to add theoretical and empirical flesh to the typological skeleton, but also that it would then be possible to compare and integrate the individual elaborations of the framework and thereby lay the foundation for a viable and comprehensive linkage theory.

The limitations of such a strategy now seem clear.   To believe that unelaborated categories will lead to precise comparison is to be misled by the apparent tidiness of a typology.   Cooperative and committed as they may be, researchers need more than a broad matrix and a common focus if they are to coordinate their efforts and produce a highly integrated volume. Viewed in this way—and with the advantages of hindsight—it is hardly surprising that the ensuing chapters are marked by variability.

Equally clear are the outlines of another strategy that could have been pursued and that might have yielded more comparability.   If some predictions about the phenomena embraced by each cell of the matrix had been hazarded, those using it would have at least had some guidance as to the kinds of questions to explore and the kinds of data to gather.   Comparisons might have then revealed that the predictions were erroneous or farfetched, but at least extensive analysis would have been undertaken and a clearer picture thereby obtained of the conditions under which linkage processes are inoperative.   Bad theory, in other words, would have been better than no theory—both as a means of achieving coordinated effort and as a way of extending comprehension.

Of course, self-criticism as to how the jailbreak might have been negotiated more successfully is only possible from a vantage point beyond the prison walls.   For, to repeat, initial steps toward an escape were taken and

---

[24] See Table 3.2.

the pages that follow are pervaded with insights into linkage processes. Notwithstanding the regret over what might have been achieved, the nine empirical chapters are full of findings that stimulate thought and press for further inquiry. Hopefully these will move the reader to join in the task of constructing a coherent body of linkage theory, the testing of which will expand and refine our understanding of the linkages between national and international political systems.

Part I

The Confluence of Systems

CHAPTER TWO

The Global System and its Sub-Systems:
*A Developmental View**

J. David Singer

WHEN someone looks at a complex visual scene, there is little certainty that he will see the same configuration in the scene as do others. In "op art," color-blindness test charts, aerial photographs, TAT cards, and Rorschach blots, a wide variety of patterns and configurations will be discerned, depending on such disparate variables as age, sex, education, culture, physical stamina, mental well-being, political ideology, and the like. Certain cues are salient for some and virtually nonexistent for others. The same holds true not only for auditory "scenes" in which one listener's signal is another man's "noise," but in purely conceptual scenes as well. This tendency is equally strong in the perception of complex biological, physical, geographical, and societal scenes. Among the societal, few are more complex than those which confront the students of world politics.

The problem in our case is not only to discern the most relevant social

* Thanks are due to James N. Rosenau, who inspired the general effort of which this is only a part, to the others who participated in the planning conference at Princeton, and to Bruce M. Russett and Karl W. Deutsch, both of whom read and commented on an earlier draft.

entities (be they largely tangible or essentially constructs of the imagination) but to sort out the relations and interactions which allegedly occur among them. I think it can safely be said that any systematic effort to begin this sorting out is fairly recent, and the explicit efforts to do this via a focus on the national-international linkage is more recent still. On the basis of the two most concerted efforts in this direction—the Northwestern conference of 1964 culminating in the Farrell volume (1966) and the Princeton and New York conferences of 1966 culminating in the present series of papers—it seems clear that we have made important strides toward increasing our signal-to-noise ratio. Therefore, it might seem a sound research strategy to continue along this route, hoping to work out a conceptual framework of increasing clarity, and a set of linkages which are increasingly meaningful and operational.

Despite this present and projected advance—and perhaps even because of it—I should like to propose here a modestly revisionist point of view. While it is to some extent an extension of, and supplement to, the formulation which focuses on the international system and its regional and national sub-systems, it is a formulation which does tend to muddy the conceptual waters and blur some of the clarity which is only now emerging.[1] My defense is simple. Any theoretical formulation intended to help describe and explain the phenomena which occur in a given social system must do more than permit an accurate cross-sectional analysis of a small slice of time in the system's evolution. Rather, it must make possible, and encourage, an analysis which takes account of a time span far enough back in the system's life to help explain the present state of the system. Moreover, the formulation must also help to predict future and as yet unobserved states of the system under investigation.

If these guidelines seem reasonable, it follows that our formulation must not concentrate too heavily on those social entities whose empirical referents exist as central actors for only a part of the time span under consideration. Such entities certainly must not be ignored—but they must not be permitted to overshadow those other groupings which, at one stage or another in the system's evolution, played an equal or superior role.[2] My contention here, therefore, is that the national state is—in most theoretical formulations—assigned too prominent a role, and that competing entities must be more heavily emphasized than has been customary.

[1] A system exists largely in the eye of the beholder; examining a cluster of individuals and/or groups, and discerning certain regularities and patterns of interaction among them, the researcher may legitimately label as a system that which he observes. In the terminology used here, then, "the global system" is composed of national, subnational, and extranational social entities, most of which are to some extent interdependent, and all of which operate within the common larger environment. Several alternative formulations are found in Alger (1963), Masters (1964), Parsons (1961a), Russett (1963), and Sondermann (1961). [Full bibliographical information for works cited is given under *References* at the end of this chapter.—Ed.]

[2] Evolution is used here only in the descriptive sense, and no teleological or explanatory implication is intended.

This is not the appropriate place to go into a detailed defense of this contention, but the relative potency of the national state vis-à-vis other actors at various points in time seems to be a researchable question, and I would hope that a serious empirical examination of it will not be too long in coming.[3] Let me move, therefore, to the matter at hand, noting only that as long as we use paradigms which assign a dominant (or occasionally exclusive) role to one class of social organization, we will never know how critical other, and alternative, actors may be—or have been—in world politics.

SUB-SYSTEM CLASSES IDENTIFIED

Having urged the need for the explicit inclusion of a variety of sub- (or intra-) and extra-national entities alongside of the nation itself, let me now turn to a specification of such entities, or more accurately, a specification of certain classes of them. A developmental model of world politics, then, might well include the following.

Intra-National Entities

First there are the two major types of primary group, the family and the face-to-face work group. While not important actors in industrial societies and while only a very few families are direct actors even in traditional societies, the family plays a critical *in*direct role in world politics, first as a socializing agency, and second as a mediating, "reality-testing" agency for its members (E. Katz, 1957). And in the more traditional societies, if we think of the extended kinship system or family, and the tribal form it may take in Africa for example, it is clear that this social group *can* play a more direct and important role in world politics. The face-to-face work group, likewise, may often play a critical role in the diffusion and legitimation of ideas, especially in those societies for which the family is not an important source of social norms and expectations.

At the secondary association (and more important) level, there are two sub-classes which, though conceptually distinguishable, may often be far from mutually exclusive in reality: governmental and non-governmental. Among the latter are such entities as trade unions, industrial-commercial associations, banking and investment institutions, professional societies, avocational groups, ethnic, ideological, and religious organizations, separatist movements, and finally, political parties. That these groups can not always

---

[3] In an earlier draft, I sketched in just enough "evidence" to confuse the issue, and in attempting this revision I assembled a fair amount of conflicting data on trade, industrial organization, tourism, communications, public opinion, and related indicators; see, for example, Deutsch and Eckstein (1961), Haas (1964), and Russett et al. (1964). But it became increasingly evident that the resulting digression would be long enough to deflect the reader, but too short to edify him. Quite relevant here is the prescient article on "The Rise and Demise of the Territorial State," published a decade ago (Herz, 1957).

be classified as non-governmental is obvious, especially if we bear in mind that parties for example, on assuming office, often become virtually indistinguishable from "the government" and that any of the others may often operate as pressure groups, which in turn easily become part of those coalitions which generally form the basis of political parties.

On the *governmental* side—at local, provincial, and national levels—there is always some type of "representative" body, normally acting on behalf of territorial and/or functional groupings, some of which are noted in the previous paragraph. Within the government proper or what we call the executive or administrative branch—and which often includes members of the representative branch—there are the fairly standard ministries or agencies. Those most immediately germane to world politics are of course the defense ministry and the foreign ministry, but for many theoretical purposes we cannot ignore such others as interior or internal security, trade or commerce, information or education, power or atomic energy, and the like.

The mere itemization of these secondary, sub-national associations shows the difficulty of any consistently clearcut set of distinctions that could be expected to hold over extended domains in time or space. That, of course, is much less critical to our enterprise here than the fact that many such secondary associations play key roles in world politics. In some nations, they work primarily as members of coalitions which legitimize and/or control the governmental agencies officially responsible for foreign policy. In others, they may often bypass the formal agencies and act in a variety of direct roles vis-à-vis foreign governments or vis-à-vis their opposite numbers within other national societies.

Here, of course, is the salient point in this formulation. If we think of nations as very complex and often unstable social coalitions, in which the formal leadership may not always exercise effective control over the coalition members, it becomes reasonable to expect that a fair amount of world political interaction will take place directly between and among intranational associations other than foreign ministries, or any official agencies at all for that matter.[4] In fact, this was precisely the case for much of Europe between the Middle Ages and the German and Italian unifications, and remains true not only for the developing nations today but for those modern mobilized ones which seem at first blush to have an effective monopoly on the information and energy sources essential to the formulation and execution of foreign policy.[5]

---

[4] Needless to say, my view is that interaction need not involve governmental agencies directly in order to be political. Nor do I consider it useful or necessary to define the boundaries among social, economic, or political phenomena; whereas Parsons (1961b, pp. 34–35) and others make much of the distinction among society, economy, and polity, my view is that the distinction is artificial and misleading. The trend toward a more unified social science can be accelerated by a somewhat greater overlap at the boundaries of the various disciplines (including, of course, history).

[5] Among some recent illustrations are: Donovan's negotiations with the USSR over the exchange of Powers and Pryor for Colonel Abel, his tractors-for-prisoners

Before shifting our focus from intra- to extra-national sub-systems, two important aspects of the former class should be noted. First, they are not necessarily territorial in nature, even when membership appears to be regionally defined. On the governmental side, non-territorial criteria are likely to be quite critical in the selection of the executive members, and legislators are often quite free to "carpet bag" from one region or district to another. On the non-governmental side, even though memberships are often based on territorial districts, the "delegates" often tend to be only moderately responsive to their home constituencies. A second impression worth noting here is the fact that these intra-national entities need not be legitimate in the eyes of (those who control) the nation or other intra-national entities. Illegitimate entities ranging from discussion groups to armed insurgents must certainly be included. Furthermore, such entities are equally, if not more, likely to have extra-national linkages.[6] Moreover, the criteria for inclusion in such entities may be quite complex and unorthodox, as, for example, the recently created association of Negroes who hold elected office at all levels of government in the United States.

Extra-National Entities

More important than the exhaustiveness or the mutual exclusiveness of our typology of intra-national (or sub-national) actors is the general nature of the relations and interactions which develop among them. In addition to the *domestic* coalitions they form in order to influence the official diplomacy of their own nation, they manifest two other kinds of linkage. First, there is the informal (and often tacit) linkage pattern *across* national boundaries. In this case, an intra-national entity (such as a group of educators or religious leaders) may privately or publicly appeal to opposite numbers in another nation to press their own government to adopt a specific foreign policy position. Or, less directly still, an association of manufacturers in nation A may be able to reward a labor union in B by cutting back their exports of a given item to B—thus increasing the union's job opportunities due to increased demand for the domestically produced item; in exchange, that union's leadership might press its government to give A's government more of a "free hand" to exploit the markets or raw materials in a third nation or region. In the noncooperative category (to take a recent example) the

---

dealings with Castro, the role of Union Minière in Katangan diplomacy, and the many cases of intelligence agencies subverting or replacing diplomatic missions abroad, the private trade and cultural delegations which deal with opposite numbers or others' foreign ministries. In some of these cases, of course, it is not so much a matter of government *inability* to control such activities as it is a matter of reluctance to do so.

The complementary aspect of this problem is dealt with in an insightful way in Scott (1965); his "informal penetration" deals with the intentional efforts of one national government to bypass the official agencies of another government.

[6] Two recent anthologies which shed considerable light on the intra-extra-national linkages of insurgency and revolution are Eckstein (1964) and Rosenau (1964).

media in nation F might publicly praise the domestic opponents of adversary nation G's policy, with a resultant weakening of the prestige of that opposition; this "kiss of death" effect then strengthens those entities in G who advocate policies even more hostile to F, which may or may not have been the original intent.

Equally interdependent, more symbiotic, but less overt is the extent to which the armed forces of one nation impinge on and link up with the "military-industrial" complex of another. If, for example, a sector in the latter group in nation J has been advocating the acquisition of a given new weapon system (such as the ABM) with little success, and then the defense ministry in K announces an increase in its number of offensive missiles, the task of the intra-national group in J is considerably eased. And if such information about K's capability can be generated by "usually reliable sources" or intelligence agencies in nations "friendly" to J, it may not even be necessary that K actually make such a decision. Such permutations and combinations of direct and indirect participation of intra-national groups in world politics could be spun out indefinitely, but the point should now be clear: A large number of informal associations and coalitions of an extra-national nature have always operated in world politics and every indication is that their number and potency is on the rise. And while the importance of these extra-national non-governmental associations of the less formal variety—especially those concerned with trade and investment—has not gone unnoticed (Feis, 1966), we really have little hard evidence regarding their size, scope, efficacy, and prospects.

On the more formal side, intra-national entities will often band to-together in extra-national associations of an increasing number and variety. Embracing groups from stamp collectors to political parties, such non-governmental organizations grew from about twenty-two in 1900 to approximately three hundred in 1954.[7] Many more can be expected to form in the future, embracing such sub-national groups as French-speaking citizens in Canada, Switzerland, and Gabon, or opponents of the supersonic transport plane in the USSR, France, and the United States.

National States

To this point, I have urged with some vigor that the nation be relegated to a more modest role in any theory-building activity, but it is now time to retreat slightly and recognize that this form of social organization displays an impressive degree of staying power. That is, even as the alleged trend toward the demise of the territorial state sets in during this century, the countervailing trend is definitely still with us, no matter how erratic the fluctuations in its strength. To put it another way, national govern-

---

[7] Some basic historical data (albeit incomplete and often inaccurate) are in Union of International Associations (1957) and a more up-to-date and detailed analysis of these trends is in Angell (1965).

ments remain the most important mediating agency between individuals at home and others abroad. This recognition is, of course, implicit in my use of the intra- and extra-national labels. Let me return, then, to the more traditional point of view now and try to examine the various forms that national, inter-governmental associations might take. The two basic classes are the coalition and the organization, but there is a third type of inter-nation association, which is more a natural clustering than an intended institution. Reference is to those groups or sub-systems of nations which manifest strong similarities in attributes or behavior or which turn out to be highly interdependent, and while such groups often tend to institutionalize these similarities and common interests, such association is not inevitable.[8]

Inter-Nation Coalitions

The most ancient and well-established form of inter-nation coalition is the military alliance, based on written or tacit agreements and embracing a limited range of more or less reciprocal commitments. An arrangement by which national governments seek to protect a flank, neutralize a potential ally of one's enemy, deter a revisionist power, compensate for an inadequate domestic power base, or increase the probability of military victory, the formal or informal alliance continues to serve useful short-run purposes. More binding[9]—if not more effective—than is often asserted, the more formal coalition or written alliance has been subjected to considerable scrutiny by historians and political scientists, yet its effect upon the total system—and vice versa—still remains one of our more perplexing theoretical issues.[10]

The military alliance, however, is only one of the forms which an inter-nation coalition may take. Among others which come under this rubric, while falling short of what we normally think of as IGOs (inter-governmental organizations), are such general political associations as the Arab League, Western Union, British Commonwealth, Comintern, and the Organization of African Unity. Somewhat closer to this latter group than

---

[8] The most comprehensive empirical analysis to date, showing the extent to which nations cluster together on such criteria, is Russett (1967).

[9] In a quantitative analysis of written alliances from 1815 to 1939 we found a strong difference between the war performance of allies and of all nations in general. Whereas the "expected" probability of fighting alongside another nation was .05, of remaining neutral was .91, and of fighting against him was .04, formal allies fought alongside in 23 per cent of the opportunities, remained neutral only 74 per cent of the time, and turned against the ally only 3 per cent of the time. When the allies had a more specific defense pact, they fought alongside 33 per cent of the time, and when they had a neutrality pact, they did indeed remain neutral 93 per cent of the time (Singer and Small, 1966a, pp. 16–19).

[10] Among the more recent papers with such a theoretical focus are Waltz (1964), Deutsch and Singer (1964), and Rosecrance (1966); some statistical measures of the short-run effect of formal alliances on the frequency, severity, and magnitude of war are found in Singer and Small, 1966b and 1968a, and a thoughtful critique of the latter is in Zinnes (1967).

27

to the simple alliance would be an alliance which has experienced an accretion of functions and acquired some sort of permanent bureaucracy; NATO is perhaps the classic contemporary case.

Inter-Nation Organizations

Although some scholars and many practitioners tend to minimize the difference between coalitions or alliances on the one hand, and inter-governmental organizations on the other, the distinction seems well worth preserving. Admittedly, the motives behind both are often similar, and the degree of formal institutionalization today is sometimes not very different, but certain fundamental distinctions remain evident.

Clearly, the alliance tends to (a) embrace a smaller territorial area or number of member governments; (b) focus on a set of contingencies which is more restricted and recognizable; (c) make most decisions by unanimity, with every member holding a veto of some credibility; and (d) have a shorter life-span in practice as well as intent.[11]

Inter-governmental organizations, then, may be said to differ appreciably from what we have labelled here as coalitions. But they also differ among themselves, with two basic types being predominant. The first type tends to be quasi-global in membership, explicitly responsive to the legal doctrine of sovereign equality, indefinite in expected longevity, and perhaps most important, not directed against any specific nation or group of nations; the League, the UN, and most of the Specialized Agencies typify this class. The second type tends to be considerably more supra-national in the sense that the veto is more informally utilized (if at all) and is more reflective of the would-be user's relative power, the membership is more restricted, and some degree of incompatibility between members and non-members is assumed, no matter how implicitly; most customs unions and economic communities would fall into this class, with EFTA, EEC, and Euratom serving as contemporary illustrations.

Within these two types of IGO, we may of course find sub-system coalitions of the partial membership. Other sub-systems in these organizations also exist, particularly in the secretariats and the bureaus and divisions therein. Occasionally, coalitions between national delegations and secretariat groups are formed, and with perhaps less frequency, such secretariat groups find themselves coalescing with intra-national entities (non-governmental, such as pro-disarmament pressure groups, or governmental, such as an intelligence agency) concerned with a specific policy problem.

[11] Whereas the League endured for 19 "effective" years, the UN and most of its specialized agencies for 23 so far, the ILO for 49 already, the UPU for 94, and the ITU for 103, the 112 formal alliances entered into by members of the international system between 1815 and 1939 lasted an average of only 7.7 years, with defense pacts running for an average of 9.8 years, neutrality pacts for 6.6 years, and ententes just 6 (Singer and Small, 1966a). Since 1693, one source estimates that there have been approximately 178 IGOs founded, of which 132 still existed in 1954 (Union of International Associations, 1957).

National Environments

Two additional sub-systems to be considered are those specified by Rosenau in Chapter 3. Highly territorial in nature, and serving as spatial milieux for the nations are the contiguous and the regional environments. There are as many of each such nesting environment as one's theoretical needs of the moment require, with the number depending upon the clusters of nations under investigation. Thus, the most immediate (or *contiguous*) environment may range from the given national borders on out until it blends with the *regional* environment, normally thought of as more or less equivalent to a continental or oceanic region marked not only by certain boundaries of some salience, but by discernible similarities within these boundaries. The dimensions along which we might compare these two types of environment (or sub-systems of the total system) as well as the *great power* environment—which I take to be synonymous with the total system—will be examined in the following section.

An alternative way of looking at regions is to think of them as spatial areas in which the effects of the global system and its many sub-systems upon any specific national or intra-national entities may be examined. The distance out from a nation's boundaries at which its influence matches that of the global system itself might very well mark a line of system-nation equilibrium, within which we find the individual nation's zone of dominance.[12] The outer limits of that zone would vary, depending upon the type of activity (or issue) involved, as well as upon the capacity of the nation to resist or overcome the constraints imposed either by the system or by other nations. For struggling new nations, the line of system-nation equilibrium would tend to be fairly close in, whereas for each of the super-powers, the line would be further out into the global environment. Furthermore, the same scheme could be applied to nation vis-à-vis nation or coalition vis-à-vis coalition, but would not, of course, be applicable to the non-territorial entities discussed above.

One of the virtues of this sort of conceptualization, providing we could devise the measures, is that it would permit us to estimate the extent to which, in Kaplan's phrase (1957) the system remains "sub-system dominant" at any point in time. Moreover, one might use it to ascertain whether the zone of dominance varies markedly for nations which differ on dimensions ranging from recency of independence to ethnic homogeneity, and to see

[12] While semantically and conceptually similar to the "sphere of influence," a different label is used to suggest the possibility of greater precision. As in the more traditional construction, the zone *need* not be contiguous to a nation's borders, providing some territorial (or nautical or aerial) base is available. A closely related concept developed by Boulding (1962) is the national "loss-of-strength gradient"; his point is that when the gradient has a steep slope for most nations, the system is a fairly safe one for many actors and wide competition. But as the gradient extends out great distances without much loss of national strength, "conflict is likely to become more acute, games of ruin ensue, and the number of parties decline until there are few enough parties that can be far enough away from each other to avoid games of ruin. . . ." (p. 79)

whether given classes are experiencing differential rates of expansion or contraction in their zones of dominance.

SYSTEM AND SUB-SYSTEM PROPERTIES

Having specified a range of sub-systems within the global system, the next question is whether we can devise a set of dimensions by which they may, however great their diversity, be compared. My own view is that we can, especially if we eschew—for the moment—any great *explanatory* aspirations, and begin with more modest *descriptive* goals. I certainly do not argue that there is any such thing as a theory-free paradigm, but would urge that we can approximate that condition if we strive for "pure" (some might say "mere") description and pass up the premature temptations of such teleological models as those found under the "functional" rubric. Without getting into a lengthy epistemological debate, I would urge that one of the reasons for the sorry state of our field is the tendency to by-pass existential description of an operational nature in the search for original theoretical formulations with strong explanatory power. My view is that, while such an enterprise ought to be continued by some, more of us should be developing operational descriptions, applying them to comparative analyses, and producing data-based empirical generalizations. Theory may be the intelligent man's substitute for empiricism, but when so much of our theory is little better than superstition (tribal, at that) and so much depends on accurate knowledge, we cannot afford to ignore the inductive road to such knowledge.

Properties and Behavior

Turning, then, to the global system and its many conceivable sub-systems, the position here is that every one of them may be described and compared with the others, or with itself over time. A single and partial exception is the global system itself. It can, of course, be compared with its various sub-systems, but for the moment there is no known system at the same level or echelon against which it might be compared, or with which it might experience relationships or interactions.

A critical point here is that there is only one global system on and around the planet Earth, and that this system may be thought of as having a range of political, economic, and social properties as will be outlined. That is, it makes little sense to differentiate among polity, economy, and society, intertwined as they are, unless one is trapped in the "functionalist" matrix. With most social entities being multi-functional and few of them being uni-functional, any effort to ascertain the sole or dominant function of an entity or class of entities seems to be destined for certain failure.

Moreover, I would hold that it is conceptually disadvantageous to postulate a number of such systems on earth over time, as do Rosecrance

(1963) and Kaplan (1957), for example. To postulate on a priori grounds that System V endured from 1848 to 1871, to be replaced by System VI after the German states were unified, or that the balance of power system obtained from before the Napoleonic Wars to World War II, to be replaced by the loose bipolar system, may be intuitively reasonable but not very useful scientifically. Why, for example, should we mark the end of one system and the onset of another merely because certain of the nations' properties or behavioral patterns showed appreciable change at the designated time? The periods before and after these cutting points always turn out to have a great many properties in common, and from several viewpoints could be classed as more similar than different. And, what are the empirical operations by which we ascertain the cutting point?

My objections to this sequence-of-systems approach are three. First, as suggested above, it is an empirical question as to whether certain specified properties of the system changed to a sufficient degree at a given point (or during a given few years) to permit the drawing of a chronological boundary. Second, for certain theoretical purposes, we may be quite interested in a particular set of system properties but utterly indifferent to others, and it seems undesirable to impose one set of criteria upon a researcher whose theoretical concerns are quite different from the prior system designator. The alternative solution of having each scholar settle upon a unique set of systems ending at unique points in time, is hardly an improvement either. Third, and perhaps most critical, how can we theorize on the basis of longitudinal data (over appreciable periods of time) when we are confronted with an allegedly new system at certain fairly frequent intervals?[13]

The preferred strategy, it seems to me, is to select certain very gross phenomena whose development marks the appearance, and perhaps the future disappearance, of "the" global system and then go on to develop more refined measures by which the state of the system may be operationally described at any particular point in time, depending on the properties which are most relevant to one's immediate theoretical needs. This also explains why "global" seems more useful than "international" or "nation-state" as our adjective, permitting as it does a much longer time span within which longitudinal and comparative analyses may be carried out.[14]

Returning from this digression, then, my point here is that the concept

---

[13] One might, of course, identify such sub-systems as the central or the peripheral ones, with a nation assigned to one or the other on the basis of its activity level, its influence, or its status in world politics. In several of the Correlates of War studies, we make this distinction for the period 1815–1920, but argue that the distinction becomes less credible and relevant after World War I (Singer and Small, 1966b and 1968a). Further, one might single out the major powers or the nonaligned nations as other possible sub-system types.

[14] A recent example of the confusion which can emerge is an article which distinguishes between the nation-state system and the international system (at the same point in time) on the grounds that only nations are treated as actors in the first, while such additional actors as international organizations are included in the second (Smoker, 1967).

of the global system is quite a useful one, but that whereas all of its sub-systems may (a) behave and interact, as well as (b) have relationships and (c) manifest comparable properties, the global system itself is restricted to the final dimension only.[15] Serving only as an environment within which our many sub-systems may exist, experience changes in their attributes, develop relationships, and behave or interact, the global system (to borrow from Allport, 1955) may manifest a particular state of *being*, and via changes in its attributes, experience a version of *becoming*, but it does not manifest *behaving* characteristics in the literal sense used here. With this exception, each of the systems delineated here may be thought of as an entity itself in a larger (spatially or conceptually) environment, and all may therefore be thought of as social organizations or social systems; thus a common taxonomic framework becomes quite appropriate. The descriptors are of three basic types: physical, cultural, and structural, and we will examine them in that order.

It should be noted at the outset, however, that these three sets of properties, attributes, or characteristics are all essentially of a static nature. That is, they tend to change at very slow rates, meaning that the time axis is almost irrelevant when they are being considered, whereas the spatial axes ("real" or conceptual) are extremely critical. Furthermore, in this formulation, these attributes provide a partial basis from which we can predict the behavior of the entity under consideration. In summary, and partly to reiterate, we observe structural, cultural, and physical properties of a system in order to describe it in being; we observe the rates and direction of change of such properties in order to describe or predict what it is becoming; and we observe their propensities to interact with one another and to respond to external inputs in order to predict, and partially explain, the system's modes of behaving.[16]

Physical Properties

Turning, then, to a discussion of the dimensions by which a system's state of being may be described—but remaining within the spatial limits and conceptual needs of the present assignment—let me list a few of the

[15] While this is essentially a definitional matter, my view is that a cluster of identifiable and interdependent social units need not manifest coordinated and collective behavior *as a group* (or coalition) in order to qualify as a system. Thus, those clusters of interdependent units which do not have discernible and legitimate agents who act on their collective behalf are viewed as systems, but as ones which do not behave or interact vis-à-vis other systems. This position does not, of course, preclude interaction among systems or sub-systems at different levels of analysis, but only among those which have no legitimate agents of the system *qua* system.

[16] A critical issue in our field, and one on which only limited evidence is available, is the amount of variance in an entity's behavior which can be accounted for by that entity's properties. My own view is that we have tended to exaggerate this at the expense of such other factors as the entity's prior relationships and the behavior of other entities, as well as the properties of the larger system. Some findings which tend to support my bias are Rummel (1967), Tanter (1966), and Alker and Russett (1965).

physical ones first. Within this category, there are three sub-dimensions. The first is the obviously *geographic* one and it includes area, topography, climate, internal and external distances, natural resources, water power, and the like.[17] The second is *demographic* and embraces the number of inhabitants, their age, sex, and ethnic distributions, and rates of change in these. It does not, however, apply to such structural phenomena (discussed in a later section) as urban-rural distribution, social mobility, kinship and marriage patterns, and so forth, even though it may correlate with them. In the third sub-category of physical attributes—the *technological*—we find those dimensions which affect the entity's capacity to exploit or control its physical geography and its social environment. Included are such attributes as industrial capability, access to scientific knowledge, population skill distributions, transport and communication nets, armed forces size and weaponry, and the like. These three types of physical attributes depend, in turn, upon the cultural and structural attributes of the system, with the former accounting for much of the motivation for, and style by which, physical resources are utilized, and the latter affecting the probability that such utilization will be effective.

Cultural Properties

But cultural and structural attributes embrace more than this. Looking at cultural ones first, I would propose that we can describe a great many (but certainly not all) cultural properties of human groups in terms of individual *psychological* properties. In my recent paper ("Man and World Politics: The Psycho-Cultural Interface," 1968b) I go into these problems in detail, but here let me do nothing more than summarize the most important dimensions. Before doing so, however, it is important to avoid at the outset any suggestion of anthropomorphizing. Not only do I not want to suggest that collectivities or groups can experience such psychological processes as cognition or affect, but also to recognize that there may well be certain "emergent properties," peculiar to a *group* of some minimum size or complexity, and not found at the level of individual psychology.

Three of the more useful dimensions by which an individual's way of looking at the world may be described are: personality, attitude, and opinion. These three psychological dimensions range in an ordinal fashion along three dimensions: (a) generality, (b) stability, and (c) observability; personality is most general, most stable, and least susceptible to direct

---

[17] While a central point in this scheme is that important sub-systems of a "non-territorial" nature have existed and may become more critical in the future, the phrase must not be taken too literally. That is, every social system embraces individual people, and while these people need not be clustered in a contiguous or compact physical region, they definitely occupy a given physical location at any point in time. As a matter of fact, an important property of relatively non-territorial entities or sub-systems might be the mean physical distance, or the rate of its change, between all possible pairs in that sub-system.

observation, while opinions tend to be quite specific, relatively transitory, and more readily observable.

One might, for the population of individuals comprising any social group which constitutes a sub-system of interest to the world politics scholar, describe the statistical distribution of any of these three dimensions within the group. That distribution might be in terms of such factors as the percentage falling into any one of a number of personality, attitude, or opinion classes; the normality (or skewness or peakedness) of the distribution curve; its dispersion in range of standard deviations; and so forth. And, for the purposes outlined here, one might quite legitimately use these distributions of individual psychological properties as descriptions of certain group properties. In my view, the personality distribution provides several dimensions of national (or any other sub-system's) character; attitudinal distributions provide the basis for measuring ideology; and opinion distributions give us an operational measure of mood, or climate of opinion.

In combination, the statistical distributions of these three psychological phenomena within a given population provide the basis for getting at much of that population's cultural attributes. They may be reasonably subdivided in three separate content areas. One embraces *perceptions* of the way things *are* done, or modes; the second refers to *preferences* for the way things *should* be done, or norms; and the third covers *predictions* as to the way things *will* be done, or expectations. The position taken here is that this approach not only gets at some of the most critical ideational attributes of a sub-system, but does so in a highly operational fashion.

Structural Properties

When we speak of the structure of a social system, reference is to the way in which relationships—and the role expectations which surround them—are arranged. The concept is highly spatial in tone (at least for Westerners) and is best exemplified in tables of organization or flow diagrams. Another aspect of structure is that it reflects as well as shapes both culture and behavior to a considerable extent, with formal structure tending to reflect norms (the way things should be done) and the more informal structure reflecting modes (the way things are done). Needless to say, there is usually a fair degree of tension between the two.

In the formal group are such political and social attributes as the types and powers of legitimate political and economic institutions handling legislative, administrative, judicial, banking, commercial-industrial regulation, social welfare, information control, and related functions. In the informal structure category might be not only those items which were specifically excluded from the physical group above (urban-rural distribution, social mobility, kinship and marriage patterns, and so on) but such additional ones as citizen access to and influence over the decision-making process; size, centralization, and scope of political parties and other unofficial or quasi-official associations (including pressure groups); number, power and role of religious, ethnic, and linguistic groupings, and the like. Also relevant as aspects of informal structure are the extent of pluralistic cross-cutting ties, and the general coalition configurations which develop among the system's many sub-systems.

INTER-ENTITY RELATIONSHIPS

The more interdisciplinary of my readers will by now have noticed an important difference between the conceptual scheme outlined here and that found in much contemporary social science theory. For reasons not altogether clear to me, political science, sociology, and to a lesser extent, anthropology, have shown a growing tendency to theorize around the concepts of relationship and of role. One consequence of this emphasis has been a gradually diminishing concern with the social entities which share these relationships and fill these roles; one almost gets the feeling that the entity which experiences these relationships and occupies these roles is of no consequence, and that its immanent properties have *no* effect on the way in which the role or relationship is handled. At the risk of looking like an unreconstructed "institutionalist," my preference is to begin with, and concentrate upon, the key entities in one's theoretical framework, keeping them and their properties very much in mind as we move on to the more dynamic and behavioral variables. If the empirical and theoretical streams in social science are to be rejoined, it seems clear to me that our observation and measurement operations will have to be carried out on individuals and groups of individuals—however these groups are conceptualized—and not upon hypothetical constructs which have no observable referents in the empirical world, and which manifest no behavior in the literal sense.[18]

With this departure taken care of, let me turn now to a summary of the relationships and interactions which occur between and among the systems and sub-systems delineated above. Implicit in this formulation is the notion that such relationships and interactions—with the partial exception of the global system as noted earlier—can occur not only in the horizontal plane (among entities of the same sub-system class) but in the vertical and diagonal planes as well, linking up entities in different sub-system classes. Let me move from the passive to the active ends of this conceptual continuum by examining relationships in this section and going on to behavior and interaction in the next section.

[18] While the formulation here departs in certain ways from the general systems approach as found in Miller's *Living Systems* (forthcoming) or those whose work appears in *General Systems*, it shares fully the strong entity-orientation of that literature. Needless to say, we appreciate that science deals only with *representations* of reality, and that every measurement and recorded observation requires an inferential leap of some magnitude; but this hardly justifies making that leap any longer than necessary.

Relationship as Similarity of Attributes

Relationships among the sub-systemic entities of the global system (and between them and the system itself) may be thought of in terms of two distinct types. One type of relationship concerns bonds or links of *interdependence* and will be dealt with in the following sub-section; the other type concerns similarity or difference in *attributes* and may be disposed of readily in a few words here. The distinction may seem self-evident, yet our literature abounds with illustrations of the tendency to assume or imply that the more similar a cluster of entities may be on certain relevant attribute dimensions, the more likely they are to exhibit high interdependence, co-operation, responsiveness, and so forth. Likewise, scholars as well as practitioners often succumb to the fallacy that sharp differentiation on such attributes implies isolation or incompatibility between or among the entities at hand. This tendency not only overlooks some impressive evidence to the contrary, but ignores such popular notions (from other settings) as the attraction of opposites and the complementarity of disparateness.

For the sort of paradigm suggested here, the distinction is quite critical. Consider, for example, the general concept of "social distance," which, while originally intended for application to inter-personal relations (Bogardus, 1928), may also be extended with care to inter-collective relations. We may speak of the "distance" between two nations or other sub-system entities as being great or small on such dimensions as (a) the degree to which each is ideologically unified, or (b) the degree to which each entity's population holds negative stereotypes of the other's (Cantril and Buchanan, 1953). The first clearly refers to *relationship as similarity*, measured as the distance between their two positions on some sort of ideological unity scale, while the second refers to *relationship as interdependence* (perceptually in this case). To take another more obvious illustration, we may speak of the distance between two nations on a population per acre scale, as distinguished from the distance in airline miles between their capital cities. For the sake of clarity, we might refer to the first case in each illustration as *difference* or *discrepancy* in regard to a given attribute, and reserve the words "close" or "distant" for the second of the cases in which some sort of psychological, physical, or economic involvement or linkage or bond is under consideration.[19]

Relationship as Interdependence

Whereas relationships defined as similarity of attribute(s) may readily be appraised and measured on the basis of a common scale or indicator, relationships concerning mutual involvement tend to be more elusive. One reason for this elusiveness is that the distinction between relations and *interactions* has never been made as explicit as it might be, in all of the social sciences as well as in world politics. The very label which we have tended

[19] A highly suggestive scheme for the measurement of such distances is in Deutsch and Isard (1961).

to pin on our field—"international relations"—has helped to obscure a distinction which is as important to conceptual clarity as it is to operational measurement.

When two or more entities behave vis-à-vis one another, and there is a sequence of at least two discernible acts such that the first can "reasonably" be interpreted as partly responsible for the second, we may speak of *interaction*. Before and after, as well as during, a given interaction sequence, the entities continue to be *related* in some fashion, however distant and remote.

The specified sub-systems of the global system may be related merely to the extent that they are located on the same continent, or belong to one or more extra-national associations, or contain representatives of the same linguistic minority. Less passive relationships might be based on joint membership in a truce observation commission, regularized exchange visits between elites, leaders who are cousins or siblings, or heavy flows of reciprocal mail and tourism. More intense relationships might be on the basis of high economic interdependence, alliance commitments to (or against) one another, or actual participation in war as allies or adversaries. Note that relations may not only range from active to passive, but from friendly to hostile as well, and that even though the illustrations are largely drawn from inter-*nation* relations, they need not be so restricted.

More important still is the fact that relationships are constructs which are imposed on a cluster of entities by the observer with some particular theoretical purpose in mind. In line with the suggestion in my opening paragraph, one may look at the vast buzzing welter of world politics and not only discern a wide range of sub-systems, but a wide range of relationships among those sub-systems, depending on one's intellectual needs and interests, even though many of us will disagree as to the single most effective way of "slicing" the system or the relationships which emerge within it.

Closely related to this point, and one of the main reasons for the formulation proposed here, is the need to achieve maximum descriptive payoff with a minimum of costly observation and measurement. The scheme used here explicitly seeks to exploit that principle; therefore, a great many of the *relationships* among entities at any given sub-system level provide the empirical base from which *structural* attributes of a larger sub-system (including the total system) may be inferred. For example, one could describe a structural attribute such as the degree of political integration in a given continental region on the basis of such relational phenomena as the degree of economic interdependence among the component nations of that region; likewise, the centralization of a given extra-national entity might be measured by the extent to which the income of its intra-national components is redistributed among them. Further, a structural attribute of the global system such as its "lateral mobility" could be measured by observing the rate of change at which nations move into and out of alliance commitments.

37

INTER-ENTITY INTERACTIONS

In the preceding section, I suggested that we must recognize not only the distinction between the two types of relationship but between inter-dependence type relationships and interactions. Let me develop the latter concept more fully now and then proceed to a brief discussion of the way in which each affects the other. When two or more entities show some degree of interdependence—that is, a relationship whose strength exceeds the minimum threshold of relationship or bond which is due to mere coexistence in some larger system—it is safe to assume that some appreciable interactions have already occurred between or among them and that more such will follow. Moreover, it is equally safe to assume that the prior bonds will partially determine the kinds of interactions which follow, and that these in turn will have an impact on future bonds. Further, since each may partially predict to the other, it is perfectly legitimate—despite the important conceptual distinction—to use one as an *indicator* of the other, within the standard constraints and demands of validity.[20]

Despite their operational substitutability, however, it should be remembered that interaction and interdependence are conceptually distinct, especially in regard to the importance of the time and space axes. One describes interaction in terms of a sequence of behavioral events, with considerable attention to the movement of energy and information across space within brief but critical periods of time; these behavioral events occur in sufficiently rapid sequence to permit their identification and classification as relatively discrete episodes, well-bounded in time. One describes relationships, on the other hand, largely in spatial terms, with the time dimension of negligible importance; time becomes important only when the change in relationships over an appreciable period is one's preoccupation. Another way to emphasize this qualitative distinction is to note that if the observation of behavior is not carried out at a specific moment (even if in an ex post facto fashion) it may either be lost forever or an event other than the one which concerns us may be the one which gets recorded. Behavioral events which add up to interaction take place in fairly quick succession, requiring observational procedures whose validity and reliability are highly dependent upon the moment at which they are carried out. But since relationships and bonds show moderately slow change, it is seldom critical whether the observation is perfectly timed or not; as a matter of fact, the social scientist will often fall back upon interpolation to get a missing measurement of a relationship which existed between two other measurements in time, and will seldom go wrong in doing so. Such a procedure for the measurement of interaction events could be disastrous.

---

[20] Perhaps the most useful discussion of validity in its various forms, as it applies to world politics, comes (not surprisingly) out of the simulation literature; see Hermann (1967).

INTERACTION AND CHANGES IN SYSTEM ATTRIBUTES

Although space limitations preclude any specific illustrations of inter-action types, the abstract formulation which is outlined above should make the concept sufficiently clear. Assuming that this is so, let me move on to the final section and propose one possible mode of looking at the way in which the attributes of system and sub-system impinge upon, and are affected by, various types of behavior and interaction. Adhering to the ecological point of view which is implicit in the approach used here, a sum-mary of the effect of the system (and its attributes) upon the behavior of its sub-systemic components would seem to be in order. To put it simply, any system which serves as a social and/or physical environment imposes con-straints and provides incentives which must exercise an appreciable impact on the behavior of the component sub-system entities, and therefore on the interaction patterns which these entities display.

An excellent demonstration of this phenomenon is found in the game theoretic literature of the past five years or so. In prisoner's dilemma ex-periments, for example, psychologists have found that one of the most potent factors influencing the behavior of the subjects is the payoff matrix. Thus, when the rewards for cooperative moves are moderate or low, but those for so-called "defecting" moves are high, both players will regularly adopt strategies which result in a lose-lose outcome. But as the so-called "temptation" payoffs are reduced, or the mutual defection payoffs become more costly, the probability of cooperative moves will increase sharply; when these magnitudes are sufficiently large, both players will adopt strate-gies which produce a win-win outcome. However, these magnitudes must come very close in magnitude to the temptation or defection reward in order to overcome (at least among American college students) the cultural predisposition to defeat the adversary. Moreover, once the players lock into a consistent defect-defect (and therefore lose-lose) interaction pattern, it requires an extremely radical change in the payoff matrix to induce mutually cooperative moves (Rapoport and Chammah, 1966; Minas et al., 1960). Without pressing the analogy too far, it is evident that somewhat the same effect is exercised by the payoff matrix which other environments offer.

For nations, the global system's attributes provide such a payoff matrix, and for sub-national associations, the nation's attributes do the same. Elsewhere, I have gone into some detail outlining the implications of the interplay between the demands of the global system and the temptations of most national sub-systems. Standing as they do at the interface between these two environments, it is little wonder that national political leaders stumble as often as they do into the sort of defecting behavior which leads to the lose-lose outcome of modern war (Singer, 1965a). More specifically, all three sets of the global system's attributes affect—and perhaps even largely determine—the behavior of the nations. Distances, resources, and weapons, for example, constitute important *physical* constraints. The way

39

nations often do behave (modes) and may be expected to behave (predictions), despite decision-makers' preferences (norms) to the contrary, combine to provide a strong set of *cultural* incentives. And the decentralized, cumbersome, and oligarchic nature of its *structure* offer few incentives for any appreciable change in national behavior.

The point, of course, is that system attributes and sub-system interaction patterns can never be too dissonant from one another. Just as successful political parties adapt to and thus reinforce the structure and culture within which they operate, and durable business firms adapt to and reinforce the structure and culture of the commercial sub-system, nations which survive in the global system generally adapt to and therefore help reinforce its structure and culture. On the other hand, all actors occasionally find their environments unsatisfactory and may sometimes attempt to modify them. Such modification must, of necessity, be attempted via behavior change, and with some regularity, innovative behavior on the part of one entity or actor can induce changes in the reciprocal behavior of others, producing modified interaction sequences in due course.

When and if such deviations in interaction are picked up and responded to by other pairs and clusters of actors, a cultural change begins to set in. That is, the behavioral modes are no longer the same, and somewhat later they are no longer perceived as being the same. Once modes begin to change—whether toward or away from norms, which may also be in flux—predictions about future behavior can be expected to shift. And since predictions and expectations are important determinants of behavior, there is a strong likelihood of reinforcement for the new behavior and interaction patterns. Needless to say, when different cultural attributes and interaction patterns emerge in a system, the likelihood of its structure remaining the same is not great. Partly by conscious behavior of those who act on behalf of the entities, and partly by some combination of the deterministic and the probabilistic, the system's structure will—if the system is to function even moderately well—be brought into consonance (harmony is too strong a word here) with the culture and the now more regularized interaction patterns. Even the physical attributes of the system may be modified as a consequence, with (for example) a new spurt in population growth, or a slowdown in resource depletion, or an increase in weapons dispersion.

Two final points regarding the interplay of system attributes and interaction patterns are in order here. First of all, not all changes which set in as a result of this interplay are likely to endure. Some changes in system and/or behavior turn out to be self-reinforcing or self-aggravating, thus producing an entirely new state of affairs. But some changes turn out to be nothing more than minor (or indeed, major) perturbations which, before too long, are slowed down and reversed by the self-correcting propensities of the system-behavior interplay. Moreover, there is nothing inherent in this interplay to guarantee whether or when a given self-reinforcing process will run down or stop in response to certain negative feedback inputs, or will continue in response to positive feedback, on a runaway course that is indeed irreversible. Closely related to these opposing tendencies is the matter of range or amplitude in the perturbations or oscillations which develop. The range may indeed be small, as in the household thermostat or as postulated in many equilibrium models of social science; or it may be large, as in industrial economies which eschew the negative feedback mechanisms of fiscal and monetary control, and thus experience the heights and depths of inflation and depression, or as in global politics which have often gone from relative harmony to the slaughter of war and back again within less than a single decade.

The second point is that neither change nor stability in this interplay is necessarily "adaptive." Under certain conditions, neither behavioral change nor system change is desirable; under other conditions, such change may be adaptive for one sub-system but not for another, or adaptive for certain sub-systems in the short run but maladaptive for the larger system in the middle run, and so forth. The problem, of course, is that sub-national, national, and extra-national decision makers often believe that they know what sorts of stability or change are adaptive for their own entities; they may often be correct, at least in the short run. But the pages of diplomatic history are strewn with the wreckage of sub-systems whose leaders turned out to be poor judges of adaptiveness. It is by no means certain that those who act for the many components of the global system today will be any more adaptive in their behavior than have their predecessors. But given the physical attributes of the contemporary system, maladaptive change or lack thereof could be so disastrous as to be irreversible for all.

CONCLUSION

One thing, however, is clear. If system and sub-system decision-makers are uncertain as to what constitutes adaptive behavior and adaptive change or stability in system attributes, those who profess to study these phenomena are not much better off. And therein lies one of the strong justifications for the enterprise which this volume represents. Differentiating between adaptive and maladaptive behavior requires knowledge which we do not yet have, but the present volume should move us closer to such knowledge. And if this particular paper suggests a way to more effectively appraise the changing systemic context within which decision makers must so differentiate, it will have served a useful purpose.

References

ALGER, CHADWICK F., "Comparison of Intranational and International Politics," *The American Political Science Review*, 57/2 (June, 1963), pp. 406–19.

ALKER, HAYWARD, and BRUCE M. RUSSETT, *World Politics in the General Assembly* (New Haven: Yale U.P., 1965).

ALLPORT, GORDON W., *Becoming: Basic Considerations for a Psychology of Personality* (New Haven: Yale U.P., 1955).

ANGELL, ROBERT C., "An Analysis of Trends in International Organizations," *Peace Research Society Papers*, III (1965), pp. 185–95.

BOGARDUS, EMORY S., *Immigration and Race Attitudes* (Boston: Heath, 1928).

BOULDING, KENNETH, *Conflict and Defense* (New York: Harper & Row, 1962).

CANTRIL, HADLEY, and WILLIAM BUCHANAN, *How Nations See Each Other: A Study in Public Opinion* (Urbana, Ill.: U. of Illinois Press, 1953).

DEUTSCH, KARL W., and ALEXANDER ECKSTEIN, "National Industrialization and the Declining Share of the International Economic Sector, 1890–1959," *World Politics*, 13/2 (January, 1961), pp. 267–99.

———, and WALTER ISARD, "A Note on a Generalized Concept of Effective Distance," *Behavioral Science*, 6/4 (October, 1961), pp. 308–11.

———, and J. DAVID SINGER, "Multipolar Power Systems and International Stability," *World Politics*, 16/3 (April, 1964), pp. 390–406.

ECKSTEIN, HARRY (ed.), *Internal War* (New York: Free Press, 1964).

FARRELL, R. BARRY (ed.), *Approaches to Comparative and International Politics* (Evanston, Ill: Northwestern U.P., 1966).

FEIS, HERBERT, *The Diplomacy of the Dollar, 1919–1932* (New York: Norton, 1966.)

HAAS, ERNST B., *Beyond the Nation-State* (Standford: Stanford U.P., 1964).

HERMANN, CHARLES, "Validation Problems in Games and Simulations with Special Reference to Models of International Politics," *Behavioral Science*, 12/3 (May, 1967), pp. 216–31.

HERZ, JOHN, "The Rise and Demise of the Territorial State," *World Politics*, 9/4 (July, 1957), pp. 473–93.

KAPLAN, MORTON, *System and Process in International Relations* (New York: Wiley, 1957).

KATZ, ELIHU, "The Two-Step Flow of Communications," *Public Opinion Quarterly*, 21 (1957), pp. 61–78.

MASTERS, ROGER D., "World Politics as a Primitive Political System," *World Politics*, 16/4 (July, 1964), pp. 595–619.

MILLER, JAMES G., *Living Systems* (New York: Wiley, forthcoming).

MINAS, J. S., A. SCODEL, D. MARLOWE, and H. RAWSON, "Some Descriptive Aspects of Two-Person Non-Zero-Sum Games II," *Journal of Conflict Resolution*, 4/2 (June, 1960), pp. 193–7.

PARSONS, TALCOTT, "Order and Community in the International Social System," in Rosenau (ed.), *International Politics and Foreign Policy* (New York: Free Press, 1961a).

———, "An Outline of the Social System," in Parsons et al. (eds.), *Theories of Society* (New York: Free Press, 1961b).

RAPOPORT, ANATOL, and ALBERT CHAMMAH, *Prisoner's Dilemma: A Study in Conflict and Cooperation* (Ann Arbor, Michigan: U. of Michigan Press, 1966).

ROSECRANCE, RICHARD N., *Action and Reaction in World Politics* (Boston: Little, Brown, 1963).

———, "Bipolarity, Multipolarity, and the Future," *Journal of Conflict Resolution*, 10/3 (September, 1966), pp. 314–27.

ROSENAU, JAMES N. (ed.), *International Aspects of Civil Strife* (Princeton: Princeton U.P., 1964).

RUMMEL, RUDOLPH J., "The Relationship Between National Attributes and Foreign Conflict Behavior," in Singer (ed.), *Quantitative International Politics: Insights and Evidence* (New York: Free Press, 1968), pp. 187–214.

RUSSETT, BRUCE M., "Toward a Model of Competitive International Politics," *Journal of Politics*, 2 (1963), pp. 226–47.

———, and HAYWARD ALKER, KARL DEUTSCH, and HAROLD LASSWELL, *World Handbook of Political and Social Indicators* (New Haven: Yale U.P., 1964).

———, *International Regions in the International System* (Chicago: Rand-McNally, 1967).

SCOTT, ANDREW, *The Revolution in Statecraft* (New York: Random House, 1965).

SINGER, J. DAVID, "The Level of Analysis Problem in International Relations," *World Politics*, 14/1 (October, 1961), pp. 77–92.

———, "The Political Matrix of International Conflict," in Elton McNeil (ed.), *The Nature of Human Conflict* (Englewood Cliffs, N.J.: Prentice-Hall, 1965a).

——— (ed.), *Human Behavior and International Politics: Contributions from the Social-Psychological Sciences* (Chicago: Rand-McNally, 1965b), pp. 453–7.

———, and MELVIN SMALL, "Formal Alliances, 1815–1939: A Quantitative Description," *Journal of Peace Research*, 1 (1966a), pp. 1–32.

———, and MELVIN SMALL, "National Alliance Commitments and War Involvement, 1815–1945," *Peace Research Society Papers*, V (1966b), pp. 109–40.

———, and MELVIN SMALL, "Alliance Aggregation and the Onset of War, 1815–1945," in Singer (ed.), *Quantitative International Politics: Insights and Evidence* (New York: Free Press, 1968a), pp. 247–86.

———, "Man and World Politics: The Psycho-Cultural Interface," *Journal of Social Issues* 24/3 (July, 1968b), pp. 127–56.

SMOKER, PAUL, "Nation State Escalation and International Integration," *Journal of Peace Research*, 1 (1967), pp. 61–75.

SONDERMANN, FRED A., "The Linkage Between Foreign Policy and International Politics," in Rosenau (ed.), *International Politics and Foreign Policy* (New York: Free Press, 1961), pp. 8–17.

TANTER, RAYMOND, "Dimensions of Conflict Behavior Within and Between Nations, 1958–60," *Journal of Conflict Resolution*, 10/1 (March, 1966), pp. 41–64.

Union of International Associations, *The 1978 International Organizations Founded Since the Congress of Vienna* (Brussels: rue du Petit Sablon, 1957).

WALTZ, KENNETH N., "The Stability of a Bipolar World," *Daedalus*, 43/3 (1964), pp. 881–909.

ZINNES, DINA A., "An Analytical Study of the Balance of Power Theories," *Journal of Peace Research*, 3 (1967), pp, 270–88.

CHAPTER THREE

Toward the Study of National-International Linkages

James N. Rosenau

AS indicated in Chapter 1, the purpose of the framework presented here is a modest one. It does not pretend to be an analytic model or even to provide a set of initial propositions about the interdependence of national and international systems. Rather its purpose is simply that of identifying points at which the two types of systems overlap and of precipitating thought about the nature and scope of the phenomena that fall within the area of overlap. What follows, in other words, is intended as an agenda and not as a design for research. It is hoped that the agenda—and the elaboration of it presented in subsequent chapters—will seem sufficiently compelling to stimulate the formulation and implementation of manageable research designs.

THE CONCEPT OF A LINKAGE

Our approach to the phenomena bounded by the overlap of national and international systems is strictly an empirical one. We wish to identify and analyze those recurrent sequences of behavior that originate on one side of the boundary between the two types of systems and that become linked to phenomena on the other side in the process of unfolding. Since the boundaries can be crossed by processes of perception and emulation as well as by direct interaction, allowance must be made for both continuous and intermittent sequences. Hence we will use a *linkage* as our basic unit of analysis, defining it as any recurrent sequence of behavior that originates in one system and is reacted to in another.

In order to distinguish between the initial and the terminal stages of a linkage, we shall refer to the former as an *output* and to the latter as an *input*. Each of these in turn will be classified in terms of whether they occur in a polity[1] or its external environment (i.e., the international system).[2] That is, *policy outputs* are defined as those sequences of behavior that originate within a polity and that either culminate in or are sustained by its environment, whereas *environmental inputs* are considered to be those behavioral sequences in the external environment to which the polity outputs give rise. Similarly, *environmental outputs* are those sequences of behavior that start in the external environment of a polity and that are either sustained or terminated within the polity, whereas *polity inputs* are those behavioral sequences within a polity to which environmental outputs give rise.

Conceptual clarity also requires distinguishing outputs and inputs in terms of their purposefulness. Some outputs, conventionally called foreign policy, are designed to bring about responses in other systems. These we shall call either *direct policy outputs* or *direct environmental outputs,* depending on whether the intentional behavior was designated by a polity for its environment or vice versa. Yet there are a host of other patterns of behavior within a polity or its environment that are not designed to evoke boundary-crossing responses but that nevertheless do so through perceptual or emula-

---

[1] In order to distinguish national political systems from the societies of which they are a part, we shall henceforth refer to the former as polities.

[2] Although the term "environment" has special meanings for students of international politics (cf. Harold and Margaret Sprout, *The Ecological Perspective on Human Affairs* [Princeton: Princeton U.P., 1965]), in this discussion it is employed in the more general, systems theory sense with which students of comparative politics are familiar. It is conceived as an analytic entity consisting of all the human and nonhuman phenomena that exist external to a polity, irrespective of whether their existence is perceived by the actors of the polity. Our use also posits the environment as having external and internal dimensions, with the "external environment" referring to the human and nonhuman phenomena located external to the geographic space of the society of which the polity is a part and the "internal environment" referring to those phenomena that are external to the polity but exist within the geographic space of the society. Since we shall be mainly concerned with the external environment, however, we shall simplify matters by referring to it as the "environment," while always using the proper designation when we have occasion to mention the internal environment. Furthermore, as a result of this formulation the external environment of a polity is conceived to be equivalent to the same phenomena as comprise any international system of which the polity is a component part. Thus we shall be using the notions of environment and international system interchangeably, depending on whether we wish to refer to the phenomena in the context, respectively, of a single polity or of the interaction of two or more polities.

tive processes. Elections and _coups d'état_ that provoke reactions abroad exemplify outputs of this latter kind, which we shall call either _indirect polity outputs_ or _indirect environmental outputs_ depending on the locus of their origin. A similar line of reasoning results in four types of inputs and the corresponding labels of _direct polity inputs, indirect polity inputs, direct environmental inputs,_ and _indirect environmental inputs._

A final dimension of our formulation concerns the way in which outputs and inputs get linked together. Three basic types of linkage processes are identified, the penetrative, the reactive, and the emulative. A _penetrative process_ occurs when members of one polity serve as participants in the political processes of another. That is, they share with those in the penetrated polity the authority to allocate its values. The activities of an occupying army are perhaps the most clearcut example of a penetrative process, but the postwar world has also seen foreign aid missions, subversive cadres, the staffs of international organizations, the representatives of private corporations, the workers of certain transnational political parties, and a variety of other actors establish linkages through such a process.[3] Virtually by definition, penetrative processes link direct outputs and inputs.

A _reactive process_ is the contrary of a penetrative one: It is brought into being by recurrent and similar boundary-crossing reactions rather than by the sharing of authority. The actors who initiate the output do not participate in the allocative activities of those who experience the input, but the behavior of the latter is nevertheless a response to behavior undertaken by the former. Such reactive processes are probably the most frequent form of linkage, since they arise out of the joining of both direct and indirect outputs to their corresponding inputs. Recurrent reactions to a foreign aid program illustrate a reactive process involving direct outputs and inputs, whereas instances of local election campaigns in the United States being responsive to trends in Vietnam exemplify a reactive process stemming from indirect outputs and inputs.

The third type of linkage process is a special form of the reactive type. An _emulative process_ is established when the input is not only a response to the output but takes essentially the same form as the output. It corresponds to the so-called "diffusion" or "demonstration" effect whereby political activities in one country are perceived and emulated in another. The postwar spread of violence, nationalism, and aspirations to rapid industrialization and political modernization are but the more striking instances of linkages established through emulative processes. Since the emulated behavior is ordinarily undertaken independently of those who emulate it, emulative processes usually link only indirect outputs and inputs.

Several aspects of this formulation require emphasis and elaboration.

[3] For a more elaborate formulation and analysis of penetrative processes and linkages, see my "Pre-Theories and Theories of Foreign Policy," in R. Barry Farrell (ed.), _Approaches to Comparative and International Politics_ (Evanston: Northwestern U.P., 1966), pp. 65–71.

In the first place, it should be noted that our terminology has been deliberately chosen. In order to stay out of the conceptual jails built by national and international specialists, we have purposely employed definitions and terminology that are not identified exclusively with either group. The concept of linkages formed out of outputs and inputs appears neutral in this regard and is at the same time easily grasped. Furthermore, the concept is neutral with respect to the question of whether the growing overlap of national and international systems represents a subtle process of integration and the emergence of a world political community. Polities are increasingly dependent on their environments and interdependent with each other in the sense that, increasingly, what transpires at home would unfold differently if trends abroad were different. However, this interdependence may or may not involve greater integration among the polities. Some linkages may in fact be founded on enmity and be highly disintegrative for polities, international systems, or both.[4] Communist China's linkages to its environment are a case in point. Hence, so as to avoid the positive evaluation that often is implicit in the notion of interdependency, we have opted for the less elegant but more neutral terminology of linkages.

Another advantage of this terminology is that it neither denies nor exaggerates the relevance of national boundaries. While it is tempting to conclude that because a shrinking world is linking polities ever more firmly to their environments it is also making them increasingly indistinguishable from their environments, such is not necessarily the case. Many political continuities still occur solely within the boundaries of a single polity and cannot be understood without reference to the existence and character of the boundaries. Transnational politics are a long way from supplanting national politics and, if anything, the world may well be passing through a paradoxical stage in which *both* the linkages and the boundaries among polities are becoming more central to their daily lives. In affirming the existence of national boundaries, however, it is easy to obscure the sequential nature of many behavioral patterns that cross over them. Such sequences often go unrecognized because the existence of the boundaries lead the analyst to treat their initial phase as a foreign policy action that comes to a halt once it crosses into the environment of the initiating polity. Consequently, the responses to foreign policy action in other polities are viewed as new and separate sequences of behavior rather than as the next phase of the same sequence. Although the concept of national-international linkages may not prevent such a practice, it should inhibit undue

---

[4] One observer has estimated the prospect of disintegrative linkages as follows: "Since there is small chance that international politics will diminish in importance and salience in the next half century, and since judgments of alternative policies and proposals will necessarily rest on highly controversial assessments of very great risks, gains, and costs, a variety of foreign policies, military affairs, treaties, regional and international organizations and alliances all promise a steady flow of internal conflict." Robert A. Dahl, "Epilogue," in R. A. Dahl (ed.), *Political Oppositions in Western Democracies* (New Haven: Yale U.P., 1966), p. 398.

segmentation of behavioral sequences. It should provide a context for the analysis of foreign policy in which the importance of polity boundaries is acknowledged but not accentuated.

Another aspect of this formulation that requires emphasis is the concept of recurrent behavior. Outputs, inputs, and the linkages that they form are not conceived to be single events. Theory building would hardly be possible if individual actions or discrete occasions served as analytic units. Rather in order to move beyond the case method to productive theorizing, outputs, inputs, and linkages are conceptualized to be events which recur with sufficient frequency to form a pattern. To be sure, any discrete event can, at some level of generalization, be regarded as an instance of a more encompassing pattern and we do not preclude examining any event with a view to determining whether it is a case of what we have classified as a national-international linkage. If such a determination cannot be made, however, the event itself will not hold our attention for long. If, for example, an official of a stable polity is assassinated or an official of the United Nations killed in an airplane crash, such events will not be treated as outputs or inputs. They might well have boundary-crossing repercussions, but, being unexpected and nonrecurrent, their repercussions are likely to be short-lived and more habitual modes of behavior are likely to be quickly reestablished.

In other words, it is the recurrence and not the occurrence of events that serves as our focus. We are interested, to use a more commonplace example, in how the elections of a polity affect and are affected by its external environment, not in the international consequences of a specific election. The immediate consequences of a particular election might be extensive, but they would be treated as reflections of linkages rather than as linkages themselves. Similarly, given a recurrent behavior within a polity, external reactions to it are not considered to form linkages with it unless they too are recurrent. In polities where elections are held regularly, for example, these would not be treated as indirect polity outputs unless they fostered a recurrent pattern of responses in the environment. National elections in Norway and the United States are illustrative of this distinction. They recur with equal regularity in both polities but only in the case of the latter do NATO deliberations and East-West relations consistently come to a halt during the preceding campaign period. American presidential elections, in short, are integral parts of environmental patterns, whereas the equivalent events in Norway are not. The former would thus be viewed as indirect polity outputs, while the latter would not.[5]

---

[5] The example of American electoral consequences also serves to highlight another aspect of our formulation, namely, that the same behavior pattern can be part of more than one linkage. If it recurrently fosters similar consequences in two or more polities or international relationships, as the quadrennial contests for the White House apparently do, then obviously it must be treated as a different output in a number of different linkages. Likewise, if a behavior pattern is conditioned by a variety of international developments, it would be treated as a different input in each case. It follows that the

Summing up our formulation thus far, we seem to have uncovered an almost unlimited number of possible national-international linkages that can, without undue simplification, be clustered into a manageable set of nine basic types of linkages. Eight of these stem from the convergence of the four types of outputs and inputs (see Cells 3, 4, 7, 8, 9, 10, 13, 14 in Figure 3.1). The ninth, which we shall call the *fused* linkage, arises out of the possibility that certain outputs and inputs continuously reinforce each other and are thus best viewed as forming a reciprocal relationship. In other words, a fused linkage is one in which the patterned sequence of behavior does not terminate with the input. Stated in positive terms, a fused linkage is conceived to be a sequence in which an output fosters an input that in turn fosters an output in such a way that they cannot meaningfully be analyzed separately.[6]

THE COMPONENTS OF A LINKAGE FRAMEWORK

In order to facilitate the development of linkage theory, we now expand the foregoing into a larger framework in which twenty-four aspects of polities that might serve as or give rise to outputs and inputs have been identified along with six aspects or (from a polity perspective) subenvironments of the international system that might generate or receive outputs and inputs. The prevalence of linkage phenomena becomes immediately apparent when the two sets of variables are combined into a matrix that yields 144 areas in which national-international linkages can be formed. This matrix is presented in Figure 3.2. The number of possible linkages is actually much greater than 144, since in many cells of the matrix all three types of linkage processes can occur and all of the aforementioned nine basic types of linkages can be established. To convey the full array of possible linkages, in other words, the matrix should be reproduced three times to account for the varying linkage processes and then each of these should in turn be reproduced nine times, eight of them covering all the

---

same behavior pattern can also serve as *both* an output and an input. We are concerned about a wide range of linkages and do not lose interest in a particular pattern just because its role in one type of linkage has been identified. The practice of giving CIA briefings to American presidential nominees, for example, has become recurrent in response to seemingly permanent aspects of the Cold War. So have certain campaign themes and possibly even certain voting patterns. Thus, just as American presidential elections can serve as outputs in one set of linkages, so can they simultaneously operate as inputs in another. Similarly, to the extent that elections in Norway are significantly conditioned by regional or Cold War issues, they would be treated as inputs in some linkages even though they do not seem to be outputs in any.

[6] An obvious example of a fused linkage is the foreign policy of a polity that serves the function of unifying its citizenry and provoking reactions abroad that further solidify the unity and thus reinforce the impetus to maintain the policies. The current reciprocity between American public opinion and the conflict in Vietnam is an even more specific illustration of this fusion.

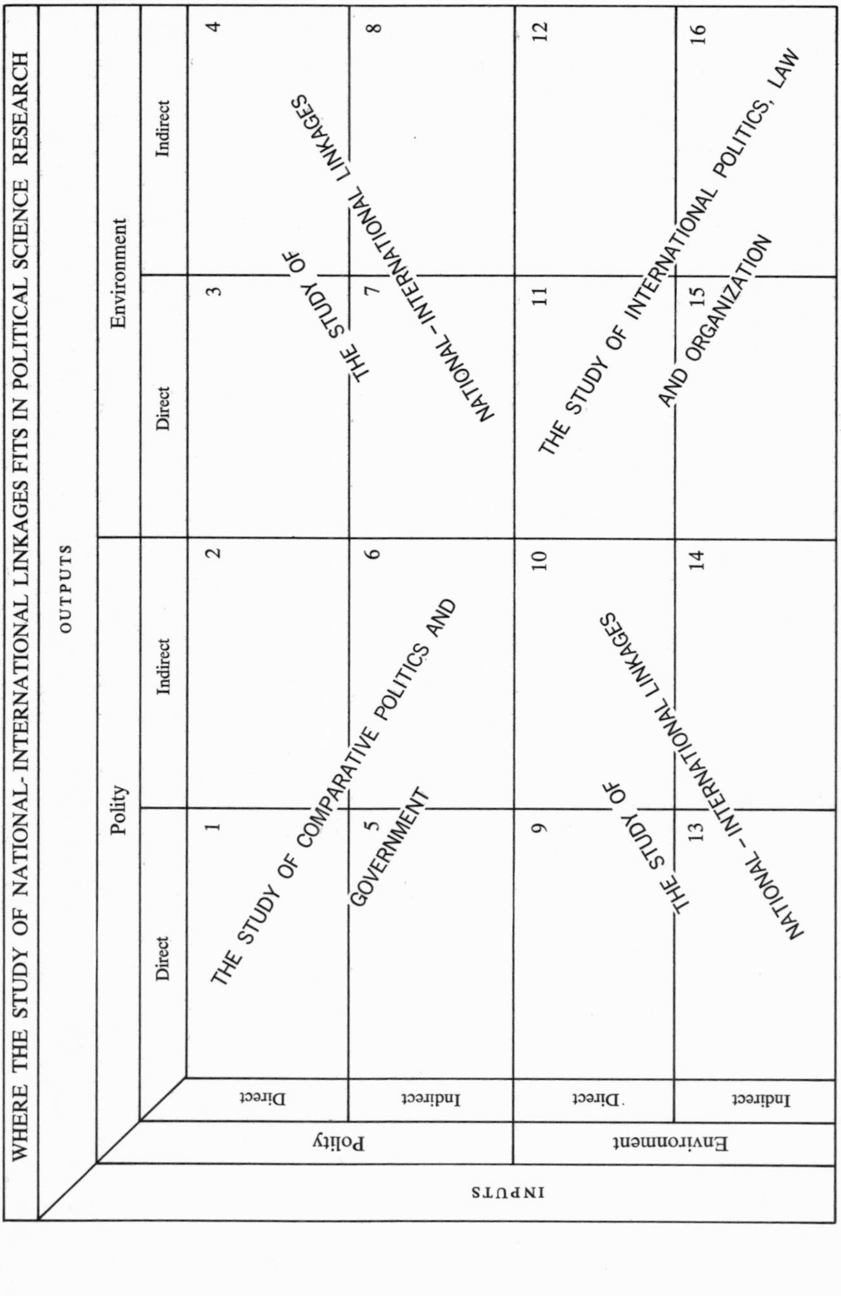

Figure 3.1. Where the Study of National-International Linkages fits in Political Science Research

possible combinations of the direct-indirect and output-input distinctions and the ninth allowing for the identification of fused linkages.

While an inquiry into each of the 27 forms of linkage that can occur in each of the 144 different cells of the matrix is feasible in an age of high-speed computers, and while all of them might well be investigated—at least to the point where it is established that their empirical existence is insufficient to make them theoretically relevant—this is not the place to undertake such a full analysis. Here we can only indicate some of the more fruitful lines of linkage theory that are suggested by such a framework. Before doing so, however, the limitations and tentative character of the framework represented by the matrix must be briefly acknowledged, lest the reader be so put off by its proliferation of categories that he overlooks its advantages and the many interesting theoretical questions to which it points. Most notably, it must be admitted that the various categories are imprecise, incomplete, impressionistic, and overlapping. Our purpose at this stage is to be suggestive, not exhaustive, and thus we have made no effort to formulate precise definitions or to delineate mutually exclusive boundaries between categories. Further refinement would no doubt result in the merging of some categories and the replacement of others. In the case of the twenty-four polity subcategories, we have merely listed some of the more obvious determinants of outputs and inputs, trusting that their general characteristics are self-evident.[7] The listing includes phenomena that sustain behavior at different levels (actors, attitudes, institutions, and processes)[8] and that unfold in different settings (the government, the polity, and the society). Likewise, in the case of the environmental categories, we have proceeded on an equally simple and impressionistic basis. The only rationale for the categorization is the impression that both actors and observers tend, often unknowingly, to think about international phenomena in terms of the units represented by the six subenvironments.[9] Again no claim is made that these six are exhaustive or mutually exclusive. Further inquiry may well

---

[7] All but the last six subcategories listed in Table 3.2 are quite commonplace in the study of Western and non-Western politics and the abbreviated labels for them should convey a general sense of the phenomena they encompass. Those listed as Rows 19–23 are taken from the formulation in Gabriel A. Almond and James S. Coleman (eds.), *The Politics of the Developing Areas* (Princeton: Princeton U.P., 1960), pp. 16–58, while the last subcategory is intended to facilitate analysis of how such phenomena as social change, group cleavage, societal stability, and so on, shape the direction and quality of direct polity outputs.

[8] By an actor is meant any concrete persons or collectivities who engage in the specified set of activities. Attitudinal determinants are conceived to be those mental-emotional states (e.g., moods, preferences, cultural norms, intellectual habits) which guide the behavior of actors. Institutions are regarded as stylized patterns or structures of inter-personal relationships through which the specified set of activities can be performed. Process refers to interactive relationships that exhibit describable patterns through time.

[9] That is, the tendency to attach relevance to location, distance, and space, as perceived and reacted to in the perspective of historical experience, would seem to be a widespread one and underlies establishment of the "contiguous environment" and the "regional environment." Equally common is the inclination to attach relevance to the

A PROPOSED LINKAGE FRAMEWORK

ENVIRONMENTAL → Outputs and Inputs / POLITY →		The Contiguous Environment	The Regional Environment	The Cold War Environment	The Racial Environment	The Resource Environment	The Organizational Environment
Actors	1. Executive Officials						
	2. Legislative Officials						
	3. Civilian Bureaucrats						
	4. Military Bureaucrats						
	5. Political Parties						
	6. Interest Groups						
	7. Elite Groups						
Attitudes	8. Ideology						
	9. Political Culture						
	10. Public Opinion						
Institutions	11. Executive						
	12. Legislatures						
	13. Bureaucracies						
	14. Military Establishments						
	15. Elections						
	16. Party Systems						
	17. Communications Systems						
	18. Social Institutions						
Processes	19. Socialization and Recruitment						
	20. Interest Articulation						
	21. Interest Aggregation						
	22. Policy-Making						
	23. Policy-Administration						
	24. Integrative-Disintegrative						

Figure 3.2. A Proposed Linkage Framework

reveal that other output or input phenomena, such as those of a legal, technological, and military kind, are so important as to justify the establishment of additional categories. We do contend, however, that these six environments are operative in the minds of actors and that they are thus at least a meaningful sample for our purposes here. (Indeed, this contention is, in effect, a basic hypothesis about national-international linkages that can and should be subjected to empirical verification.)

Despite the crudeness of the categories, the framework outlined in Table 3.2 offers a number of advantages. In the first place, it prevents perpetuation of the analytic gap between comparative and international politics and compels thought about the way in which they are linked. By juxtaposing aspects of systems, we identify a number of points at which they can overlap and make it easier to break the habit of separately examining political systems from an exclusively national or international perspective.

Second, the framework prevents us from focusing on only manifest linkages. By subdividing polities and their environments into many components, we call attention to a number of unfamiliar and latent linkages that might go unrecognized or be quickly dismissed as being of no importance if a less explicit framework were employed. Although many of the linkages derived from the framework may not prove to be worthy of extended analysis, at least they will have to be considered and their relevance assessed.

Third, the polity side of the framework should greatly inhibit the tendency to treat national governments as having undifferentiated internal environments and thus to rely on the national interest as an explanation of international behavior. By breaking down polities into aspects that are not ordinarily considered in an international context, we have encouraged inquiry into the processes by which the needs and wants of a polity are determined and discouraged the assumption that its outputs merely serve interests. Moreover, by identifying nongovernmental actors, attitudes, institutions, and processes, as well as those connected with formal decision-making, we have made it possible to examine fused linkages and to pose functional questions about the ways in which external behavior serves the internal workings of polities.

Similarly, and fourth, the environmental side of the framework should substantially curb the tendency to regard polities as having undifferentiated external environments. By identifying several international systems of which polities are a part, we have made it difficult to presume that events

---

particular pattern of Great Power relationships that prevail at any moment in history; hence the selection of the "Cold War environment." Similarly, associating relevance to certain types of trans- and subnational group or individual relationships is widely practiced and the "racial environment" and the "resource environment" have been chosen to reflect this manner of categorizing phenomena. Still another practice is that of ascribing relevance to the existence and activities of international organizations and thus we have separated out the "organizational environment." For an elaboration of the boundaries and nature of these subenvironments, see Appendix A.

abroad operate as constants rather than as variables in the functioning of polities.   Such a procedure also permits comparisons of the stability of different international systems in terms of the varying ways in which polities may be linked to them.   If, for example, the consequences of the historic differences between India and Pakistan, France and Germany, Korea and Japan, Greece and Turkey, and Israel and Egypt are any indication, it would seem that the close-at-hand environment of a polity can dominate its foreign policy and internal life far more extensively than other, more remote, environmental ties.[10] These differential environmental ties have never been subjected to the systematic and comparative analysis that is inherent in the linkage framework.

Fifth, all of these advantages are further served by the distinction between direct and indirect linkage phenomena.   By emphasizing that behavior sequences can be either intentional or unintentional, we allow for the analysis of two basic sets of linkages that tend to be ignored.   One involves those initiated by the direct outputs of polities.   Obviously a preponderance of the actions purposefully directed at the environment are undertaken by the governments of polities, so that the primary category of direct outputs consists of all those activities, both decisional and implementive, that are usually described as the foreign policies of a nation.   In the context of nation-international linkages, foreign policies are recurring forms of action— or inaction—that the duly constituted authorities of a polity initiate toward one or more objects in their external environment, with a view to either preventing the object from hindering the satisfaction of polity needs and wants or obtaining resources from it that will facilitate satisfaction of polity needs.   But foreign policy activities are not the only direct outputs of polities.   A major advantage of the linkage framework is that it calls attention to another major category of purposeful behavior that is often overlooked and that ought to be subjected to extensive inquiry, namely, those recurrent activities that private persons or groups undertake with the intent of preserving or altering one or more aspects of the polity's external environment.   Corporations, religious bodies, professional organizations, labor unions, some political parties, special interest groups, distinguished citizens, and a variety of other private actors sometimes pursue, in many polities, goals designed to establish desired patterns of behavior abroad.   An obvious example of the importance of these nongovernmental direct outputs is provided by the overseas activities of U.S. corporations.   As Samuel P. Huntington puts it,

> There is the whole question—which is far from just a Marxist myth—of the impact which private economic groups have on the politics of undeveloped countries where they have investments and on their developed home countries.   This is a

[10] For some evidence along these lines, see Leonard Binder, *The Ideological Revolution in the Middle East* (New York: Wiley, 1964), pp. 261–2.

54

subject which political scientists have avoided, but my own very limited studies on Latin America convince me that it is of fundamental importance. . . . The international corporation which owns property in a dozen or more countries today escapes control by government and has much the same relationship to weak developing governments that the American railroad corporation had to our state governments in the 1870s. A comparative study of the politics of the supra-national corporation, of how ITT, Shell, Standard Oil, General Motors, General Electric, etc. respond to and influence the politics of the countries in which they function seems like a high-priority item for any study of national-international linkages. Another interesting issue would be the more general problem of why economic bodies (like corporations and, to some extent, unions) can function effectively across international lines, while purely political bodies, e.g., parties, cannot. To the best of my knowledge, every attempt to maintain an international political party has foundered on the rocks of nationalism. The RDA and the Baath are only the latest examples in a list strewn with the wreckage of the second and third internationals. If this is true internationally, why is this the case, and what implications does it have for the probable success of the efforts by parties and other groups to integrate countries like Burma, Malaysia, Nigeria, or the Congo?[11]

Likewise, on the input side the direct-indirect distinction has the advantage of emphasizing that the life of a polity is conditioned by far more than the purposeful actions that other polities direct at it. This point is often ignored in research. Many analysts rely heavily on the concept of intervention as a means of analyzing the international situation of polities and focus on the ways in which actors in a polity's environment intervene in its affairs. In doing this, they tend not to question whether a number of its activities have been unintentionally affected by events and trends abroad. Intervention implies resistance, or at least the conscious interposition of foreign elements that must be brought under control and managed: Subversion must be contested, economic penetration offset, military threats countered, diplomatic demands bargained with, propaganda charges answered. Yet, obviously, there is more to life in a world of other polities. While we do not minimize the importance of the behavioral patterns that are precipitated by purposeful interventions, we would argue that there are also myriad ways in which polities adjust to circumstances in their external environments that were not designed to affect them. Hopefully the concept of indirect inputs will encourage more extensive inquiry into these adjustment patterns.[12]

[11] In a personal communication, dated July 7, 1965.

[12] Recognition of indirect inputs, it might be added, is facilitated by investigation of those political roles in a polity that either have undergone recent changes or are newly

Finally, but no less importantly, the linkages framework responds to the need for more genuine comparisons in the study of foreign policy. As we have implied here and elaborated elsewhere,[13] the great preponderance of foreign policy analyses focus on the international behavior of a single polity and most of them do so by moving back and forth indiscriminately between explanations that posit the polity's foreign policies as stemming from, say, geocultural factors in one situation, from the personality of leaders in another, and from resource and other capability variables in still another. Rare indeed are attempts to identify and assess the causal potency of key variables through a comparison of their operation in two or more polities. By bringing both the internal and external variables together in a framework that can be applied to any polity, hopefully we have provided a way of overcoming this deficiency and a basis for assessing and comparing the relative potency of the variables underlying the international behavior of any two polities.

AN AGENDA FOR RESEARCH

Of course, the test of such a framework lies not in the advantages that are claimed for it, but in the theoretical questions that it generates. One innovative line of inquiry suggested by the matrix in Table 3.2 involves a focus on linkages per se, so as to compare their origins, duration, flexibility, stability, and functions irrespective of the kind of polity that sustains them. The impact of the contiguous environment on party systems, for example, could be contrasted with the way in which the Cold War environment affected the competition, number, organization, and solidarity of the parties within different systems. Questions such as the following might be researched: Do dimensions of the contiguous environment create more or less divisiveness within and among parties than do aspects of the Cold War environment? Does the former tend to foster penetrative or emulative processes that divide parties and the latter reactive processes that unite them? Indeed, is one environment more likely than another to create

---

established. Such a procedure often turns up clues as to where and how the impact of the external environment is being experienced. Consider, for example, electoral politics in the United States. Where White House aspirants were once predominantly state governors because of a norm that presidents ought to have prior executive experience, today the informal requirements of the candidate role have changed to emphasis on a "foreign affairs" background, with the result that presidential nominations have increasingly gone to members of Congress in recent years. Similar indirect inputs can even be discerned at lower levels of American politics as, for example, candidates for state and local offices increasingly cite their previous international experiences as grounds for their election. Likewise, the tendency of church, labor, business, and educational organizations to create high-ranking positions that are specifically charged with responsibility for handling the organization's international contacts and interests is another reflection of the occurrence of indirect inputs.

[13] Farrell (ed.), "Pre-Theories and Theories of Foreign Policy," *op. cit.*, pp. 31–37.

issues that encourage the emergence of new parties whose existence and strength is in turn a function of the duration and intensity of the issues posed by the environment? How do party-system contiguous environment linkages differ from party-system Cold War environment ones in terms of their impact upon the capacity of parties to raise funds, recruit members, select leaders, and resolve conflicts? In contrast, what is the likelihood of one-, two-, or multi-party systems being differentially linked to the two types of environments and thus differentially affecting their structure and stability? Are fused linkages more likely to occur with respect to the Cold War than to the contiguous environment? That is, is it reasonable to hypothesize that the former is more likely than the latter to foster issues that divide parties and that in turn serve as outputs?

While these questions suggest the potentialities of comparing linkages within each row of the matrix, others indicate the utility of comparing them within each column and, more broadly, of comparisons among rows and among columns. It is interesting to ask, for example, whether the Cold War environment is more securely linked to, say, the structure of mass public opinion and the functioning of the system of mass communications than to the various processes of governmental policy-making? Indeed, is it not conceivable that public opinion-Cold War linkages are more predictable and enduring than those in which this environment is tied to the activities of parties or to the patterns of voting behavior? These questions lead to the broader one of whether such Cold War linkages are likely to be stronger, more extensive, and less flexible than those linking the resource or organizational environment to various polity institutions? Are some external environments likely to be linked to only a few selected aspects of polities, whereas with others linkage occurs across the entire range of polity activities? Are some environments more likely to foster penetrative or emulative processes than others? Or does the nature of the linkage process stem less from environmental characteristics and more from the structure of polities? Posed in systemic terms, how do the linkages that support or disrupt contiguous systems compare with those that sustain regional ones? Is it not reasonable to hypothesize that the former, consisting of especially proximate ties between polities and their environments, are more fragile and subject to greater fluctuation in intensity and direction than the latter?

A second major line of inquiry, one that will appeal particularly to students of comparative politics, would be to contrast linkages from the perspective of a single polity. A host of questions come to mind: How widespread are the linkages to which the polity contributes outputs? Are these exclusively of a direct (foreign policy) kind or also of the indirect variety? To what extent are its ties to the external world characterized by direct or indirect inputs? Are some polity actors, attitudes, institutions, and processes more subject to penetration or emulation than others? Do linkages occur primarily with one type of environment? Or is the pattern of linkages not a clear-cut one? Are, say, the polity's policy-making processes linked more extensively to the Cold War environment, whereas its processes of interest articulation and aggregation are tied more closely to the regional environment? Does the organizational environment create issues for interest groups? Or are the latter tied more closely to the resource environment, whereas bureaucracies and elite groups sustain most of the links to the organizational environment? What function does each linkage serve in terms of the polity's capacity to define its domestic goals, mobilize its resources, and implement its decisions? How is the polity's ability to identify and pursue goals in the foreign policy area enhanced or restricted by the nature of its linkages? Are some linkages more functional than others? Are some that are functional offset by others that are dysfunctional?

Questions such as these lead naturally to a third line of inquiry in which the linkage patterns of particular types of polities are traced and compared: Are democracies similarly linked to the outside world and are their linkage patterns in turn different from those of authoritarian polities? Do different types of environments press more closely upon unintegrated polities than upon integrated ones? Do superpolities have similar linkage patterns that are distinguishable from those of small polities? Is the former type of polity more subject to emulative processes than the latter type, whereas small polities are more vulnerable to penetrative processes than super ones? Are polities in, say, Latin America more closely linked to the regional environment than European ones? Are wealthy polities more successful in managing their direct linkages than poor ones?

Equally intriguing questions arise out of an approach which classifies and compares polities entirely in terms of their linkage patterns, instead of using more conventional categories. For example, four basic types of polities could be identified by classifying them in terms of the number of linkages to which they contribute outputs, by doing the same in terms of the linkages for which they are the input recipients, by dividing the two scales into low and high, and by then combining them in a fourfold table. The four types of polities created by such a scheme would be (1) those that are high on both scales; (2) those that have many linkages to which they contribute outputs and few in which they receive inputs; (3) those that have the pattern opposite to (2); and (4) those that are low on both scales. If the world's polities were to be classified in terms of these four types, such a procedure would pose the tantalizing question of whether there are other ways in which those similarly classified resemble each other. Might one find, as seems reasonable at first glance, that many outputs are fostered by superpolities and by those medium-sized polities for whose allegiance superpolities compete; that few outputs are generated by disunited new polities and by traditionally neutral ones; that many inputs are experienced by new polities and by those for which superpolities compete; and that both superpolities and traditionally neutral ones are likely to be the recipients of few inputs? In short, might research yield clusters of polities such as Figure 3.3?

		OUTPUTS	
		High	Low
INPUTS	High	Egypt Nigeria	Congo Cyprus
	Low	U.S. U.S.S.R.	Sweden Switzerland

Figure 3.3.

Another line of inquiry, one that will be especially appealing to students of foreign policy, would concentrate on those linkages in which the outputs are direct and result from governmental activities. Unlike the more conventional types of foreign policy analysis, such a focus insures that comparison will not be confined to policy content, but will also be extended to its sources and its effectiveness. By treating foreign policies as only one aspect of recurring patterns, the analyst would be compelled to assess them in terms of the factors that led to their adoption and of the behavior to which they became linked abroad. Again a variety of interesting questions seem worth pursuing. Are direct governmental outputs likely to be linked more profoundly and less transitorily to the contiguous environment than to the regional or racial environments? Are governmental linkages with the contiguous environment likely to be formed mainly through diplomatic and economic activities, whereas those with the latter are more likely to be based on propaganda or military behavior patterns? Do governments tend to be imaginative in linking themselves to the familiar dimensions of the contiguous environment, but cumbersome in coping with the obscure and uncharted terrain of the Cold War environment? For similar reasons, is public opinion more likely to underlie governmental outputs that are part of linkages to the crisis ridden Cold War environment than governmental outputs that are tied to the routinized behavior patterns of the regional environment? Are cabinet governments likely to initiate more enduring linkages than presidential governments?

Fused linkages provide still another intriguing realm for comparative inquiry. Such research would focus on the interdependence of polities and their environments, and would thus be of special interest to students of international institutions and to those concerned with the prospects of supranational integration. The kinds of questions that might be investigated seem almost endless: Are fused linkages more likely to occur with respect to contiguous, regional, resource, or other highly structured environments than to Cold War, racial, or other more volatile environments? Are certain types of polities likely to have a predominance of fused linkages, while others have virtually none? Do such linkages tend to involve elections and public opinion more than other aspects of polities? Is fusion between interest groups and the resource environment likely to be more stable than comparable linkages involving government actors? Is the stability of a fused linkage primarily a function of its environmental or of its polity components? Do fused linkages tend to be more or less enduring than those in which fusion does not occur? Does a rapid expansion in the number of an environment's fused linkages signify that it constitutes an international system that is becoming increasingly integrated?

POSTSCRIPT

One further line of questions comes to mind: Is it irresponsible to raise questions that one neither answers nor provides the basis for answering? Is it self-defeating to propose research based on impressionistic and overlapping categories that have not been derived from a theoretical model and that may thus prove more misleading than helpful? In a discipline that is seeking to find itself as an empirical science, is it counterproductive to argue for theory building without also specifying how appropriate data might be gathered and processed? Furthermore, if the need for linkage theory is so great, why have efforts not been made to develop it? Could it be that in fact there is no such need, that present modes of analysis are more than adequate to handle the convergence of national and international systems?

The answer to these questions can be found in one's reaction to the substantive ones suggested by the framework and to the empirical analyses of the chapters that follow. If our efforts seem mundane, then the call for greater attention to linkage phenomena may well be misleading and unnecessary. On the other hand, if our agenda for research evokes curiosity and reflection, then further work would seem to be in order. And, if use of the framework does appear to have resulted in the identification of important phenomena, then the task of moving on to the construction of research designs should prove both possible and exhilarating.

Appendix A: Elaboration of the Six Subenvironments

In considering the contiguous, regional, Cold War, racial, resource, and organizational subenvironments (see Table 3.2), it must be remembered that these are a breakdown of the external world from the perspective of any polity. Looked at from an international systems perspective, these categories comprise patterns of interaction that recur, respectively, among contiguous polities; among polities in the same general geographic area (such as a continent, region, or hemisphere); among superpolities and their alliance systems (such as the United States, the USSR, the West, and the East); among those in different polities who prevent, enhance, or otherwise affect relations between races; polities who develop, distribute, and consume human or nonhuman resources; and among and within international organizations.

Before elaborating on these categories, it is also useful to locate more precisely the origins of the outputs of these subenvironments. In each of the six cases an output can be the product of behavior patterns that unfold either within or between one or more of the units comprising the subenvironment. In other words, from the perspective of a polity that receives environmental outputs as inputs, the outputs can originate either in other polities or in the interaction among them. If the outputs are purposefully designed by one of the polities in the environment, or if they result from the planned coordination of two or more of them, then they are classified as direct environmental outputs. If, for example, both the United States and NATO regularly seek to obtain, say, Sweden's support for certain arms control proposals, both patterns would be viewed as direct outputs from Sweden's Cold War environment. On the other hand, if aspects of Swedish political life were to become unintentionally linked to sequences resulting from unilateral tariff decisions taken by the United States and to others that consisted, say, of United States-British trade agreements, both would be regarded as indirect outputs of Sweden's resource environment.

Much the same can be said about environmental inputs. These can be part of behavioral patterns that unfold both within and among the polities that comprise the subenvironments of any polity. Patterned reactions to American presidential elections in England and NATO, for example, would both be treated as the environmental input components in linkages in which the outputs were contributed by the United States.

The Contiguous Environment   This category refers to any cluster of polities that border geographically upon a given polity. Hence the contiguous environment allows for the consideration of such phenomena as boundary disputes, historic rivalries, traditional friendships, and the many other distinctive features of relations among immediate neighbors.

The Regional Environment   This category is based on considerations similar to those underlying the previous one. In this case, however, the scope is extended to include the entire region in which a given polity is located. The concept of region is a flexible one, its referent depending on whether geographic, cultural, religious, or historical variables are used as the basis of delineation. Thus the size of a region can range from small areas (such as Central America or the Outer Seven) to partial continents (e.g., Subsaharan Africa, Southeast Asia, or the Arab world) to entire continents (e.g., North America or Europe). Even combined continents, such as the Western Hemisphere, can be treated as a regional environment if it is "natural" for polities to segment the external world along such lines. In other words, the regional environment falls between the close-at-hand and the remote environments to which polities must relate. As such, it would seem to play an important role in the life of many polities, or at least this impression is readily derived from the widespread postwar tendencies toward the institutionalization of regional relationships in a variety of federations, confederations, and common markets. Such integrative tendencies, as well as those of a disintegrative sort, will be among the phenomena identified by this category.

The Cold War Environment Although perhaps less so than many aspects of the contiguous and regional environments, the competition that marks relations among the world's superpolities and their blocs is obviously a highly salient element of the external world of any polity. Particular polities may be geographically removed from the question of whether there will be war or peace in Berlin, Vietnam, or the Congo, but they can hardly remain unaffected by the ways in which East and West relate on such matters. Nor is the problem of war and peace the only dimension of the Great Power or (as we shall call it here) Cold War environment. It also encompasses any pattern that is predominantly a consequence of the state of East-West relations. Questions of disarmament, foreign aid, space exploration, and cultural exchange are thus also part of the Cold War environment, as are socioeconomic policies pertaining to the economic role of government, the rights of groups, and the welfare of individuals.

The Racial Environment This is a frankly experimental category that encompasses phenomena that might perhaps be subsumed under any of the others. It is designed to include all those expectations, trends, and conflicts external to a polity that pertain to relations between racial or ethnic groups. Our purpose is to determine whether categorization at the level of a major issue area is likely to yield significant insights that might not otherwise be developed into the nature of national-international linkages. If inquiry along these lines does prove fruitful, then an attempt to establish other categories of this sort could be undertaken.

The Resource Environment Encompassed here are all the activities through which goods and services in the external world of any polity are created, processed, and utilized. By "goods" is meant nonhuman resources of all kinds, from unmined ore to foodstuffs to advanced machinery. By "services" is meant human resources, including such diverse phenomena as the training of technicians, the education of youth, and the skills of armies. But it is *the activities that result in the utilization of goods and services*, and not the goods and services themselves, which comprise the resource environment. While nonhuman goods are crucial to the satisfaction of a polity's needs and wants, satisfaction results from the use and not the existence of resources. Hence it is the activities in the environment which permit, foster, limit, or prevent usage by the polity of given resources that can become linked to activities within it and which thus constitute this subenvironment.

National-international linkages, in other words, are conceived to occur exclusively among humans. In one sense, to be sure, men are "linked" to their physical surroundings, but these are not linkages as we conceive them here because they can be sustained or altered by the action of only some, but not all, of their components. Physical surroundings impose limits or provide opportunities, but in themselves they cannot act as causal agents in a relationship. What varies is the use (or disuse) of the physical world—the decisions men make about the resources they possess, the resources they desire to possess, and the means they will employ to narrow the discrepancy between their possessions and their desires. Conceived in this way, the resource environment consists of such regularized activities as trade and fiscal relations, economic development programs, attempts to acquire nuclear weapons or, indeed, attempts to acquire any capabilities that will facilitate the conduct of foreign policy.

The Organizational Environment The proliferation and growth of international organizations has required polities to devote increased attention to institutionalized patterns of activity that transpire in their environment. This category is designed to facilitate analysis of the linkages that have thereby been created. It encompasses all those organizations that have structure and personnel apart from the polities belonging to them, such as the United Nations, the Organization of American States, and the International Court of Justice. It does not include, however, the many alliances and agreements in which elaborate specifications for interaction and cooperation are not accompanied by the establishment of implementing machinery that has an identity of its own. Such agreements might be part of the contiguous, regional, Cold War, or resource environments, but here we are interested only in separate organizations, which by virtue of being separate, introduce an additional set of actors into the environment of all polities.

Part II

Regional Circumstances

CHAPTER FOUR

Developing on the Periphery: External Factors in Latin American Politics

Douglas A. Chalmers

LATIN American nations are developing in a far different environment than did the nations of Europe, or even other areas presently classified as developing. Latin America's long-standing ties with an immensely more powerful Europe and United States, the rapidity of communications that send people, money, and resources swiftly back and forth, a century and a half of legal independence, but high economic and cultural dependence, these are elements of the distinctive relationship the area has with its environment. And this relationship profoundly affects politics in the area. Latin American political leadership must constantly deal with the advantages and dangers which such an environment presents. But even more, the political systems are linked to the environment not only as a whole, through the responsible elite, but also through the manifold linkages that exist between groups and institutions within and outside of the area. It is this pattern of linkages, its changes over time, and the consequences that it has for Latin American politics that is the subject of this chapter.[1]

[1] James N. Rosenau, in Chapter 3, defines linkages as "any recurrent sequence of behavior that originates in one system and is reacted to in another." His challenge is

The first task in analyzing the importance of linkages is to evolve a framework sufficiently flexible to describe the many variations involved in the relationships polities have with their environment. Based on this framework, some as yet highly speculative propositions will then be advanced concerning the impact of linkage patterns on Latin American paths to development.

ASPECTS OF LATIN AMERICAN LINKAGE PATTERNS

Some of the dimensions that come to mind in trying to describe the relation of a polity to its environment are colonial dependency versus independence, cooperation versus exploitation and intervention versus nonintervention. However suggestive these terms might be, they are rigid, difficult to measure, and too gross to detect variations between countries and over a period of time. In addition, they are part of the language of polity-to-polity relationships whereas what is needed are categories that deal with the environment and the polity in more flexible terms, since many of the actors and events having an impact on Latin American politics are only loosely, if at all, identified with another polity.

To provide a framework for the description of the general Latin American type of linkage pattern, four aspects are explored:

1. The character of the international system.

2. The external linkage groups (polities, actors, or structures with whom the polity in question has most direct relations) and the relationship of the polity to those external linkage groups.

3. The internal linkage groups (groups, actors, or structures most directly responsive to external events) and the relationship of the internal linkage groups to the polity.[2]

4. The character of the polity.

Within each of these categories, variables can be identified which,

---

to develop systematic analysis of linkages not only as international events affect domestic politics, but also vice versa. The present chapter, however, takes up only the first part of this challenge. It should be noted, too, that this chapter does not explore variations in linkage patterns and their consequences among Latin American polities, thereby perpetuating what for many experts is the lamentable tendency to generalize about a very diverse area. At this preliminary stage of analysis, however, I feel that the similarities are sufficient basis for a general treatment, although verification and refinement in the hypotheses offered here will surely require a more discriminating treatment of the area.

[2] The term linkage groups comes from the suggestive analysis of Karl Deutsch in his essay, "External Influences on the Internal Behavior of States" in R. Barry Farrell (ed.), *Approaches to Comparative and International Politics* (Evanston: Northwestern U.P., 1966), p. 5.

taken with the others, determine the sort of impact that the linkage pattern has on the polity. The following chart illustrates the categories by roughly indicating their content in several periods of Latin American history.

The International System

Rosenau has pointed out that the relevant environment of a polity is made up not of one system, but many—the contiguous, the regional, the global, and so on.[3] A lasting characteristic of the linkages Latin American polities have with the world, however, has been the overwhelming importance of the central arenas of international politics—Europe, the United States and the Soviet Union. It is true that ignoring the contiguous and regional environments has drawbacks, particularly in the period of boundary disputes and Latin American wars of the nineteenth century, and perhaps now with the growth of inter-American economic cooperation and communications. In general, however, it is the characteristics of the "central" system that is of primary concern and consequence for Latin America.

Another important characteristic has been the salience of the economic dimension. The world powers have, in the five centuries since the conquest, been competing with each other for economic advantage in Latin America—for precious metals, raw materials, markets and possibilities for investment. It is true, however, that the character of this economic dimension has changed, most importantly by virtue of the fact that the increasing economic interdependence of the major powers and the effects of the world wars has created a situation that makes possible violent economic instability.

One of the most important characteristics of the international system relevant to Latin America emerged after World War I. The central international system expanded to include the United States and the Soviet Union. At the same time ideologically oriented political conflict was generated as both the Soviet Union and Nazi Germany defined their objectives and needs in world-wide terms. The fact that these conflicts led to world-wide war conditions—hot with respect to Nazi Germany and cold with respect to the Soviet Union—reinforced the ideological drive to build support among polities in such areas as Latin America. The competitive aspects of the international system ceased to be remote and Latin America has, on occasion, become the arena for great power confrontations.

External Linkage Groups

No matter what the state of international relations, the impact on a polity will vary according to the particular nations, structures and groups to which the polity is linked and the nature of that link. Nations do not react to the international system as a whole, but to the way it is reflected

[3] Cf. Rosenau, *op. cit.*

69

Table 4.1—Summary of Latin America's Linkage Patterns in Selected Historical Periods

Aspect	Colonial	PERIOD Late Nineteenth Century	Inter-War	1950 and After
International System	Colonization and mercantile competition	Aggressive commercial competition	Highly instable international economic situation; emergence of ideological conflict	Somewhat stabilized international economy; intensified political conflict increasingly oriented towards winning "third world" allies
External Linkage Groups	Colonial powers who see Latin America as area for exploitation and religious conversion	The major commercial powers, especially Great Britain, who see area as source of raw materials, markets	The international trade pattern, in which LA is a subordinate participant; the major ideological powers begin to see LA polities as allies	The USA—economically sees LA as field of investment and markets; politically as area to be secured against Communism; International agencies, UN, ECLA, IMF, etc., with increasing attention to stimulating the area's development
Internal Linkage Groups	Colonial administrators, church officials	Exporting and commercial elites often dominant. Intellectuals looking to Europe, US. Military establishments. Immigrants	Exporting and commercial elites, still often dominant. Intellectuals looking increasingly to all competing powers. Agents and agitators from all major powers	Government authorities and technicos receiving advice and aid. Intellectuals. Agents and agitators. Middle sectors, aware of external high standard of living. Church groups, especially lay
Nature of the Polities	Bureaucratic-authoritarian	Unstable oligarchy	Unstable oligarchy, with broadening to middle sectors and sporadic agitation from labor groups	Unstable, and broader oligarchy, much divided. Governments increasingly committed to broad development. Forceful nationalist reaction and efforts to control foreign influence

in particular actors with whom they have the most contact. One of the most enduring features of Latin American linkages has been the predominance of one other nation—a colonial power to begin with, and then a dominant commercial one, and finally, despite the growing importance of international markets and agencies, the United States. One might say that with marginal exceptions, for five hundred years each Latin American polity has been in someone's sphere of influence.

Further, after Independence, the linkages have generally been with countries considerably more developed economically than those in Latin America, creating a sharp inequality of capabilities. One may speak of the enduring peripherality of Latin America. Despite the presence of valuable resources that are needed by the major powers, Latin America's bargaining position has generally been weak. This has been modified with the evolution of a politically competitive international system in which major powers showed an increasing interest in winning Latin American allies. The countries with significant strategic value in World War II, for example— Brazil, Argentina, Panama, and Mexico—gained bargaining power with the United States. And in the post-war period, Latin American countries have sporadically been seen as important in the Cold War. This is a growing trend, although still a limited one, but it has led to a significant increase in the resources involved in the linkages.

The linkage pattern of Latin America is distinguished from other parts of the "third world," of course, by the fact that direct colonial ties were severed 150 years ago. This, in a way, has contributed to Latin America's peripherality, since a lack of authoritative bonds meant that the major powers had neither the opportunity nor the responsibility for a thoroughgoing and direct intervention in Latin American politics. Only in the areas near the United States like Cuba and Mexico did this country try, and sometimes succeed temporarily, in direct imposition.

A final point in this category of external linkage entities is the considerable growth and diversification of subsidiary, but still important sources of influence, especially in the various sorts of international agencies— such as the Economic Commission on Latin America of the United Nations, which has been important in providing orientation and technical assistance, and the various international financial institutions, such as the International Monetary Fund, which is important in defining the economic issues, and, when there is a financial crisis, in applying direct pressure on political leaders. Although it would be too early to speak of a differentiated and specialized international set of linkage groups, the Latin American pattern is clearly moving in that direction.

Internal Linkage Groups

With the possible exception of a full-scale invasion, the various elements of a political system do not respond equally to international events.

Groups and structures within the polities have different levels of interest and awareness in the international environment. Another significant way of describing the linkage pattern, then, is to indicate the character and distribution of the most directly linked groups in the polity, and their position with respect to its decision-making processes.

The variables within this category which appear most significant in explaining the impact of the pattern on the polity are:

1. the dependence of the linkage groups on foreign sources of support and their loyalties abroad, or, conversely, their commitments to the polity;

2. the extent to which important linkage groups are filling or controlling authoritative decision-making roles, or more vaguely, but flexibly, their influence;

3. the range of issues in which internal linkage groups are involved, and;

4. the coherence of the linkage groups—i.e., whether they are similarly oriented and coordinated, or whether they are diverse and competitive.

The Independence eliminated the viceroys and bureaucrats who were fully committed and dependent on foreign support and in positions of authority. Following the Wars of Independence in the nineteenth century, the influence of linkage groups was still very great, however, through the dominance of the exporting oligarchs—although the degree of their loyalty, and the permanence of their influence varied according to the degree to which they were nationals or foreigners, and the degree to which they were able to establish hegemony. Since that time the linkage groups have certainly not decreased in size or importance, but they have become more diversified, less coherent, and more domestically oriented. Even foreign businessmen, wherever their loyalties lie, have become more dependent on internal factors, as indicated by the general shift in investment from exporting industries to manufacturing for the local market. Further, the competition of major powers for support has generated competing political groups (Communist parties, guerilla groups, rightist parties, and more recently business and military groups) with fairly strong ties abroad. The technocrats and intellectuals who are in general sensitive to foreign ideas are less committed to particular foreign models, in general due to increasingly complex and differentiated sources, and their loyalties and perceptions appear to become somewhat more autonomous, as is shown in part by their growing espousal of nationalism.

Standing back, the relatively permanent characteristics of Latin American linkage patterns with respect to internal linkage groups in the last century and a half include the absence of direct colonial experience, but an expanding range of linkage groups having considerable influence. As was apparent from discussing external linkage groups, the constant theme has been linkages based on economic factors. While other groups have emerged, the foreign business community and the foreign-tied domestic banking, commercial, and manufacturing interests have been consistently important.

The Character of the Polity

The structure and behavior of the polity become the dependent variables in the next part of the chapter, but however much the linkage patterns influence the political system, it is clear that the relation is two-way, and that no matter what the international system and the pattern of linkage groups are, the impact will be different if, say, the polity in question is forcefully unified in an authoritarian fashion, or if it is a loose and conflict-ridden system.

The variables most useful in assessing the impact of linkage patterns are:

1. the unity and distinctiveness of national culture,

2. the demand-performance ratio with regard to socio-economic development,

3. the legitimacy and stability of existing decision-making procedures, and

4. the capability of the system to regulate the actors within the system—in particular the linkage groups.

Compared with other areas of the world each Latin American polity's national culture must be scored as unified but not sharply differing from each other or that of the major powers. It is relatively unified in that there are few "primordial" loyalties strong enough to threaten a fragmentation of the society. Latin America, despite the presence of the Indian, who is relatively quiescent politically, escapes the threat of national dissolution so prominent in Africa, Asia, and Central Europe. The last foreigner to use "divide and conquer" techniques (based on cultural cleavages) with any grand success was Cortez in the conquest of Mexico.

On the other hand, the culture of Latin American countries has always been heavily oriented toward Europe and the importance of Latin American culture as a source of political opposition to the foreigner has always been rather half-hearted, despite the existence of eloquent advocates. Even the relatively strong "latin" rejection of "anglo-saxon" attitudes seems to be of only peripheral importance.

With respect to the demand-performance ratio, Latin America has certainly experienced a "revolution of rising expectations" in ways to be discussed below, and also experiences relatively sharp crises engendered by the various strategies involved in satisfying those demands. There is no question but that inflationary spirals, political crises over demands to expand and make more effective the suffrage, or other crises associated with the

73

process of development, provide an entry for direct political intervention by outside groups—such as the power given to the International Monetary Fund and foreign bankers in the periodic monetary and payments crises that Latin American countries have recently been undergoing. If anything, this type of problem appears to be increasing.

The high turnover of regimes, and more particularly of presidents and groups in power, which has long provided the central topic for political scientists studying Latin America, also seems plausibly related to the significance of the pattern of linkages. This pattern has been variously termed a "lack of legitimacy," or "instability," although it is commonly noted that such instability rarely indicates major changes in policy orientation. More recently it has been suggested that there is, in addition, a relatively high degree of predictability about the *golpes* and sudden shifts in top personnel—at least in that they reflect a basic set of relationships among a series of elite groups, the "tentative" solution to which may change in detail, but not in general character.[4] In any case there is a weak sense of legitimacy about any fixed procedures of resolving political conflicts, and weak legitimacy for any particular set of top executive leaders. Once again, this would appear to provide opportunities for influence by exogenous groups that would be absent otherwise.

All of the factors so far discussed influence the regulative capability of the system, particularly as it is or can be applied to foreign-based groups. Fundamental and superficial crises impair this ability, as does the lack of a cultural base on which to reject the foreigner. In Latin America, in general, though, there has clearly been a significant increase in this regulative capability, based in part on the strength of nationalistic movements, but probably more importantly, on the development of bureaucratic techniques to control the in and outflow of money and resources, and the improving ability to provide for security, as in the increasingly sophisticated "insurgency" control tactics of the Latin American military (assisted by the United States military). It is obviously an uneven, and unevenly applied capability, but perhaps one of the strongest trends is in the direction of its improvement, most evident in Mexico, where the government appears to be able to absorb a very high degree of foreign involvement and foreign-tied linkage groups without losing control.

THE IMPACT OF LINKAGES ON LATIN AMERICAN POLITIES

Any effort to assess the over-all impact of this pattern of linkages on the structure and development of Latin American polities immediately

[4] For a discussion of the more or less enduring rules of the Latin American political game despite apparent instability, cf. Charles W. Anderson, *Politics and Economic Change in Latin America* (Princeton: Van Nostrand, 1967), ch. 4.

runs up against the obvious complexity of the relationships involved. Linkages may affect the system, for example, in the following ways:

1. Groups with special ties abroad may emulate policies, organizations, standards of living, and so on, introducing exogenous patterns of behavior that may stimulate chains of disequilibria;

2. unequal access to foreign resources may alter the distribution of power;

3. unstable or exceptional demands may be injected into the system by groups acting "under orders" from abroad, or by local groups seeking to compensate for deprivations experienced in their dealings abroad, and;

4. linkage groups, especially foreigners, may be under special constraints with regard to their participation in political life, which may be important enough to affect the style of politics and influence the range of viable political institutions.

Further, the impact of the linkage pattern may be felt in a very general and indirect way in changes brought about in the socioeconomic and cultural bases of the polity, or in a very specific way on the form and output of the day-to-day decision-making process. In order to provide some depth for the tentative conclusions about the over-all impact of linkages, the following pages will suggest some important "middle-range" hypotheses about the impact of linkages on the infrastructure of politics in Latin America, the issues facing decision makers and the policies they adopt, and the institutions through which the system operates.

Impact on the Infrastructure

At the most general level, the history of socioeconomic change in Latin America has been strongly influenced by its linkage patterns. In the colonial period the impact was most direct, with decisions about land tenure, the treatment of the Indians and slaves, and the social status of foreigners and creoles being the subject of legislation in Spain and Portugal. Since the beginning of the nineteenth century, the impact has been more indirect, but strong enough so that histories of social and economic changes are taken up in large part with references to the impact of situations abroad with respect to markets, investments, immigration, and the like.

In a very general sense, the long-term trend, stimulated at least partly from abroad, has been in the direction of modernization—that is, the increasing secularization and differentiation of the population of Latin American polities and their social mobilization attendant on the processes of education, urbanization and industrialization. The question is, however, whether this process of modernization takes on any special characteristics by virtue of the linkage patterns. The answer is clearly in the affirmative, although it is difficult to be precise about distinguishing the importance of linkages from other factors—such as the particular patterns of resources and the influence of more or less indigenous cultural characteristics. A few of these special characteristics most plausibly related to linkages deal with the relationships to authority often denoted as paternalism, the sudden rise in political demands from the "revolution of rising expectations," and the existing pattern of political inequality.

Paternalism

One of the most often noted characteristics of Latin American politics is the tendency of many elements of the population to look to their leaders, political and otherwise, for the initiation, execution, and evaluation of policies, and to resist a mass, "class-conscious" mobilization to make demands. This has received various names, including the *authoritarian tradition*, the diffusion of *patron mentality*, the *subject culture*, and *paternalism*. It is manifested in the relation of the peasant to the landowner, the labor union members to their leaders, the businessmen to the government, and the followers of personalistic leaders in politics. As the terms used to describe it indicate, this phenomenon is usually described or explained in terms of cultural attitudes. It can, however, at least in part be related to the pattern of linkages. This can best be demonstrated by looking at some particular groups.

With regard to the largest set of groups in Latin America, the peasantry, for example, the manner in which Latin American economies were tied into the world market contributed to the perpetuation of large-scale paternalistic social organization in the rural areas and has severely limited the rise of group-conscious small farmers or peasants. The purely Indian communities were destroyed or isolated, and the dominant early patterns of rural organization were large-scale land holdings based on slavery or debt peonage. Major changes in agriculture came with the development of more and more crops for export, rather than commercial production for domestic consumption. Such export production often entailed the perpetuation of the large paternalistic *hacienda* or *fazenda*. Even the most technologically advanced modern agricultural producers of the present time—a fair proportion of which, incidentally, are foreigners—employ a sort of modern paternalism designed to keep their workers tied to the land through provision of housing, schools, churches, and the like. As mechanization and the domestic demand grows, this paternalistic structure will probably change, but it seems clear that up to now, the typical pattern of a fragmented peasantry, tied closely with a local patron, has survived by virtue of the particular linkage pattern Latin America has experienced.

There are also factors related to the linkage pattern which affect the outlook of the urban working class, and may account for its low level of group or class solidarity, a generally low and probably declining level of radical political ideology, and the tendency to opt for rather diffuse "populistic" leadership rather than specific organizational leaders.

To begin with, Latin America's status as a late-comer has produced a particular pattern of industrial growth that emphasizes the demand for highly skilled labor in capital-intensive industries, creating incentives for paternalistic devices by management to hold these workers. At the same time the high levels of immigration to the cities—much faster than the creation of industrial jobs (the industrial work force is declining as a percentage of the total in many countries) leads to a high level of internal stratification within the work force and has been suggested as a reason for the lack of solidarity.[5]

More directly, the pattern of linkages contributes to working-class dependency and involvement with agencies of the government. This dependency—with its resultant lack of labor militancy—can be seen most readily in countries like Mexico and Brazil, where the labor unions are more or less official, but it exists in more subtle ways throughout the continent.[6] Linkages play a role in creating this situation through the emulation by elites in the 1930s and 1940s of world-wide trends toward adoption of "advanced" labor codes and welfare legislation, which in Latin America has created the legal and financial basis for tying the worker to the government. The fragile nature of Latin American industrialization in the face of international competition also makes public policy with regard to tariffs, exchange rates and regulation of credit exceptionally important for industry. If this makes the industrial and commercial interests of the country closely involved with the government, it also means that the workers, too, must depend more on government than on collective bargaining for significant economic gains. Although this orientation sometimes ends with the participation of labor leaders in government, for the rank and file the opportunity and incentive to form militant unions designed to win concessions from management is limited.

Some of the same factors have led to the prevalent posture of industrial and commercial groups, who are periodically chastised by North American writers for their preferences for personalistic dealings, family enterprises, and dependency on the favors of the government.[7] These groups have only recently approached the status of a coherent, politically organized group, and then only in the economically advanced Latin American countries. Developing on the periphery, however, has meant that such groups have always had more to gain—in terms of markets, credit, and technology— through direct dealings with the foreigner, or through favors gained,

[5] Cf. Frank Bonilla, "The Urban Worker," in John J. Johnson (ed), *Continuity and Change in Latin America* (Stanford: Stanford U.P., 1964). Also Henry A. Landsberger, "The Labor Elite: Is it Revolutionary?" in S. M. Lipset and Aldo Solari (eds.), *Elites in Latin America* (New York: Oxford U.P., 1967).

[6] Cf. Robert Alexander, *Organized Labor In Latin America* (New York: Free Press, 1965), and for an analysis of the strategies used by labor in dealing with this situation in Peru, James L. Payne, *Labor and Politics in Peru* (New Haven: Yale U.P., 1965).

[7] Cf. Albert Lauterbach, *Enterprise in Latin America* (Ithaca: Cornell U.P., 1966) and Frank Brandenburg, *The Development of Latin American Private Enterprise* (Washington: National Planning Association, 1964).

often individually, from a government which increasingly controls access abroad.

Probes into the behavior and structure of other groups, I believe, would show similar patterns, providing a partial explanation, at least, for the failure on the part of many Latin American polities to evolve what in Gabriel Almond's terms would be a series of differentiated and autonomous interest groups.[8] Despite the general impulses from abroad towards socio-economic development, which perhaps will produce this pattern in the long run, the combination of unequal levels of development, the pattern of emulation fostered by the cultural and political orientation towards Europe, and the necessarily crucial position of the government authorities in the highly linked economic system, all provide brakes to this process of modernization.

The Revolution of Rising Expectations

The concept of a *demonstration effect* producing a rising level of demands as the people of Latin America become aware of the high standards of living in the more developed countries is a familiar one. The basic conditions necessary—a sharp international inequality and a high level of communications—are clearly part of the Latin American linkage pattern. Some qualifications need to be made, however.

To begin with, the proposition must be applied separately to the various groups in the population. Access to information about the gap in living standards is unevenly distributed, for example, as are opportunities for use of nonpolitical means to satisfy the demands created. Further, any reaction to awareness of the gap depends on the ability of the persons to empathize—imagine themselves on the other end of the scale of inequality—and to have the necessary instrumental attitudes which would lead them to believe that action on their part (i.e., expressing those demands) would be useful in bridging the gap.[9]

Taking these variables together, it seems a plausible and valid hypothesis that it is the middle sectors who would be most affected. The upper classes would either not find a gap between themselves and their reference group abroad, or, in many cases they would be able to rectify it not by pressure on the government, but by manipulating their contacts abroad—even moving there. The lower end of the socioeconomic scale, on the other hand, would be limited in its reaction by lack of access to detailed information, and because of attitudes which would limit their direct action.

These propositions seem in general to be valid in Latin America, since it is clearly this complex middle segment that provides much of the pressure for increasing output by governments. The image called forth by the notion

[8] Cf. Gabriel Almond and B. Powell, *Comparative Politics: A Development Approach* (Boston: Little, Brown, 1966).

[9] Cf. Daniel Lerner, *The Passing of Traditional Society* (New York: Free Press, 1958).

of the *revolution of rising expectations*, that of the masses battering at the gates of the wealthy, is not, therefore, very appropriate. Latin American middle sectors are largely bureaucratic and white collar, and have a long-standing orientation towards assimilation into upper-class patterns. In many countries they are closely tied with the military. In Brazil in the early 1960s, for example, one segment of the much divided middle class was to be found toying with appeals for a fundamental social change, only to be stopped short by another segment—equally insistent on development, but with different ideas about its achievement—supporting a military *coup d'état*.

The impact of the *demonstration effect* is very real in Latin America, and is providing some of the most important factors in its present dynamics, but as yet, in any case, it has not produced a clear confrontation, nor a general mobilization of energies, but conflicting and contradictory trends that have added a new stimulus to diffuse political instability.

The Distribution of Power: Linkages and Political Resources

One of the most enduring consequences of linkages in Latin America has been the influence they have had on the distribution of economic resources, social status, and the means of violence among various groups, contributing thereby to the particular patterns of inequality of power in the system. For centuries, the special advantages that the top elite possessed in controlling the technology and finances from abroad, or the benefits of international trade, made possible a highly oligarchical system. The resources most crucial to maintaining the power of this oligarchy changed—the military technology of the conquerors, the access to markets and financing in the nineteenth century on the part of the exporting oligarchy, and the technical and bureaucratic skills available to governments throughout Latin American history. Until recently, however, the net impact has been to reinforce inequality.

The recent situation is changing, not through creation of an egalitarian society, but by a trend towards so called dispersed inequalities[10] in which there is more diffusion and, to some extent, competition among powerful groups. The way linkages have contributed to this latter phenomenon suggests some hypotheses concerning the conditions under which they affect the distribution of power.

1. The resulting power inequality will be greater the greater is the disparity between the resources available from abroad and those available domestically. Although technologically and in terms of wealth, the gap between Latin America and the rest of the world is increasing if it is changing at all, industrialization has generated competing resources within the country, and improved transportation has made the mobilization of political forces internally better able to counter the use of foreign resources.

[10] Cf. Robert A. Dahl, *Who Governs?* (New Haven: Yale U.P., 1961).

2. Power inequality will be greater the greater is the capacity of relatively small groups to monopolize the access to foreign resources. The competitive nature of the international system and the proliferation of internal linkage groups has created a situation in which opposition groups as well as ruling elites, industrialists as well as exporters, and varying groups of technicians, intellectuals, academics, and civil servants have some opportunity to gain access to foreign resources of various types. The situation has become, therefore, considerably more diffuse.

3. Power inequality will be reduced, on the other hand, to the extent that either the outside source, or the government of the polity, is able to effectively limit the use of externally derived resources for general political purposes. There has been a continuing and probably, on the whole, not very successful effort on the part of United States authorities to prevent aid monies from being used for pay-offs and all sorts of political uses going under the name of corruption. The attitude of the United States has been much more equivocal and much more explosive with respect to the use of military assistance for domestic political objectives.[11] Given the apparently rather confused state of United States policies in this regard, the ability of foreigners to control the use of resources cannot yet be regarded as sufficient to or directed towards reducing political inequality.

More important, however, has been the growing capacity of domestic governments to control the use of resources. Better means of detecting arms shipments across the borders, better administration of export-import and exchange transactions and increasing capacity to regulate the use of foreign aid, sometimes through planning, have all limited the traditional concentration of power in the hands of the traditional oligarchies and their foreign allies within the system. This is an ambiguous trend, of course, since increasing the regulative capacity of government merely accentuates inequality if an oligarchy controls the government. It would seem fair to say, however, that political control of government has become increasingly diversified, although in widely differing degrees from one country to another.

The Impact on the Issues of Latin American Politics

One of the striking things about Latin American politics is the extent to which prominent issues are loaded with international overtones. Even, apparently, purely domestic issues, such as automobile and traffic control, have international dimensions, such as recently when the chief of a traffic department in Rio de Janeiro resigned with a statement blaming his failures on the fact that the United States government had not come through rapidly enough with a promised financial grant for equipment. This rather extreme example points to the fact that one of the ways linkages affect

[11] There is a considerable literature on the uses and abuses of military assistance. With respect to Latin America, Edwin Lieuwen's *Arms and Politics in Latin America* (New York: Praeger, 1960) provided a basic critique which in many respects still stands.

Latin American polities is through making certain types of issues prominent within the system and influencing the ways in which others are faced.

Two of the many aspects of the problem are first, the reflection of external ideological conflict within the polities, and second, the use of "imported" policies and programs in dealing with contemporary problems.

The Reflection of External Conflicts

Ideological conflict in Latin America has long reflected the conflicts of ideologies beyond its borders. The conflict over the role of the Church in civil society, for example, generated vehement controversy which borrowed a great deal from the ideological arguments in Europe. In the twentieth century, the conflicts between the Allies and the Axis and between the Communist and non-Communist world have provided much of the language used in internal political disputes in Latin America. Mere use of the language, however, is not enough, and the problem is to assess the degree to which international conflicts have real significance for Latin American politics. Such significance has had two forms in Latin America, first in the occasional situation in which the conflict among groups directly influenced by foreign powers is important, and second, when this is not the case but when some elites take over the means and definitions of political conflict used by international groups to identify and deal with their enemies.

The direct conflict of internationally responsive groups has been an occasional factor from earliest times—e.g., among commercial groups tied to England and to Spain in the later days of the colonial empire—but they have unquestionably become more important in the time since World War I as the major powers have sought directly to create allies among various groups in Latin America. A whole range of political groups in Latin America can be identified with foreign ones. Increasingly, on the left this identification is with foreign powers—the Russian groups, the Chinese groups, the Cuban groups—whereas on the right and center, since World War II, at least, the identification has been with such entities as the international Christian Democratic movement, the economic groups tied to international business, the military tied to the United States military, and so forth.

It is a mistake to believe, however, that because these groups exist and clearly do conflict, that the major political conflicts within Latin America always revolve around them. Despite the use of international ideological language, and the tendency of journalists to pick up and report such language, the importance of this domestic-international conflict appears to rise and fall, correlated, it would appear, with the intensity of the international conflict, and the crises—from whatever origin—within the polity.

For example, the sharpening of international conflict leading to World War II saw numerous attempts at *coups* by fascist-sympathizing groups against those aligned with Great Britain and the United States, as in

Argentina. The sharp rise in the temperature of the Cold War in the late forties saw a rise in the importance of conflicts with the Communists in Latin America. The conflict between Castro and the United States in the early 1960s also clearly accentuated the political conflict between sympathizing groups in Latin America, and this conflict was sharply diminished after the missile crisis of 1962 both on the domestic and international front.

Internally, crises within the polities also appear to provide opportunities for international involvement and an escalation of domestic-international conflict. By crisis is meant more than a *coup d'état*, of course, although specifying just what characteristics of an internal crisis lead to its internationalization is difficult. In any case, the Guatemalan upheaval that culminated in direct foreign intervention in 1954 is an obvious and extreme example. The Brazilian crisis following the resignation of Janio Quadros that led ultimately to the military overthrow of Goulart in 1964 also saw heightened activity on the part of foreign powers and also by groups on the left and right who may be considered as directly responsive to them, even though the Brazilian crisis stemmed largely from internal factors, and was resolved largely by internal forces.

Although the consequences of these sorts of situations are complex, it might be suggested that since the United States so far has a much superior capacity of providing assistance to groups sympathetic to it, crises strengthen such groups; and that the apparent availability of external support in times of crisis may account to some extent for the sometimes puzzling fact that Latin American political leaders often seem strangely unwilling to build a political base within the country that they might call on in times of crisis. These must remain tentative suggestions, but they invite further investigation.

Even when direct conflict between internationally linked groups is not present, groups often adhere to strategies evolved internationally for "fighting communism" or "overthrowing the imperialists" in their domestic conflicts. There seem to be fashions on the left and the right. For example, left wing strategy has gone through accommodative and revolutionary phases, and a segment of it at present seems to have accepted the Mao-Castro emphasis on rural guerilla war as the road to power. On the right, the influences of United States doctrine about fighting left-wing agitation have had their impact, too. Hemispheric defense to counter the Soviet military threat in the 1950s, support for the "non-Communist left" through diplomacy, private agencies and the CIA, and counter-insurgency tactics have all had their impact on thinking in Latin America, perhaps especially among the military. The conditions under which such transfer is likely are unclear, but it would appear to be a useful area of investigation, since the cues which are used to trigger political action by such groups as the military, or the tools that are likely to be used in internal conflict seem to be influenced by such factors.

Linkages and Latin American Problem Solving

Linkages affect the issues in Latin American political systems in another, more subtle way. Any decision-making process obviously responds to the demands of groups within the system, but the interpretation of those demands depends on the attitudes and perceptions of the decision makers as to the nature of the problem and the resources available. In Latin America these attitudes and perceptions are very often the product of linkages. The methods of collecting data, problem identification and diagnosis, and the programs and policies used often derive from experience in other countries. They are transmitted by a local intelligentsia that has worked and studied abroad, through international agencies such as the Economic Commission for Latin America, or through the technical advisers from foreign governments.

Faced with unrest, declining or stagnant economies, inflation, separatist tendencies, or whatever the problem, leaders in all countries at all times have, of course, cast about in international experience for guidelines for their responses. But because of the long-standing European orientation of Latin American elites and the importance of Latin America's colonial and then economic satellite status, the importance of these foreign definitions and policy models has always been very great. Perhaps the most often noted example of such borrowing was the imitation of European and North American constitutions in the establishment of the Republics after Independence. Despite increasing nationalism, this importation of ideas is more important than ever.

There are many reasons for its growth, primary among which is the vast increase in the rate of communication of ideas to and from Latin America. More Latin Americans are going abroad to study or to work, more international agencies are paying specific attention to Latin American problems, the number of North Americans alone who are involved in conveying advice, plans, and programs, aided by the leverage of financial and material assistance, is very great. Even the growth in the field of the social sciences in the United States dealing with Latin America—however deficient it may still appear in the eyes of specialists—constitutes a vast core of people and institutions giving advice, which is sometimes taken. Latin American decision makers at all levels of authority are increasingly bombarded with suggestions as to what their problems are and what they should do about them. Technical assistance is sometimes thought of in narrow terms of specific governmental programs. Looking at the overall linkage pattern, however, it is clear that generally construed as the transfer of ideas, technical assistance constitutes by now a very broad movement, and this cannot fail to have an effect on the approaches that decision makers take to the problems they face. And those effects come not only from the particular content of the advice that is given, but also in the channels through which it is given.

POLICY INSTABILITY

With regard to the content, one of the most obvious consequences for the system comes when policies or institutions evolved in foreign contexts are applied to quite different situations in Latin America—which happens quite often given Latin America's close ties with Europe and the United States. That such policies do not produce the expected results may contribute to (a) a disillusionment with the policy makers and the possibilities of reform, and (b) a highly volatile style of decision making, in which policies are adopted with fanfare and high hopes, only to be thoroughly condemned as useless when the expected results do not appear. This latter has been described as part of the Latin American decision-making style by Albert O. Hirschman.[12]

Again, the classic example of such a syndrome may be found in the adoption of liberal-democratic constitutions at a time when the social and economic structure of the Latin American republics could turn them into instruments of oligarchic rule. Although the continued prestige of the constitutions has been remarkable—in part no doubt because they could serve the interests of the oligarchies, there is a notable cynicism about them, and also a *de facto* shift back and forth in many countries from at least partial adherence to constitutional procedures and flagrant violation of them. Another example, admittedly covering many particular situations too generally, might be the Alliance for Progress concepts. This time, the projects are much more tailored to the Latin American reality, but they still reflect international strategies of stimulating economic growth, and the gap between expectations and reality has produced cynicism and waves of rejection and support. At least some of the instability in policies in Latin America, and the widespread cynicism about the effectiveness of official action must be credited to the continued and understandable efforts of Latin American decision makers to adopt the latest international program.

PRESERVING FOREIGN INFLUENCE

Although it is a highly explosive topic, it is also unquestionable that the content of much of the advice that comes from abroad has the effect of perpetuating certain kinds of arrangements and ties and particularly the power of some of the most important linkage groups. Given the dominance of the United States in the flow of ideas and resources, it is not surprising that much advice, along with sometimes subtle and sometimes blatant pressure to take such advice, tends to influence the system in the direction of approximating North American ideas about the organization of society and economy, and more particularly, to protect North American interests in Latin America. The policy of urging Latin American elites to define communism as a chief internal threat, or the austerity program for com-

---

[12] Cf. Albert O. Hirschman, *Journeys Toward Progress* (New York: Twentieth Century Fund, 1963), esp. ch. 4.

bating inflation urged by the International Monetary Fund, or the recommendations on the importance of encouraging foreign investment as a basic development strategy are all obvious cases in point. One should not make as much of this as some critics of North American foreign policy do, perhaps. Policies may be intended to protect North American interests but actually do the opposite—as when Latin Americans are brought to the United States for training and return as convinced anti-Yankees. Also there are competing groups within the United States and therefore competing interests to be protected. Finally, it is obviously not true that anything that serves United States interests is necessarily against the interests of Latin America. Nevertheless, as a general characteristic, it is still true that the predominance of a single power in the Latin American environment has shaped the systems and, in a manner of speaking, allowed for a circular reinforcement of that tie.

Both policy instability and the reinforcement of foreign interests are probably diminishing, not because the borrowing of policies is any less, but because the sources of such borrowing are gradually becoming more numerous and competing, and because the growth of scientific interest in Latin America has meant that the facts of the Latin American case are becoming more important in the policies suggested by foreigners or suggested by foreign oriented Latin Americans. There are other effects, however, which do not seem so likely to diminish, but rather to be reinforced by the swelling volume of ideas, advice, and resources in the linkage pattern.

ANTICIPATING DEMANDS AND BUREAUCRATIC OVERLOAD

Despite the authoritarian and bureaucratic traditions presumably inherited from the colonial period, a fairly strong tradition approximating laissez-faire doctrines evolved in Latin America in the nineteenth century, represented by the Liberal parties in many countries. The prominence of such doctrines in Europe was at least partially responsible. Probably equally important, however, was the fact that much economic growth was stimulated by large scale foreign investment in primary commodity production, whose main political needs were to secure favorable concessions and then be left alone as much as possible, since the technology, personnel, transport, and physical construction was largely handled directly by the concerns themselves. The need for support from the local authorities had mostly to do with securing the necessary labor, and not with providing the elements of infrastructure, or a favorable internal market.

By mid-twentieth century, however, the situation changes completely. Not only are foreign investors more dependent on local conditions, but doctrines in the "developed" world have shifted strongly in the direction of an activist state, and much of the technical and financial resources available from abroad are being channeled through government bureaucracies. To this may be added the fact that international economic and political instability—another characteristic of the linkage pattern—makes it difficult to solve many problems without the active representation of Latin American interests in international negotiations on commodity prices, external financing, and so forth.   The linkage pattern has come to reinforce an old tradition which assigns to the leaders the responsibility to identify problems, evolve strategies and apply them, which they do often by applying the latest model solution current in international circles.

Major innovations in governmental policy in Latin America over the last decades would include the introduction of labor codes and welfare policies, the various strategies designed to stimulate industrialization, the extension of the suffrage, and the beginnings of land reform.   In each of these cases, the actions of leaders cannot be adequately explained as responses to the organized pressures of interested groups.   With respect to the labor codes adopted in the 1930s and 1940s, for example, one can find sporadic strikes and unrest, but, at least on paper, the elites overreacted, creating extensive legislation to protect workers often before there were many workers, much less irresistible pressures.   Part of the reason for this can be found in the importance that even minor outbreaks of violence have for the delicately balanced arrangements among the governing elites in many Latin American countries.   But at least in part, the availability of models from abroad—designed to deal with more serious threats in other countries—must be considered as a cause.   Such influence is very easy to perceive with respect to labor codes, for which the Latin Americans could adopt all or part of the legislation being urged by such agencies as the International Labor Organization.   In the case of extended suffrage, the models were more diffuse and varied.   Land reform, perhaps the most recent general vogue in policy making, has also been imposed prior to organized peasant demands, either as part of a general revolutionary ideology, as in Cuba, or as part of a general developmental plan, as in Venezuela.   However much these programs are adopted to the local circumstances, the fact remains that they are imposed rather than being demanded, at least in part because they are parts of the international models of what the problems of underdevelopment are, and what should be done about them.

The consequence of this anticipation of demands, although very complex, appears to entail a reinforcement of the role of the leadership in a paternalist fashion, a great emphasis on the administration of reform, and the opportunity for elites who initiate and execute these reforms to manipulate them in such a way as to avoid serious threats to their position. Thus, land reform can be turned in the direction of increasing productivity rather than destroying the power of the traditional landed oligarchs, as in many countries in Latin America today, or to becoming an instrument for cementing national political control of the countryside, as in Cuba and Mexico.

More fundamentally, this situation produces a particularly delicate problem for the "reform-mongers" who apparently are given a great advantage in the ability to make use of relatively sophisticated reform measures, but who must face the problem of maintaining these reforms in the absence of a firm political base which, having actively campaigned for the measure, might provide the necessary support for the leaders when opposition from entrenched interests develops.

Another consequence of the government-initiated problem solving stimulated by the pattern of linkages is the great load placed on the administrative apparatus. For example, land reform policies are adopted which require detailed knowledge of existing patterns of landholding, productivity and types of exploitation. Such information is often not available nor easily gathered by the existing agencies. It is often difficult to answer the criticism levelled at the advocates of planning that they assume a veritable miracle of administrative development.

In the long run, demands on the bureaucracy will no doubt produce investments in the training and organization of officialdom, but in the short run, the result is often inefficient operations, reinforcement of cynical attitudes toward the bureaucracy and a rise in personal favoritism and graft.

It would obviously be an exaggeration to consider the linkage pattern chiefly responsible for the attitudes and practices just discussed—corruption has long-standing roots in Latin American politics, for example—but the impact of developing on the periphery clearly plays some role. Of course the advantages of being able to exploit the latest and most sophisticated analyses and policies are not to be overlooked, but as conditioning factors of the political system, they clearly have many unintended consequences.

Linkages and the Pattern of Institutionalization

Another aspect of the political systems of Latin America for which the pattern of linkages has been important is that of the manner and form of regular organized political action, or more simply, political institutions. In particular cases, external forces such as the United States have played a very important role in directly influencing the form of political institutions. Financial and military support for Batista in Cuba and Perez Jimenez in Venezuela, for example, helped to perpetuate the dictatorial pattern established in those countries for a short period at least. Intervention in Guatemala in 1954 forestalled the imposition of a radical leftist and perhaps Soviet style institutions in that country, and led to the return of oligarchical institutions of a particularly instable type.

I do not intend to discuss this further, however, since I am not sure there is any general effect, but rather contradictory and changing ones. The left in Latin America contends that United States policy promotes dictatorships and the defenders of the United States contend that it promotes democracy. They both seem to be right at different times and different places.

At a somewhat more general level, however, it seems a plausible hypothesis that the type of linkage pattern characteristic of Latin America has some share of responsibility for the instability of political institutions in Latin America. The general argument would be as follows: Stable and effective institutions require among other things a high level of mutual expectations, shared norms, and an effective set of rewards and sanctions that will secure behavior in accordance with the norms. When there exists in a political system linkage groups with limited knowledge of, or allegiance to, the host system, the institutions are likely to be weakened. An obvious example is the threat that a large immigrant group might pose, although in Latin America the sanctions available to the government are quite large enough to prevent a fundamental threat to the system from that source.

The actors in contemporary systems in Latin America that are the most problematical, however, are foreign businessmen, foreign diplomats and military missions, and the foreign-linked revolutionary groups. Although I cannot cite particular examples of how faulty information, or lack of commitment of these groups directly stimulated the breakdown or change of political institutions in Latin American polities, it is hard to believe that the presence of these "foreign bodies" in the political system has no effect. It is at least interesting to speculate on the possibility that the ignorance of local patterns by powerful foreigners, or their unwillingness to play the game, might enter into some examples of institutional breakdown.

A more consistent influence, however, is that of the presence of foreigners and foreign-tied groups on the workings of liberal democratic institutions. The classic democratic institutions of Western Europe and the United States have been representative ones—parliaments linked with the electoral systems and political parties. The operation of these institutions has never completely replaced or pre-empted the networks of personal relationships among the elites even in the developed countries, and the pattern of interest groups interacting directly with administrative agencies in Europe and the United States has become increasingly important. The system of parties, elections, and parliaments, however, manages to establish basic legitimacy and carry out an over-all regulation of the political game, chiefly by their control over the chief executive.

In Latin America, however, it is notorious that the system of representative institutions is weak. Elections have been manipulated and legislatures have been dominated by the executive or set aside by the military. Although this has many causes, it seems plausible to argue that the linkages have something to do with it in at least two senses. First, the powerful linkage groups, especially the foreigners, are usually not able, constitutionally or practically, to participate openly and fully in the kind of public competition which is demanded for party-political activity, participation in elections and representation in Congresses and parliaments. Although at an earlier stage it would be easy to identify the local representatives of foreign interests who might act quite openly as such, with the rise of nationalism this becomes more and more difficult. The natural habitat of the foreign businessman, the military attaché, the technician providing assistance, is not on the electoral hustings, but rather in the halls of bureaucracy, or in the personal interactions that take place with high government officials at cocktail parties and informal discussions.

In other words, linkages contribute to the tendency to develop means of resolving conflicts, aggregating and articulating interests, through traditional informal means, or through the more or less "private" representation through the bureaucracy. Although this does not necessarily lead to an authoritarian type of system, it would seem to increase its likelihood, especially in circumstances such as those often found in Latin America in which the evolution of pressure groups and regularized means of consultation—which might assure a more or less equal set of opportunities for all existing or potential participants—is, to say the least, not well developed. It is very often not a harsh form of authoritarianism, and may be highly paternalistic rather than ruthless. In part it is moderated, too, by the networks of personal relationships, in which friends can arrange that laws are not too harshly enforced in particular cases. Foreign businessmen, for example, who often have the advantage of rather substantial resources with which to buy such friends, apparently find this game not too difficult to play.

One might look at the same sort of factor from a somewhat different point of view, from that of the political leader faced with the problem of building the necessary type of long-term support for his policies. The strategies that he adopts are limited by the fact, that, as in all systems, he must find a "political base" which will not only return him or his friends to office and pass his legislation in Congress, but will secure the necessary cooperation for the policies that he adopts, or that will find ways to control potential opposition. The high incidence of linkage groups commanding important resources in Latin America means that in one fashion or another, he has to have their support. Also, many of his problems have to do with international questions. The ability of the political leadership to adjust to, say, changes in international prices or the shifting fortunes of international political conflict is limited in any case, since many of the events are far beyond his control. But they are much more uncontrollable if he cannot count on the groups within his own system who are closest to, and have some influence over those external events. The problem of securing their support is more complicated than for domestic groups. First of all, if he brings pressure on them, they will either withdraw (to his detriment) or escalate the pressures they command in the international arena. To build them into his political base, however, requires concessions and communication which usually cannot be carried out as the president might attempt with his "domestic" support—that is, in organizing them through political parties and interest groups acting openly. The contacts must be more or less informal, or expressed—as they often are—in the innumerable "protocols" and "agreements" that are negotiated with foreign governments and international institutions.

The Latin American executives are, very often, caught in a rather difficult position in which their public (electoral and party) base sometimes differs radically from their informal base of support. There results what might be called the "Frondizi syndrome" after the Argentinian president who campaigned on a vigorously nationalistic program in 1958, and once elected, carried out a policy of courting various linkage groups, in particular the American Embassy and the international oil companies. His open political base, in other words, was quite at variance with his necessary base of support once in office. Although there are many factors which undermine the effectiveness of electoral and party systems in Latin America, this complex of national, linkage group and international interests, and the differentials in the ability or desire of these groups to express themselves in an acceptable manner in party and electoral competition is certainly an important factor.

Once again I have treated all linkage groups in the same fashion, and I believe that in general there is a consistency in the pattern, but it is true that there are great variations in the activities of foreign-based groups. In the late part of the nineteenth century, for example, the foreign business firms principally engaged in export trade were no doubt the most important groups in question. With the emergence of foreign business firms more tied to local markets, foreign business seems to play less of a role in promoting a personalistic-bureaucratic type of structure. This would not be true, however, of the huge firms that still remain as powerful entities, such as the United Fruit in Central America, the copper companies in Chile (at least until recently) and the oil companies, particularly in Venezuela.

The business community has been replaced by the embassies and international financial representatives, however, as the main actors of this type. But the basic problem remains the same, and until systematic relationships can be worked out and integrated into Latin American political institutions, the net effect will continue to be that of making the search for stable and secure political bases a complex and difficult task.

CONCLUSIONS

Given the highly speculative nature of the propositions offered here, any conclusions must be tentative. Assuming the validity of even some of these propositions, however, important implications follow for the study of comparative politics and for our understanding of Latin American political processes.

First of all, it is clear that any theories of comparative politics must pay more attention to external factors than has usually been the case. Economists have long done so, particularly with respect to Latin America, where economic history is largely a discussion of external factors and their influences. Political scientists have been much less assiduous about such analysis, however. The reasons for this are many, but one of them, perhaps, has been the dominance of an extremely simple model for analyzing external factors, namely that of polity-to-polity relationships. Overwhelming attention is given externally to the actions of the colonial power, of the intervention of the United States, and only very unsystematically to the impact of groups within other polities, international groups, or the characteristics of the international system as a whole. Further, the emphasis has been on the responses of the polity as a whole—the general "revolution of rising expectations" or the national response to external military threats—and again, only very unsystematically to the differentiated responses of particular groups or institutions. The four-term model offered at the beginning of this essay: (1) the international system; (2) the external linkage groups; (3) the internal linkage groups; and (4) the polity, may point the way to a rather more flexible type of analysis, and one which will allow for a more useful classification and analysis of linkage patterns.

The importance of this effort can be seen from a tentative conclusion about the impact of the linkage patterns on Latin American political systems. Developing on the periphery of a set of powerful and technologically advanced polities, and linked to them in manifold and sometimes subtle ways, the character of Latin American polities cannot help but be different from that of a country at some hypothetically equivalent stage of development in Europe or North America. Not only does the pressure generated by the example of developed countries subject the decision makers to a greater sense of urgency, but the technological and material resources available to them are very much greater than for the leaders of polities developing earlier or in greater isolation. These resources and techniques are not an unmixed advantage—since they must be painfully adapted to the Latin American reality. Building support for the adoption of a foreign-inspired anti-inflationary policy or a set of civil service regulations, for example, requires tactical skills on the part of the leadership quite different from those required in implementing proposals that originate within the polity. A much higher emphasis on something akin to education is part of this, perhaps, as is the discovery of means to avoid or make use of the very wide swings in opinion which are likely to occur without a firmly fixed basis of political support.

The problem of building support for policies and political leadership is also profoundly affected by the presence of large numbers of foreigners and foreign-tied nationals in positions that are crucial to the economy, defense, and cultural affairs. Securing the support of such people is different from that of fully committed citizens by virtue of the special guarantees that must be given (or forceful but subtle means of control) to maintain their cooperation without making them choose the option of leaving the country. The pattern of institutionalization of such support-building practices, too, is different from a more isolated or less dependent polity, because the foreigners are far more difficult to integrate into the public framework of political parties and openly active organized interest groups.

Further, the ideological conflicts of the international system introduce special sorts of frictions into the open political system in Latin America, especially when they are linked with determined outside powers, or when they involve the question of the position of the foreigner within the system. Once again, the linkage pattern, therefore, presents obstacles to the institutionalization of the kind of representative institutions that we are familiar with in Western Europe and the United States.

For a long time, the speculation of political scientists about Latin America centered around the notion of the "pathology of Latin American democracy." Very often executive instability, weakness of parties, manipulation of elections, and *caudillo* type of leaders—taken as the indices of this pathology—were explained in terms of the Iberian Colonial heritage or from cultural factors. If the analysis presented here has any validity, however, the causes must be found also in the linkage pattern that has characterized the area.

But "pathology" is probably not the right word, or it may be applied wrongly to the over-all character of the political systems in Latin America. North Americans and Europeans are perhaps too ready to identify democracy with the health of the representative institutions with which they are familiar, despite the acknowledged signs of weakness into which many of their own have fallen—as is witnessed by the long-standing analysis of the "decline of parliaments." Without judging whether Latin American democracy is "healthy" or not, the analysis here suggests that the forms in which representation and popular influence on the choice of executives and policy making are likely to be quite different in Latin America than in Europe and the United States. Along with other factors, the linkage pattern appears to encourage the evolution of bargaining and negotiation within the framework of the bureaucracy or the executive.

Concentrating the political process among the myriad agencies of the administration, stimulated by the linkage pattern and conforming to the traditional personalistic and paternalistic elements of Latin American political culture, unquestionably opens the way for elite manipulation and nondemocratic practices. But despite the conventional opinion which associates bureaucracies with nondemocratic and manipulative behavior, such is not necessarily the case. It may well be that in Latin America, as in Europe and the United States, the process most crucial to democratic values is the so far largely unobserved interactions that are going on behind the large solid doors of the ministries, autonomous agencies, and mixed enterprises of Latin American governments. The analysis of linkage patterns, in any case, appears to provide an explanation for the importance of these sorts of processes, and ought to stimulate political scientists to consider them as fundamental to the process of political development.

A final conclusion to be drawn relates to the changes in the Latin

American linkage patterns. Although some features have remained constant—the basic peripherality, for example—the pattern has changed by virtue of the increasingly interdependent international system, the more competitive and more numerous external linkage groups, and finally, the increasingly integrated polities of Latin America. The sometimes expressed desire of Latin Americans to eliminate the influence of the foreigner seems quixotic in the face of such changes. But the very increase in the complexity of the linkages, coupled with increasing capacity of Latin American bureaucrats and decision makers, makes possible an increasingly rational control of the domestic situation within Latin American nations, in which the internal linkage groups are more systematically dealt with and their demands related to national objectives. The modern paradox of an increasingly interdependent world with increasingly "nationalist" assertion in such areas as Latin America is, perhaps, not a paradox at all, but rather a logical outcome of the particular ways in which polities are linked to international systems.

Whatever the validity of these analyses or projections, it is clear that techniques will have to be devised to systematically explore patterns of national-international linkages in order to obtain a satisfactory understanding of the factors involved in development. This essay has taken a small step in that direction.

CHAPTER FIVE

Sub-Saharan Africa: Case Studies of International Attitudes and Transactions of Ghana and Uganda*

William G. Fleming

AFRICA offers a rich source of material for scholars interested in developing international systems. Most of the countries of that continent have become independent within the last decade. Most of them have found it necessary to organize foreign offices, establish diplomatic relationships, acquire economic aid, and develop external policy in an extraordinarily short period.[1] Several interesting questions are presented by this process:

* This paper is a preliminary examination of international attitudes and transactions of two African polities—Ghana and Uganda. An attempt is made to provide operational meaning for the categories of the framework set out in Chapter 3. No attempt will be made here to redefine or explore theoretically the concepts of that chapter and it will be assumed that the reader is familiar with them. The purpose here is rather to report empirical findings in terms of the linkage framework. Because the conditions of research were somewhat less than desirable, it must be admitted that the findings of this exploratory investigation remain highly tentative and open to revision. Nevertheless, there is heuristic value in such an exercise and it is hoped that this work will help to illuminate a fresh approach to the study of international and comparative politics. The author wishes to express his appreciation for the support received from the Research Council at the University of North Carolina for this study.

[1] For recent examinations of African international affairs see: V. McKay (ed.), *African Diplomacy* (New York: Praeger, 1966); I. William Zartman, *International*

How is economic underdevelopment related to international political relations? Does the African region exhibit peculiar characteristics as a developing interstate system, or does it share these with other parts of the non-Western or underdeveloped world? Does Africa constitute an international subsystem on its own—or do most African nations interact more frequently with countries outside the continent?

Contemporary specialists in international relations such as Kaplan, Rosecrance, McClelland, and Deutsch have focussed attention upon the continuing pattern of interactions between states and have employed the concepts of systems analysis in their research.[2] Snyder and Robinson have suggested that international maps be constructed for depicting the relations between units in the international system.[3] The Rosenau approach set forth in Chapter 3 attempts to account for the effect that both national and international systems have upon each other.[4]

In the present research both international attitudes and transactions are examined for Ghana and Uganda. These two countries were chosen because of the availability of research materials and because they represent African nations on different parts of the continent and different kinds and stages of political development.

Ghana was the first independent black African country of this century. Since her freedom was gained in 1957 through 1965 she had followed a radical path in both internal and external affairs. Kwame Nkrumah and his party, the Conventions People's Party, had outlawed all opposition and embarked upon an almost reckless policy of intensive social mobilization. This led, eventually, in 1966 to the total breakdown of the system, a military *coup*, and the removal of Nkrumah from office. In foreign affairs the late President was one of the chief proponents of "Pan-Africanism" in which he envisaged Ghana as the nucleus of a continental-wide political union. He espoused socialism, and was in favor of close relations with the Communist

---

Relations in the New Africa (New Jersey: Prentice-Hall, 1966); see also, Patrick J. McGowan, "Africa and the Cold War: A Statistical Study of Comparative Foreign Policy," mimeograph, Department of Political Science, Northwestern University (July, 1967), a paper delivered at the annual meeting of the African Studies Association, New York City, Nov., 1967.

[2] Morton Kaplan, *System and Process in International Politics* (New York: Wiley, 1957); Richard Rosecrance, *Action and Reaction in World Politics* (Boston: Little, Brown, 1963); Charles A. McClelland, *Theory and the International System* (New York: Macmillan, 1966); Karl Deutsch, numerous articles and books among which, *Political Community and the North Atlantic Community* (Princeton: Princeton U.P., 1957), "Toward an Inventory of Basic Trends and Patterns in Comparative and International Politics," *American Political Science Review*, 54 (1960), 35–47, "Transaction Flows as Indicators of Political Cohesion," Chap. 3 in P. E. Jacob and J. V. Toscano (eds.), *The Integration of Political Communities* (New York: Lippincott, 1964).

[3] Richard C. Snyder and James A. Robinson, *National and International Decision-making* (New York: The Institute for International Order, 1961), see project 6.

[4] See also James N. Rosenau, "Pre-Theories and Theories of Foreign Policy," in R. B. Farrell (ed.), *Approaches to Comparative and International Politics* (Evanston: Northwestern U.P., 1966), pp. 27–92.

nations.   Indeed, his downfall occurred while he was away from home on an official visit to China.

In contrast, Uganda, at the time of the research, was a multi-party state, semi-federal in the distribution of political power, and independent only since late 1962.   Its Prime Minister, Milton Obote, was not considered a charismatic leader nor a dynamic Pan-Africanist.   In foreign affairs Uganda was concerned with her Kenya and Tanzania relations and the East African Federation.   The Federation was little more than a customs union and common market, which quickly began to disintegrate after the departure of Britain.

Ideally, it would have been appropriate to include some Francophonic countries in this study.   But given the limitations of this exploratory research it was not possible.   The main goal, here, is to discover dimensions of international attitudes and interactions and to generate propositions for further investigation.   The emphasis is upon fitting some empirical data into the Rosenau conceptual framework, to test its utility and provide suggestions for its refinement.   As the reader is well aware, by now, the theoretical thrust of this volume concerns the effect which internal and external phenomena have on the behavior of any given polity.   It is the nexus between national and international events that is the focus of the analysis.

In this chapter Ghana and Uganda represent emerging African societies which are economically underdeveloped and are members of a growing international subsystem.   For the most part, all of the major directing decisions in foreign policy are made by a select elite.   This elite have undergone similar socialization and recruitment experiences.   Both Ghanaian and Ugandan leaders were raised in the colonial era, both shared in the battle against British colonialism—though in Uganda it was a mild, almost indifferent rebellion against paternal power.   However, there are also some significant differences.   Ghana, in the period under study, could have been characterized as a closed polity.   Elites could rise only through the party apparatus which was highly controlled by Nkrumah and his leading circle.   The natural tribal pluralism of almost all African states was managed in Ghana through a centralized regime which utilized many different combinations of coercion, communication manipulation, and psychological rewards.   The Uganda system, on the other hand, allowed expression of traditional pluralism in its institutional structure.   At the time of the investigation there were three political parties in Uganda, a ceremonial head of state chosen from among the traditional kings of the Bantu states, a prime minister who was not Bantu, and a cabinet of mixed tribal membership.

Uganda is a landlocked nation of some 91,134 square miles and a population of seven million.   Only 1 per cent of the people lived in localities over ten thousand in the period under consideration.   It is estimated that in 1964 about 7.4 per cent of the population were in various levels of education.   While the equator bisects the country, its relatively high altitude and the moderating influence of the great East African lakes provide it with a potentially favorable environment for agricultural production. Most of its earnings are based on coffee and cotton exports. Its Gross Domestic Product was just under $500 million in 1963 and was increasing at about the rate of 7.6 per cent in 1960–64.

Ghana covers 92,100 square miles and had a population of nearly $7\frac{1}{2}$ million in the time studied. Over 11 per cent of its population lived in localities of 100,000 or more and it enjoyed access to the sea with good port facilities. Almost 19 per cent of the population were estimated to be in school of some type in 1964. It has a more advanced and diversified economy than Uganda, although it still depends heavily on the agricultural sector, especially cocoa, for its foreign earnings. In 1963 its Gross Domestic Product was just over $1\frac{1}{2}$ billion, three times that of the East African nation, and it was increasing at the rate of 9.3 per cent in 1960–64.

CONCEPTUAL AND OPERATIONAL VARIABLES

Polity Variables

One of the major categories in the Rosenau Typology of Direct Output Determinants is that of "attitudes" (see Table 3.2). The problem facing the researcher was how to give empirical meaning to this category without going to Africa and engaging in a survey of elite attitudes. It was decided to use an unobtrusive measure—content analysis—of elite opinion in Uganda and Ghana.

In the case of Ghana the best available source of elite attitudes was *The Evening News* of Accra. This paper was established in 1948 by Nkrumah as the organ of the nationalist movement. It is a tabloid published in the capital and consists generally of seven or eight pages. Advertising is sparse, much of it from the government. One page is usually devoted to sports. Date lines are rare and news sources seldom credited. During the period of investigation the *News* was thoroughly under the control of the former president and leaders of the Convention People's Party.[5] Because of this peculiar relationship between the press and the regime, this particular newspaper was considered to be a good source of data on elite attitudes.

As a more pluralistic polity, finding a source for comparable data from Uganda presented a problem. None of the Ugandan newspapers could be relied upon to provide a mouthpiece for the leadership. Since the leadership itself was fragmented it was necessary to find some source which would represent its multiple tendencies. It was finally decided that since many different facets of opinion, traditional and modern, were represented in the National Assembly that the records of its debates would be an appropriate source of information.[6]

[5] See Zartman, *op. cit.*, p. 61.
[6] *Uganda Parliamentary Debates*, Vols. 19–30 (1963–64), Entebbe, Uganda; *The*

Environmental Variables

For Uganda the contiguous environment of *East Africa* is deemed to consist of Kenya, Tanzania, Ethiopia, and the Congo, and for Ghana it is defined as *West Africa*, specifically those nations which border upon her—Ivory Coast, Upper Volta, Togo—and those nearby—Nigeria, Mali, Senegal, Guinea, Sierra Leone, Liberia, Dahomey. The regional environment consists of the remainder of Africa, and by the subregions of East Africa, North Africa, West Africa, and the Organization for African Unity. (South Africa, Rhodesia, Angola, and Mozambique are omitted.)

For both Ghana and Uganda interactions with or attitudes expressed toward the Western systems or the Socialist system were taken as evidence of involvement in the Great Power Environment. Western systems were divided into United Kingdom and English-speaking members of the Commonwealth, the United States and nations of Western Europe. The Socialist systems consist of the Soviet Union and nations of the Eastern Bloc, as well as China and North Vietnam. Nations of the rest of Asia and Latin America represent other subsystems of the total international environment.

Outputs and inputs are conceptualized as interactions with the various environments. Inputs and outputs are divided into three main types of interaction—economic, political, and social-cultural. The economic class refers to events specifically related to the production and distribution of material wealth, trade agreements, technical assistance, commercial delegations, financial arrangements, and communications. Political acts or attitudes refer to the distribution of power both within and between countries, the power structure, national institutions, national policy, ideological exchanges of diplomatic representation, meetings of heads of state or government, special delegations from one government to another, and such hostile acts as border clashes, invasions, and so on. The social-cultural class is mainly residual and would apply to sports activities, art, music, and literary phenomena. (See Appendix I for a fuller discussion of research procedures.)

The source of data for operationalizing the above input-output concepts was the *Africa Research Bulletin*; both the political, social, and cultural series and the economic, financial and technical series.[7]

It is possible to represent the research in the following diagram:

Evening News, Dec. 2–8, 1963; Jan. 6–12, Feb. 3, 9, Mar. 9, 15, April 6, 12, May 11, 17, June 8, 14, July 6, 12, Aug. 3, 9, Sept. 7, 13, Oct. 12, 18, Nov. 15, 22, 1964, Accra, Ghana.

[7] *Africa Research Bulletin*; Economic, Financial, and Technical Series, II, numbers 1–12; Political, Social, and Cultural Series, II, numbers 1–12 (January–December, 1965); (Exeter, England: Africa Research Limited, 1965). The *Bulletin* is published monthly by Africa Research Ltd. and reports events in Africa in précis form using over ninety different national and international sources. Each event which appeared in the *Bulletin* was coded as economic, social-cultural, or political. The value of each event was further coded according to a scale of friendly or positive (+), neutral or undeterminate (0), or unfriendly or hostile (−).

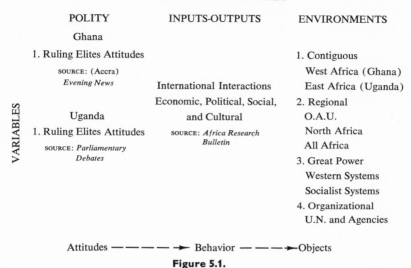

RESEARCH VARIABLES

POLITY	INPUTS-OUTPUTS	ENVIRONMENTS
Ghana		
1. Ruling Elites Attitudes		1. Contiguous
SOURCE: (Accra)		West Africa (Ghana)
Evening News	International Interactions	East Africa (Uganda)
	Economic, Political, Social,	2. Regional
Uganda	and Cultural	O.A.U.
1. Ruling Elites Attitudes	SOURCE: *Africa Research*	North Africa
SOURCE: *Parliamentary*	*Bulletin*	All Africa
Debates		3. Great Power
		Western Systems
		Socialist Systems
		4. Organizational
		U.N. and Agencies

VARIABLES

Attitudes — — — — ➤ Behavior — — — ➤ Objects

Figure 5.1.

GHANA—ELITE ATTITUDES

A 1965 survey of *The Evening News* had disclosed that elite opinion in Ghana was positively oriented toward the Soviet Union, and by comparison negatively oriented toward the United States.[8] Out of 232 mentions in the August issue, the United States received 4 per cent positive, 27 per cent neutral, and 69 per cent negative, while Russia garnered 78 per cent positive, 22 per cent neutral, and no negative references in a total of 130.

The present examination was carried out for one year, 1963 to 1964, to determine the affective orientation of the Ghanaian elite toward the several environments—contiguous, regional, and Great Power. A total of 2,635 attitudes was identified; of these 670 dealt with economic affairs, 1,465 were political, and remaining 500 social and cultural. This would seem to indicate that the elite, at least as expressed in opinions in *The Evening News*, were highly politicized.

> **1.1** Elites in developing African centralized polities are politically oriented toward the several environments and are less concerned with economic or social-cultural relationships.

[8] I am indebted to Mr. John Galbraith for this information. The attitude coding in this project was carried out by Mr. Galbraith, of the School of Journalism, and Mr. Gordon Friedman, of the Political Science Department at the University of North Carolina. Further important assistance was provided by Mr. Peter Harkins of the Political Science Department, to whom I am also grateful for drawing the graphs.

As a dynamic Pan-African government there is little surprise in the highly political orientation of Nkrumah's regime.   It may be well to point out, however, the importance of ideology as a determinant of attitudes. The famous dictum of the former President, "Seek ye first the political kingdom," was as salient for foreign affairs as for internal development. Indeed, this may indicate the propensity of a ruling elite to translate all problems into political questions.   What is needed is a comparable study of orientations in a "developed" polity and of attitudes of historical leaders in the West.   It may be that national elites of all transitional societies which seek regional hegemony in an international subsystem, including those of eighteenth- and nineteenth-century Europe and North America, are highly politicized.

Contiguous and Regional Environments

Of the total attitudes identified 31 per cent concerned Africa as a region and the majority of these were either positive or neutral (see Figure 5.2). The rather large number of negative orientations (183) were about half

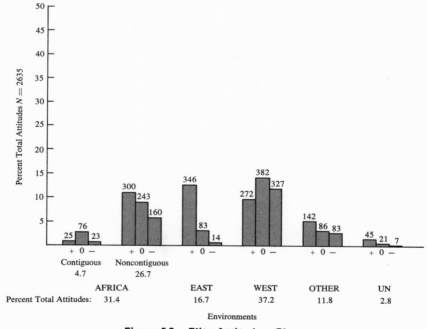

Figure 5.2.   Elite Attitudes: Ghana

Percentages represent volume of Ghanaian elite orientation toward the several environments as identified in *The Evening News*, Accra, 1963–64.   Plus, zero, minus represents the quality or value of the attitudes: positive (+), neutral (0), and negative (−) respectively.

political although 65 were economic and 28 social-cultural. The lack of an overwhelming positive orientation of the elite toward the rest of Africa is perhaps indicative of the quarrels which had already developed between Ghana and other states.

The Ghanaian elites' concern for the immediate contiguous environment was expressed only as 15 per cent of the Regional total and about 5 per cent of the grand total. This is somewhat surprising in that one might have expected more evidence of interest in the neighbors of West Africa. However, Ghana under Nkrumah had aspirations of becoming the leader of Pan-African unity and perhaps the chief power on the continent. By 1964 strained relations had already developed between Ghana and the Entente Powers (Ivory Coast, Niger, Upper Volta, Dahomey) and the Monrovia Groups (Liberia, Nigeria, Sierra Leone, Togo).

> **1.2** The higher the aspiration for regional leadership, the higher the orientation to environments beyond contiguous boundaries.

The finding that nearly one third of all attitudes expressed related to the regional environment (Africa) is of some interest. One would like to know how this compares with the orientation of elites of other states (see figures on Uganda), and with state interactions.

> **1.3** The stronger the "pan" ideology of regional environment, the more polities will be oriented toward relationships beyond immediate neighbors.

These two propositions (1.2 and 1.3) are significant in several dimensions. Ghanaian elite orientation to the wider area of Africa may reflect the importance of an encompassing political ideology which stimulated militant international behavior. Except for Guinea, Nkrumah's radical external policy had alienated Ghana from most of the surrounding polities. However, much attention was still focussed on the entire continent which indicates the leaders' preoccupation with African affairs.

One particular kind of relationship between two categories of the Rosenau framework now emerges. Contiguous environments may not represent salient objects for involvement when polity elites aspire to regional leadership. This illustrates the problems in the development of an African international subsystem. Rigid blocs and alliances have not yet appeared and the kind of jockeying implied here may mirror the fluid state of an evolving equilibrium. A "pan" ideology which pervades a geocultural area may characterize the early stages of systems growth in interstate relations. The distinction then, between contiguous and regional environments, which is highlighted by Rosenau, may be very important for the study of "underdeveloped" international systems.

101

The Great Power Environment: Western and Socialist Systems

Ghanaian elites directed 37 per cent of their attention toward western systems in the period under consideration. These were divided almost evenly—one third positive, neutral, and negative. The Socialist systems received only 17 per cent of the volume of attitudes. Of these 78 per cent were positive and only 3 per cent were negative. It is interesting to note that almost 20 per cent of the Socialist total was directed toward Communist China. China received 66 positive mentions, 19 neutral and only 2 negatives.

The larger volume of attitudes directed toward the Western systems can be interpreted in various ways. It seems rather obvious that Ghana elites were still preoccupied with their former western ties, and about evenly divided in affective orientation. There are probably several reasons for this —ties of language and common relationships built up in the colonial period, more opportunity for development assistance. However, the picture of Ghana under Nkrumah as a severe shrill critic of the West becomes somewhat blurred. Almost two thirds of all attitudes identified were either positive or neutral.

> **1.4** The higher the environment potential for providing development assistance, the higher the orientation of an African polity toward that environment.

> **1.5** The longer and stronger former relationships and common communications symbols exist with an environment (other society), the greater the orientation of an African polity toward that environment.

In proposition 1.4 "African polity" is a more specific substitute for "underdeveloped state." The problem here is to ferret out the other plausible reasons for Ghana's volume of orientation toward the West. Possibly there are more Western nations which impinge upon her area of interest. If the attitudes expressed had been predominantly negative, an ideological factor, the counterpart of that in proposition 1.6, might be cited. Both the United Kingdom and the United States received over 300 mentions and together they account for two thirds of the western total. This would lead to the hypothesis that past historical connections are still very important in determining current orientations (proposition 1.5).

Although the volume of attitudes expressed toward the Socialist systems was much smaller than that toward the West, almost 80 per cent were supportive. Thus while the image of Ghana as hostile to the West is somewhat altered by these data, the belief of her (former) positive orientation toward the Socialist systems is maintained. This may be due to the strong ideological attachment to socialist principles evidenced in the speeches and writings of the elite such as Nkrumah's work on "Consciencism."

1.6 The stronger the ideological attachments within an African polity, the higher the positive orientation toward (systems) environments possessing similar or comparable ideologies.

The importance of the ideological factor in accounting for much external behavior in Africa cannot be ignored. Ghana, and present day Guinea, are the best examples of this phenomenon. According to one specialist, ideology in African foreign affairs is not a directing force but rather a limiting one. It can provide a framework within which to justify and interpret actions and "affects the choices of allies and enemies."[9] The Socialist systems are often viewed as the best allies against real or imagined neo-colonialism of the West. Thus the Ghanaian elite were overwhelmingly positive in their orientations to the Soviet Union and China.

The Great Power Environment accounted for over 50 per cent of all Ghanaian effective involvement. This would seem to indicate the pervasive influence in Africa of the great power struggle. It might also signify the greater predisposition to "external" leadership and therefore foreign involvement of the former Ghana political chiefs.

1.7 Cleavages between the Great Powers in the international environment will remain salient for underdeveloped centralized African polities, official policies of nonalignment notwithstanding.

For any state which participates in the world system there is probably no escape from involvement in the Great Power dispute. As pointed out previously, however, even militant, radical Ghana showed a greater volume of orientation toward the West than the East. And on the whole the attitudes expressed were not negative. It is interesting to note that even though there was a small volume of orientation toward the United Nations these were favorable.

UGANDA—ELITE ATTITUDES

In this investigation of the affective orientation of Ugandan elites toward the several external environments a total of 1648 attitudes were identified. As in the case of Ghana, more of these were political (727) than economic (634) or social-cultural (287), although the politicization is not so pronounced. The economic proportion may be larger than Ghana's because of parliamentary attitudes expressed toward United Nations technical assistance. This may be a function of elites playing more responsible roles in a formal legislative setting, rather than attempting to arouse public

[9] Zartman, *op. cit.*, pp. 83–84; see also Zartman, "National Interest and Ideology," in McKay (ed.), *op. cit.*, pp. 15–54.

opinion through the medium of a political newspaper. This larger economic orientation of the Ugandan legislators may also reflect a genuine concern for development of the economy—which as noted was far less advanced than that of Ghana. In any case the political total is slightly larger.

> **2.1** Elites in developing African pluralistic polities will tend to temper political orientation toward the several environments with economic considerations.

The more temperate pluralistic regime in Uganda was characterized not only by a more pronounced concern with economic matters but also by a far larger number of neutral orientations, and corresponding fewer negative or positive ones (Figure 5.3). This moderation may be caused by several factors. Ideology was not an important determining force in Ugandan politics. The period under investigation was only the second year of independence (1963–64) and the fragmented elites were still greatly concerned with internal unity. Indeed a more pronounced positive or

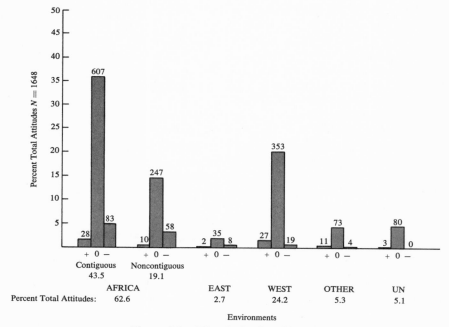

Figure 5.3. Elite Attitudes: Uganda

Percentages represent volume of Ugandan elite orientations toward the several environments as identified in the debates of the Ugandan National Assembly, 1963–64. Positive (+), neutral (0), and negative (−) categories represent the quality or value of attitudes expressed.

negative stand in the international system may come only when the leaders have more time for involvement and to develop standard responses or policy on foreign affairs.

> **2.2** The higher the elite involvement in internal problems, the lower the volume of negative or positive orientations toward international environments.

> **2.3** Elite positive and negative attitudes toward the international affairs will increase the farther from the date of independence.

The very lack of direction in the attitudes discovered is itself probably an indicator that an over-all belief system or political ideology had not yet formed in Uganda. However, to be certain it would be necessary to have comparable data from Ghana and several other African polities in the period shortly after independence.

The Ugandan elite directed over 1000 of their comments toward Africa as a region and most of these concerned the immediate contiguous environment of East Africa. The difference between the African orientations of the Ugandan leaders (63 per cent) and the Ghanaian (31 per cent) is of some importance and not easily explained. Again it is necessary to be sensitive to the sources of the data—perhaps elites as legislators are more oriented to problems with immediate international neighbors. Certainly Uganda was not an aspiring bloc or Pan-African leader as was Ghana. But then why so much concern with the entire continent and particularly with the contiguous nations of Kenya and Tanzania?

Part of the answer may lie in the peculiar events of 1964. This was the year in which the armies of all three East African nations mutinied and the East African Federation continued to disintegrate. British forces had to be called back briefly in order to re-establish stability in the area. The Zanzibar revolution, which occurred just previous to the mutinies and may have been related to them, was climaxed by the joining of that island to Tanganyika to form the new state of Tanzania. This may explain some of the Uganda elites' concern with the contiguous environment.

When compared to Ghana, Uganda showed only slightly less orientation toward the rest of the continent outside immediate neighbors. But the direction of the involvement was far less pronounced. Much of this data might be viewed as evidence in support of propositions 1.2 and 1.3 concerning regional orientations. Uganda was not a strong mover in Pan-African union and therefore her involvement in local East African matters is not surprising. Indeed the greatest number of negative attitudes expressed in the National Assembly at this time were directed toward the contiguous (83) and regional environments (58).

Until the recent extra-constitutional changes in Uganda, which smashed the old ethnic balance and pluralistic regime, the political leaders were chiefly concerned with sustaining national integration. It would be interesting to know how the country, in the earlier period, would have rated on one of Deutsch's "preoccupation ratio scales."[10] In general it might be hypothesized that leaders in all underdeveloped polities are more occupied in building internal mechanisms of unity than in foreign relations. In this context, the Ugandan concern with East Africa can almost be viewed as an internal problem. A study of the Ugandan legislature in 1961 revealed a more positive orientation toward the neighboring countries of Kenya and Tanganyika.[11]

There are of course a great many variables which might affect the different postures of Uganda and Ghana toward their contiguous and regional environments. Uganda had been part of the British Empire in East Africa and was closely tied to the other units in the Federation. Ghana, on the other hand, was the former British colony of the Gold Coast and is surrounded by Francophonic polities with which she has had little in common in the past. Not long after independence she had formed a union with Guinea and Mali which was little more than a paper agreement and never really effective after 1961.

> **2.4** The more an African polity has shared a common colonial past with contiguous neighbors, the more oriented her elite toward those neighbors.

This proposition is offered for heuristic purposes and is testable throughout a great variety of situations in Africa. It may be considered corollary or companion to **1.5** regarding former relationships and communication symbols. Again, the factor of ideology would account for some of the difference in behavior. Even though Ghana and Nigeria did not share a common boundary they were very near each other in the same area of West Africa and had shared a common colonial experience. But the Ghanaian elite were thoroughly alienated from the moderate international policies of the former pluralistic Nigerian regime and had even given assistance to subversive elements in order to bring it down.

The Great Power Environment: Western and Socialist Systems

The Western systems were the object of 24 per cent of all comments by the leaders in the Uganda National Assembly during the period under examination. Most of these were neutral (353) with about an even number divided between positive (27) and negative (19) orientations. It is interesting to note that about 50 per cent of all these were directed toward Great Britain and the older Commonwealth and that almost all of the positive responses (20) and half the negative ones (11) were likewise directed. Again

---

[10] Deutsch, *op. cit.*, 1964.

[11] See Gordon Friedman, "A Content Analysis of References to Foreign Countries in the Legislatures of Ghana and Uganda, in 1961," typescript paper (Chapel Hill: University of North Carolina, Department of Political Science, Jan., 1966).

this may be evidence that the influence of the former colonial power was still very strong in East African affairs during the eventful year of 1964. The comparable data for Ghana show something less than a third of the volume of western orientation directed toward the Anglophonic Commonwealth.

The reasons for Ugandan elite attraction to the United Kingdom are probably more than the one suggested by 1.4 above regarding economic development, though that is undoubtedly important. Indeed the only attitudes expressed at all toward the non-British members of the Commonwealth were all economic. But the preoccupation can most likely be attributed to the role the metropolitan power was still playing in security matters, development assistance, and internal administration. The ties had not yet vitiated and the new polity was independent in name only. The cultural links were also still very important in the comments of the elite. A well-integrated ideology had not yet developed as it had in Ghana, which contained myths about the past struggle against British imperialism and the dangers of neo-colonialism.

> **2.5** The closer an African polity to date of independence and more dependent on the former colonial power and the lack of militant anti-colonial ideology, then the more positive and the larger the volume of its elite orientations toward that power.

If this proposition is supportable a contemporary study should show that Uganda has drifted further from Great Britain since the date of obtaining sovereignty. This one factor would be attenuated by the need for assistance and the lack of ideological development. Zartman points out how surprised a Guinean delegation was to discover portraits of the Queen all over Ghana in the early days of independence.[12] The comparative attraction to the mother country was also characteristic of the less militant pluralistic polities of Nigeria and Sierra Leone.

Although the over-all orientation of the Ugandan elite toward the West was smaller than that of Ghana (24 per cent to 37 per cent) less than 3 per cent was directed toward the Socialist systems. This is much smaller than the Ghanaian figure (17 per cent) and reflects the lack of ideological commitment of the fragmented Ugandan elite. It is doubtful that this indicates an ideological stance favorable to the West. The data seem to suggest that the small East African country was far less effectively involved in the Great Power environment than its West African counterpart.

> **2.6** The higher the affective involvement of African elites with the contiguous environment, or internal political unity, then the lower the orientation toward cleavages in the international system or the Great Power environment.

[12] Zartmann, *op. cit.*, p. 61.

There is little doubt that the Ugandan elites were highly involved in settling problems of internal unity and East African integration during the period of investigation. However, there may be several other causal factors working here in conjunction. Again, the date of independence may be important—Uganda had not yet had enough time to become deeply involved in the international system, had not developed an ideology nor foreign policy.

Involvement in the international system might be measured by voting record within the United Nations. But this could also be a misleading measure since all members are, by definition, part of a world system. The context is one which influences all states to take positions on questions of international cleavage—any propensity to opt out or remain neutral is scarcely indulged. One researcher has found that Uganda's voting record within the 1963 General Assembly associates very highly with such radical states as Ghana and Guinea.[13] This would suggest that Uganda was playing more of an important ideological international role than the data here indicate.

The Ugandan elites directed 5 per cent of their comments toward the United Nations. These were all neutral and were concerned entirely with economic problems, this in contrast to Ghana where most of the U.N. orientations were political.

INPUT-OUTPUT TRANSACTIONS

It will be possible here to provide only a cursory examination of the transactional data and to suggest questions for further analysis. There are several important dimensions of interstate relations which can be studied through the transactional approach.[14] The first of these might be the volume or number of interactions between polities, to measure the intensity of a relationship. Another would be the type of transaction involved; in this investigation a classification of three main categories has been constructed—economic, political, and social-cultural (see Appendix I). A third significant dimension would be the quality or value of the transaction for the polities in the relationship. Again, in this study a simple ordinal scale of plus, zero, and minus has been constructed for identifying such phenomena. Last, it would be necessary to discover the balance of transactions—the number of interactions initiated with any polity to those received. This would be the political counterpart of the international balance of payments familiar in economics. It would describe the symmetry of relations between polities—to what extent interactions were reciprocal or asymmetrical.

[13] Benjamin Meyers, "African Voting in United Nations General Assembly," *Journal of Modern African Studies*, IV, 2 (1966), 213–27, and his study also showed Nigeria and Tanganyika as part of the same cluster.

[14] See Snyder and Robinson, *op. cit.*, 1961; Deutsch, *op. cit*, 1957 1964.

Eventually it is hoped that all these dimensions will be measured in this project. For the present only a few will be given as illustrations.

Ghana

A total of 220 interactions were recorded for Ghana in the period January, 1965 to December, 1965. (These do not include the totals for the organizational environments which amounts to 10 and increases the grand total 230.) This means that Ghana either initiated or was the recipient of 220 different types of relationships with the several different environments. About 39 per cent of these were economic exchanges, 50 per cent political and the remaining 11 per cent social and cultural. These appear to be somewhat associated with the attitudinal orientations reported earlier and lend support to proposition 1.1, though economic exchange is higher than would be predicted by affective orientation.

> **3.1** The higher the ideological politicization of the elite in an African polity, the stronger the tendency toward political interaction with the external environment, and the less emphasis on economic or social exchanges.
>
> **3.2** Economic interaction will remain higher than predicted by affective orientation of the elite in an African centralized developing polity.

Ideology or high politicization of the Ghanaian elite would seem to be an important factor in determining the volume and value of interactions. Out of a total of some 113 political transactions, Ghana initiated 47 friendly acts, 6 neutral and 15 unfriendly ones. She was the recipient of 63 supportive economic transactions and only initiated 20 herself. This clearly indicates the Ghanaian emphasis on political transactions.

At the same time it is apparent that the rest of the world was engaging in economic transactions with the developing African country. The Socialist systems initiated some 20 positive economic acts, the Western systems 15 and the United Nations 4. Regardless of the political orientation of the elite, economic transactions constituted an important sector of Ghanaian relations with the industrialized nations. This should not seem unusual when it is remembered that an underdeveloped country has little ability to initiate economic acts. This is reflected in the low number of economic transactions between Ghana and the rest of Africa.

Contiguous and Regional Environments

Forty-three per cent of all Ghanaian interactions were with other African regional polities, and 70 per cent (73) of these were with the contiguous states of West Africa. Economic exchanges accounted for 25 per cent of the

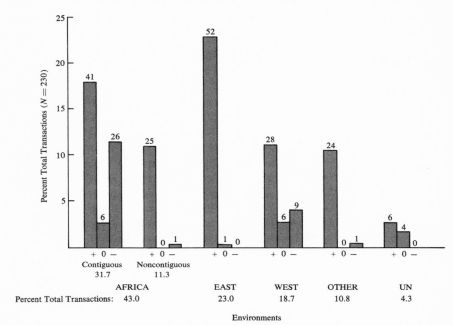

Figure 5.4. International Transactions: Ghana

Volume of Ghanaian international transactions with the several environments represented by bars. Friendly acts represented by (+), neutral by (0) and hostile by (−). Source of data: *African Research Bulletin*, 1965.

total African interaction pattern, while 69 per cent were political and only 6 per cent social-cultural.

Again, the affective orientations reported previously would not have predicted Ghana's close relationship with her regional and contiguous environments. Though elite attitudes were apparently oriented toward greater world involvements, actual interactions were more circumscribed. Nevertheless, there does appear to be some slight relationship between the volume of Africa directed opinions found in *The Evening News* (31 per cent) and the volume of regional interactions (43 per cent).

3.3 The higher the elite aspiration of regional leadership, the higher the interaction of a centralized African polity with regional and contiguous environments.

3.4 Interaction with contiguous nations will remain high regardless of large volume of elite orientations toward other environments in a centralized African polity.

110

Proposition 3.3 must remain untenable until more evidence is available. The data reported on Uganda suggest that even nonaspiring regional leaders will have a high volume of orientations and transactions with other African nations. And thus one conclusion might be that interactions of under-developed African polities will not depend necessarily upon the attitudes of the leaders but rather upon the available neighbors. With limited ability to control the international environment, the elite cannot direct the course of behavior as they would wish. Contiguous boundaries and regional neighbors thus will continue to supply the largest number of transaction partners. More research is needed to discover what factors increase a polity's ability to widen its pattern of international interaction.

It seems fairly apparent that regardless of the low volume of elite orientation Ghana dealt significantly with contiguous West African polities. As mentioned above, geographical availability would seem to play an important role here. Elite attitudes are not the only governing factor. Indeed, the orientations of the leaders toward the surrounding West African states was, if anything, highly neutral or indifferent. The interactions, however, showed well over half friendly and about one-third acts as un-friendly. Thus we might conclude, tentatively, that not only the volume of interaction with the regional environment but also its value may not depend upon the orientations of the leadership. It is also possible to speculate that in foreign affairs Ghana was not the highly centralized polity, nor was the hegemony of the elite party as complete in controlling international interactions, as might be supposed.

> **3.5** The quality of interactions in the regional environment will not necessarily be a function of the elite orientations of a developing African polity.

The Great Power Environment: Western and Socialist Systems

Western systems were involved in 19 per cent of all Ghanaian transactions, while Socialist Systems accounted for 23 per cent. Exchanges with the West are not at the same level as the volume of attitudes (37 per cent), and those with the Socialists somewhat above the level of orientations (16 per cent). The most significant finding is that 98 per cent of all Ghanaian exchanges with the Socialist systems were friendly or supportive and there were none hostile. This would tend to confirm the attitudinal orientation toward the Socialist systems.

> **3.6** The stronger the positive ideological orientation of an African elite toward an environment, the higher the friendly transactions and the lower the hostile transactions with polities in that environment.

Both the attitudes of the Ghanaian elite under Nkrumah and the actual international exchanges show a definite bias in favor of the USSR and the Socialist systems. Ghana initiated some 14 exchanges and was the recipient of 39—none of these were hostile. There is good evidence for asserting that the West African country was significantly oriented toward the East in the Great Power environment. It is doubtful if this tendency will continue under the new military regime which has already attempted to create conditions favorable for the attraction of private western capital.

Ghana appears to be highly involved in the Great Power-Cold War environment, a total of 41 per cent of all her exchanges are so directed. And she is on friendly terms with both the Western and Socialist systems, exhibiting perhaps a more positive relationship with the latter.

Another interesting observation is that the positive exchanges with the West were three times as large as unfriendly ones—but still smaller than those with the East. Relations with the western systems were still important both in volume and quality.

> **3.7** Positive African elite ideological orientations and friendly international transactions of a developing African polity with any Socialist polity in the Great Power environment will not preclude significant friendly relations with Western systems.

This is an important hypothesis. It may well indicate the conscious policy of the elite not to isolate their country nor become tied to any one camp. It could also mean that polities in the Great Power environment are willing to maintain relations with developing African polities regardless of the ideological pronouncements of their leaders. As already pointed out friendly economic exchanges were still significant with both sides. Over half of the Western and Eastern initiated exchanges with Ghana were economic. And almost a third of the Socialist initiated transactions were social and cultural.

Uganda

A total of 158 interactions were counted for Uganda in 1965. Economic exchanges accounted for 56 per cent of these, political acts amounted to 38 per cent and social-cultural to about 6 per cent. Here we find a reversal of the relative importance of political and economic exchanges when compared to Ghana. It will also be recalled that Ugandan economic attitudes were of a higher proportion than for those of the West African counterpart. The evidence tends to support propositions made concerning politicization of elites, and economic interactions. It would seem that Uganda's more conservative international posture includes realistically emphasizing economic interactions.

> **4.1** The more ideologically conservative internal African leadership, or the more internal involvement in national integration, the higher the propensity toward external economic exchanges.

112

4.2 The higher the economic orientation of an elite in an African pluralistic polity, the larger the volume of economic transactions with the several environments.

It should be noted that Uganda initiated almost as many political transactions (28) as economic ones (30), but that it received over twice as many economic exchanges (59) as it did political ones (28). In other words, the industrialized world was emphasizing economic relations with the underdeveloped East African country. This would appear to be additional evidence for proposition 3.2. The greatest imbalance occurred with the West which initiated some 18 economic transactions and Uganda reciprocated with only 2. However, the Uganda elite were definitely more concerned with economic affairs than Ghana and this would seem to account for some of the difference in the greater number of economic transactions.

It is interesting to point out that in the case of both the East African and West African polities under study most of the exchanges in the social-cultural arena took place either with other underdeveloped countries or with the Socialist systems. For Ghana out of 25 such exchanges recorded 14 were with the Socialist systems, one with the West, and the remainder with African and Asian nations. For Uganda there were no social-cultural transactions with the West, 7 were exchanges with other African systems, and two with the Socialists. Again this probably refers to the available types of "currency" which developing states can exchange with each other.

4.3 The lower the available economic exchange resources of an underdeveloped African polity, the higher the propensity to engage in social-cultural transactions with other low resource nations.

Contiguous and Regional Environments

Uganda was involved in 76 exchanges with African regional systems, which represent 48 per cent of the total. Of these 40 per cent were interactions with the contiguous states of East Africa. Economic transactions in Africa amounted to 41 per cent, political exchanges to 50 per cent, and social-cultural 9 per cent.

Attitudes expressed in the Uganda National Assembly revealed a high concern for both Africa and the contiguous states of East Africa. However, both percentages reported here for exchanges in the regional and contiguous environments are lower than those of the affective orientations. This, again, is almost the reverse of the Ghana case—where attitudes were lower than recorded interactions. Both Uganda and Ghana had similar interaction rates with the regional environment (49 per cent and 43 per cent respectively). This would seem to indicate that exchanges with African regions are not necessarily determined by ideology, politicization, aspirations for bloc leadership, nor affective orientation.

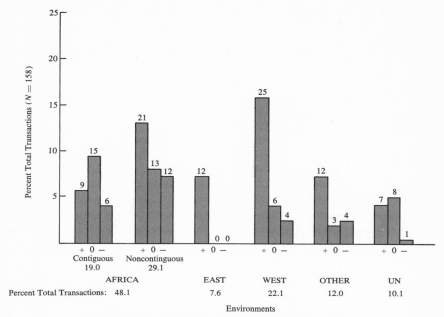

Figure 5.5. International Transactions: Uganda

Volume of Ugandan international transactions with the several environments represented by length of bars. Friendly acts represented by (+), neutral by (0), and hostile by (−). Source of data: *Africa Research Bulletin*, 1965.

4.4 The volume of exchange of polities in the African Regional environment will not necessarily be determined by the volume of attitudinal orientation of the internal elite.

This proposition is a companion to **3.4** above. The volume of exchanges between African polities will apparently not depend upon the orientations of the elite. Attitudinal involvement of the Uganda elite with the contiguous environment of East Africa amounted to 43 per cent but transactions only to 19 per cent. In the case of Ghana only about 5 per cent of elite orientations were directed toward West Africa while almost 32 per cent of actual interactions took place there.

These cases are difficult to explain. Why do the elite of a newly independent "reconciliation" polity orient their attitudes toward large-scale involvement with neighboring East African states when their actual interactions account for only a small portion of their international behavior? Why do the leaders of a supposedly militant "mobilization" polity reveal intentions of limiting transactions with the contiguous West African

114

societies when the actual volume of their relations is far greater? In both kinds of polities it would seem that the elite possess little control over their international environment or portions of it.

The Great Power Environment: Western and Socialist Systems

The Socialist systems accounted for 8 per cent of the volume of Uganda's international transactions while the Western systems were involved in 22 per cent of the total. Seventy one per cent of all actions directed toward the West were friendly and only 11.5 per cent were negative. Again, as in the case of Ghana 100 per cent of all the transactions between Uganda and the Socialist systems were friendly. However, this represents only a total of 12 exchanges recorded.

Uganda would appear to be less involved in the Great Power environment than Ghana. Only about 30 per cent of all her exchanges were with the Western and Socialist systems as compared to 41 per cent for Ghana. However, she is on friendly terms with both systems. This again would seem to indicate that African polities need not be deeply involved in the global struggle and may maintain amicable relations with both blocs, though the pervasive influence of the Cold War is still evident.

> **4.5** The higher the exchanges with the Regional environment in a developing African polity, the lower the involvement in the Great Power cleavage.

The data here support this proposition only slightly. Uganda had a higher transaction rate with the Region than Ghana and a lower score for involvement in the East-West conflict. Again it could be suggested that a newly independent nation, greatly concerned with problems of internal unity, has not had the time nor the inclination to become part of the Cold War cleavage.

A recent preliminary study found that, generally, all African states had a low interaction rate with the Socialist bloc. Other tentative findings from the same study revealed a tendency for small African "reconciliation" polities (e.g., Uganda) to be nonaligned or pro-West and for the larger, more developed "mobilization" polities to be more oriented toward the Eastern bloc. It should be noted that no relationship was found between number of years independent and pro-communist orientation, and that the smaller the polity the lower the interaction rate with either side in the Great Power cleavage.[15]

Transactions Patterns

In transactions with the several environments Ghana initiated a total of 92 exchanges and was the recipient of 132. This is a slightly asymmetrical balance of almost 3:4. Ghana initiated **75** friendly (+) acts

---

[15] McGowan, *op. cit.*, 1967. It is regretted that this valuable study only came to the author's attention after the main part of this paper was completed.

toward other polities and received 101 supportive exchanges in return. She was the object of 22 hostile or unfriendly acts by other polities and produced 15 such acts herself.

Within the regional environments Ghana initiated 45 friendly acts toward other African polities, but was the recipient of only 21 in return. She directed 9 hostile acts toward other regional states and received 18. The contiguous states of West Africa initiated 18 hostile exchanges with

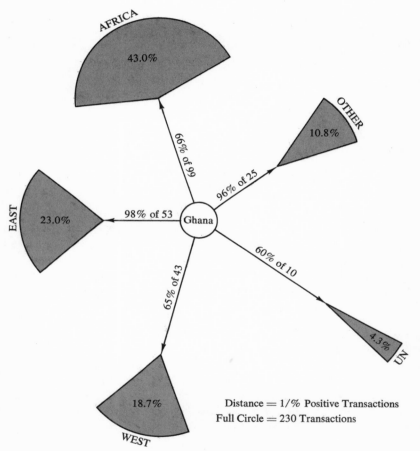

Figure 5.6. International Transaction Map: Ghana, 1965

Ghana is located at center of map.   Distance from Ghana is determined by per cent positive transactions of total transactions: the farther away, the less friendly.   Size of environment is determined as per cent of total interactions directed by Ghana toward that environment and the total interactions directed toward Ghana by the environment: the larger the environment, the more transactions it has had with the focal polity.

Ghana, while she produced only 8 with them. Ghana initiated 25 friendly interactions with her neighbors but received only 16 in return. Thus the balance of transactions between Ghana and her contiguous and regional environments was both asymmetrical and unfriendly.

Figure 5.6, the transaction map, attempts to depict graphically the relationships between Ghana and the several environments. Ghana is at

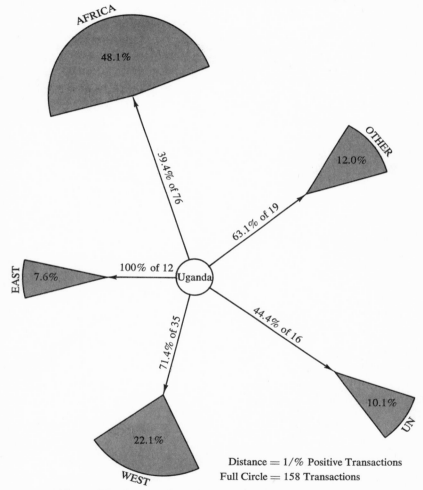

Figure 5.7. International Transaction Map: Uganda, 1965

Uganda is located at center of map. Distance from Uganda is determined by per cent positive transactions of total transactions: the farther away, the less friendly. Size of environment is determined as per cent of total interactions directed by Uganda toward that environment and the total interactions directed toward Uganda by the environment: the larger the environment, the more transactions it has had with the focal polity.

117

the center of the figure.   The distance between her and an environment is the per cent positive of friendly transactions of all exchanges with the environment.   The size of the various environments is determined by the per cent of all transactions which Ghana engaged in with the other polities in that particular category.   Thus although the East (Socialist systems) is very close to the West African country it is not as large as Africa which represented 43 per cent of all transactions.   The West is just about the same distance away from Ghana as is Africa, but is much smaller in size since it represents only about 19 per cent of her foreign exchanges.

Eighty-eight per cent of Uganda's initiated exchanges with the several environments were reciprocated (73/83).   This is fairly symmetrical.   She initiated 37 friendly acts and received 49 (70 per cent) and 93 per cent of her hostile acts were reciprocated (13/14).

Within the African region Uganda initiated 20 friendly exchanges but received only 10 in return.   But her hostile acts were returned equally at 100 per cent (9/9).   In the East African setting her contiguous neighbors returned double the amount of friendly interactions which she initiated (3/6) and also returned double her negative acts (2/4).

Uganda's transactional map (Figure 5.7) shows that East African polity at about the same distance from the Socialist systems as Ghana, but with them representing far fewer of her total international exchanges.   The West, on the other hand, is both friendlier and more important in terms of her over-all relationships.   Africa is an important source of transactions for Uganda, almost half of all her exchanges took place there—but she appears more distant from the polities there than Ghana.

CONCLUSIONS

This has been an exploratory study of the international attitudes and interactions of two developing African polities.   One, Ghana, was a West African centralized regime guided by a strong leader and ideological elite. The other, Uganda, was an East African pluralistic regime led by a more fragmented elite and only recently independent.

The goal of this chapter has not been to present substantive findings about the behavior of these two polities in the international system.   The research procedures were too limited and the data gathered too qualified. The purpose was, rather, to illustrate what might be done under more favorable conditions, to utilize the Rosenau framework for the exploration of theoretical linkages between national and international politics.   Propositions have been suggested for testing and refinement.

Political, economic, and social-cultural dimensions of elite attitudes in Ghana and Uganda were tapped in Time 1 (1963–64) and then compared with the same kinds of international interactions of these nations in Time 2 (1965).   Similarity between these two sets of data was not pronounced.

Transactions were measured between the two polities and their several environments—contiguous, regional, and Great Power. These were represented in transactional maps which graphically displayed the "political" distance between the focal polity and the nations in the environments. Eventually, it may be possible to construct several different kinds of maps showing how nations relate to each other beyond simple geographic boundaries.

In terms of substantive findings, Ghana was far more ideological or opinionated in the elite attitudes identified and more saliently directed in its international transactions than Uganda. The data summarized in Figure 5.8 show the more positive-friendly and negative-hostile orientation of Ghana in comparison to possible neutral responses.

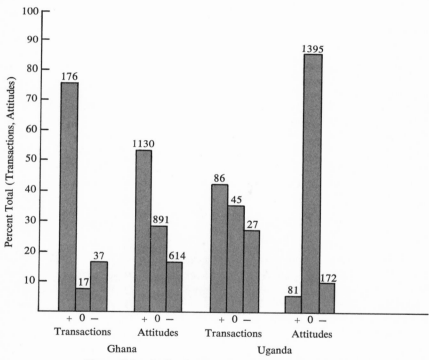

Figure 5.8. Attitudes and Transactions Compared

In the text several reasons were suggested for the configurations of attitudes and transactions. This project will continue and further evidence will be reported in the future. However, in this initial investigation the purpose was mainly to generate propositions within the context of the linkages framework. There are so many sources of competing explanations in uncontrolled research of this type that a heavy caveat must be entered and the highly tentative nature of the findings acknowledged.

Appendix

RESEARCH PROCEDURES

Social science theory would specify, generally, that attitudes and opinions precede behavior, though the two phenomena affect each other. On the basis of this tenet it was decided to measure the polity variables— attitudes expressed in legislative debates and a party newspaper—before the interactional or behavioral variables. Consequently an analysis of the (Accra) *Evening News* and the Uganda *Parliamentary Debates* was carried out in Time 1 (December–October, 1963 to November–July, 1964). This was followed by a measurement of the transactional patterns as recorded in the *Africa Research Bulletin* in Time 2 (January, 1965–December, 1965).

The point of this exercise, as underlined previously, is exploratory. It can be suggested that future diachronic research in this area should tap dimensions of attitudes and interactions over shorter time periods.

Polity—Attitudinal Data

1. The Accra *Evening News* was analyzed in bi-weekly periods beginning December 2, 1963 and ending the week of November 22, 1964. The context unit and the unit of analysis was the paragraph. The analyst was instructed to code information in the general classes of economic, political, and social-cultural events. He was further required to make a judgment on the quality of the attitude expressed. Positive attitudes were classed as plus ($+$), neutral or undetermined ones as zero (0), and negative as minus ($-$). Entries were made on the coding sheet in rows next to the country to which they pertained, and in columns under the general classes and in the categories of $+$ 0 $-$.

2. The *Uganda Parliamentary Debates* (proceedings of the National Assembly) were analyzed completely for the period October 9, 1963 through July 10, 1964, volumes 19–30. The coder was instructed to use the same procedures as outlined above. The name of a foreign country was the unit of analysis. Fewer positive or negative values of the attitudes expressed could be identified and thus more neutral entries appeared on this coding sheet than on that for *The Evening News*.

Input-Output—Transactional Data

All information listed under Ghana and Uganda in the *Africa Research Bulletin* from January to December, 1965 was coded and placed in the content categories. A distinction was made between actions initiated by Ghana or Uganda and actions of which they were the recipient. Thus it was possible to show the balance of transactions between the polities under investigation and their several environments—contiguous, regional, and so on.

Because of financial limitations it was possible to use only three coders —one for the Accra *Evening News*, one for the *Uganda Parliamentary Debates*, and one for the *Africa Research Bulletin*. Ideally the analysis should have been carried out by a panel, and inter-coder and intra-coder reliability tested.

The lack of rigorous control in the research is freely admitted. There are many competing hypotheses for explaining relationships. This is an exploratory investigation to suggest problems for future research.

Part III

Systemic Roles

CHAPTER SIX

National-International Linkages: Superpolities*

Bernard C. Cohen

AS part of the planned effort to explore the interactions between national political systems and aspects of the international political system, our purpose here is to study the linkages that exist between the particular national systems that we call superpowers and the international system of which they are so central a part. The possible points of intersection and impact are so numerous that some arbitrary bounds need to be set: We shall focus on the top political leadership of the superpolities, which offers a convenient and meaningful point of articulation between national and international political environments.

* This paper was first prepared for delivery at the 1966 Annual Meeting of the American Political Science Association while I was on leave as Visiting Research Scholar at the Carnegie Endowment for International Peace, New York. In the two years since then, I have—for better or worse—resisted most of the temptation to modify or to reassert particular hypotheses in the light of the Vietnam war; we are too much in the midst of that war, it seems to me, to know for sure what its short- and long-term impacts on American political life are going to be.

James N. Rosenau has served as valuable critic as well as editor from the very beginning.

Super-status in the ranks of the world's political systems is of relatively recent origin. As World War II moved into its final stages, William T. R. Fox wrote a book called *The Superpowers*,[1] by which he meant the great great powers of the postwar world, the United States, the Soviet Union, and Great Britain. But many nuclear explosions have gone up in smoke since then, along with colonial possessions, and the disparities in power that super-status connoted have come to differentiate the United States and the Soviet Union from all the other polities of the world. This is not to argue that it will ever be thus, but only that it is currently the case, as it has been for most of the post-war period. These two polities stand head and shoulders above all the others in the scope of their international power—in their ability to assert, to protect, and to advance their political, economic, and military interests around the globe.

The sample of superpolities is thus small; it could be made larger by including those political systems in the past that have been vastly more powerful than their neighbors, like Sparta and Athens. For many purposes this makes much sense; but it seems to me that our present purposes suggest otherwise: There is too great a disparity in the effective reach of power, and thus in the impingement of external environments, of a Greek city-state and a global power that is rapidly conquering outer space, for such polities to be treated as equal members of the same class of polities.[2] We are left, thus, with only two.

For the purposes of this paper, furthermore, the sample of superpolities will be somewhat less than two in a practical sense: There is a serious problem of access to relevant and reliable information about the Soviet Union that has no ready parallel in the United States. Under the best of circumstances, the available data concerning the two countries are not commensurate. And the circumstances are less than the best, for I cannot pretend to specialized knowledge about the Soviet Union in any event. With these reservations in mind, we can nonetheless try to study not one or two countries but a class of polities having vastly superior politico-military standing vis-à-vis all other powers. We want to inquire into the relative potency, the comparative impact, of four environments—three international: the dominant or super-power, the regional, and the contiguous or neighboring; and the internal or domestic—on certain political leadership variables within the superpolities.

We are concerned, also, with both the *inputs* from the four environments to the domestic leadership variables, and the reverse flow, the *outputs* from the domestic political environment to the international environment. We often talk as if the distinguishing feature of superpolity status were the

---

[1] New York: Harcourt, 1944.

[2] But at some point it will be worthwhile testing the merit of this assumption, by studying the "superpolities" of the past in their own settings, to see which of the linkages between nuclear superpolities and their environments have parallels or counterparts in the linkages between what we might call bireme superpolities and their environments, and which do not.

dominance of its outputs—i.e., its capacity to affect the political systems of other countries. But, a priori, the inputs seem to be as much a feature of superpolity status as outputs: why should a country have any reason to affect other political systems unless it were in some important ways affected by what happens in those systems? Our assumption, in other words, is that superpolity status is marked not only by inputs as well as outputs, but also by high levels of both. If subsequent comparative analysis should show a decreasing volume of inputs and outputs, accompanied perhaps by changes in their ratio, as one moves from apparent superpolities to apparent small polities, then we might even have at hand a satisfactory empirical means of arbitrarily dividing polities into power-categories or classifications. Hopefully, for example, this would provide a better basis than the one we used above for deciding whether or not to treat the dominant Greek city-states as superpolities.

We shall look at four aspects or characteristics of leadership: the techniques of power manipulation, the social background of leaders, the socialization of leaders and their political attitudes, and the structure of leadership and its bases of support. These are not simply arbitrary items of interest or foci of concern. To the extent that linkages between the international and national systems are indeed operative, we would expect to find evidence of them in the characteristics of a nation's top political leaders that define their attainment of, and accommodation to, power. The evidence that we do find, and which we will evaluate in the following pages, is more than ample to suggest effective linkages. But it does not unequivocally point to many linkages that are common to superpolities as such. The linkages between the international and the national systems seem to work in the same way for the two nuclear superpolities insofar as social background and political socialization variables are concerned, to work in opposite ways insofar as techniques of power manipulation are concerned, and to be too obscure in the case of the bases of leadership support to sustain any generalization. The latter two variables, however, seem to be especially sensitive to differences in the internal political systems themselves, which override any similarities in the role these two super-polities play in the international political system. Let us look at each of these leadership variables in detail, to see what the linkages look like.

THE TECHNIQUE OF POWER MANIPULATION

The largest of the international environments, the overarching one, is variously called the Cold War, the global, the dominant, or even the Great Power environment. We mean by this the context of interaction—chiefly hostile but not exclusively or even necessarily so—among those powers that have the capacity to engage in major war. There can be no question but that this basic international power competition is used as a technique of power manipulation—i.e., as a means of mobilizing or organizing support for the acquisition and the exercise of political power—in those countries that are most active and most heavily involved in that competition, but there is some question about how important that use is, and whether it is an inevitable concomitant of intimate and intense (we might call it super) involvement or of superior power capabilities.

There has not been a Presidential election in the United States since the end of World War II where the major candidates have not sought to ride the Cold War, or a particular manifestation of it, to power. The use that Richard Nixon made, in his 1960 campaign, of his finger-wagging debate with Khrushchev in the kitchen of a model American home at a trade fair in Moscow has its parallels, most of them more subtle to be sure, in the campaigns of all the major Presidential candidates in the post-war period. Once in power, American Presidents have not been reluctant to use these issues in an effort to mobilize political support for more general purposes, nor have they failed to profit in the coin of political popularity from a particularly vivid confrontation of United States and Communist power. And what holds at the Presidential level is also the case, though with much less uniformity, at the level of Congressional and even state and local office. The Communist question generally, and the specific problems of the Soviet Union, Communist China, Korea, and Vietnam, have been issues in many local contests (leading men to believe, with and without evidence, that they have been responsible for the outcomes), and they have been deliberately used to launch at least a few notable political careers.

But, while this is often the language of political discourse and debate, one has only to look at repeated surveys of public opinion on political questions to understand the limits of this proposition: Individuals in the United States may make small and in some cases highly strategic political gains by using Cold War issues, but in no sense can it be said that American politics turn consistently or importantly on these issues—or indeed on any issues.[3] This is due in part to the remoteness even of these questions for the vast majority of the American people, and in part to the fundamental similarity—despite all the noise—in the approach of the major parties and their candidates toward these questions. The Johnson-Goldwater campaign may look at first blush like an exception, but the lopsidedness of the vote is a reaffirmation of the essential one-sidedness of the American approach to the Soviet Union.

We have fewer instances of overt power manipulation in the Soviet Union, most of the maneuvering and the selection processes being hidden from public view. We are not, therefore, in a very good position to say whether the competition with the United States figures in Soviet internal political calculations in the same way that it figures in American. In a broad sense, of course, the international power relationship is an ever present

[3] Cf. Angus Campbell, Philip E. Converse, Warren E. Miller, and Donald E. Stokes, *The American Voter* (New York: Wiley, 1960), pp. 168–87.

factor in Soviet policy; and from time to time it visibly spills over into Soviet politics. There seems to be agreement among Soviet specialists that foreign policy was one of the major issues Khrushchev used in the process of building up and consolidating his leadership position in the mid-1950s. Between 1953 and 1955 he undermined Malenkov's position by taking, *inter alia*, a "hard line" on foreign policy. Having secured that flank, he then moved against the Stalinists in 1955 with softer foreign policy positions, including the Geneva summit meetings and the overtures to Yugoslavia.[4] Apart from this set of circumstances, however, there is no strong evidence that there are sufficient openly expressed differences of opinion among the relevant constituencies in the Soviet Union with respect to the United States and to international policy to make the international power competition a major and continuing technique of internal power manipulation. On the other hand, there are abundant inferences that the transfer of power from Malenkov to Khrushchev, and from Khrushchev to the collective leadership of Brezhnev and Kosygin, and the major realignments of policy at least since Malenkov's time, have turned more substantially on questions of bloc relationships and of internal economic development.[5]

What about the reverse connection—the subsequent import *for* the United States-Soviet competition of these limited techniques of internal power manipulation that derive initially *from* that Cold War relationship? In the United States, both Presidents Eisenhower and Kennedy came to power with promises involving a somewhat more militant posture toward the Soviet Union, and both of them instituted policies to carry out these promises—e.g., Dulles' Massive Retaliation doctrine, and Kennedy's program for economic growth and for an enlargement of the defense budget, which was ostensibly matched by the Soviets. President Johnson's campaign against Senator Goldwater rejected any sharp increase in militancy,

---

[4] Cf., e.g., Zbigniew Brzezinski and Samuel P. Huntington, *Political Power: USA/ USSR* (New York: Viking, 1965), pp. 241–7; Arnold L. Horelick and Myron Rush, *Strategic Power and Soviet Foreign Policy* (Chicago: U. of Chicago, 1966), pp. 19–31.

[5] Brzezinski and Huntington, for example, argue that Khrushchev concentrated on three issues to build up his position against Malenkov between 1953 and 1955: the need for reform in agriculture, the defense of the priority for heavy industry, and the hard line in foreign policy. Yet their own distribution of attention among these three issues puts foreign policy a very poor third in importance (*op. cit.*, pp. 241–4).

There will always be problems in the interpretation of evidence about Soviet political behavior. For example, Boris Nicolaevsky argues—in Janet D. Zagoria (ed.), *Power and the Soviet Elite* (New York: Praeger, 1956)—that Beria was removed in 1953 over a foreign policy question: "The facts at our disposal leave virtually no room for doubt that the decisive dispute and rupture occurred in the realm of foreign policy, in the matter of concessions to the West which Beria considered necessary. There is almost no doubt that these concessions were to be very substantial and go as far as withdrawal from East Germany. . . . It was, however, the very scale of the concession contemplated by Beria which stretched the patience of his colleagues to the breaking point and which led to his arrest." (p. 137) Nicolaevsky may well be right; but given what we know about the personal competition for power at that juncture in Soviet affairs, and given the genuine difficulty in establishing unequivocal motivation even in so accessible a government as our own, we would be wise to be a bit chary of such dogmatic assertions about the motives of Soviet leaders.

but his use of the Gulf of Tonkin incident to undercut Goldwater's position was itself a militant gesture. But the striking feature of all of these Administrations was the continuing and progressively successful attempts of the Presidents, once in office, to *moderate* the international rivalry and to seek to defuse it as an issue both of internal and international politics. Even President Johnson's most strenuous pursuit of the war in Vietnam has interfered only marginally with this progressive moderation. Nevertheless, the political successes of Senator Joseph R. McCarthy, Senator Goldwater's inability to break away from his extreme right wing into at least a semblance of the center, and the resilience of the John Birch Society all testify to the existence of political techniques and strategies that have not only benefited from the Cold War confrontation but have in the process kept the confrontation alive.[6]

Again, the situation in the Soviet Union is less clear. The major power transitions from Stalin to the current leadership have been accompanied by a secular trend toward a relaxation of the confrontation with the United States, but there have been significant eruptions of hostility at intervals, such as the Berlin crisis of 1961–62, and the Cuban missile crisis of 1962, which one cannot arbitrarily dismiss in the present context. It is certainly reasonable to assume that some of the pressures behind or at least some of the support for these policy acts came from internal political constellations and maneuvers that were themselves the products of the bipolar relationship; those who may have ridden to power in the Soviet Union on the strength of the Cold War antagonism would have as much interest as their counterparts in the United States in demonstrating the continued reality of American hostility, or at least in periodically testing it in order to take advantage of its absence. When Malenkov took moderate international positions after the death of Stalin, subordinating the international competition to the consumer needs of the Soviet people, he apparently aligned against himself the men who saw their positions in the Soviet system jeopardized—high-ranking military officers, men whose careers were built on the drive for heavy industry, and important elements of the Communist Party apparatus—men who subsequently shifted their crucial support to Khrushchev.[7]

These are suggestive rather than rigorous comparisons, to be sure; and I do not see how they can be otherwise. But one conclusion emerges very strongly from all the accounts of the differential uses of the Cold War com-

---

[6] Milton J. Rosenberg explores some of the psychological dimensions of this process in his essay on "Attitude Change and Foreign Policy in the Cold War Era," in James N. Rosenau (ed.), *Domestic Sources of Foreign Policy* (New York: Free Press, 1967), p. 111–59.

[7] Cf. Vernon V. Aspaturian, "Internal Politics and Foreign Policy in the Soviet System," in R. Barry Farrell (ed.), *Approaches to Comparative and International Politics* (Evanston: Northwestern U.P., 1966), pp. 242–3, 256–77. Aspaturian goes on to argue, however, that the vested interests in the Cold War within the Soviet Union are a minority: ". . . those social groups which tend to benefit from a relaxation of international tensions . . . make up the overwhelming proportion of the population." (p. 278)

petition as a technique of power manipulation: These differential uses appear to be a function less of superpolity involvement in the Cold War competition than of the different internal political systems in the two superpowers, and of the fact that in free and open competition for broad-based political support, men make use of those issues and techniques that they believe will gain them that support.[8] This is an important point, and I shall come back to it more than once.

The regional environment looks much the same as the Cold War or superpolity environment insofar as the techniques of power manipulation are concerned, except that it impacts in just the opposite way: Whereas the Cold War environment seems to play a greater role in United States politics and political strategies than in the Soviet Union, the regional environment seems to play a greater role in Soviet internal politics and political strategies than it does in the United States.

For the United States, the relevant regional environments are the Latin American and the North Atlantic. Their connection to the United States is historical, geographical, and institutional, with strong political, economic, and military dimensions. Yet one would be hard put to claim that either of these has had (in the years of United States superpolity status) more than a minor role in United States politics, or been more than minimally affected by the techniques of power manipulation employed in American politics. With the exception of Cuba (which we shall consider more fully as part of the contiguous environment) and an occasional event like the intervention in the Dominican Republic, Latin America is hardly more important or exciting an issue area than Antarctica. One might expect, hope, or even urge otherwise, but that does not alter the situation. Both the Cuban case and the Dominican intervention in April, 1965, indicate that Latin America becomes significant for contemporary American politics only as it involves questions of Communism—i.e., as it takes on aspects of the Cold War environment; but as a *regional* consideration it is without much weight. Senator Robert Kennedy believed it worthwhile to deliver a major speech in the Senate on Latin American policy in early 1966, but the reaction among political commentators indicated no widespread support for that belief.

It is not surprising that there is little political mileage for American officials or politicians in the ordinary issues (i.e., other than Communism) of Latin American political and/or economic life. With the very minor exception of the maltreatment of American public figures in Latin America, which has created a momentary fund of sympathy for them in the United States, no one in recent years has been able to use Latin America as a springboard to significant general policy influence or to high office. Latin America is more readily affected by political techniques in the United States than the

---

[8] Cf., e.g., Brzezinski and Huntington, *op. cit., passim*; and R. Barry Farrell, "Foreign Politics of Open and Closed Political Societies," in Farrell (ed.), *op. cit.*, pp. 167–208.

other way around. Just as Communist movements within Latin America become an important input into United States domestic political competition, Cold War politics in the United States have an impact on United States policies in Latin America. Thus one of the factors behind President Kennedy's acquiescence in the Bay of Pigs invasion was his fear that to abort the mission would make him appear to be soft on Communism.[9] And President Johnson's Dominican intervention clearly drew some of its inspiration from his reading of the domestic political pressures attending the whole Cuban imbroglio.[10]

The North Atlantic region, the central concern of American foreign policy through two hot wars and one cold one within a half-century, is surprisingly in the same general classification as Latin America, as a region that has had no great impact on the techniques of power manipulation in the United States; nor has it been in any particular way affected by the competition for political power in this country. James Reston recently noted with wonder the lack of political reaction, the lack of note in the United States press or the Congress, to the fact that the United States is now responsible for the main defense of the European continent, that "U.S. conscripts stand between the Elbe River and the North Sea. . . ."[11] Perhaps it is the very centrality of Europe in American policy, the fact that most American political figures are "Atlanticists," that has served in recent years to insulate these European policies, active as they are, from the influence of political competition. These policies were much less insulated in the years immediately after World War II, when the United States response to the new distribution of power in the world was being forged. But particularly since General Eisenhower's victory over Senator Taft at the Republican nominating convention in 1952, a large area of bipartisan commitment has made the region one of administrative or specialist rather than political concern. There are, of course, some localized exceptions to this—cases where the ties between American political constituencies and European populations are close, and where the politics of the mother country are intimately involved in the politics of the constituency. These instances are oft-told tales, because they make striking examples, but it may not be inaccurate to describe their impact on American politics or policies as something less than stunning. Where all office seekers in such constituencies have to bow to the same idols, the bow itself often becomes ritualistic rather than central to the competition for power; and officials who make decisions can discount much of this presumed "pressure." There do remain incidents, however—the local snubbing of visiting kings, the refusal to load or unload ships trading with particular countries—that although unimportant in the large do represent a visible connection, running in both directions, between

---

[9] Theodore C. Sorensen, *Kennedy* (New York: Harper & Row, 1965), pp. 294–309.
[10] Cf. James Reston's column in *The New York Times*, June 8, 1966.
[11] *The New York Times*, June 1, 1966.

a regional environment and the search for and use of political power in the United States.

The links between the power competition in the Soviet Union and the regional environment of that country appear to be rather more important than their counterparts for the United States. Partly this may be due to the fact that a major part of the Soviet regional environment, the bloc countries, is substantially also a contiguous environment, and the relative significance of each is difficult to determine. There is, furthermore, an important political-ideological connection between the Soviet Union and most of the bloc countries that makes her relationship with them different in kind from the relationships that characterize the United States and its regional (or even contiguous) environments. Having said all this, it remains obviously true even through the obscure haze surrounding Soviet politics that developments in the bloc, issues and events in the large Communist world, are powerful factors shaping the rise and fall, successes and failures, of Soviet leaders. China is to the Soviet Union, as Cuba is to the United States, an important feature both of a contiguous and a regional environment; and the public eruptions of the Sino-Soviet dispute strongly suggest that this relationship has been for several years perhaps the single most important *external* consideration in Soviet internal politics, dominating even the Vietnam issue. In view of the rather immediate attempts at a Sino-Soviet rapprochement following on the downfall of Khrushchev, it is not unlikely that his opponents inside and outside the Soviet Union used his China policy as one of the elements in fashioning the coalition that brought him down.[12] And certainly the dispute has colored Soviet relations with all the bloc countries, as the Soviet has sought to strengthen its position and isolate the Chinese party within the world Communist movement.

The contiguous environment of the superpolities is not greatly different from the regional environment both in its concrete dimensions and in its impact. Although the differences we just observed between the United States and the USSR still hold for the contiguous environment, it is worth noting nonetheless, that for both the United States and the Soviet Union, immediately neighboring countries have a bearing on internal politics that is generally greater than the disparities in power between those superpolities and their immediate environments would lead one to expect. We have already mentioned some of the ways in which Cuba has become important to American politics. In another example, the period surrounding the Cuban missile confrontation in 1962 saw several Senators trying to use the possibility of Soviet missiles and the continued presence of Soviet troops in Cuba as a lever for expanded political power—and while they may have failed on the strictly personal level, they helped to shape the way the President made *his* political calculations in the crisis. Within the United States government, also, the CIA has apparently been able to use the possibilities

[12] Cf. Vernon V. Aspaturian, *op. cit.*, pp. 212, 227–35, 272.

of Cold War intrusion into the neighboring environment in Central America as a means of seeking a more substantial base of power. But apart from the projection of the Cold War confrontation into the immediate neighborhood,[13] this environment is of little continuing significance for American politics.

Everything that has been said about Latin America applies with even greater force to Canada. In the ordinary course, Canada might as well be on the far side of the moon so far as the competition for power in the United States is concerned. But any sign of special Soviet attention to Canada evokes the same nervousness that Communism in Latin America gives rise to.[14]

In the case of the Soviet Union, the China problem stands out at the moment; but the Soviet government has always been concerned about the countries on its borders, and since the establishment of the Communist regimes in Eastern Europe at the end of World War II Soviet politics and policies have been intimately connected with events in these countries. But the regional and the contiguous environments are virtually identical for the Soviet Union, and apart from stressing once again the apparently distracting importance of China for the Soviet leadership there is no point in covering the same ground twice. Except for China, the growing independence of the bloc countries changes the form but not the fact of their subordination to Soviet political initiatives. While the impact of its immediate environment on the Soviet Union is generally high (much higher than in the corresponding United States case), the Soviet impact on this environment appears to be higher still; policies in the countries around the Soviet Union are subject to a greater measure of influence by emanations from the Soviet political system than vice-versa. In this one respect the Soviet Union and the United States interact similarly with their intermediate and close-in environments.

The significance of the relative potency of these three international

---

[13] Note the parallel in the World War II period, when Nazi inroads in Latin America were a matter of great concern to the United States.

[14] See, e.g., the article by Harry Schwartz in *The New York Times*, July 25, 1966: "Canada's geographic position and strategic importance combine to suggest that the recent signs of new warmth in Soviet-Canadian relations deserve more attention in this country than they have received."

The situation is different, of course, for these countries when they face the United States. In other words, the present considerations of American politics and public policies generate demands that are centrally important for these countries. Castro's use of the United States invasion scare as a technique of political manipulation and control is obvious, as is the much longer history of responses to the manifestations of American economic and political interest in Central America. And the magnitude of the United States-Canadian relationship for the Canadian surfaces from time to time in political discussions of economic "domination," and in the rarer and more dramatic form of the defeat of Diefenbaker's Conservative Party following official American criticism of him during the Canadian elections of 1962.

For an illustrative example of the great impact of the United States on Canadians, see A. D. P. Heeney, "Dealing with Uncle Sam," in J. King Gordon (ed.), *Canada's Role as a Middle Power* (Toronto: Canadian Institute of International Affairs, 1966), pp. 87–100.

environments for the techniques of power manipulation within the two superpolities can be assessed only after a further comparison with the impact that the domestic environment has on such techniques. In other words, to what extent are political calculations and manipulations a result of *domestic* rather than (a variety of) international stimuli, and to what extent do the domestic and international environments variously bear the brunt of these aspects of political leadership? This question, like so many others in this paper, is much easier to ask than to answer. As a first approximation of an answer, however, it appears that the domestic environment is a more important factor than any of the international environments in the techniques of power manipulation for the United States—witness, e.g., the issues that dominate political campaigns, and the kinds of questions that the polls repeatedly suggest are "troubling" people. The substance of public debate and controversy in the Soviet Union suggests that domestic issues may be more important than international issues for the Soviet also,[15] but by a much narrower margin than in the United States: Soviet leadership being rather independent of popular support at home, at least in the short run, techniques of power manipulation can more easily turn on the demands from more importunate and less easily controlled constituencies in the several international environments, near and far.

As a second approximation, we might note that in the case of each of the superpolities, changes have been taking place that are generally in the direction of the position occupied by the other power. The achievement of superpolity status by the United States has meant the acceptance of what looks like an increasing amount of responsiveness to the outside world, and a concomitant increase in the extent to which domestic political behavior is conditioned by this responsiveness—though, of course, satisfactory empirical measures of this are lacking. For the Soviet Union, the sudden emergence into superpolity status was equally marked by a heightened priority accorded to the international environments; but with the passage of time the subordination of the domestic to the international environments has apparently become more and more onerous to the population, and Soviet politics seem to be ever more responsive to domestic pressures and opportunities.

SOCIAL BACKGROUNDS OF LEADERS

Political scientists have done quite a bit of work on the social backgrounds of men in responsible positions in government and public life—e.g., Congressmen, Foreign Service Officers, military officers, federal executives, and so forth. It has been easier to explain, even though in general ways, the *causes* for the recruitment or selection of leaders with these particular backgrounds than to explain the *consequences* of these backgrounds for

[15] Cf., e.g., Brzezinski and Huntington, *op. cit.*, Chap. IV, "Power and Policy," pp. 191–232.

public policies. In the United States top political leadership has tended to be drawn from the middle and upper-middle classes, to be well educated, white and Protestant; in the Soviet Union it has been proletarian or peasant, substantially Russian, and increasingly better educated.[16] Part of the difficulty in explaining the meaning that these particular backgrounds have for public policy is due to the lack of comparisons: The national political culture in both countries is reasonably well homogenized, and we have no systematic way of examining the consequences of leadership by radically different groups. The very homogenization of political culture suggests the possibility that the differences might be so slight that they would be difficult to attribute to particular social-background variables, such as class. One thing we can say with certainty, however, is that the relationship between social background and public policy is sufficiently obscure to warrant further exploration and clarification.

The present inquiry offers an opportunity to look at the question of social background of top leadership from a new perspective: What is the relative import of the various international environments and the domestic environment on the recruitment or selection of leaders with particular social backgrounds; and what consequences does such leadership have for these environments?

For the United States there is no strong evidence suggesting any *causal* relationship of a positive sort between international environments and the selection of leaders from particular social backgrounds, conventionally defined. To the extent that one can even distinguish different backgrounds among top American political leadership, we might be said to have run their gamut in the past four national administrations, in the absence of any really substantial change in the external environments. It would take some abstract speculation to delineate any causal relationship between the slow and subtle changes in the three international environments, on the one hand, and the shift from the mixture of professional public servants and the business and professional types of the Truman Administration, to the wealthy businessmen and lawyers of the Eisenhower Administration, to the young intellectuals and experienced political practitioners of the Kennedy Administration, and back to what looks like the Truman-type mixture of the Johnson Administration.[17]

We should also consider the interesting (though not readily testable) possibility that the outside world may have been helping to shape our leadership recruitment in a negative way: The Cold War confrontation, which is manifested in all three international environments, may have been instrumental in preventing any shift away from establishment-type leadership in the United States—or at least in supporting all the other political and social institutions that have made such a shift very unlikely.

There remains the paradoxical possibility that the Cold War confronta-

[16] *Ibid.*, Table 1, pp. 132–3, and Table 6, p. 161.
[17] For data on the first three of these administrations, see *ibid.*, Table 5, p. 158.

tion, far from *preventing* any such shift in American political recruitment, is only now just beginning to have discernible positive effects of precisely this kind. The stultifying nature of this confrontation, running through all of the three international environments and coloring American relationships even with small and weak neighbors, is stimulating the emergence of a new kind of political leadership, or potential leadership. This is the New Left, a coalition of angry young men who are hostile to all middle-class efforts dedicated to the support of middle-class values, and militants of all races who are marrying the earlier civil-rights movement with a movement of foreign policy protest.[18] The connection between civil rights and Vietnam serves to underline the importance of the domestic environment in this one place where any shift in the social background of American political leadership may be taking place.

Finally, we can note the positive effect of the international environment on the selection of leaders from particular *political*, rather than social, backgrounds. In recent years the Presidency has been unavailable, for all practical purposes, to anyone who lacks an image of international statesmanship, no matter what his reputation in domestic political life. Consequently, the serious contenders for the Presidency have tended more and more to come from the Senate, where they have had the opportunity to get involved in foreign affairs and to gain some experience and reputation in statesmanship, and less and less from the state Governorships or from private life, where the opportunity to demonstrate competence in international affairs is much rarer. The Vice-Presidency is increasingly subject to the same selection criteria as the Presidency; and where incumbent Vice-Presidents in recent administrations have not had much of an international reputation to begin with, the Presidents have quickly given them assignments that would help them acquire it.

On the Soviet side, too, clear signs of any positive causal relationship between the international environments and social-background variables are hard to see. The slow change in Soviet leadership from the old Bolshevik type to the industrial manager, the scientist, the engineer, the intelligentsia, might in a very indirect sense be attributed to the outside world, since the creation of these types of people is a by-product of the kind of society that the Soviets have created under forced draft, as it were, to survive and expand in the world. But in a more proximate as well as more realistic sense, these new classes of leaders are a response to a changed domestic environment, the coming to the age of responsibility of a generation that is more familiar with the industrial revolution than the Bolshevik revolution, and more absorbed in its problems and potentialities.[19] In other words, for the

---

[18] Cf. Tom Kahn, "The Problem of the New Left," *Commentary*, 42, 1 (July, 1966), pp. 30–38.

[19] After describing the scale of Soviet economic development, Brzezinski and Huntington observe that "the political leadership has to be responsive to the needs of an increasingly complex, and hence also differentiated, society" (*op. cit.*, p. 195).

Soviet Union as for the United States, the domestic environment seems to be more important than all of the international environments as a determinant of the social backgrounds of leaders.

If the social background of political leadership in the superpolities is mostly indifferent to inputs from the international environments how does the proposition look when we turn it around? There is at least a possibility that social background variables have more significance as outputs for the three international environments, than vice-versa. Here, too, however, the homogeneity of the political cultures makes it rather difficult to discover the extent to which policy outputs of the political systems are attributable to small differences in the social construction of political leadership. The Soviets, in fact, ostensibly see no differences whatsoever in the social background of American political leaders; they are all representatives of the same capitalist, exploitative, class. (The New Left shares this monochromatic view of American leadership, though in less explicitly Marxist terms.) But those of us with better vision (or is it worse, since we may not be seeing the forest for the trees?) may be indulged if we suggest that there may be some slight differences in the social backgrounds of American political leaders that seem to have policy consequences. In the early years of our superpolity status, for example, there was a discernible tendency for men with a middle-class business background to be chary of all "socialist" governments, Communist and non-Communist alike, and in economic dealings with democratic socialist regimes to want restrictive clauses that would presumably help the cause of free enterprise. Subsequently, the big-business men in the Eisenhower administration pursued a rather rigid and uncompromising opposition to Communist regimes, whereas the intellectual-politicians of the Kennedy administration were more predisposed to "bridge-building" gestures and policies toward the Communist world. But it must be acknowledged once again that this is very speculative indeed, and that we have no way of knowing that the differences, however slight, were in fact a consequence of the social-background variables rather than of other factors, like political party affiliation.

On the Soviet side, there is an interesting parallel to the circumstance in which the Soviets profess to see no difference in the social backgrounds of the "ruling groups" in the United States: American observers, applying a neo-Marxist stratification theory to the Soviet Union,[20] clearly hope that a shift in that country toward a ruling class composed of managers and at least a technical intelligentsia will mean a new set of international relationships, less hostile and more collaborative, with countries in all the international environments. The interesting question in this context involves the political leadership variable to be discussed next, political socialization: Might not such a shift in Soviet leadership, assuming it does occur, take place

---

[20] Brzezinski and Huntington call it "anti-Soviet Marxism" (*ibid.*, p. 10).

at such a slow pace that the new leaders will be absorbed into the political and policy perspectives of the old, obscuring the operating significance of any new social-background variables? The very possibility should induce even greater caution in our approach to social background as a political variable.

We have treated the international environments mostly in an undifferentiated way in this section, because there seemed to be little difference from one environment to another. Over-all, we find that we still cannot say very much, on the basis of the obvious evidence, about the tie between social background and polity inputs or policy outputs. It may be that social background is simply not a relevant variable within any given socio-political order—that it becomes important only at the point of revolutionary change in the social order and in the political system. Only then are there likely to be changes of such magnitude as to have consequences, if not causes, in the political world outside. That possibility might explain the apparent indifference of social background to the international environments of the superpolities in the period of their superpolity status.

SOCIALIZATION OF POLITICAL LEADERS

By political socialization I mean here the learning by men in important leadership positions of responses appropriate to the political circumstances confronting them. By looking at the range of those responses (including those discussed above as "techniques of power manipulation"), we can get some rough sense of the impact that the several environments have had in defining the contemporary political culture for the top leadership in the superpolities. We have greater difficulty, however, in getting at the learning process itself, at the socialization process as it takes place at less prominent stages of a man's career. To twist Harold Lasswell's lapidary phrase, we could study with profit the question, "Who learns what, when and how?" in the field of governance. But even without a new line of political biography—one that emphasized less the import of personality for decision making and more the import of political experiences on political behavior (mediated of course by personality)—we can find in the history of the two superpolities some striking and suggestive evidence of political socialization processes at work in which the international and domestic environments are differentially involved.

For the United States, two important socialization experiences worth some careful study are (1) those involving the movement of the Republican Party to an acceptance of international responsibilities, and more generally (2) the learning by American leadership, without regard to party, of the political culture of deterrence—the learning of nuclear restraint and the rules for collective survival.

The political socialization of the GOP stretches from the very beginning of our superpolity status to the present time, and it may be viewed as a struggle of the international environments, and especially the "great power" environment, to dislodge the domestic environment from its central, commanding position in the political culture of Republicans. World War II was the socializing agent of large elements of the Republican Party, and the "conversion" of Arthur Vandenberg is a good semi-public document marking the event and revealing some of its dynamics.[21]   The work of the following half-dozen years, the remarkable "revolution" in American foreign policy, was the product of a coalition between the Democrats in the Administration and the Congress, and a sizable group among the Republicans in the Congress some of whom had become "internationalists" by conviction and others of whom were simply responding to a series of specific and inescapable challenges.   But there was a significant dragging of heels and expressing of doubts on the part of some powerful Republicans during this period.   The 1952 Republican Presidential nomination was an important landmark in the socialization of the party.   General Eisenhower, who represented the claims of the international environments, so to speak, was the instrument of the already internationalized Republicans against the nationally oriented Republicans led by Senator Robert Taft.   In his remarkable electoral victories and in his eight years in the White House, President Eisenhower went a long way toward making positive involvement in and responses to the international environments acceptable to the rank and file of Republican voters in the United States.   In 1964 Senator Goldwater tested that degree of political socialization, and found that it was both effective and extensive. This is not to say that the dominant political culture will not be challenged again by those who oppose it.   Nevertheless, we can see in this series of events some of the stages in the process by which Republicans have learned to accept the "requirements" of all of the international environments (even though still favoring, perhaps, the Cold War environment) as being at least as compelling of their attention as the "requirements" of the domestic environment.

The process of socialization of American political leaders in the requirements of deterrence is much harder to sketch out than the more visible steps involving the change, through success and failure, of Republican political orientations.   It can be traced in the development of a specialized literature exploring the political and military implications of a strategy of deterrence in a bipolar international political system, and, trailing somewhat behind, in the arguments and justifications of political debate on the comcomitants of the strategy itself.   The 1960 political campaign and the handling of the 1962 Cuban missile crisis may be compared with the theory and practice of deterring the Japanese in 1940–41 and the naval and airpower debates of the late 1940s to see how sophisticated the understanding of American political leaders has become.   In the same vein (though I

[21] Cf. Arthur H. Vandenberg, Jr. (ed.), *The Private Papers of Senator Vandenberg* (Boston: Houghton, 1952).

reserve the right to be wrong) a comparison of the political debates attending the Korean War and the Vietnam War so far suggests a certain measure of learning among the political leadership of the nation about the conduct of limited wars. At the least, there has not yet been a repetition of the argument that in war there is no substitute for victory.[22]

These two examples treat political socialization as a dependent variable, the inputs coming from heightened perceptions of and sensitivity to the international environments. On the output side, we mentioned earlier the rapid socialization of aspiring American politicians into the politics of anti-Communism and the Cold War, and the significance that this in turn has had for the international environments. The Soviet Union, the neutral nations, the Central American Republics, our allies—indeed, most nations in the world—have had to learn to live with this aspect of the political culture of the United States and its peculiar rigidities and provocations.

While we must be especially tentative in claiming to perceive any patterns of political socialization among Soviet political leadership, there are several obvious candidates for that description that merit our attention. When George Kennan explained containment of the Soviet Union as a policy of holding the line against Soviet expansionism until a process of "mellowing" took place among Soviet leadership,[23] he was explicating a probable theory of the international political socialization of the Soviet elite. The events in the intervening years have suggested that Kennan's socialization hypothesis was essentially correct: The persistent opposition of the United States to Soviet military and political expansion—i.e., our assumption of the obligations of the Cold War—was apparently an important learning experience for the Soviet leadership. Whenever the Soviets made a major effort to test the firmness of our policy, the learning experience was reinforced at great cost to them: the expansion in central Europe and the North Atlantic treaty; the Berlin Blockade and the ensuing airlift; the Korean War and the tripling of the American defense budget; the Berlin crisis of 1961 and the mobilization of American reserves; the Cuban missile crisis and the very brink of war and forced Soviet retreat. While this is apparently not the kind of containment that Kennan had in mind originally, the Soviet leaders seem to have accepted, at least for the time being, the alternative of moderation and accommodation to continued hostile provocation—a lesson the Chinese have not learned first hand and which the United States is hopeful they might learn in Vietnam.

Containment was a form of political socialization relating to the circumstances of the Cold War or the Great Power environment. A comparable bit of socialization from the Soviet regional environment is also

---

[22] These particular examples lend force to Karl Deutsch's suggestion that a political generation lasts only 15 years. See his "External Influences on the Internal Behavior of States," in Farrell (ed.), *op. cit.*, pp. 25–26.

[23] "X," "The Sources of Soviet Conduct," *Foreign Affairs*, XXV, 4 (July, 1947), 566–82.

discernible. It has proved entirely too costly, if indeed not totally infeasible, for the Soviet Union to maintain Communist Party leadership in the bloc countries that is always subservient to the leadership of the Soviet Union itself. The periodic reassertion of national identity and national policy by Communist elites in Poland, Rumania, and Czechoslovakia, for example, not to mention Yugoslavia, China, and Albania, has finally been reflected in a greater tolerance for Communist dissent, a modified pluralism, on the part of the Soviet party leadership.

This description of both containment and the spreading disease of national communism as having ineluctably "socialized" the Soviet leadership into a posture of peaceful coexistence on both fronts, may be attributing excessive force to these external phenomena as inputs for the Soviet leaders. It is at least possible that there are some substantially domestic factors at work that have had as an output this moderation toward the international environments. Peaceful coexistence and an increasing toleration of dissent may be in part an outgrowth of a rapidly modernizing industrial society, a by-product of a new internal political culture as well as a learned response to the effective limits of international action.[24]

The problem of distinguishing between the domestic and the international environmental contribution to the political socialization of a given set of top leaders is difficult, and worth continued study. One part of the problem, of course, is that the environments do not interact uniformly for all leaders; there may be modal aspects to a political culture without there being uniformity. In the case of the United States, for example, the record of Democratic leaders richly suggests that domestic inputs, like a concern for poverty and the remnants of a "depression mentality" are at war with the international inputs; while for the Republican leadership the struggle has been more lopsided in favor of the domestic environment (though the policy concerns are not the same as those that preoccupy the Democrats). For the Soviet Union balances of this kind are less easy to strike; here again the lack of open political competition makes the "learning" process different, and more difficult to observe. But these hasty comparisons suggest some possible lines of future research. In the U.S., it might be instructive to make comparisons between the distribution of political campaign attention to various policy subjects, and the distribution of actual policy attention to those subjects by the same people once they are in office. This would permit us to distinguish somewhat more easily between a fundamental change in attitude, a real learning process, on the one hand, and a tactical expediency, a "technique of power manipulation," on the other. For example, an impressionistic hypothesis would be that, in the period of our superpolity status to date, the domestic environment is stressed rather more than the international environments during the campaigns, but that once an administration is safely in office the international environments become the

---

[24] Brzezinski and Huntington, *op. cit.*, who focus on the internal dynamics of the two superpolities, help to create such an impression.

most prominent subjects of policy discussion, the most prominent conditioner of thought and action. In any case, and for both superpolities, it would be desirable also to have longitudinal studies of relevant attitudes of political elites, so that we could make more careful measures of changes over time, of the kinds of political learning that take place, in some sort of correspondence with external and internal events. But since we are not likely to get that kind of data in any equal measure for both sets of political leaders, we will have to make do with more impressionistic evidence.

THE STRUCTURE OF LEADERSHIP
AND BASES OF SUPPORT

Let us look, finally, at the connection between the various environments and the support structure underlying the political leadership of the superpolities.

The political system in the United States, including its electoral aspects, ensures that the leadership structure will be highly permeable to groups in the population that are both creating and responding to a variety of stimuli in the political environment. This increases the opportunity for interactions among all of the political environments both foreign and domestic, the supporting groups, and the leadership itself; but it says nothing about the relative impact of any of the environments. We have to devise empirical measures that will distinguish among these. The situation is rather different in the Soviet Union. There the absence of open electoral competition and the strictures on the formal organization of competitive political associations means that the leadership structure is far less permeable to individuals or groups in the population having policy interests that are not currently in favor. But where the American political system is structurally more or less indifferent as between the impingement in this way of foreign and domestic environments, the Soviet political system seems to be biased in favor of the impingement of the domestic environment. This is so because the domestic environment is experienced directly by Soviet population groups, who can operate with respect to it through the normal Soviet processes we summarize as "the aggregation of interests"; but the international environment is not experienced so directly, and the regime can to a much greater degree control what is heard about the international environment as a consequence of what it says and permits to be heard about that environment.[25] But while the United States political leadership is structurally vulnerable equally to groups having domestic and foreign affairs interests at heart, the actual situation may not be greatly different most of the time as between the two countries: Voting studies in the United States indicate the predominance of domestic orientations in the United States population

[25] Cf. Robert Angell, "Social Values of Soviet and American Elites: Content Analysis of Elite Media," *Journal of Conflict Resolution*, VIII, 4 (December, 1964), p. 380.

at large; and interest groups in the foreign policy field do not seem to be notably effective.[26]

In the United States, the major political parties are perceived by large numbers of voters as having distinctive positions on both domestic and foreign policy, and they are identified with particular supporting groups or blocs that reinforce the distinctiveness of those positions. In the foreign policy field these patterns of support do not neatly categorize into the three international environments we have been considering, but we may nonetheless recognize different levels of international concern and responsiveness.

The Democratic Party, thus, draws much of its political strength and support from the urban minority groups, ethnic, racial and religious. It gets a high proportion of the votes, and no doubt also of the political money, of the Jews particularly in the largest cities. And the periodic contretemps involving the Saudi Arabian Kings in New York City are a convenient illustration of the impingements of Middle Eastern politics on American politics, and vice-versa. Similarly, the Negro has in recent years been voting overwhelmingly Democratic, and Negro groups have taken advantage of their new accretions of political power to bring the African states more centrally into their policy initiatives. Other ethnic groups, like the Poles and the Italians, also constitute visible links between high Democratic leaders and the politics of particular foreign countries, but these are less strategic politically and hence less effective than the other groups mentioned. And we can note also the high Democratic vote among Catholics, who have been especially articulate opponents of Communism especially in the European countries where Catholic populations and institutions are extensive.

The Republican Party draws an important measure of its support from men in business, industry and finance, from rural populations up- and down-state of the big cities and in the middle reaches of the country, and in some places from small clusters of extremely conservative individuals, some of whom overlap the above mentioned groups. And each of these sources of support brings a mixture of inputs from both domestic and international environments into the calculations of the party leaders. On the international side, the support from business, industry and finance introduces international trade questions from a variety of environments; these are both restrictive and liberal in their orientations, in a fine balance that has kept the top Republican leadership only slightly on the liberal trade side.[27] The support from rural populations has tended to be more concerned with the domestic environment than the international, a source of the inertia within the party on the question of international involvement and commitment. But both of these groups display a strong anti-Communism, which

---

[26] Angus Campbell et al., *op. cit.*; Bernard C. Cohen, *The Influence of Non-Governmental Groups on Foreign Policy-Making* (Boston: World Peace Foundation, 1959). Vietnam, I would argue, is a very rare and exceptional case.

[27] Cf. Raymond A. Bauer, Ithiel de Sola Pool, and Lewis A. Dexter, *American Business and Public Policy* (New York: Atherton, 1963).

has made the national Republican leadership particularly responsive to this dimension of the largest international environment we have been examining, and sensitive also to the threats of Communist encroachment in areas nearer to the United States.   And this particular pattern of environmental interest has been reinforced by the small but vocal injection of radical-conservative opinion, from the John Birch Society and similar organizations—people whose Republicanism is so strong and whose ideology is sufficiently resonant that their support will be solicited, or at least not disavowed, by some Republican leaders at all levels of the party.

The Soviet system eliminates the possibility of private interest groups shaping policy decisions, or forming enduring political coalitions.[28]   Beyond that, however, the absence of open political competition and electoral choice in the Soviet political system deprives us of really comparable data or insights into the group supports of the Soviet political leadership and their environmental connections.   Lacking such open data, we have to make gross inferences about which socio-political institutions or groups in Soviet society— the Army, the intelligentsia, the party, the plant managers, etc.—are supporting which trends or bodies in the Soviet leadership at any particular point in time.   It is important to beware of the gross oversimplifications that attend these gross inferences.   What does it mean when we say that any group of Soviet leaders has Army support, for example?   More fundamentally, how is such support obtained?   By the political leaders accepting military perspectives on international competition (i.e., the Army as a channel for inputs from the international environment), or by well-developed techniques of Party cooptation of Army leaders, by political influence in and supervision of military organizations, and so on?   Clearly, we do not know enough about the bases of support for Soviet political leadership to be able to relate the various political environments to specific political groups in any meaningful way.

AFTERTHOUGHTS

Since nothing so conclusive as conclusions can be drawn from this first effort, a few final words may be allowed which will both summarize a few leading thoughts and hopefully establish the importance of some additional lines of research and speculation.

1.   There are so many gaps in our knowledge at so many crucial points that we cannot render a very satisfactory verdict.   The obvious evidence is mixed on the central point, which is the relevance of the superpolity classification as a definer of a distinctive set of linkages between national and international politics.   For two of the variables under scrutiny, political socialization and social background, there is some evidence that the linkages

[28] Cf., e.g., Vernon V. Aspaturian (*op. cit*), pp. 283–4.

tend to be similar for the two superpolities. But for the other two variables, the techniques of power manipulation and the bases of political support, the linkages seem to be quite different. And these differences seem to be a function more of the disparate political systems in the two polities than of any other factor. To put it differently, we might say that the character of the political system seems to be so important both in creating and in revealing the national-international connections in both countries that at best it obscures any readily identifiable and generalizable superpolity behavior.

2. There is some question whether Communist China or France will ever achieve superpolity status, whether measured by conventional (and intuitive) standards or by some more objective yardstick such as a ratio of inputs to outputs between the environment and the polity, which was mentioned earlier in this paper. But there is no doubt that each aspires to greater independence of national decision-making and greater equality on the international scene with the United States and the Soviet Union. Each thus merits scrutiny now and in the future, as a rare experimental laboratory to determine whether any shifts in the patterns of linkage take place as these two countries take on additional characteristics of the superpolities. If any such shifts do in fact take place, we will have better grounds for distinguishing political-system variables from type-of-polity variables.

3. There lurks in my mind the hypothesis that the conditions of geography, economy, society and polity that have led to superpolity status in the twentieth century virtually guarantee to the states that possess it a very substantial measure of self-sufficiency in both an economic and a strategic sense. An integral element of such self-sufficiency is the very great importance that the political system and the political leaders accord to their domestic environments, in comparison with other and smaller polities that are more vulnerable politically, economically, and culturally, to the structure of international politics. The character of the polity may turn out to be related more to the substantive nature of the environmental inputs and outputs than to their volume or their sources in the several environments. But we need to wait on comparative studies of other polities for the evidence that would confirm or alter this hypothesis.

CHAPTER SEVEN

*National-International Linkages: France and China As Nonconforming Alliance Members**

Ole R. Holsti
and John D. Sullivan

INTRODUCTION

AMONG the more spectacular developments in recent international relations has been the disintegration of unity within the two great alliances which emerged after World War II. France's withdrawal from NATO and the bitter public dialogue between Moscow and Peking since 1963 are only two indications that the era of international bipolarity is coming to an end. The Cold War alliances may endure in some form for a number of years, but it seems unlikely that political relations within them can ever again take the form that they did during the 1950s. For example, discordant personalities and political styles among American, French, Soviet, and Chinese leaders have contributed to the disintegration of alliance unity. Yet if the consequences for Sino-Soviet relations of Nikita Khrushchev's political eclipse are an indication, it would appear unlikely that the eventual passing of

* For assistance and valuable criticism in preparing this paper we are indebted to Richard Fagen, Nazli Choucri, Dennis Doolin, David Finley, K. J. Holsti, Terry Hopmann, Joanne Loomba, Michael Oksenberg, and Randolph Siverson. Charles Hermann and James N. Rosenau also offered useful suggestions. Indispensable secretarial assistance was provided by Mrs. Violet Lofgren and our wives.

Mao Tse-tung, Charles DeGaulle or Lyndon Johnson will restore Soviet and American hegemony over their alliances to the degree that it existed during the first decade after World War II.

This chapter will examine one aspect of these events by comparing France and China as representatives of a politically interesting type of nation—nonconforming members of alliances. Our perspective and many of our concepts derive from the "national-international linkages" framework presented in Chapter 3.[1] Hence the discussion will explore some of the domestic and international factors which appear linked to similarities and differences in recent French and Chinese alliance policies.

The next section investigates some aspects of internal political processes that may be related to alliance policy. Some *similarities* in present French and Chinese political processes will be described, and we will consider how these may give rise to foreign policies which deviate from alliance norms. From the many domestic political processes which contribute to policy making, we have selected the socialization experiences of political elites and the stability of top leadership for examination.

Our consideration of internal political processes also explores some of the clear *differences* between French and Chinese politics that may be linked to the degree of their disassociation from the western alliance and communist system respectively. The analysis stems from two observations. First, France and China are more or less representative of pluralistic and authoritarian political systems. Second, as indicated by data to be presented later under "Findings," the fissures between China and the Communist system are more extensive and severe than is the rupture between France and the western alliance. Our discussion considers whether there is any systematic link between these two points; that is, are there attributes of authoritarian polities which may give rise to a relatively complete break from an alliance? What characteristics of pluralistic nations may act to limit the disruption of relations with allies?

The analysis then turns to an external aspect of the problem—the nature of the alliances of which France and China are members. The western alliance and communist system differ in a number of important respects. We will consider how these environmental variations may be linked to different patterns in French and Chinese alliance policies.

In the final part of the chapter we present quantitative data on some aspects of French and Chinese relations with their allies to shed some light on hypotheses developed in previous sections.

One point should be made explicit at the outset. We are not attempting to identify the event or events that "caused" the Sino-Soviet conflict or the

---

[1] We have also profited from reading James N. Rosenau, "Pre-Theories and Theories of Foreign Policy," in R. Barry Farrell (ed.), *Approaches to Comparative and International Politics* (Evanston: Northwestern U.P., 1966). We are aware of the distinction sometimes made between "blocs" and "alliances." We will use the terms interchangeably only for literary reasons.

differences between Paris and Washington, nor do we seek to allocate the blame in the disputes which may have led to French and Chinese deviation from bloc norms.[2] If Kremlinologists, Sinologists, and Gaullologists cannot agree among themselves on such matters—an assessment that can be verified by a random selection of any half-dozen recent books on NATO or Sino-Soviet relations—surely the limited observations and data to be presented here will not resolve these issues. Although we cannot offer a definitive assessment of French and Chinese alliance policies, we are trying to suggest possible explanations in terms of national-international linkages. Thus, our speculation about French and Chinese policy and our decisions regarding the types of data to be sought were governed by the definition of a linkage as "any *patterned sequence of behavior* that originates in one system and is reacted to in another."[3]

The national-international linkages framework opens up for investigation an almost limitless number of theoretically significant questions. This can be illustrated by considering a few of the questions one might ask about a single type of activity—the recent Chinese purchases of wheat from western nations. A linkage analysis is initially concerned with the complex political processes by which a need for wheat was transformed into a demand on the political system and then into a decision to negotiate a contract with wheat suppliers. Among the many interesting questions one might want to ask are the following: "Through what channels were demands for wheat communicated?" "What alternative means of meeting these demands were suggested, by whom, and within which institutions?" "What attitudes were engaged by a decision to purchase wheat from an 'enemy' nation?" A linkage analysis considers not only the internal sources of the Chinese policy, but also its consequences for the environment—for example, for the Canadian political system. "What activities by interest groups preceded the sale of wheat to China?" "How did leaders, parties, and publics respond to the wheat sale?" As the primary beneficiaries of the sale were farmers in the English-speaking provinces, what was the impact of the decision on tensions between the English and French communities?" "What effect did the wheat sale have on the 1965 national elections?"[4] In

[2] Some would maintain that it is the United States and the Soviet Union, rather than France and China, which have deviated from bloc norms. We shall not address ourselves to this question; to do so would be to stray from our purpose of examining national linkages to various international environments and place us back in the position of weighing the merits of claims made in current controversies within the two alliances.

[3] The quote is from the Rosenau formulation in Chapter 3. (Italics added.)

[4] Such a list of questions could be endless. Spinning out all determinants or consequences of any polity output would be limited only with the advent of a developed theory of "linkages" which predicted specific consequences as a result of polity or environmental outputs. Were such a theory available, it would be necessary to examine only those consequences predicted by the theory in order to evaluate it.

Yet these few questions indicate that even if we leave to the historian the task of reconstructing unique events in all their complexity, identifying and describing theoretically important national-international linkages will require the collective energies

short, a full investigation into the sources and consequences of national-international linkages goes far beyond the scope of a single paper, and especially beyond that of an exploratory study such as that undertaken here.

INTERNAL POLITICAL PROCESSES AND NONCONFORMING ALLIANCE POLICIES

Of the many processes, institutions, actors, and attitudes which may be linked to foreign policy, we confine ourselves to the socialization of political elites, the stability of top leadership, and certain characteristics of open and closed polities. Even within these limited areas our discussion is necessarily speculative and illustrative rather than exact.

The Socialization of Political Elites

French and Chinese leaders appear to share some striking similarities which may be related to deviation from their alliances. Mao Tse-tung and Charles DeGaulle are intellectuals, leaders of great personal stature, intensely nationalistic, and both are convinced that their vision of history gives them better insight than their allies into the features of the politically relevant future.[5] At least to some extent these characteristics appear to reflect some widely shared traits of their societies. A general attribute cited by virtually every student of French and Chinese politics is the nationalism, bordering on xenophobia, which permeates these nations. The Chinese philosophical tradition has long emphasized China's cultural superiority in contrast to the surrounding "barbarians" and has viewed China as the center of the world. French commentators have expressed similar views regarding France, the superiority of its culture, language, way of life, and its *mission civilisatrice*. These sentiments currently find their most eloquent expression in DeGaulle's pronouncements about France's international role, such as in a statement made at his twelfth press conference.

> Indeed, the independence thus regained is enabling France to become, despite the ideologies and hegemonies of the colossi, for all the racial passions and prejudices, above and beyond the rivalries and ambitions of nations, a champion of cooperation, failing which the troubles, the interventions, the conflicts that lead to world war would go on spreading. Now, France is, par excellence, qualified to act in this way.[6]

of a substantial proportion of those who consider themselves students of comparative or international politics. This is not said in criticism of the enterprise or to discourage what seems to us a clearly desirable course of events.

[5] Zbigniew Brzezinski and Samuel P. Huntington, *Political Power: USA/USSR* (New York: Viking, 1964), p. 390.

[6] Ambassade de France, Service de Presse et d'Information, "President de Gaulle Holds Twelfth Press Conference," *Speeches and Press Conferences*, No. 228 (Sept. 9, 1965), p. 8.

Such feelings are often cited as a basic source of deviation from alliance norms: "The evidence suggests that where the [Chinese] communists move with the tide, i.e., nationalism, they are more successful than when they seek to move against it, i.e., 'the Russians are our brothers.' "[7]   Diffuse cultural factors are clearly not sufficient to explain French and Chinese foreign policy during the 1960s, because they also existed in the previous decade.[8] They may, however, be viewed as background factors which have contributed to the political "education" of present leaders, and which provide at least latent support for current foreign policies.

For present purposes the most relevant socialization experiences of French and Chinese leaders are those related to international politics in general and alliance politics in particular.   Historically France and China have been among the "great powers."   But after experiencing considerable political instability during the inter-war years, both nations suffered invasion and catastrophic military defeats during the initial years of World War II, and only the military power of their allies enabled them to emerge victorious.   During the war French and Chinese leaders often experienced disappointment and humiliation.   Consider, for example, the key meetings of Allied leaders to which neither French nor Chinese representatives were invited, despite their nominal status as members of the "Big Five."

Like leaders in other nations who have successfully challenged their alliance leaders (e.g., Yugoslavia and Albania), Mao and DeGaulle owe their present positions to personal and national factors rather than to the intervention of their allies.   But even before achieving national leadership, they experienced similar incidents with allies which may have convinced them of the virtues of self-reliance.   Both developed something less than cordial relations with the leaders of their respective alliances.   DeGaulle's frustrations in his dealings with Anglo-American leaders during World War II are well documented, as are Mao Tse-tung's disappointment with the half-hearted Soviet support for the revolution in China before and during World War II, and through a considerable period of the subsequent Chinese civil war.   It is worth noting that these experiences were not limited to DeGaulle and Mao.   Most of China's present leaders were with Mao during the revolutionary period, and eight French Cabinet members were associates of DeGaulle during World War II.[9]

The political instability which had characterized China and France

[7] Robert A. Scalapino, "The Foreign Policy of the People's Republic of China," in Joseph E. Black and Kenneth W. Thompson (eds.), *Foreign Policies in a World of Change* (New York: Harper & Row, 1963), p. 563.

[8] See, for example, Benjamin I. Schwarz, "The Maoist Image of World Order," *Journal of International Affairs*, XXI (1967), pp. 92–102, who demonstrates some of the dangers of assuming that Chinese decision makers merely reflect uniform cultural attributes.

[9] Computed from Ambassade de France, Service de Presse et d'Information, "Re-Election of General de Gaulle as President of the French Republic and Composition of the New Pompidou Cabinet," *French Affairs*, No. 186A (January 10, 1966).

continued after the war, and only after the present regimes came to power in 1949 and 1958—after a civil war and near civil war—was internal stability restored.   China and France were accorded some of the symbols of "Great Power" status but the realities of international politics during the Cold War left little doubt that they were very junior partners in the alliance established by the Soviet Union and the United States.   For economic reconstruction and national security both nations were heavily dependent upon the Soviets and Americans.   In many important respects France and China could be characterized as "penetrated" political systems (to borrow a term from Rosenau)[10] during this period. Although both were successful in resisting certain overt attempts by alliance leaders to force integration of their armed forces into those of the alliance—France rejected the European Defense Community in 1954 despite Dulles' threat of an "agonizing reappraisal," and China resisted Soviet overtures for some types of military integration in the late 1950s—the United States and the Soviet Union had an important influence on domestic and foreign policies in France and China.

From the point of view of French and Chinese leaders, the imbalance of costs over benefits deriving from their respective alliances must have become increasingly clear as a result of various international crises during the 1950s and early 1960s.   As examples of the risks inherent in alliance membership they could point to the apparent Soviet and American willingness to drag their alliances close to the brink of nuclear war over Berlin and in other Cold War disputes—or even over a few missiles on a small Caribbean island populated by neither Russians nor Americans.   But if the potential risks of alliance membership were clear, the benefits must have appeared considerably more questionable.   The Chinese were unable to count on Soviet support to regain offshore islands in the Taiwan Straits, and they were publicly chided by Moscow for the frontier campaign against India in 1962.   Promised Soviet support for China's nuclear weapons program was unilaterally broken off.   Even Soviet economic aid was increasingly being diverted from China to nations in the "Third World" whose commitment to international revolution was suspect, and whose needs were not demonstrably greater than those of China.

Similarly, when interests defined as vital by the French were at stake— as in Indo-China and Algeria—they found that support from the alliance in general and from the United States in particular could scarcely be relied upon.   Decisive French action to preserve control of the Suez Canal failed to elicit even a benevolent American neutrality, much less aid or sympathy. Indeed, during the height of the Suez crisis Vice-President Nixon and Secretary Dulles publicly lectured France on the obligations of international law, while proclaiming American "independence" from the interests of "colonial" powers.   Nor were the French more successful than the Chinese

---

[10] Rosenau, "Pre-Theories and Theories of Foreign Policy," *op. cit.*, pp. 65 ff.

in gaining support for a nuclear weapons program. While General DeGaulle was in temporary retirement during several of these episodes, it seems likely that they had considerable impact on his attitudes toward the western alliance.

Finally, whatever may have been the motives of American and Soviet leaders in signing the Nuclear Test-Ban Treaty of 1963, the Chinese and French interpreted the treaty as a direct effort to retard their own nuclear weapons program. Thus, as they defined their interests, both Mao and DeGaulle had ample reason for dissatisfaction with their alliances and with the leadership provided by Moscow and Washington. If Cold War crises have taught Soviet and American leaders that great caution is necessary to avoid a thermonuclear holocaust, the same events appear to have confirmed Chinese and French suspicions of the asymmetrical nature of their alliance commitments.

In part as a result of these and other experiences, both French and Chinese leaders have tended to define international alignments in a manner somewhat different from their bloc leaders, and these differences appear important for alliance relations. DeGaulle's call for a Europe from the "Atlantic to the Urals" assumes an end to the European sector of the Cold War, and Lin Piao's thesis of a confrontation between the "cities of the world" and the "countryside of the world" is similarly predicated upon major changes in international alignments. In both definitions of the international system Cold War alliances are transformed, for each view envisions a completely new role for Eastern Europe and the Soviet Union.

In summary, then, recent experiences of French and Chinese leaders appear analogous in a number of respects. The explanatory power of such anecdotal and unsystematic evidence may be quite limited, and certainly it provides no base from which to generalize to other nonconforming members of alliance. It seems reasonable to suggest, however, that these experiences have helped to shape the political attitudes and predispositions of French and Chinese elites. That is, might not a generation of leaders who had not shared these experiences have been somewhat less prone to deviate from alliances which have been, in the main, products of American and Soviet policy?

The Stability of Top Leadership

A second internal political characteristic which may be related to alliance policy is the stability of top leadership. The literature on alliance cohesion generally focuses on political attributes of the bloc leader. It is often asserted that alliance cohesion depends upon stable leadership within the leading nation.[11] These propositions appear to have high face validity.

[11] Karl W. Deutsch et al., *Political Community and the North Atlantic Area: International Organization in the Light of Historical Experience* (Princeton: Princeton U.P., 1957); and George Liska, *Nations in Alliance: The Limits of Interdependence* (Balti-

But recent disintegrative tendencies within the communist system and western alliance cannot be explained by the absence of elite stability in the United States and Soviet Union during the past decade. Individuals occupying top leadership positions have changed from time to time in both nations, but transitions from one set of leaders to another hardly appear to have arisen from irrepressible demands for changes in foreign policy. Indeed, as Cohen points out, all members of the Soviet and American "establishment" have effectively used the Cold War to maintain power.[12] Nor have transitions in leadership had a great impact on subsequent foreign policies. Even the most sudden and unexpected personnel changes, such as the assassination of President Kennedy in 1963 and the removal of Chairman Khrushchev a year later, produced few basic policy changes. Thus it seems necessary to turn elsewhere in order to explain French and Chinese deviation from bloc norms.

On the other hand, stable and effective leadership in nations other than the bloc leader may be a necessary, if not sufficient, condition for successful deviation from alliance norms. A casual survey of notable nonconforming bloc members—China, France, and Albania; Yugoslavia during the late 1940s and the 1950s; and Great Britain during the nineteenth century—appears to support this proposition. It may be that only leaders relatively secure from internal dissent are likely to undertake external policies which violate important bloc norms,[13] and that unless leadership is stable and effective, bloc leaders may successfully appeal to and provide support for an alternative group of leaders within the nonconforming nation. While a study limited to two cases can only be suggestive, it is perhaps instructive to speculate about the consequences for alliance unity had the positions of Mao and DeGaulle been vulnerable to challenge by a strong opposition within China and France during the early 1960s. Might such circumstances have deterred Peking and Paris from challenging their alliance leaders? And if not, would the Soviets and Americans have been tempted to support actively a potentially more tractable leadership group?

In France, instability of leadership characterized politics during the

---

more: Johns Hopkins Press, 1962), p. 93. On the other hand, Jacob and Teune suggest that governmental ineffectiveness, which presumably indicates the absence of stable and effective leadership, may provide added incentives for seeking larger units of community. Philip E. Jacob and Henry Teune, "The Integrative Process: Guidelines for Analysis of the Bases of Political Community," in Philip E. Jacob and James V. Toscano (eds.), *The Integration of Political Communities* (Philadelphia: Lippincott, 1964).

[12] Bernard Cohen, "National-International Linkages: Superpolities," paper read at American Political Science Association meeting (September, 1966), a revised version of which appears as Chapter 6 of this volume.

[13] This interpretation is at variance with that of Peter S. H. Tang, who asserts that the relative absence of internal competition for political leadership in China and the Soviet Union supports cooperation, rather than conflict between them. Tang, *Communist China Today*, 2nd ed. (Washington: Research Institute on the Sino-Soviet Bloc, 1961), p. 488.

Fourth Republic and, although personnel turnover was less spectacular than changes in governments, it was manifestly a source of difficulties in the formulation and execution of foreign policy. Not every American effort to dominate French policy was a success; witness Dulles' failure to force France into the European Defense Community. Nevertheless, French political instability may have permitted greater American influence in French Foreign policies at that time, whereas the absence of alternatives to DeGaulle during the Fifth Republic has left the United States with little choice but to accept Gaullist policies.

Similarly, few students of Chinese politics have failed to comment upon its stable leadership. Through the mid-1960s virtually every top position was filled by those who had been among Mao's leading lieutenants during the pre-1949 revolutionary period. With only a few exceptions—notably those of Kao Kang in 1954 and Peng Teh-huai in 1959—China had been free from periodic purges which seem to be a recurring feature of politics in other communist nations.

This has, of course, changed recently. Yet the current purges do not necessary nullify the proposition that stable leadership is a necessary condition for successful deviation from alliance norms. The period of China's break with its alliance *was* one of elite stability, and by 1966, when the current wave of purges started, China's split with the Soviet Union and the communist system was probably already beyond repair. Moreover, there is neither evidence that any top leaders in China have embraced a pro-Soviet position, nor that they could enhance their prospects for success by doing so. Recent Soviet expressions of sympathy[14] (and material aid, according to un-confirmed reports) for anti-Mao factions within China also suggest that un-stable leadership within the nonconforming nation will tempt the alliance leader to interfere in its internal political processes. If this hypothesis is valid, we might expect that the eventual passing of General DeGaulle will lead to American efforts on behalf of potential successors who are more favorably inclined toward NATO.

Stable leadership may be a necessary condition for an effective policy of deviation from bloc norms. Conversely, nonconforming alliance policies may serve to solidify the position of top leaders. This is, of course, a variant of the popular theory that antagonism toward foreign nations may prove the smoothest road to maintenance of domestic political power. Cohen's suggestion that Cold War competition has been instrumental in maintaining the American and Soviet "establishment" in power is a case in point. There is evidence that the symbols of intra-alliance composition have similarly been used by French and Chinese leaders.

General DeGaulle has effectively employed nationalistic and anti-alliance rhetoric in his various political campaigns. Even results of the 1967 parliamentary elections, in which the Gaullist parliamentary majority

---

[14] See, for example, Kosygin's press conference in London (February 10, 1967).

was severely reduced, do not appear to reflect voter dissatisfaction with DeGaulle's foreign policies. Supporters of Jean Lecanuet, the so-called "American candidate," suffered even worse losses than the Gaullists. Moreover, the largest gains were made by the Communists. This pattern suggests that issues other than French alliance policies were responsible for the election results.

A more dramatic version of the same political process appears to be taking place in China. It is often suggested that the current "cultural revolution" and its attendant political purge were triggered off by Maoist efforts to cleanse Chinese society of all threats—manifest and latent, real and imagined—to revolutionary purity. To some extent this may be a general reaction against all foreign influences. But among the most salient and immediate threats to Maoist ideology and institutions are those of the Soviet "modern revisionists," who are not only geographically proximate, but who have also had the most opportunity for "subversion." The United States may be viewed by the Chinese as the greatest threat to national security, but there is scarcely any danger that an emerging generation of Chinese leaders will emulate American social, political, ideological or cultural norms. Maoist leaders may feel far less secure, however, that the Soviet patterns of Marxism will not prove an attractive and viable model for future Chinese elites. Thus, the external enemies used to generate political activity in behalf of those in power in China are no longer confined to the "imperialist" nations, for the Soviets have joined the United States as the most important negative symbols in China. As one observer has commented, "The rift with the Soviet Union has been critically important in maintaining the CCP suspicion of domestic heterodoxy and its determination to resist any political and economic concessions that might smack of 'revisionism.' "[15] Liu Shao-chi, Teng Hsiao-ping, Tao Chu and others who have fallen from Mao's grace have been attacked for following a pro-Soviet line. Whether they have in fact done so is far from evident; what is clear is that anti-Soviet symbols have become a major part of political rhetoric in Chinese political processes. Thus competition and conflict within the alliance appears to be having at least as much impact on Chinese internal politics as competition between alliances.

Pluralistic and Authoritarian Polities

To this point we have suggested—anecdotally and impressionistically—some of the shared political attributes which may be linked to similar patterns of French and Chinese foreign policy toward their respective alliance leaders. We have treated these two political systems as members of a single class and we will present data to indicate that both have indeed deviated from important bloc norms. But there is some danger in attempting

---

[15] James R. Townsend, "Internal Politics Since 1956," *Bulletin of the Atomic Scientists* (June, 1966), p. 65.

to carry the parallels too far. To do so would be to suggest: (1) that patterns of Chinese and French alliance policy are similar in all respects; (2) that manifest differences in the French and Chinese polities are politically less relevant than the similarities already discussed; and (3) that alliance policy is solely a reflection of internal political factors, and that striking differences in the nature of the western alliance and the communist system— that is, the intra-alliance environment—are irrelevant to French and Chinese policy. The remainder of this chapter will address itself to a critical examination of these three points by identifying some important dissimilarities in French and Chinese alliance policies and by attempting to link them to differences in polity and alliance attributes.

Our initial hypotheses indicate that French and Chinese alliance policies, while sharing a tendency toward deviation from norms of their respective alliances, diverge in the extent of their break with their alliances in general and with the alliance leaders in particular. That is:

> French nonconforming behavior has remained confined to a few issue-areas, with a low tendency for it to "spill over" into all issue-areas.

> Chinese nonconforming behavior has tended to spill over into all issue-areas.

These hypotheses appear to have face validity in that the Sino-Soviet rift and Moscow's ability to mobilize other Communist nations in a polemical battle against Peking seems to exceed by a considerable margin the disruption within the western alliance. However, these hypotheses do not indicate the significance of national-international linkages. To do so we will turn first to attributes of the French and Chinese political systems in an effort to illustrate, if not demonstrate, the linkages between some basic dissimilarities in internal political processes and the alliance policies to which they give rise.

By most familiar methods of classifying political systems the differences between France and China are considerably more obvious than the similarities. It has been suggested that a "pre-theory" of comparative foreign policy might be developed by classifying political systems on three dimensions: *open polity-closed polity*; economically *developed-underdeveloped*; and *large-small*.[16] On the first two dimensions France and China are virtually on opposite ends of the continuum and they differ, if somewhat less spectacularly, with respect to size. This discussion will focus on the first of these factors—the political dimension.

The hypotheses can be restated in terms which link polity differences to differences in alliance policy.

---

[16] Rosenau, "Pre-Theories and Theories of Foreign Policy," *op. cit.*

Nonconforming alliance policy of an open polity tends to remain confined to a few issue-areas; that is, there is little tendency for disputes to "spill over" into all issue-areas.

Nonconforming alliance policy of a closed polity tends to spill over into all issue-areas.

These hypotheses derive from the view that in a pluralistic system foreign policy elites operate under significant constraints against sudden and complete changes in policy. These include multiple internal and external channels of communication, relative freedom for divergent interests to make political demands and a limited ability of top leaders to mobilize all politically relevant groups and institutions in support of their policies.

One significant barrier against a complete French break from its alliance exists in the many national and international organizations—governmental, semi-governmental and private—through which French elites can communicate with their counterparts in allied nations. Even if effective communication between top leadership (e.g., between Presidents Johnson and DeGaulle) is disrupted, other formal and informal channels of communication remain. Such organizations tend to generate multiple interests and loyalties which cut across national boundaries. The existence of these ties, which are likely to survive alliance disunity in one issue-area, have been used to explain the relatively moderate rupture in Franco-American relations.

In both countries, the political "Establishment" contains a large cadre of men deeply involved in the development of NATO and European unity, and in the application of American aid to the recovery of France; this has created a special bond of understanding and shared interest. In each country there were prominent individuals pleading for reciprocal restraint and cooperation. To the United States, individuals such as Jean Monnet or Robert Schumann were an important source of reassurance that the basic ties were not being severed. To the French leader, the voices of General Norstad, Ambassador Gavin, and Governor Rockefeller meant that his conceptions had important American interpreters; and this too was vital in maintaining a relationship of continuing discussion.[17]

Equally important, a pluralistic polity is generally characterized by at least a moderate degree of functional autonomy. Public officials who owe their positions in part to technical expertise, rather than merely to political loyalties, are likely to be more numerous and influential in policy making. Individuals, groups and institutions responsible for policy in various issue-areas may represent quite different values, loyalties and interests. They are

---

[17] Brzezinski and Huntington, *op. cit.*, pp. 404–5. For a more general discussion of the advantages enjoyed by open polities in formulating foreign policy, see Kenneth N. Waltz, *Foreign Policy and Democratic Politics* (Boston: Little, 1967), esp. Ch. 11.

likely to serve as barriers against central control of policy in all issue-areas and therefore may act as a conservative force against radical policy changes. That technical experts in an open polity may develop interests and loyalties which resist complete control by top political leaders is illustrated in a study of agricultural politics in the European Economic Community.

> The relative power and prestige of "technical ministers," such as agriculture, have typically been enhanced . . . generating further interest on their part in maintaining the system [EEC]. Ministers of foreign affairs who have tried to maintain control of community matters by preserving the distinction between foreign policy and domestic policy have, in general, been fighting a losing battle.[18]

Other potential internal constraints operating against a complete rupture of French alliance policy can be illustrated by some recent opinion surveys. French political elites approved of the trend toward increasingly nationalistic policies in a world which is becoming more multipolar. But they also indicated a preference for maintaining strong links to the United States, they agreed that French security is largely dependent on the United States and they seemed confident that American commitments to European security will be honored. Public opinion data revealed a similar ambivalence to Gaullist foreign policies. A majority opposed alignment with the United States; at the same time most respondents indicated that France's interests are closely tied to the United States and public attitudes toward the United States have become more favorable during the period of the Fifth Republic. A similar pattern of attitudes existed toward Great Britain and its possible entry into the Common Market. Despite DeGaulle's emphasis on an independent nuclear force, there was limited support for this program either among elites or the public. Finally, while elites, masses and newspapers indicated reservations about NATO, these doubts have not spilled over into other areas of international cooperation such as trade and cultural activities.[19] In a relatively open political system such divergent views are likely to act as at least partial constraints against revolutionary and thoroughgoing changes in policy, even when a leader as commanding as DeGaulle heads the nation.

Hence, whether policy formulation is considered vertically (i.e. hierarchical levels of responsibility for policy) or horizontally (i.e., responsibility for policy in different issue-areas), in a pluralistic polity there are

---

[18] Leon N. Lindberg, "Decision Making and Integration in the European Community," *International Organization*, XIX (1965), 74.

[19] The data in this paragraph were derived from Karl W. Deutsch, "Integration and Arms Control in the European Political Environment: A Summary Report," *American Political Science Review*, LX (1966), 354–66; W. W. Kulski, *DeGaulle and the World: The Foreign Policy of the Fifth French Republic* (Syracuse: Syracuse U.P., 1966), pp. 65–67; and Michel Gordey, "The French People and DeGaulle," *Foreign Affairs*, XXIV (1964), 546–8.

likely to be sufficient cross-cutting interests and loyalties to preclude a complete break from pre-existing policies.

A similar line of reasoning suggests that the linkages between political processes in an authoritarian polity and its international environments will differ from those of pluralistic political systems. On the one hand, the "party line" on foreign policy in an authoritarian political system tends to define acceptable policy in all issue-areas. Within nations in the communist system, the sources of these guidelines include the all-encompassing world view of Marxist-Leninist thought. Once it is determined that the alliance leader is among the "enemies," as the Chinese now appear to categorize the Soviet Union, this designation is expected to guide policy makers in all issue-areas. On the other hand, authoritarian polities tend to lack institutionalized barriers against radical changes in policy—of which nonconforming alliance behavior is an example—in all issue-areas. Minimal channels of communications with allies, a relative absence of elites and groups representing multiple interests and possessing multiple loyalties, and centralization of policy formulation functions reduce the probabilities that alliance disunity in one issue-area can be contained within limited spheres of alliance activity.

Because an authoritarian polity such as China possesses limited channels of communication with allies, a rupture at the top leadership level has more severe consequences for alliance policy than would be the case for a pluralistic nation. Once the Sino-Soviet conflict had engulfed top levels of Chinese and Russian leadership, there were no effective channels of communication at lower levels through which the ties could be maintained and perhaps repaired.

> Because of the monolithic structure of the Soviet and Chinese systems, any such informal and indirect ties would have automatically threatened the stability of their respective leaderships. Formal communication exhausted all communication, with no safety valve of the indirect approach and no commonly shared experience in constructive understandings as a cushion. The Soviet and Chinese leaders met only on several formal occasions; there was simply no "Sino-Soviet Establishment" to plead the cause of unity and to moderate the increasingly immoderate language of the debate.[20]

This interpretation does not necessarily contradict the more specific reasons often given for the rift between Peking and Moscow, for example, explanations which locate a major source of conflict in personality differences between Mao, Khrushchev, and others.[21] It is precisely because few external channels of communication exist in authoritarian polities that personality differences between top Chinese and Soviet leaders take on great political importance. Such differences also exist between Presidents Johnson and

[20] Brzezinski and Huntington, *op. cit.*, p. 405.
[21] David Floyd, *Mao Against Khrushchev: A Short History of the Sino-Soviet Conflict* (New York: Praeger, 1964), p. 77; Scalopino, *op. cit.*, p. 568.

DeGaulle, but their political consequences are less far-reaching. Stated more generally, idiosyncratic factors such as personality are likely to have a more significant impact on formulation of foreign policy in a closed political system.[22]

Authoritarian political systems also lack effective internal barriers against a spill over of alliance disputes from one issue-area to all of them. Leaders responsible for policy in all issue-areas are likely to embrace similar attitudes and policies toward the alliance and its members. As one observer has noted, "Mao has implicated most of his immediate subordinates in this vitriolic war of words" [with the USSR].[23] Hence one polity consequence of the dispute with the Soviet Union has been that officials responsible for policy in *all* issue-areas have been drawn into an anti-Soviet position. This has in turn contributed to an increasingly intransigent Chinese policy toward Moscow.

The absence of effective constraints appears not only in the top level of leadership but also at all levels in the bureaucracy, where political loyalty tends to take precedence over competence, especially during periods of crisis. Moreover, the nature of Chinese bureaucracy tends to preclude the development of cliques which represent interests other than those of the political leadership. The kinds of extra-national bureaucratic loyalties which have developed in France are unlikely to be found in China, for, "The balance of power is clearly in the hands of the higher authorities, and the systematic breaking up of possible cliques by sending in outsiders, and transferring out insiders in a rudimentary clique prevents true cliques from developing."[24]

Other evidence also suggests an increasing concentration of decision making, and a concomitant standardization of policy in all issue-areas, during the period in which the Sino-Soviet break developed. Senior party leaders were sent from Peking to assignments in regional bureaus, reversing an earlier tendency to promote the most capable regional leaders to Peking; ambassadorial appointees were increasingly drawn from party operatives rather than from experienced foreign-service officers; and in the Central Control Commission closer links were established between top leaders in Peking and the provinces.[25] Whatever the reasons for these changes, they reduced potential constraints on a mobilization of internal support against the Soviet Union in all issue-areas.

Finally, it is sometimes said that freedom from broadly-based domestic constraints permits China to pursue an aggressive policy against the West.[26]

[22] Cf. Rosenau, "Pre-Theories and Theories of Foreign Policy," *op. cit.*, pp. 90–91.

[23] Donald W. Klein, "Succession and the Elite in Peking," *Journal of International Affairs*, XVIII (1964), 8.

[24] Ezra Vogel, "Politicized Bureaucracy: Communist China," paper read at American Political Science Association meeting (1966), p. 8.

[25] Donald Klein, "Chinese Communist Leadership: Some Problems of Control, Mobility and Policy Making," paper read at American Political Science Association meeting (1966), pp. 3–4.

[26] Tang, *op. cit.*, p. 488.

But such freedom may be even *more* important to mobilize a vast population against a nation once hailed as the vanguard of the international socialist movement.

In their analysis of western and communist alliance management, Brzezinski and Huntington conclude that "factors peculiar to the American and Soviet political systems" were "decisive" in containment of the Franco-American dispute and in escalation of the Sino-Soviet split.[27] The point we have been developing here is a complementary, not a contradictory, one. That is, political factors in France and China—some of which have been described in this discussion—have also contributed to different patterns of deviation from alliance norms. Or, to use linkage terminology, basic differences in the French and Chinese political processes appear systematically linked to different patterns of relationships within their intra-bloc environments.

ALLIANCE STRUCTURE AND NONCONFORMING ALLIANCE POLICIES

In the preceding sections we speculated about some of the ways in which internal political processes might be linked to patterns of nonconforming alliance policies. At this point we shift our focus to consider how characteristics of the intra-bloc environment may be linked to differences in alliance policy.

Theorists who have considered problems of alliance cohesion and disintegration by comparing the communist system with the western alliance have differed rather sharply in their analyses and predictions. Liska and Morgenthau tend to judge recent developments within the two alliances as rather similar in character, whereas Dinerstein and Kissinger emphasize differences between the blocs, viewing schisms within the communist system as far more serious.[28] Explanations of deviation from alliance norms also take many forms. Among the more plausible are those which point to a decreased level of inter-bloc conflict,[29] the nature of bloc leadership,[30] or the diffusion of military technology.[31] Others have attempted to explain a

---

[27] Brzezinski and Huntington, *op. cit.*, p. 407.

[28] George Liska, *op. cit.*, pp. 12–13; Hans J. Morgenthau, "Alliances in Theory and Practice," in Arnold Wolfers (ed.), *Alliance Policy in the Cold War* (Baltimore: Johns Hopkins Press, 1959), p. 185; Herbert S. Dinerstein, "The Transformation of Alliance Systems," *American Political Science Review*, LIX (1965), 593; and Henry A. Kissinger, *The Troubled Partnership* (New York: McGraw-Hill, 1965).

[29] Liska, *op. cit.*, pp. 89–90; Morton A. Kaplan, *System and Process in International Politics* (New York: Wiley, 1957), pp. 62–63; and Kissinger, *op. cit.*, p. 9.

[30] Liska, *op. cit.*, pp. 87–89; Kaplan, *op. cit.*, pp. 79–80.

[31] William H. Riker, "Politics in the Age of Maneuver," in Morton Berkowitz and P. G. Bock (eds.), *American National Security: A Reader in Research and Policy* (New York: Free Press, 1962), p. 182; R. W. Tucker, *Stability and the Nth Country Problem* (Washington, D.C.: Institute for Defense Analyses, 1962), p. 13; George Modelski,

somewhat different aspect of the problem—the *form* that nonconforming behavior takes—with propositions linking the nature of the alliance to patterns of nonconforming behavior. Each of these propositions is testable within a linkage framework, but we will limit ourselves to an assessment of hypotheses relating attributes of alliances and forms of deviation from alliance norms. The following discussion defines some differences between monolithic and pluralistic alliances. Two propositions, which predict differences in *forms* of nonconforming behavior by members of monolithic and pluralistic alliances, are derived from these definitions. An assessment of these will be undertaken with data on France and China.[32] However, it should be made clear that, being unable to reject competing explanations for the same behavior on the basis of two cases, we can only undertake the most preliminary examination of the hypotheses.

Monolithic Alliances

We assume that a monolithic bloc exhibits a rigidly hierarchical organization with the relationships between the bloc leader and its followers clearly defined. This in turn implies that status differences of alliance members will be explicit. Thus,

> **Definition 1.** A monolithic bloc is hierarchically organized.

Monolithic blocs are characterized by a common outlook and orientation, often imposed by the bloc leaders, to each other and to the external environment. This outlook is "total" in the sense that it enters into all aspects of bloc and polity activities. This seems especially true of the communist system, which has been described as "a functionally diffuse grouping in which cooperation is not tied to one specific goal, but potentially embraces all spheres of international activity."[33] Thus,

> **Definition 2.** A monolithic bloc has a wider sectorial scope; that is, it operates in more issue-areas.

A bloc that operates in many issue-areas has more potential sources of conflict than one with more limited functions. As Modelski has noted,

The Communist International System (Princeton: Center for International Studies, 1960); A. L. Burns, "Military Technology and International Politics," *Yearbook of World Affairs* (London: Stevens, 1961), p. 188; R. N. Rosecrance, *Problems of Nuclear Proliferation* (U.C.L.A.: Security Studies Paper No. 7, 1966), pp. 26 ff.; and Richard A. Brody, "Some Systematic Effects of the Spread of Nuclear Weapons Technology: A Study Through Simulation of a Multi-nuclear Future," *Journal of Conflict Resolution*, VII (1963), 663–753.

[32] These propositions are intended to describe "ideal types" which no actual alliance is likely to match in every detail. Thus we do not imply that the communist system is absolutely monolithic or that the western alliance is pluralistic in all respects.

[33] Modelski, *op. cit.*, p. 7. See also Zbigniew K. Brzezinski, *The Soviet Bloc: Unity and Conflict* (Cambridge: Harvard U.P., 1960), p. 395.

> . . . the Communist system creates a type of difficulty which
> is not very apt to reach the governmental level in non-Com-
> munist countries but which does so in the Communist system
> because of the complete state control over economic and other
> fields of life. Hence within the system the likelihood is
> greater of disputes over prices set in trade agreements, over
> the quality of goods delivered, over quantity of foreign aid,
> over the behavior of Soviet civilians, troops, and specialists,
> over special privileges granted to one state, etc.[34]

Two solutions to the problem of maintaining cohesion suggest themselves; a
reduction in the number of alliance members or a reduction in heterogeneity among them.[35] Expulsion of Yugoslavia from the Cominform illustrates the first method, and repression of Hungary in 1956 is an example of
the second. From the perspective of the bloc leader the latter approach
may seem preferable. Thus,

> **Proposition 1.** The wider the sectorial scope of an alli-
> ance, the greater the necessity for consensus.

The existence of status differences, the large number of issue-areas
within which the alliance operates and the requirement for consensus in a
monolithic alliance imply that the leading nation will tend to become dominant in all issue-areas. For instance, within the more pluralistic western
alliance the United States is not dominant with respect to cultural relations,
as all members tend to relate to each other as equals in this area, whereas
within the communist system the Soviet Union dominates all issue-areas,
including cultural relations. Thus,

> **Proposition 2.** The more monolithic the alliance, the
> more likely it is that the alliance leader is dominant in all
> issue-areas.

An alliance leader intent on maintaining both its dominant position
and bloc cohesion is likely to use coercive means to repress strains on any
major issue.[36] To bargain with subordinates implies some lessening of
differences in status. Within the more pluralistic western alliance a tradition of compromise and adjustment has contributed to containment of
disputes. Perhaps equally important has been the general lack of com-
pulsion to force each issue to complete resolution. Recent Franco-American
relations illustrate the latter point; each side appears more or less resigned
to the other's policies, and both have tended to ignore the issues which divide

---

[34] Modelski, _op. cit._, p. 63.

[35] Amitai Etzioni, "The Dialects of Supranational Unification," _American Political Science Review_, LVI (1962), 931.

[36] Liska, _op. cit._, p. 73; Brzezinski, _op. cit._, pp. 394–5; and Bruce M. Russett, "To-ward a Model of Competitive International Politics," _Journal of Politics_, XXV (1963), 227.

them. Within the communist system, on the other hand, the pragmatic style of conflict resolution is quite alien. When opposing views on substantive issues are couched in doctrinal terms, each dispute in effect becomes two—one substantive and one ideological—and demands buttressed by claims of ideological purity do not lend themselves easily to compromise. Thus,

> **Proposition 3.** The higher the necessity for consensus and the more explicit the status differences within the alliance, the more likely it is that the alliance leader will use repression rather than bargaining to resolve strains.

The observation that nonconforming behavior is less likely to occur in hierarchical alliances because they are capable of acting with greater energy with respect to intra-bloc and inter-bloc issues is a recurring one in the alliance literature.[37] Moreover, status differences associated with a monolithic alliance are likely to be based in part on the leader's superior coercive capabilities, further suggesting that successful deviation by subordinate members of the alliance is unlikely. Thus,

> **Proposition 4.** The more monolithic the alliance, the lower the probability that nonconforming behavior will be successful.

According to Proposition 2, the leading nation within a monolithic alliance is likely to maintain a hegemonic position in all issue-areas. Within such an alliance deviation from bloc norms in any issue-area is likely to be construed as a challenge to the leader in all of them. On the other hand, a nation within a pluralistic alliance, not faced with a leader supreme in all areas of activity, may more readily be able to deviate from alliance norms in some issue-areas without doing so "across the board." Thus,

> **Proposition 5.** The more monolithic the alliance, the more likely is successful nonconforming behavior in any issue-area to be treated as a challenge to the leader's dominance.

Successful defiance of the alliance norms is improbable in a monolithic bloc. But such behavior by subordinate nations, in any issue-area, is unlikely to be tolerated by the bloc leader. Hence any deviation from alliance norms is likely to spur the leader into renewed action in all issue-areas to maintain a dominant position. And, characteristically, the means are likely to be coercive; as Brzezinski notes with respect to the communist

---

[37] Roger D. Masters, "A Multi-Bloc Model of the International System," *American Political Science Review*, LV (1961), 795; Kaplan, *op. cit.*, pp. 40–41; 75–76; and Richard C. Snyder, *Deterrence Weapons Systems and Decision-Making* (China Lake, Calif.: United States Naval Ordnance Test Station, 1961), p. 70.

system, "The suppression of diversity and the forceful imposition of unity almost inevitably result in excessive reliance on force."[38] Thus,

> **Proposition 6.** In a monolithic alliance, unsuccessful efforts to repress nonconforming behavior in one issue-area will impel the bloc leader to maintain its position and alliance consensus by reasserting its dominance in other issue-areas.

One of the interesting questions posed by integration theorists is that of "role differentiation" versus "spill-over" theories.[39] According to the former theory, cooperation between political units in one issue-area neither depends upon, nor enhances the prospects for, collaboration in other types of activities. Spill-over theory, on the other hand, asserts that agreement for concerted action in one issue-area induces the partners to make further agreements in other enterprises; for example, proponents of foreign trade or cultural exchange programs often assert that they will result in closer political relations between the participating nations. As suggested by the somewhat contradictory conclusions in the integration literature, the superiority of either theory, or the conditions under which each is more valid, remains to be demonstrated conclusively.

Little attention has been paid to the reverse process—the extent to which *nonconforming* or *disintegrative* behavior in one issue-area is likely to affect alliance relations in others—although several observers have suggested the likelihood of a general erosion of unity within the communist system: ". . . the cohesion of the Communist alliance system, once pressed into a rigid mold, will suffer much greater disintegration than the always loose non-Communist system."[40] Proposition 7 (and 7a below) can be viewed as a way of suggesting that role differentiation and spill-over theories may also be applied to disintegrative processes, and that the latter may be more valid in monolithic alliances, whereas the former theory is more applicable to pluralistic ones. Thus,

> **Proposition 7.** In a monolithic alliance, if nonconforming behavior should be successful in one issue-area, there is a high probability that such behavior will "spill over" into other issue-areas.

Pluralistic Alliances

The propositions identifying the characteristics of pluralistic alliances are, in effect, the converse of those describing monolithic alliances.

[38] Brzezinski, *op. cit.*, pp. 394–5.

[39] Karl W. Deutsch, "Transaction Flows as Indicators of Political Cohesion," in Philip E. Jacob and James V. Toscano (eds.), *The Integration of Political Communities* (Philadelphia: Lippincott, 1964), p. 95. The concept of "spill over" is derived from Ernst B. Haas, *The Uniting of Europe* (Stanford: Stanford U.P., 1958).

[40] Dinerstein, *op. cit.*, p. 601; Brzezinski, *op. cit.*, pp. 394 ff.; Kissinger, *op. cit.*, p. 251.

Definition 1a. A pluralistic alliance is less hierarchically organized than a monolithic one.

Definition 2a. A pluralistic alliance has a narrower sectorial scope, operating in fewer issue-areas, than a monolithic alliance.

Proposition 1a. The narrower the sectorial scope of an alliance, the less is the necessity for consensus.

Proposition 2a. The more pluralistic an alliance, the less likely it is that the leader is dominant in all issue-areas.

Proposition 3a. The less the necessity for consensus and the less explicit the status differences within an alliance, the more likely it is that the leader will bargain to resolve strains rather than attempt to repress them.

Proposition 4a. The more pluralistic the alliance, the higher the probability that nonconforming behavior in one issue-area will be successful.

Proposition 5a. In a more pluralistic alliance, successful nonconforming behavior is likely to be treated as a challenge to the bloc leader in only limited issue areas. (This follows from Proposition 2a which states that the bloc leader is unlikely to be dominant in all issue-areas.)

Proposition 6a. In a more pluralistic alliance, unsuccessful efforts to forestall nonconforming behavior are less likely to result in attempts by the bloc leader to assert dominance in other issue-areas.

Proposition 7a. In a more pluralistic alliance, if nonconforming behavior within a specific issue-area is successful, there is a low probability that such behavior will spill over into other issue-areas.

The relevance of these propositions to the study of Chinese and French nonconforming behavior depends upon the assumption that the definitions spelled out above are applicable to the communist system and the western alliance; namely, that the communist system is intended to operate across a wider spectrum of issue-areas than is the western alliance, and that the former is more hierarchically organized than the latter. If these assumptions are valid we would expect, according to Propositions 7 and 7a, to find Chinese deviant behavior in nearly all issue-areas, and French relations with its allies to remain intact in several issue-areas. The intervening propositions (1-6 and 1a-6a) linking the definitions with predictions about differences in nonconforming behavior are testable, but we will not do so. The data presented below are intended only to shed light on the differences between Chinese and French policies as predicted by Propositions 7 and 7a.

FINDINGS

Nations which are members of an alliance establish characteristic patterns of interaction with various international environments. A conforming bloc member adheres to certain predictable patterns of behavior with other members of the alliance, the leading nations in the bloc, nations within the opposing alliance and nonaligned states. In these terms, deviation from bloc norms is the establishment of qualitatively and quantitatively different patterns of interaction with various international environments.

The data to be presented here do not exhaust all relevant aspects of alliance relations, but they are assumed to index at least some important dimensions of adherence to or deviation from bloc norms. Data on actions, elite attitudes, international trade, foreign aid, and treaties and agreements are presented in a partial attempt to assess how differences in internal political processes and in the nature of the intra-bloc environment are linked to patterns of alliance policy.[41]

The categories into which our data are coded are derived largely from the national-international linkages framework. *International environments* are defined according to political (*intra-bloc, inter-bloc, non-bloc*) and geographical (*contiguous, regional*) criteria. The test of bloc membership is a treaty commitment—either multi-lateral or bilateral—of a military/security nature. Thus membership in such organizations as NATO, SEATO, CENTO or the Warsaw Pact defines bloc assignment, as does a bilateral agreement linking such nations as Spain, Japan, Taiwan, or Cuba to one alliance or the other. Nations without such agreements were coded into the nonbloc category. The *contiguous* environment is defined as those nations with which a polity shares a common frontier. Thus the contiguous environment for France includes Belgium, Luxembourg, Germany, Switzerland, Italy, Spain, and Andorra. As used here the *regional* environments of France and China are based primarily upon geographical and cultural factors. East and Southeast Asia are included in China's regional

---

[41] The importance of such data as indicators of Chinese foreign policy is not universally accepted. Karl Wittfogel, for example, asserts that, "In the course of this intricate process the leading Communist countries may have grave differences of opinion on details of economic cooperation and domestic and foreign policy. But any analyst who, because of such secondary differences, disregards the primary ties between Moscow and Peking, appraises the Communist power system with the standards of a Babbitt or a Colonel Blimp."—Wittfogel, "A Stronger Oriental Despotism," *The China Quarterly*, No. 1 (Jan.–Mar., 1960), 34.
At the risk of being guilty of Babbitry, we assume that our data do in fact shed some light on the current state of Sino-Soviet relations.

environment, while continental Europe and the British Isles are included in France's regional environment.[42]

Because nations often undertake a wide variety of activities within the framework of an alliance—military cooperation, foreign aid, technical assistance, trade agreements and the like—an approach which permits a separate analysis of linkages in each issue-area is particularly relevant for our purposes. We will consider activities in five issue-areas: *security* (military aid, bases, weapons, military actions, etc.); *territory* (boundary definitions, colonies, etc.); *status* (diplomatic recognition, consular and diplomatic relations, status of representatives, membership in organizations, etc.); *human resources* (cultural activities, education or training program, travel, and so forth); and *nonhuman resources* (trade, foreign aid, transportation, exchange rates, and many other activities relating to the acquisition and deployment of nonmilitary goods).

Action Data

Chinese and French actions from 1950 through 1964 were coded to provide a broad index of changes toward nations in various international environments. All French and Chinese activities, physical or verbal, which crossed their respective national boundaries were coded from these sources.[43]

In coding these data, each action was given an identification number indicating the source, the year, month and day of the action. The target nation was recorded as well as any third party mentioned in the action. Each action was coded into one of six issue-areas identified previously. The "other" category includes actions which encompassed more than one issue-area.

[42] Determination of the regional environments for France and China involved some arbitrary decisions, one of which was to consider the Soviet Union as a European rather than an Asian nation, and therefore within the French but not the Chinese regional environment. One reason for this decision was that it would be useful to have an environment which cuts across Cold War alignments. Perhaps French and Chinese leaders would define regions similarly. DeGaulle has talked of a Europe from "the Urals to the Atlantic," and Chinese leaders have sought to exclude the Soviet Union from the "Afro-Asian" world.

[43] *The New York Times Index*, 1950–1964; Charles McClelland et al., *The Communist Chinese Performance in Crisis and Non-Crisis: Quantitative Studies of the Taiwan Straits Confrontation: 1950–1964* (China Lake, Calif.: Naval Ordnance Test Station, 1965), and William H. Vatcher, *Panmunjon* (New York: Praeger, 1958). The McClelland and Vatcher sources were chronologies and it was necessary only to record each action as it appeared. *The New York Times Index* employs a system of cross-referencing which necessitated the following approach. The main section for each country contained cross-references indicating international actions by both countries. These cross-references were to geographical, issue, and organizational items. With one exception, we coded all actions appearing in these sources. We abandoned efforts to report every military engagement in Korea, Indo-China, Algeria, and other former French dependencies. The problem of determining what level of engagement (e.g., squad, company, battalion) should be included was not readily solvable. Moreover, such activities were often described as "reported" military encounters and verifying them would have proved a virtually impossible task.

The final classification used was type of action. The original coding of types of actions included 24 categories; for example: defend, propose, accuse, demand, threaten, sign agreement, send aid, confer, seize property, troop mobilization, attack, etc. For present purposes these were collapsed into only two categories—positive and negative actions.

There are several potential sources of systematic error in these data. First, our sources may have employed biased selection procedures and we have no control over such error. There are also two potential types of errors in cross-referencing the *Times Index*. If an action was not properly cross-referenced, it would be missing from our data. But we did search for all actions which were cross-referenced more than once, and duplicate cards were removed. The final source of error is coder error in identifying or classifying data into appropriate categories. These operations required relatively little judgment once the categories had been defined, but limited time and resources did not permit use of two coders and tests of inter-coder reliability. Hence we cannot estimate the level of error attributable to coding. Nevertheless, while some error no doubt exists in our action data, we assume that at least major trends in Chinese and French policy are accurately portrayed.

Chinese actions toward nations in all international environments are summarized in Table 7.1. Over the period 1950–1964, the most striking changes are the patterns of Chinese action toward the inter-bloc and the intra-bloc environment. Primarily owing to a single type of recurring activity—the armistice negotiations directed at ending the Korean War—Chinese actions toward nations in the western alliance appear quite positive during 1951–1953. Except for the period of the armistice negotiations, Chinese actions toward nations in the inter-bloc environment were consistently negative.

For the present purposes Chinese relations with other nations in the Communist system are of most interest. These data indicate a widening fissure between China and other communist nations,[44] and especially between Peking and Moscow. When data are analyzed according to issue-area (Table 7.2), the hypothesis of worsening relations between China and its allies in all types of activities is generally supported.

There has been a marked deterioration of Chinese intra-bloc relations between 1950–1962 and 1963–1964. But merely examining the total figures for all members of the communist system may be misleading; that is, the Sino-Soviet conflict accounts for most of the change between these two periods. As will become clear when we examine other types of data in more detail, the worsening relations between China and most of the eastern European nations (including the USSR) were accompanied by closer ties with North Vietnam, Cuba, Albania, and, until recently, North Korea.

[44] Chinese verbal attacks against Yugoslavia account for the results in 1958, during which only 62 per cent of Chinese actions toward members of the communist system were positive.

Table 7.1—Chinese Actions Toward Nations in Various International Environments: 1950–1964

Environment of Target Nation	1950	1951	1952	1953	1954	1955	1956	1957	1958	1959	1960	1961	1962	1963	1964
Inter-bloc:															
Positive	14	108	114	86	40	76	67	31	54	16	19	24	14	20	30
Negative	105	89	83	28	203	229	117	85	324	97	107	88	57	55	107
% Positive	11.7	54.8	57.8	75.4	16.4	24.9	36.4	26.7	14.2	14.1	15.0	21.4	19.7	26.7	21.9
Intra-bloc:															
Positive	20	14	14	29	26	11	25	35	13	31	43	60	40	19	55
Negative	3	1	2	0	0	0	4	1	8	7	6	8	25	29	45
% Positive	87.0	93.3	87.5	100.0	100.0	100.0	86.2	97.2	61.9	81.6	87.8	88.2	61.5	39.6	55.0
Non-bloc:															
Positive	5	5	11	5	16	0	49	15	26	26	44	31	28	55	66
Negative	3	1	2	1	0	0	5	1	5	21	10	6	64	18	13
% Positive	62.5	83.3	84.6	83.3	100.0	0.0	90.7	93.8	83.9	55.3	81.4	83.3	30.4	75.3	83.5
General:*															
Positive	11	8	4	6	19	15	9	5	7	9	16	21	10	11	17
Negative	19	1	2	3	7	2	3	4	1	14	8	15	1	6	11
% Positive	36.6	88.9	66.7	66.7	73.1	88.2	75.0	55.6	87.5	39.2	66.7	58.3	90.1	64.7	60.7
Total:															
Positive	50	135	143	126	101	102	150	86	100	82	122	136	92	105	168
Negative	130	92	89	32	210	231	129	91	338	139	131	117	147	108	176
% Positive	27.8	59.4	61.6	79.7	32.5	30.6	53.8	48.6	22.8	37.1	48.2	53.8	38.5	49.3	48.8
USSR:															
Positive	16	12	10	24	16	10	18	15	6	15	14	18	11	6	25
Negative	1	0	2	0	0	1	1	0	0	1	3	5	13	25	38
% Positive	94.1	100.0	83.3	100.0	100.0	90.1	94.7	100.0	100.0	93.7	82.4	78.3	45.8	19.4	39.7
Contiguous:															
Positive	24	18	25	31	31	11	45	26	13	34	47	40	37	30	45
Negative	6	0	8	1	0	0	4	0	1	22	9	10	76	42	51
% Positive	80.0	100.0	75.8	96.9	100.0	100.0	91.8	100.0	92.9	60.7	83.9	80.0	32.7	41.7	46.9
Regional:															
Positive	11	11	19	17	35	4	57	26	36	33	43	38	35	43	51
Negative	21	11	18	2	105	117	62	52	162	78	41	17	83	32	24
% Positive	34.4	50.0	51.4	89.5	25.0	3.3	47.9	33.3	18.2	29.7	51.2	69.1	29.7	57.3	68.0

*Target nation unspecified, or target nation in more than one environment

171

Table 7.2—Chinese Actions Toward Nations in the Communist System

Issue-Area	ACTIONS TOWARD ALL MEMBERS OF THE COMMUNIST SYSTEM		ACTIONS TOWARD USSR	
	1950–1962	1963–1964	1950–1962	1963–1964
Security:				
Positive	98	17	49	6
Negative	30	13	17	11
% Positive	76.6	56.7	74.2	35.5
Territory:				
Positive	6	3	5	2
Negative	2	7	0	7
% Positive	75.0	30.0	100.0	22.2
Human Resources:				
Positive	13	3	6	3
Negative	2	2	1	1
% Positive	86.7	60.0	85.7	75.0
Non-human Resources:				
Positive	47	5	22	1
Negative	0	11	0	10
% Positive	100.0	31.3	100.0	9.1
Status:				
Positive	97	27	37	8
Negative	11	7	2	6
% Positive	89.8	79.4	94.9	57.1
Other:				
Positive	100	19	66	11
Negative	20	34	6	28
% Positive	83.3	35.8	91.7	28.2
Total:				
Positive	361	74	185	31
Negative	65	74	26	63
% Positive	84.7	50.0	87.7	33.0

The French action data are also generally consistent with our hypotheses. Since 1960 there has been a moderate decline in friendly relations with members of the western alliance in general, and with the United States in particular (Table 7.3). But any friction in French intra-bloc relations does not approach in intensity the rupture between China and many of its allies. The Chinese and French data also reveal one other difference: The increasingly bad relations between China and members of the communist system have not been accompanied by significantly more friendly actions toward the west. By 1964, however, French actions were characterized by friendly overtures toward communist countries.

When French actions during the Fourth and Fifth Republics are analyzed according to issue-area, the pattern is one of only moderate changes

Table 7.3—French Actions Toward Nations in Various International Environments: 1950–1964

Environment of Target Nation	1950	1951	1952	1953	1954	1955	1956	1957	1958	1959	1960	1961	1962	1963	1964
Inter-bloc:															
Positive	15	31	22	28	23	35	21	4	21	14	10	4	6	1	18
Negative	24	36	15	8	29	29	11	9	19	6	18	23	10	6	4
% Positive	38.5	46.3	59.5	77.8	44.2	54.7	65.6	30.8	52.5	70.0	35.7	14.8	37.5	14.3	81.8
Intra-bloc:															
Positive	245	205	209	177	165	146	143	65	98	100	77	74	66	80	85
Negative	80	27	39	29	16	41	20	14	7	16	8	11	18	22	35
% Positive	75.4	88.4	84.3	85.9	91.2	78.1	87.7	82.3	93.3	86.2	90.6	87.1	78.6	78.4	70.8
Nonbloc:															
Positive	6	12	13	16	22	58	50	28	47	34	32	42	23	19	33
Negative	6	11	27	12	3	8	35	19	31	11	18	20	2	4	1
% Positive	50.0	52.2	32.5	57.1	88.0	87.9	58.8	59.6	60.3	75.6	64.0	67.7	92.0	82.6	97.1
General:*															
Positive	21	26	20	25	31	36	39	20	22	36	13	16	8	11	28
Negative	7	5	24	8	4	17	23	10	12	14	14	22	6	12	12
% Positive	75.0	83.9	45.5	75.8	88.6	67.9	62.9	66.7	64.7	72.0	48.1	42.1	57.1	47.8	70.0
Total:															
Positive	287	274	264	246	241	275	253	117	188	184	132	136	103	111	164
Negative	117	79	105	57	52	95	89	52	69	47	58	76	36	44	52
% Positive	71.0	77.6	71.5	81.2	82.3	74.3	74.0	69.2	73.2	79.7	69.5	64.2	74.1	71.6	75.9
United States:															
Positive	42	51	34	39	32	19	31	30	28	23	16	24	22	13	18
Negative	11	11	15	6	1	15	8	5	1	7	2	6	10	8	10
% Positive	79.2	82.3	69.4	86.7	97.0	55.9	79.5	85.7	96.6	76.7	88.9	80.0	68.8	61.9	64.3
Contiguous:															
Positive	36	14	20	15	22	25	15	9	10	20	13	8	15	17	17
Negative	16	4	7	5	6	6	3	0	2	1	1	0	0	0	7
% Positive	69.2	77.8	74.1	75.0	78.6	80.6	83.3	100.0	83.3	95.2	92.9	100.0	100.0	100.0	70.8
Regional:															
Positive	99	98	91	91	79	74	71	26	45	48	37	24	38	43	46
Negative	44	42	23	17	33	38	17	10	20	10	16	25	15	11	16
% Positive	69.2	70.0	79.8	84.3	70.5	66.1	80.7	72.2	69.2	82.8	69.8	49.0	71.7	79.6	74.2

*Target nation unspecified, or target nation in more than one environment.

173

(Table 7.4).   There has been some deterioration of intra-alliance relations in the security issue-area, but in many issue-areas French ties to other members of the alliance (including the United States) have remained stable. These conclusions will be supplemented by an examination of data on elite attitudes, trade and treaties.

Table 7.4—French Actions Toward Nations in the Western Alliance

Issue-Area	ACTIONS TOWARD ALL MEMBERS OF THE WESTERN ALLIANCE		ACTIONS TOWARD UNITED STATES	
	1950–1957	1958–1964	1950–1957	1958–1964
Security:				
Positive	719	279	184	83
Negative	176	78	54	35
% Positive	80.3	78.1	77.3	70.3
Territory:				
Positive	17	4	3	0
Negative	4	0	1	0
% Positive	81.0	100.0	75.0	0.0
Human Resources:				
Positive	28	3	6	0
Negative	7	1	2	0
% Positive	80.0	75.0	75.0	0.0
Non-human Resources:				
Positive	164	37	31	10
Negative	17	3	5	1
% Positive	90.6	92.5	86.1	90.1
Status:				
Positive	296	150	26	35
Negative	44	5	6	2
% Positive	87.1	96.8	81.3	94.6
Other:				
Positive	131	107	28	16
Negative	18	30	4	6
% Positive	87.9	78.1	87.5	72.7
Total:				
Positive	1355	580	278	144
Negative	266	117	72	44
% Positive	83.6	83.2	79.4	76.6

Elite Attitudes

A crude index of elite attitudes relevant to nonconforming behavior was obtained through content analysis of Chinese and French documents. The content analysis data may be considered both as elite responses to activities initiated in international environments and as elite predispositions to undertake certain policies toward these environments.   But we can identify only in the most general sense the events which gave rise to these attitudes or their consequences for policy formulation.

A random sample of 400 Chinese editorials (25 per year) published in the newspaper *People's Daily* and the biweekly magazine *People's China* was selected for analysis. The French documents consisted of the speeches, press conferences and similar statements made by the President, Premier, and Foreign Minister. All 219 French documents located in a half dozen sources, rather than a sample of them, were coded. After pretesting a number of content categories, only a few of which are reported here, coders were instructed to determine whether these categories appeared as a "major theme" within each document and, if they did, to record them as present and to indicate the issue-area being discussed.[45] The scoring method thus indicates the number of documents within which a content category appears as a major theme; it does *not* take into account the frequency with which a given theme might appear in a single document.[46]

Results of the content analysis are summarized in Table 7.5 and 7.6. French data are divided into two periods corresponding to the Fourth and Fifth Republics. No such obvious division of the Chinese data suggested itself so the periods 1950–62 and 1963–65 are arbitrary ones, suggested in part by events during 1962–63—the Cuban missile crisis, the Sino-Indian border conflict, and the Nuclear Test-Ban Treaty—and in part by the data themselves.

Comparison of Chinese and French attitudes reveals both similarities and differences. Both view the opposing alliance, its leader and other member nations critically, but there is somewhat greater ambivalence in the French attitude during the DeGaulle years. This result is supported by a recent opinion survey in which 99 per cent of French elite respondents expected relations with countries in eastern Europe to become more cordial.[47] Sharper differences emerge with respect to attitudes about the intra-bloc environment. Chinese and French elites are considerably more critical of their alliances and bloc leaders during the more recent periods. But if their attitudes are analyzed according to issue-areas the Chinese appear consistently critical of the Soviet Union in *all* issue-areas and praise them in none. Even the abundant praise voiced by the Chinese toward the communist system as a whole through the early 1960s has virtually ceased. On the other hand, French attitudes about the western alliance and its leading member have become more critical with respect to security and status, but

[45] Space limitations do not permit a detailed description of data gathering and data analysis methods. These have been described in Ole R. Holsti, "Research Memoranda," Nos. 1–10, mimeo. (1966), available upon request.

[46] This method of scoring is similar to that used by Lasswell, Lerner, and Pool in their RADIR studies of editorials appearing in elite newspapers. See their *The Comparative Study of Symbols* (Stanford: Stanford U.P., 1952).

[47] Karl W. Deutsch, "Integration and Arms Control in the European Political Environment: A Summary Report," *op. cit.*, p. 361. See also Morton Gorden and Daniel Lerner, "The Setting for European Arms Control: Political and Strategic Choices of European Elites," *Journal of Conflict Resolution*, IX (1965), 419–33.

Table 7.5—Themes Relating to the Communist System and the Western Alliance in Chinese Editorials

NO. AND % OF DOCUMENTS IN WHICH THEMES APPEAR

Theme and Issue-Area	1950–1962 (325 Documents)		1963–1965 (75 Documents)	
	N	%	N	%
Praise USSR				
Security	38	11.7	0	0.0
Territory	0	0.0	0	0.0
Human Resources	2	0.6	0	0.0
Nonhuman Resources	34	10.5	0	0.0
Status	5	1.5	0	0.0
Other	36	11.1	0	0.0
Criticism USSR				
Security	0	0.0	9	1.2
Territory	0	0.0	1	1.3
Human Resources	0	0.0	2	2.7
Nonhuman Resources	0	0.0	3	4.0
Status	1	0.3	5	6.7
Other	0	0.0	16	21.4
Praise "Socialist Camp"				
Security	23	7.1	1	1.3
Territory	0	0.0	0	0.0
Human Resources	0	0.0	0	0.0
Nonhuman Resources	11	3.4	1	1.3
Status	14	4.3	2	2.7
Other	25	7.7	0	0.0
Criticism of "Socialist Camp"				
Security	0	0.0	0	0.0
Territory	0	0.0	0	0.0
Human Resources	1	0.3	0	0.0
Nonhuman Resources	0	0.0	0	0.0
Status	1	0.3	2	2.7
Other	1	0.3	1	1.3

NO. AND % OF DOCUMENTS IN WHICH THEMES APPEAR

Theme and Issue-Area	1950–1962 (325 Documents)		1963–1965 (75 Documents)	
	N	%	N	%
Criticism US				
Security	167	51.2	37	49.4
Territory	20	6.2	3	4.0
Human Resources	5	1.5	2	2.7
Nonhuman Resources	13	4.0	3	4.0
Status	10	3.1	2	2.7
Other	41	12.6	26	34.7
Criticism Western Alliance				
Security	41	12.6	3	4.0
Territory	1	0.3	0	0.0
Human Resources	1	0.3	0	0.0
Nonhuman Resources	6	1.8	0	0.0
Status	2	0.6	1	1.3
Other	11	3.4	5	6.7
Criticism of any Western Nation (except US)				
Security	48	14.8	8	10.7
Territory	11	3.4	1	1.3
Human Resources	7	2.2	2	2.7
Nonhuman Resources	1	0.3	0	0.0
Status	8	2.5	3	4.0
Other	30	9.2	8	10.7
Praise Western Alliance or any Western Nation				
Security	4	1.2	1	1.3
Territory	1	0.3	0	0.0
Human Resources	1	0.3	0	0.0
Nonhuman Resources		0.3	0	0.0
Status	2	0.6	0	0.0
Other	8	2.5	2	2.7

Table 7.6—Themes Relating to the Western Alliance and the Communist System in French Documents

Theme and Issue-Area	1945–1957 (103 Documents)		1958–1966 (116 Documents)	
	NO. AND % OF DOCUMENTS IN WHICH THEMES APPEAR			
	N	*%*	*N*	*%*
Praise US				
Security	15	14.6	6	5.2
Territory	3	2.9	0	0.0
Human resources	2	1.9	0	0.0
Nonhuman resources	11	10.7	6	5.2
Status	4	3.9	0	0.0
Other	4	3.9	10	8.6
Criticism US				
Security	2	1.9	13	11.2
Territory	0	0.0	1	0.9
Human resources	0	0.0	2	1.7
Nonhuman resources	0	0.0	4	3.4
Status	0	0.0	0	0.0
Other	1	1.0	4	3.4
Praise Western Alliance				
Security	14	13.6	24	20.7
Territory	1	1.0	0	0.0
Human resources	1	1.0	1	0.9
Nonhuman resources	2	1.9	2	1.7
Status	4	3.9	2	1.7
Other	4	3.9	9	7.8
Criticism of Western Alliance				
Security	1	1.0	9	7.8
Territory	0	0.0	0	0.0
Human resources	0	0.0	0	0.0
Nonhuman resources	1	1.0	1	0.9
Status	0	0.0	7	6.0
Other	0	0.0	5	4.3

Theme and Issue-Area	1945–1957 (103 Documents)		1958–1966 (116 Documents)	
	NO. AND % OF DOCUMENTS IN WHICH THEMES APPEAR			
	N	*%*	*N*	*%*
Criticism USSR				
Security	14	13.6	22	19.0
Territory	10	9.7	12	10.4
Human resources	2	1.9	3	2.6
Nonhuman resources	1	1.0	5	4.3
Status	3	2.9	2	1.7
Other	2	1.9	3	2.6
Criticism Soviet Bloc				
Security	3	2.9	3	2.6
Territory	4	3.9	2	1.7
Human resources	1	1.0	3	2.6
Nonhuman resouces	0	0.0	2	1.7
Status	1	1.0	2	1.7
Other	0	0.0	1	0.9
Criticism of any Communist Nation (except USSR)				
Security	0	0.0	3	2.6
Territory	1	1.0	3	2.6
Human resources	0	0.0	2	1.7
Nonhuman resources	0	0.0	3	2.6
Status	0	0.0	0	0.0
Other	0	0.0	0	0.0
Praise Soviet Bloc or any Communist Nation				
Security	6	5.8	3	2.6
Territory	3	2.9	0	0.0
Human resources	2	1.9	5	4.3
Nonhuman resources	2	1.9	2	1.7
Status	2	1.9	3	2.6
Other	0	0.0	3	2.6

have not changed significantly in other issue-areas. Again the previously cited survey reveals similar public and elite attitudes: French skepticism toward supra-national organizations seems focused largely on NATO. Thus these data are at least consistent with the proposition that nonconforming behavior is more likely to spill over across issue-areas within the more monolithic bloc.

International Trade and Foreign Aid

Elites and political analysts of many ideological persuasions have looked upon international trade as an integrating force. In the decades prior to World War I it was fashionable to argue that while competition for international markets might exacerbate international conflict in the short run, over the long run trade ties would make war unthinkable. At the more limited level of the region or alliance, some theorists have suggested that the effects of economic cooperation would spill over into other issue-areas, and at least one of them assigns the highest spill-over potential to economic cooperation because its effects are felt by all sectors of society.[48] similarly, Nikita Khrushchev predicted in 1959 that,

> . . . the further development of the socialist countries will in all probability proceed along the lines of consolidation of the single-world socialist economic system. The economic barriers which divided our countries under capitalism will fall one after another. The common economic basis of world socialism will grow stronger, eventually making the questions of borders a pointless one.[49]

Whether or not these predictions overstate the political significance of economic factors, trade data should provide one important quantitative index of alliance relations. If the hypotheses of a higher spill-over effect resulting from nonconforming behavior in the more monolithic bloc are valid, we should find that Chinese intra-bloc trade patterns have been disrupted more than those of France.

Perhaps more clearly than any other indicator, foreign trade data (Table 7.7) reveal how extensively Chinese relations with the Soviet Union and other nations in the communist system have changed in recent years.[50]

---

[48] Etzioni, *op. cit.*, pp. 931–2. Cf. Karl W. Deutsch et al., *op. cit.*, p. 197; and Kissinger, *op. cit.*, p. 39.

[49] Quoted in Brzezinski, *op. cit.*, p. 402.

[50] Chinese trade data have been gathered from Alexander Eckstein, *Communist China's Economic Growth and Foreign Trade* (New York: McGraw-Hill, 1966); United States Mutual Defense Assistance Control Act Administrator, *Reports to Congress*, annual; Pauline Lewin, *The Foreign Trade of Communist China* (New York: Praeger, 1964); and *Current Scene* (Feb. 1 and Feb. 15, 1966). The latter source, from which the 1965 data presented in Table 7.7 are derived, includes some estimates.

Some controversy surrounds determination of the exact value of goods exchanged within the communist system. See, in addition to the above, Kang Chao, "Pitfalls in the Use of China's Foreign Trade Statistics," *China Quarterly*, No. 19 (July–Sept.,

Table 7.7—Distribution of Chinese Trade in International Environments

	1952	1953	1954	1955	1956	1957	1958	1959	1960	1961	1962	1963	1964	1965
Total Imports (US $ millions)	890	1107	1260	1321	1465	1391	1865	2011	1912	1414	1139	1228	1475	1770
Intra-bloc %	79.4	82.6	82.5	78.3	72.4	63.8	60.4	67.8	66.7	54.2	48.3	40.6	27.8	27.1
Inter-bloc %	12.7	8.0	9.5	11.6	16.6	19.9	29.3	21.4	23.0	34.0	38.9	45.5	55.1	67.2
Non-bloc %	7.9	9.4	8.0	10.1	11.0	16.3	10.3	10.8	10.3	11.8	12.8	13.9	17.1	5.7
From Bloc Leader (USSR) %	62.2	63.0	65.6	56.6	50.0	39.1	34.0	47.4	42.7	26.0	20.5	14.8	9.2	11.3
Regional %	14.9	8.5	11.3	14.0	15.8	17.3	13.4	10.7	11.2	19.0	24.4	27.3	*	*
Contiguous %	64.8	63.8	63.5	63.4	56.2	44.9	38.9	51.9	48.4	39.0	35.3	30.9	*	*
Total Exports (US $ millions)	871	1093	1119	1345	1612	1615	1911	2211	2010	1571	1597	1605	1780	2085
Intra-bloc %	66.8	65.9	72.8	69.1	66.4	67.1	66.5	71.7	65.3	67.6	59.4	53.4	39.9	32.6
Inter-bloc %	26.3	26.6	21.4	25.2	24.2	24.5	24.0	19.2	24.7	27.3	29.2	35.2	42.1	56.2
Non-bloc %	6.8	7.5	5.8	5.7	9.4	8.4	9.5	9.1	10.0	10.1	11.4	11.4	18.0	11.2
To Bloc Leader (USSR) %	47.8	45.7	51.7	47.8	47.4	45.7	46.1	49.8	42.2	35.0	32.3	25.7	17.6	14.4
Regional %	25.1	23.3	21.1	23.6	25.6	26.6	25.3	21.5	25.5	32.1	36.2	42.5	*	*
Contiguous %	64.6	57.9	63.4	60.4	61.5	61.2	61.0	63.8	59.2	58.1	57.5	53.3	*	*

* 1964 and 1965 data are not detailed enough to permit analysis of trade with regional and contiguous partners.

During the first decade of its existence more than two thirds of China's trade was with partners within the communist system. As late as 1960 there appeared little reason to believe that China's economy was not becoming increasingly dependent upon bloc members, and especially the Soviet Union. Since then China's trade relations within the communist system have changed dramatically. Some of the increase in trade with western nations may be attributed to factors other than intra-alliance strife; for example, it is unlikely that China's emergency grain requirements in recent years could have been met within the communist system, as the Soviet Union has also been forced to purchase wheat on the world market. Nevertheless, the dramatic change in the distribution of China's trade and the decline in the total value of goods traded with alliance partners cannot be accounted for merely by the emergency in Chinese agriculture.

That differences within the communist system have spilled over into trade relations is further confirmed when Sino-Soviet trade data are examined. The decline both in Russia's proportion of total Chinese trade and in the absolute value of goods exchanged is even sharper than that with the communist bloc as a whole, thereby supporting the conclusion that the Sino-Soviet rift has severely disrupted trade relations.

Nonaligned nations appear to have played a relatively minor role in Chinese trade, at least in economic terms. That is, the costs and benefits (if any) to China of its trade with non-bloc states apparently must be assessed primarily in political rather than economic terms. Despite China's professed interest in the Afro-Asian and other emerging nations, at no time has trade with these partners reached 20 per cent of the total turnover, and it has usually remained at about half that level. Moreover, while the 1965 data include some estimates, they indicate a rather clear decline from the previous year's trade with non-bloc nations; in fact, China appears to have imported fewer goods from these nations in 1965 than in any year since 1952, despite a two-fold increase in the total value of imports in the intervening years.

The value of China's international trade has been increasing despite the disruption of its economic relations within the communist system because trade with the West has expanded uninterruptedly since 1960. Even disregarding large purchases of grain from Canada, Argentina and Australia, trade with leading members of the western alliance has increased markedly. Among the more influential western nations, only the United States has not increased its trade with Peking during the past few years. China's twelve most active trade partners now include Japan, Australia, Great Britain, West Germany, Canada, Italy, and France.

1964), 47–65; and Feng-hwa Mah, "The Terms of Sino-Soviet Trade," *China Quarterly*, No. 17 (Jan.–Mar., 1964), 192–204. But such discrepancies should not affect our results, which are concerned with comparisons across time, rather than with the absolute level of trade in any given year.

Further insight into ties between China and the communist system in the nonhuman resources issue-area may be derived by examining foreign aid data. It is difficult to determine with precision the level of aid received by China from other members of the communist system. The problem is, at least in parts, one of defining "foreign aid." Some sources use the term only for outright grants, others include credits and loans, and at least in a few cases, some parts of foreign trade are included in the calculation of "aid."[51] Despite these discrepancies all sources agree on one point: China has been the recipient of little, if any, aid during the last decade. Eckstein's data, which are consistent with the trends if not with the exact amounts in other sources, indicate that China received something under $1.5 billion aid from the Soviet Union through the first half of the 1950s and that since 1957 such aid has "virtually ended."[52] Assistance from other bloc members, never at a level comparable to Soviet aid, also appears to have ceased.

Whether Soviet aid even during the early years of the Peking regime was considered adequate by Chinese leaders—at least one observer suggests that Stalin's niggardliness in negotiating the February 1950 aid agreement was the initial source of Mao's disaffection with the Soviets—there is little reason to doubt that withdrawal of economic and technical aid has been a major irritant in relations between Moscow and Peking.[53] According to one of many similar Chinese statements,

> In July 1960, the Soviet authorities . . . suddenly and unilaterally decided on a complete withdrawal of the 1390 experts who were in China to help in our work, they tore up 343 contracts for experts and the supplements to these contracts and abolished 257 items for scientific and technical cooperation and since then, they have reduced in large numbers the supplies of complete sets of equipment and key sections of various other equipment. This has caused our construction to suffer huge losses, thereby upsetting our original plan for the development of our national economy and greatly aggravating our difficulties.[54]

Such statements are clear evidence of a linkage between Soviet actions and significant consequences within China. Unfortunately, beyond the rather trivial observation that these Soviet actions have contributed to a change in elite attitudes toward Moscow (see Table 7.5), we cannot trace out the

[51] This becomes evident if one compares the figures in Choh-ming Li, "China's Industrial Development," *China Quarterly*, No. 17 (Jan.-Mar., 1964), 3–38; Eckstein, *op. cit.*; David Floyd, *op. cit.*; Kang Chao, *op. cit.*; Boris Meissner, "The People's Commune: A Manifestation of Sino-Soviet Differences," in Kurt London (ed.), *Unity and Contradiction: Major Aspects of Sino-Soviet Relations* (New York: Praeger, 1962); and Leonard Shapiro, "The Chinese Ally from the Soviet Point of View," in Kurt London (ed.), *op. cit.*

[52] Eckstein, *op. cit.*, pp. 181–2.

[53] Floyd, *op. cit.*, p. 12.

[54] Editorial in *People's Daily* (Dec. 4, 1963), quoted in Choh-ming Li, *op. cit.*, p. 32.

specific consequences on political processes in China. Among the questions which might be asked within a national-international linkages framework are the following. Have patterns of recruitment into the Chinese Communist Party changed to place heavier emphasis on technically trained personnel? What bureaucratic changes resulted from the withdrawal of Soviet aid? What institutions and elites (party, military, bureaucracy, and so on) gained or lost influence as a result of this development in Sino-Soviet relations? Unfortunately these and many other intriguing questions can be asked but not answered here.

Whereas there is some disagreement on what constituted Soviet aid to China, there seems to be more consensus on the calculation of Chinese grants to other nations, the first of which was made in 1953.[55] The data in Table 7.8 are consistent with trends in trade relations—an increasing proportion of aid has been going to nations outside the communist system since 1956. By itself, increased Chinese attention to non-bloc nations is not proof of deviation from bloc norms. Indeed, this could be interpreted as Chinese emulation of a pattern established earlier by the Soviet Union. But there are a number of indications that Chinese aid, both within and outside the communist system, has been granted in direct competition with Moscow. For example, Floyd asserts that,

> Competition between Russians and Chinese for the friendship of non-Communist countries, especially those which had freshly acquired independence, was apparent elsewhere. In May Chou En-lai visited Outer Mongolia . . . to conclude a treaty of friendship and mutual aid and to extend a loan of 200 million roubles. It is perhaps not without significance that in August, 1960 Khrushchev's critic, Vyacheslav Molotov, was withdrawn from the Soviet embassy in Ulan Bator. The extension of a $35 million loan by Russia to the new state of Guinea in Africa was followed by one of $25 million from the Chinese. Khrushchev's effort to make a firm friend of Fidel Castro in Cuba by extending economic and military aid were [sic] followed by a Chinese undertaking to trade with Cuba and lend her $21 million. Even in the Middle East, an area of predominantly Russian interest, the Chinese were competing for influence, for example in Iraq.[56]

Moreover, nearly all aid within the communist system has been granted to nations which have tended, at least until very recently, to support China's

[55] Table 7.8 was constructed from data in Eckstein, *op. cit.*; Lewin, *op. cit.*; and Maurice D. Simon, "Communist System Interaction with the Developing States, 1954–62: A Preliminary Analysis," *Stanford Studies of the Communist System*, mineo (1965). It should be noted that the figures in Table 7.8 refer to *grants*, not to actual *deliveries*, which may be considerably smaller in many cases, or which may be spread out over a number of years. Cf. Eckstein, *op. cit.*, p. 162; and A. M. Halpern, "China in the Postwar World," *China Quarterly*, No. 21 (Jan.–Mar., 1965), 54.

[56] Quoted in Floyd, *op. cit.*, p. 81. See Also W. A. C. Adie, "China, Russia, and the Third World," *China Quarterly*, No. 11 (July–Sept., 1962), 200–13.

Table 7.8—Chinese Foreign Aid

		1953	1954	1955	1956	1957	1958	1959	1960	1961	1962	1963	1964
Total Aid (US $ mil.)		344.0	15.0	204.0	105.9	89.8	120.6	150.2	296.5	456.0	16.3	88.1	287.9
Recipients													
Intra-bloc	%	100.0	100.0	100.0	46.7	60.1	68.0	79.2	74.2	61.8	0.0	0.0	0.03
Inter-bloc	%	0.0	0.0	0.0	0.0	0.0	0.0	0.0	0.0	0.0	0.0	0.0	20.8
Non-bloc	%	0.0	0.0	0.0	53.3	39.9	37.0	20.8	25.8	38.2	100.0	100.0	79.1
Regional	%	100.0	0.0	98.0	86.6	39.9	86.2	86.6	68.3	64.0	89.0	0.0	22.3
Contiguous	%	100.0	0.0	98.0	49.7	0.0	68.2	66.6	59.4	55.0	24.5	0.0	0.03

position against that of the Soviet Union: Albania, North Vietnam, and North Korea.

In summary, the pattern of Chinese foreign aid, like that of foreign trade, indicates increasing attention outside the communist system. But whereas patterns of trade appear to be based on considerations of economic necessity—since the disruptions of Sino-Soviet trade relations, only nations of the west are in a position to provide for China's requirements for grain and capital goods—aid has been supplied to nations which appear most likely to support China's policies vis-à-vis the United States, Soviet Union and India.[57]

The pattern which emerges from French foreign trade data (Table 7.9) is markedly different from that of China, and these differences are consistent with the proposition of limited spill-over of intra-bloc conflicts in more pluralistic alliances.[58] Whatever the nature of French disagreements with the United States and other allies, they appear not to have had an adverse effect on French trade with members of the alliance. The value of intra-alliance trade has expanded virtually every year since World War II, and even the proportion of total trade within the alliance has risen consistently. The sharpest increases have been with nations within the contiguous environment, which is nearly coterminous with the Common Market, and while trade with the United States has remained a relatively constant proportion of the total trade turnover, the value of goods exchanged has increased consistently. Trade with nations in the communist system has increased during the 1960s, but it continues to represent a very minor part of both French imports and exports.

The internal sources and consequences of international trade are considerably easier to assess for France than for China. Opinion surveys indicate that French mass and elite attitudes about NATO are unfavorable, but opinions toward economic and cultural organizations remain favorable. For example, French respondents favored the Common Market over NATO by a ten-to-one margin.[59] Other studies have shown a significant effect on political socialization, interest articulation and aggregation, and decision-making in France as a result of trade activities in Europe. Some of these consequences are described in a study of agricultural policies in the European Economic Community:

> In a real sense public discussion of agricultural policy is carried on in terms of a single political arena covering the six countries. Increasingly there is a common set of issues, of institutions, of personalities, and these are known to all the actors in the

[57] The first aid to a member of the western alliance, a grant of 60 US $ million to Pakistan, was announced in 1964.

[58] Table 7.9 was constructed from data in *The Yearbook of International Trade* through 1963, and from figures made available by the French Embassy, Washington, D.C., for 1964 and 1965.

[59] Deutsch, "Integration and Arms Control in the European Political Environment," *op. cit.*, p. 360.

Table 7.9—Distribution of French Trade in International Environments

		1947	1948	1949	1950	1951	1952	1953	1954	1955	1956	1957	1958	1959	1960	1961	1962	1963	1964	1965
Total Imports (bil. new francs)		4.0	6.7	9.3	10.7	16.1	15.9	13.8	15.2	16.7	19.8	22.7	26.6	25.2	31.0	33.0	37.1	43.1	49.7	51.1
Intra-bloc	%	60.0	49.9	51.6	50.6	50.3	47.7	46.8	46.6	48.8	52.8	53.8	49.1	52.8	58.0	59.3	61.1	63.8	67.1	67.3
Inter-bloc	%	0.5	0.8	0.6	0.4	0.2	0.5	0.5	2.2	1.6	1.9	1.9	2.6	3.3	2.7	2.5	2.6	2.8	3.1	3.4
Non-bloc	%	39.5	49.2	47.8	49.0	49.5	51.8	52.7	51.2	49.6	45.3	44.3	48.3	43.9	39.3	38.2	36.3	33.4	29.8	29.3
From Bloc Leader (US)	%	30.2	17.6	17.6	12.3	11.3	10.0	9.8	8.8	9.6	12.1	13.3	10.0	8.4	12.5	11.0	10.3	10.3	11.3	10.5
Regional	%	21.2	23.0	25.6	27.8	27.8	29.3	28.6	32.2	30.6	37.1	35.6	37.2	41.6	42.9	46.7	49.5	52.8	54.3	55.5
Contiguous	%	11.6	12.8	14.4	17.2	15.8	16.8	17.0	17.5	19.9	20.8	21.4	22.7	26.3	28.7	31.0	33.5	35.3	36.0	37.4
Total Exports (bil. new francs)		2.2	4.3	7.8	10.8	14.8	14.2	13.2	15.0	17.4	16.2	18.9	21.5	27.7	33.9	35.7	36.4	39.9	44.4	49.6
Intra-bloc	%	38.3	36.9	39.4	45.0	41.2	35.2	41.2	40.9	47.7	46.1	45.9	44.1	50.8	51.6	50.0	59.3	60.2	61.9	64.6
Inter-bloc	%	1.1	0.8	0.8	0.4	0.2	0.3	0.5	1.5	2.3	2.1	2.0	2.3	4.1	4.0	3.6	4.1	3.7	3.9	4.3
Non-bloc	%	60.6	62.3	59.8	54.6	58.6	64.5	58.3	57.6	50.0	51.8	52.1	53.6	45.1	44.4	46.4	36.6	36.1	34.2	31.2
To Bloc Leader (US)	%	2.7	3.6	2.0	4.1	5.9	3.9	4.8	3.6	4.2	4.8	4.7	5.9	8.4	3.8	5.8	5.8	5.2	5.2	5.9
Regional	%	40.0	38.8	37.5	42.5	37.0	37.0	36.3	43.4	47.8	48.2	45.8	41.3	46.0	50.4	49.5	60.6	62.0	63.9	65.5
Contiguous	%	21.5	19.1	16.3	22.0	19.2	22.6	22.4	26.4	27.8	30.3	29.0	23.6	29.7	32.7	31.3	41.4	43.6	44.2	45.4

Table 7.10—Chinese Treaties in Various International Environments, All Issue-Areas

		1949	1950	1951	1952	1953	1954	1955	1956	1957	1958	1959	1960	1961	1962	1963	1964	1965
TOTAL		12	36	24	57	60	94	92	115	76	91	75	85	97	84	88	90	133
Intra-bloc*	N	6	26	23	34	46	70	70	69	43	55	58	35	40	51	38	54	54
	%	50.0	72.2	95.8	59.6	76.7	74.5	76.1	60.0	56.6	60.4	77.3	41.2	41.2	60.7	43.2	60.0	40.6
Non-bloc	N	2	8	1	10	6	17	22	39	25	27	17	50	54	26	34	33	62
	%	16.7	22.2	4.2	17.5	10.0	18.1	23.9	33.9	32.9	29.7	22.7	58.8	55.7	31.0	38.6	36.7	46.6
Inter-bloc	N	4	2	0	8	6	7	0	7	6	8	0	0	3	5	16	3	17
	%	33.3	5.6	0.0	14.0	10.0	7.4	0.0	6.1	7.9	8.8	0.0	0.0	3.1	6.0	18.2	3.3	12.8
Others†	N	0	0	0	5	2	0	0	0	2	1	0	0	0	2	0	0	0
	%	0.0	0.0	0.0	8.8	3.3	0.0	0.0	0.0	2.6	1.1	0.0	0.0	0.0	2.4	0.0	0.0	0.0
With bloc leader (USSR)	N	1	20	7	9	6	16	10	12	6	10	12	3	11	8	1	3	4
	%	8.3	55.6	29.2	15.8	10.0	17.0	10.9	10.4	7.9	11.0	16.0	3.5	11.3	9.5	1.1	3.3	3.0
Regional	N	7	6	1	14	15	38	28	38	27	35	23	41	34	22	32	25	49
	%	58.3	16.7	4.2	24.6	25.0	40.4	30.4	33.0	35.5	38.5	30.7	48.2	35.1	26.2	36.4	27.8	36.8
Contiguous	N	8	23	8	15	14	47	34	34	24	34	28	30	39	26	17	24	26
	%	66.7	63.9	33.3	26.3	23.3	50.0	37.0	29.6	31.6	37.4	37.3	35.3	40.2	30.1	19.3	26.7	19.5

* Includes 24 multipartite intra-bloc treaties; all non-bloc and inter-bloc treaties are bilateral.

† Multipartite treaties and general international agreements with partners in more than one international environment.

system and to the attentive public. New patterns of interactions and communication are involved, as well as new political
styles. Agricultural committees of these national parliaments which try to maintain some control and oversight of
agricultural policy are forced to spend the bulk of their time
on issues raised by the Community. The attention of interest
groups is similarly directed beyond the national system to the
Community system. These phenomena tend to contribute to
an increased incidence of a self-conscious sense of "European
identity."[60]

In summary, whether measured in the value of goods exchanged, in the
proportion of intra-bloc trade, or in trade with the alliance leader, Chinese
and French patterns of international trade have changed as predicted by our
hypotheses. And while information on political processes is at best sketchy,
it seems reasonable to assume that altered patterns of international trade
have had a significant impact on political processes in France and China.

Treaties and Agreements

Treaties and agreements have traditionally served as an index of a
nation's relations with other nations and have thus been of interest to
students of alliances. Whatever deviations from traditional diplomatic
methods have characterized the members of the communist system, these
appear not to have extended to the use of treaties and agreements; the
sheer volume of Chinese treaties suggests a heavy reliance on formal agreements to make explicit relations in virtually every issue-area.[61] A quantitative analysis of treaties and agreements, such as that described here, inevitably ignores important questions, the answers to which depend upon
qualitative aspects of the treaty, Thus while the present data—based on
an analysis of 1308 Chinese and 1124 French treaties—reveal some interesting patterns they are most useful when combined with other data.

Until 1963 treaties with members of the western alliance accounted for
a very small proportion of all Chinese agreements (Table 7.10).[62] But while
there has been marked increase in agreements with western nations during

[60] Lindberg, *op. cit.*, p. 75.

[61] "In Stalin's lifetime the impression was widespread that the remaining forms of
state sovereignty and international procedure, the diplomatic and consular arrangements, the patterns of international legal rights and obligations . . . were 'survivals' of
the bourgeois era, destined soon to be replaced by more progessive superstructures.
More recent years have seen the negotiation and completion of formal instruments in a
variety of less important fields which earlier would not have been thought worth
troubling about." Modelski, *op. cit.*, pp. 29–30.

[62] Chinese treaties were located in the following sources: Robert Slusser and Jan F.
Triska, *A Calendar of Soviet Treaties, 1917–1957* (Stanford: Stanford U.P., 1959);
George Ginsbergs, "A Calendar of Soviet Treaties," *Ost Europa Recht*, annual; *China
Mainland Review*, I (1965), 1–3; *Peking Review*, 1958–1965; American Consulate
General, Hong Kong, "Agreements between Communist China and Foreign Countries,"
Current Background, No. 545 (Jan. 20, 1959) and No. 651 (April 19, 1961); American

the past several years, nearly all of them (28 of 36 during 1963–65) have been confined to the nonhuman resources issue-area, as might be expected given the deterioration of Chinese economic relations within the intra-bloc environment and the marked increase in Chinese trade with western nations. Thus Chinese treaty relations to the inter-bloc environment have remained rather narrowly confined within a single issue-area with little indication of a spill-over into others.

In recent years nonaligned nations have supplanted members of the communist system as China's leading treaty partners. Again the reasons are not wholly indicative of nonconforming bloc behavior; with the greatly expanded number of new nations, Chinese treaty relations with such nations would have shown some increase, even in the absence of disputes within the communist system. On the other hand, Sino-Soviet competition among the new nations has probably contributed to the frequency of Chinese trade, aid and cultural agreements with non-bloc members.

The treaties most relevant to an analysis of nonconforming alliance policies are those with other members of the alliance. Despite the limitations inherent in a quantitative analysis, some revealing patterns emerge from the data. During the first decade of its existence an overwhelming proportion of China's agreements were signed with members of the communist system. During the 1960s, however, more treaties have been signed with nations outside the bloc than within it. A more interesting picture emerges when each of China's intra-bloc treaty partners is revealed (Table 7.11). The Soviet Union was China's primary treaty partner during the first decade of the PRC's existence, but this relationship has changed markedly during the 1960s. Since 1962 only Yugoslavia has signed fewer agreements with China than has the Soviet Union. The same pattern exists with respect to other East European nations except Albania. On the other hand, Albania, North Korea and North Vietnam, minor treaty partners during the early 1950s, have joined Cuba as the nations with which most Chinese treaties and agreements are signed.

These data are consistent with propositions that China is attempting to form a bloc within the communist system consisting of the poorer and

---

Consulate General, Hong Kong, *Survey of the Chinese Mainland Press, Index*; four volumes in a series published by the Institute für Asienkunde, *Die Verträge der Volksrepublik China mit anderen Staaten* (Frankfurt: Alfred Metzner Verlag, 1957); *Verträge der Volksrepublik China mit anderen Staaten: Süd- under Ostasien* (Frankfurt: Alfred Metzner Verlag, 1962); *Verträge der Volksrepublik China mit anderen Staaten: Die Länder des Vorderen Orients und Afrikas* (Frankfurt: Alfred Metzner Verlag, 1963); *Verträge der Volksrepublik China mit anderen Staaten: Die nichtkommunistischen Länder Europes under die Länder Amerika (einschliesslich Kubas)* (Frankfurt: Alfred Metzner Verlag, 1965); and United Nations, *Treaty Series*, vols. 1–511.

Tables 7.10–7.14 include treaties, agreements, and protocols, but exclude joint statements, communiqués, exchanges of letters, minutes of meetings, and agreements with unofficial organizations in other countries, which are sometimes included in treaty collections.

Table 7.11—Bilateral Chinese Intra-bloc Treaties and Agreements, All-Issue Areas

Partner	1949–1953			1954–1956			1957–1959			1960–1962			1963–1965		
	N	%	Rank	N	%	Rank	N	%	Rank	N	%	Rank	N	%	Rank
USSR	43	32.3	1	38	19.2	1	28	18.8	1	22	17.6	1	8	5.6	11
Czechoslovakia	16	12.0	2	14	7.1	8	13	8.7	4	8	6.4	7	10	7.0	6.5
Poland	14	10.5	3	18	9.1	3.5	9	6.0	8	6	4.8	10	9	6.3	9
Hungary	13	9.8	4.5	13	6.6	9.5	12	8.1	5.5	7	5.6	8.5	8	5.6	11
E. Germany	13	9.8	4.5	17	8.6	5	12	8.1	5.5	4	3.2	12	10	7.0	6.5
Rumania	9	6.8	6	15	7.6	7	7	4.7	11	5	4.0	11	10	7.0	6.5
Mongolia	7	5.3	8	13	6.6	9.5	8	5.4	10	12	9.6	5	8	5.6	11
Bulgaria	7	5.3	8	16	8.1	6	9	6.0	8	7	5.6	8.5	10	7.0	6.5
N. Korea	7	5.3	8	18	9.1	3.5	19	12.8	2	15	12.0	2.5	16	11.2	2.5
N. Vietnam	4	3.0	10	19	9.6	2	18	12.1	3	14	11.2	4	15	10.5	4
Yugoslavia	0	0.0	11.5	7	3.5	12	5	3.4	12	1	0.8	13	2	1.4	13
Albania	0	0.0	11.5	10	5.1	11	9	6.0	8	9	7.2	6	16	11.2	2.5
Cuba	—	—	—	—	—	—	—	—	—	15	12.0	2.5	21	14.7	1
TOTAL	133	100.1%*		198	100.2%*		149	100.1%*		125	100.0%		143	100.1%*	

* Do not total 100 per cent because of rounding error.

less developed, but ideologically "purer," nations.[63] This is apparent if we compare the frequency of Chinese treaties with various partners during an early (1949–1953) and a recent (1963–1965) period with the GNP per capita of the treaty partner.[64] During the earlier period there was a very high Spearman rank-order correlation ($r_s = .79$) between the number of treaties signed by China and the wealth of the other signatory. The six wealthiest nations in the communist system (Soviet Union, Czechoslovakia, East Germany, Poland, Hungary, and Rumania) were the most frequent treaty partners, and the poorest nations (Mongolia, North Vietnam, North Korea, Albania, Bulgaria, and Yugoslavia) signed the fewest treaties with Peking. The relationship between treaties signed and the wealth of the treaty partner is markedly different for the latest period ($r_s = -.26$). The Soviet Union and some of the relatively prosperous nations of Eastern Europe have been replaced by such poor nations as Cuba, North Vietnam, North Korea, and Albania as China's leading treaty partners. In addition to their low level of economic development, these four nations also share one other attribute: They are the four members of the communist system farthest removed geographically from the heartland of the Soviet Union.

Finally, an examination of the Chinese treaties according to issue-area reveals that the decline in the number of intra-bloc agreements has tended to affect all issue-areas (Table 7.12). This is most evident in the case of treaties with the Soviet Union. Since 1962 the proportion of Chinese agreements with the Soviet Union has decreased in every issue-area.

The French treaty data are summarized in Table 7.13.[65] The distribution of the 499 bilateral and 625 multipartite treaties is similar in some respects with that of China and differs in a number of others. There has been a general decline in intra-bloc treaties and in those agreements limited to partners in the contiguous environment during the years of the Fifth Republic. However, this change is somewhat misleading because all "multiple bloc" treaties include at least one other member of the western alliance and many include contiguous nations. Concomitantly there has been a significant rise in the proportion of treaties with partners in the opposing alliance and a somewhat less marked increase in agreements with non-aligned nations and in treaties with signatories in more than a single bloc. The proportion of regional and organizational treaties remained stable between the two periods.

When French intra-bloc agreements are further analyzed according to treaty partner and issue-area (Table 7.14), the pattern which emerges differs from that of China in one important respect. Like China, France

---

[63] Brzezinski, *op. cit.*, 405–6; Jan F. Triska et al., "The World Communist System," *Studies of the Communist System*, mimeo. (Stanford: n.d.), p. 5.

[64] Gross National Product per capita figures from Triska et al., *op. cit.*, were used.

[65] French treaties were located in the United Nations *Treaty Series*, vols. 1–511; Slusser and Triska, *op. cit.*; and Ginsbergs, *op. cit.* Owing to the time lag in publication of the *Treaty Series*, the French data are almost certainly less complete than those for China for the last two or three years.

Table 7.12—Chinese Treaties and Agreements by Issue-Areas

Issue-Area	USSR	North Korea	North Vietnam	Czecho-slovakia	Poland	East Germany	Hungary	Mongolia	Bulgaria	Rumania	Albania	Cuba	Yugoslavia	All Others
1949–62														
Security (N = 25)	4	1	0	1	0	2	1	1	0	0	0	0	0	15
%	16.0	4.0	—	4.0	—	8.0	4.0	4.0	—	—	—	—	—	60.0
Territory (N = 14)	2	0	0	0	0	0	0	2	0	0	0	0	0	10
%	14.3	—	—	—	—	—	—	14.3	—	—	—	—	—	71.4
Human Resources (N = 186)	32	9	9	16	13	13	12	7	10	11	9	5	2	38
%	17.2	4.8	4.8	8.6	7.0	7.0	6.5	3.8	5.4	5.9	4.8	2.7	1.1	20.4
Non-human Res. (N = 705)	89	49	45	33	34	30	32	30	29	25	19	10	11	269
%	12.6	7.0	6.4	4.7	4.8	4.3	4.5	4.3	4.1	3.5	2.7	1.4	1.6	38.2
Status (N = 64)	3	0	0	1	0	1	0	0	0	0	0	0	0	59
%	4.7	—	—	1.6	—	1.6	—	—	—	—	—	—	—	92.2
Other (N = 2)	1	0	1	0	0	0	0	0	0	0	0	0	0	0
%	50.0	—	50.0	—	—	—	—	—	—	—	—	—	—	—
TOTAL (N = 996)	131	59	55	51	47	46	45	40	39	36	28	15	13	391
%	13.2	5.9	5.5	5.1	4.7	4.5	4.5	4.0	3.9	3.6	2.8	1.5	1.3	39.2
1963–65														
Security (N = 8)	0	0	0	0	0	0	0	0	0	0	0	0	0	8
%	—	—	—	—	—	—	—	—	—	—	—	—	—	100.0
Territory (N = 6)	0	0	0	0	0	0	0	1	0	0	0	0	0	5
%	—	—	—	—	—	—	—	16.7	—	—	—	—	—	83.3
Human Resources (N = 99)	3	9	5	5	7	5	5	2	8	6	4	8	0	32
%	3.0	9.1	5.1	5.1	7.1	5.1	5.1	2.0	8.1	6.1	4.0	8.1	—	32.3
Non-human Res. (N = 180)	5	7	9	5	2	4	3	5	2	4	11	13	2	108
%	2.8	3.9	5.0	2.8	1.1	2.2	1.7	2.8	1.1	2.2	6.1	7.2	2.2	60.0
Status (N = 10)	0	0	0	0	0	0	0	0	0	0	0	0	0	10
%	—	—	—	—	—	—	—	—	—	—	—	—	—	100.0
Other (N = 9)	0	0	1	0	0	1	0	0	0	0	1	0	0	6
%	—	—	11.1	—	—	11.1	—	—	—	—	11.1	—	—	66.7
TOTAL (N = 312)	8	16	15	10	9	10	8	8	10	10	16	21	2	169
%	2.6	5.1	4.8	3.2	2.9	3.2	2.6	2.6	3.2	3.2	5.1	6.7	0.6	54.2

Table 7.13—French Treaties in Various International Environments, All Issue-Areas

		1945	1946	1947	1948	1949	1950	1951	1952	1953	1954	1955	1956	1957	1958	1959	1960	1961	1962	1963–1965
Total		26	60	68	75	57	62	67	68	71	96	82	66	66	56	68	42	28	36	30
Intra-bloc	N	10	46	39	45	34	39	40	28	34	38	25	29	28	22	22	12	17	7	7
	%	38.5	76.7	57.4	60.0	59.6	62.9	59.7	41.2	47.9	39.6	30.5	43.9	42.4	39.3	32.4	28.6	60.7	19.4	23.3
Inter-bloc	N	3	2	2	3	0	0	0	0	3	3	0	2	6	5	8	8	0	1	2
	%	11.5	3.3	2.9	4.0	0.0	0.0	0.0	0.0	4.2	3.1	0.0	3.0	9.1	8.9	11.8	19.0	0.0	2.8	6.7
Non-bloc	N	0	2	4	1	2	1	1	6	1	4	2	4	1	4	5	2	3	5	3
	%	0.0	3.3	5.9	1.3	3.5	1.6	1.5	8.8	1.4	4.2	2.4	6.1	1.5	7.1	7.4	4.8	10.7	13.9	10.0
Organizational	N	0	2	13	17	9	3	11	7	6	20	41	6	10	9	10	9	3	8	3
	%	0.0	3.3	19.1	22.7	15.8	4.8	16.4	10.3	8.5	20.8	50.0	9.1	15.2	16.1	14.7	21.4	10.7	22.2	10.0
Multiple blocs*	N	13	8	10	9	12	19	15	27	27	31	14	25	21	16	23	11	5	15	15
	%	50.0	13.3	14.7	12.0	21.1	30.6	22.4	39.7	38.0	32.3	17.1	37.9	31.8	28.6	33.8	26.2	17.9	41.7	50.0
With bloc leader (US)**	N	3	17	10	18	3	7	4	6	2	2	5	9	3	8	7	8	9	4	2
	%	11.5	28.3	14.7	24.0	5.3	11.3	6.0	8.8	2.8	2.1	6.1	13.6	4.5	14.3	10.3	19.0	32.1	11.1	6.7
Contiguous	N	2	5	9	10	9	10	2	5	10	6	2	5	10	6	2	0	2	1	0
	%	7.7	8.3	13.2	13.3	15.8	16.1	3.0	7.4	14.1	6.2	2.4	7.6	15.2	10.7	2.9	0.0	7.1	2.8	0.0
Regional	N	9	26	26	27	28	30	16	26	42	27	14	30	42	24	36	13	6	8	5
	%	34.6	43.3	38.2	36.0	49.1	48.4	23.9	38.2	59.2	28.1	17.1	45.5	63.6	42.9	52.9	31.0	21.4	22.2	16.7

* Multipartite treaties and general international agreements with partners in more than one international environment.
** Bilateral treaties only.

concluded a substantial proportion of its agreements with the bloc leader. But whereas there has recently been a sharp decline in the number of Sino-Soviet treaties, this has not occurred within the western alliance. Rather, during the Fifth Republic the number of French agreements with the United States has shown an increase in proportion to those with other partners, and in no issue-area has there been a significant decline in agreements between Paris and Washington.

Table 7.14—French Treaties and Agreements by Issue-Area
1945–1957
TREATY PARTNER

Issue-Area		United States	Common Market Nation	"Outer Seven" Nations*	Other Intra-bloc Nations	Multi-partite Treaties	All Others
Security	(N = 24)	3	0	3	1	7	10
%		12.5	0.0	12.5	4.2	29.2	41.7
Territory	(N = 32)	2	13	3	2	3	9
%		6.3	40.1	9.4	6.3	9.4	28.1
Human Resources	(N = 238)	14	44	23	7	11	139
%		5.9	18.5	9.7	2.9	4.6	58.4
Nonhuman Res.	(N = 450)	70	38	37	59	48	198
%		15.6	8.4	8.2	13.1	10.7	44.0
Status	(N = 115)	0	1	2	3	37	72
%		0.0	0.9	1.7	2.6	32.2	62.6
Others	(N = 5)	0	0	3	1	0	1
%		0.0	0.0	60.0	20.0	0.0	20.0
TOTAL	(N = 864)	89	96	71	73	106	429
%		10.3	11.1	8.2	8.4	12.3	49.7

1958–1965
TREATY PARTNER

Issue-Area		United States	Common Market Nation	"Outer Seven" Nations*	Other Intra-bloc Nations	Multi-partite Treaties	All Others
Security	(N = 11)	4	0	0	1	1	5
%		36.4	0.0	0.0	9.1	9.1	45.5
Territory	(N = 8)	5	1	0	0	0	2
%		62.5	12.5	0.0	0.0	0.0	25.0
Human Resources	(N = 59)	2	8	6	0	4	39
%		3.4	13.6	10.2	0.0	6.8	66.1
Nonhuman Res.	(N = 151)	26	5	4	7	8	101
%		17.2	3.3	2.6	4.6	5.3	66.9
Status	(N = 26)	1	0	0	0	3	22
%		3.8	0.0	0.0	0.0	11.5	84.6
Others	(N = 3)	0	0	1	0	0	2
%		0.0	0.0	33.3	0.0	0.0	66.7
TOTAL	(N = 258)	38	14	11	8	16	171
%		14.7	5.4	4.3	3.1	6.2	66.3

* Excludes treaties with non-bloc Switzerland, Austria and Sweden (17 treaties 1945–57; 6 treaties 1958–65).

These results should be interpreted with considerable caution, in part because the French treaty data for the most recent years are almost certainly incomplete, in part because the frequency with which treaties are signed may not prove an adequate index of relations between states. For example, the recent Franco-American "agreement"[66] on withdrawal of United States Air Force units from France (not included in Tables 7.13 and 7.14) hardly indicates cooperation in the security issue-area. Despite obvious limitations in the data, differences in the patterns of Chinese and French intra-bloc treaties are consistent with the proposition that in the more pluralistic alliances, nonconforming in one issue-area is less likely to spill over into all of them.

CONCLUSION

This paper has been an exploratory effort to examine some of the linkages between polities which deviate from alliances and their environments. We have described some of the similarities and differences in French and Chinese political processes, and speculated about their consequences for alliance policy. We also considered some of the differences in monolithic and pluralistic alliances, and suggested how these might be linked to the fact that France's relations with the western alliance have been less severely disrupted than those of China with the communist system.

Data on French and Chinese actions, elite attitudes, trade, foreign aid and treaties were consistent with our hypotheses. But there are some significant limitations in the present paper which must at least be noted. In examining the linkages of nonconforming alliance members we have been able to develop indices on many of the recurring international activities which they undertake and to which they respond. But owing to space limitations, gross categories have been used to report the data. Hence some interesting aspects of nonconforming alliance policies may have been overlooked. For example, trade figures were not further broken down according to commodities, and action data were reported only as positive or negative. More refined analysis of these and other data will be undertaken elsewhere.[67] A more serious shortcoming is that we have considered only some facets of the complex interaction of actors, institutions, attitudes and processes from which foreign policies emerge and which may be directly or indirectly affected by events in various international environments. Our data reveal trends on aspects of Chinese or French foreign policy quite precisely, but many interesting questions remain unanswered, in part owing to the impossibility of examining them within the limits of an exploratory study, in part because even anecdotal information on Chinese decision-making is scarce. It

[66] *The New York Times*, June 16, 1966, 1:1.
[67] In Ole R. Holsti, P. Terry Hopmann, and John D. Sullivan, *International Alliances: Unity and Disintegration* (Homewood, Ill: Dorsey Press, forthcoming).

is easy to ask questions about how Chinese actors, institutions, attitudes and political processes contribute to foreign policy decisions or how they are affected by the policies of other nations, but it is often impossible, even for specialists in Chinese politics, to answer them.

Finally, even though the data appear consistent with our hypotheses about the consequences of domestic and alliance characteristics on patterns of nonconforming behavior, we have in fact only taken the most preliminary steps toward exploring these linkages. We have found that France, the more pluralistic nation and a member of the more pluralistic alliance, has disrupted its relations with allies in a limited manner. China, an authoritarian polity within the more monolithic alliance, has deviated from bloc norms in virtually all issue-areas. But an important question for any linkage analysis is the relative potency of domestic and international factors on policy decisions. That is, do we attribute the pattern of French policy to its internal political processes, to the characteristics of the western alliance, or to some combination of both? This question—and, unfortunately, a great many others—remain to be explored in future research.

Part IV

Geographic Conditions

CHAPTER EIGHT

Insular Polities*

Robert T. Holt
and John E. Turner

THE invitation to write on insular polities and national-international linkages is really a summons to participate in an experiment. The scholars who planned the underlying theme of this book and the topics of the individual chapters have been concerned for some time about the artificial division between the study of international politics and the study of national systems—a separation that has been responsible not only for some of the weaknesses in each area of study, but also for the absence of systematic analysis of the linkages between the two levels of political systems. As Professor Rosenau has pointed out, this book is designed to explore the nature of these linkages by using the comparative method, whenever appropriate, in an effort to discern the most fruitful way to approach the problems being raised. The purpose of this experiment is not to subject well-formulated, theoretically significant hypotheses to the hammer blows of empirical research so as to produce a verified, integrated set of propositions. The experiment is, rather, an exploratory undertaking which endeavors to

* This study was prepared under the auspices of the Center for Comparative Political Analysis, Department of Political Science, University of Minnesota.

reveal selective data, stimulating impressions, and provocative—if not fully tested—propositions.[1] So that we can make our selective data and our concluding propositions (hopefully provocative) meaningful, it will be necessary to indicate at the outset how our approach to the problem is related to the other treatises in this volume.

INTERNATIONAL SYSTEMS, NATION-STATES, AND INSULAR POLITIES

The assigned subject matter of this chapter may be defined as falling within an area that is identified by the intersection of three sets: (1) the study of international systems; (2) the study of national polities; and (3) the study of political geography. The general confines can be visually represented by a simple Venn diagram.

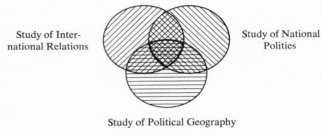

Study of Inter-
national Relations

Study of National
Polities

Study of Political Geography

Figure 8.1

Obviously, not all of the intersection is of concern to us in this work, but only that part included in a sub-set of political geography which might be called the study of insular polities.[2] In other words, we are trying to establish a basis from which one might proceed to answer the question: What variation in the interface between the international system and national polities can be accounted for by the fact that certain polities are insular?

When we pose the question in this way, it should be obvious that we shall have to be content with potential tendencies and tentative conclusions. In establishing the basic framework for this book, Professor Rosenau has indicated that the analysis of relations between international politics and national polities is a neglected research area. Indeed, it is fair to assert that, with very few exceptions, political geography has been ignored by

[1] See Chapter 3. See also James N. Rosenau, "Pre-theories and Theories of Foreign Policy," in R. Barry Farrell (ed.), *Approaches to Comparative and International Politics* (Evanston: Northwestern U.P., 1966), pp. 27–92.

[2] It must be observed, however, that only by grossly distorting a field of study would we be able to speak of the study of insular polities as a subfield of political geography.

political scientists for several decades. Thus, we are in the difficult position of trying to throw a few flickers of light on an unexplored area, from the perspective of a field of study that is virtually *terra incognita* for political scientists. Such a predicament not only fosters sensitivity to caution, but also prompts us to discuss briefly the conceptual springboard from which we shall attempt a leap into the unknown.

The Rosenau Linkage Matrix

Professor Rosenau has developed a framework which can provide some conceptual structure for the portion of our Venn diagram that is defined by the intersection of the study of international systems and the study of national polities. He conceives of the interrelationship in terms of a set of linkages, with specific categories of outputs from the domestic system into the international system, of inputs from the international system into the domestic system, and vice versa. His matrix for classifying the various types of interaction contains 9×144 cells.[3] In a short discussion of this type we cannot begin to fill systematically even a small fraction of these cells. When considering the linkages in terms of the domestic political system, therefore, we shall have to limit ourselves to a few comments on two points: (1) the way in which the fact of insularity may contribute to a distinctive kind of processing of outputs from the international system into the polity, especially with respect to political culture and social institutions (cells #9 and #18 in the Rosenau matrix); and (2) selected direct polity outputs of official decision-makers in insular polities.

When we turn our attention to linkages from the initial perspective of the international system, we encounter some conceptual problems with Rosenau's scheme that make it difficult to employ. His categories for dealing with the international side of the problem are

1. Contiguous environment.
2. Regional environment.
3. Cold War environment.
4. Resource environment.
5. Organizational environment.[4]

This conceptualization of international politics is developed solely from the perspective of the national polity. International politics is viewed simply as the environment of national polities. With the possible exceptions of the regional environment and the Cold War environment, this conceptualization ignores the system characteristics of international politics and provides no method for dealing explicitly with changes in international outputs that vary as a function of systemic modifications in the international system. Since much of what Professor Rosenau calls the contiguous and regional environments are delineated for use by the definition of insular

[3] See Chapter 3.
[4] See Appendix A of Chapter 3.

polity, and since the inputs and outputs of the international system *qua* system may be of particular consequence to insular polities, we shall not be able to follow his conceptualization, but we will suggest how the problem may be alternatively treated in systemic terms.

Insular Polities and Geopolitics

While Rosenau's framework is helpful in treating the area of study that falls in the intersection of national politics and international politics, scholars have not provided us with a ready-made scheme for analyzing insular polities.[5] We should like, however, to make a few comments about the way in which geographical factors have been treated in political analyses.

First, it is erroneous to say that geographical factors are ignored by students of international politics. Virtually every textbook in the field devotes a section, if not a whole chapter, to the treatment of geographical factors, usually as an element of state capability. It is fair to say, however, that the scholarly literature is largely devoid of any exploration of or research into geographical factors, and it shows little evidence of fruitful cross-fertilization between geography and political science.

Second, the most significant exception to this generalization is found in the work of Harold and Margaret Sprout. For a number of years they have stressed geographic factors, and they have been the most visible scholars who have transmitted the ideas, insights, and research findings from geography into the study of international relations. The major thrust of the Sprouts' work, however, has been toward the development of a useful conceptual framework for analyzing the "man-milieu" relationship.[6] After reading the Sprout studies, the student should not expect to discover that insularity (or any other single geographic feature) can account for much variation in the behavior which occurs within the overlap between domestic and international systems. Indeed, there is little in the Sprouts' recent work to suggest that much is to be gained by trying alternatively to identify the effect of any single geographic factor on foreign policy and international politics, other things being equal.

Although they provide us with little counsel on the present subject of discussion, we pay tribute to the Sprouts because they stand almost alone among political scientists in keeping in touch with the scholarship of professional geographers as they deal with environmental impact upon international politics. However, the political scientist's general lack of familiarity with recent research and theoretical writings in geography has been

[5] The difference between insular and continental polities in international relations has attracted the attention of some scholars. Long ago, for example, Alfred Mahan was impressed with the sea power advantage of insular polities; and more recently Robert MacIver has argued that, historically, the sea power-based empire of an insular country had a much different problem of control than did the land-based empire.

[6] The most complete statement of their position is found in *The Ecological Perspective on Human Affairs, with Special Reference to International Politics* (Princeton: Princeton U.P., 1965).

pointed out by a committee of distinguished American geographers who commented about a certain issue of a scholarly journal which dealt with aspects of geography and international politics: "In the several articles contributed by political scientists to a survey of geography and international conflict . . . there is almost no reference to or recognition of contemporary geographical literature or thought."[7]

If we had been writing on this subject a generation ago, we would have found a topic involving geography and international politics much more fashionable. But the literature of that era has little bearing on our present problem. While students (and pseudo-students) of geopolitics were certainly concerned with geography and politics, the trifling fact of insularity, as we shall attempt to treat it, did not command their attention. These men were searching for—and thought they had found—an all-embracing formula which could explain how national destinies were controlled by accident of geography.

In short, while political geography remains a major segment of the study of geography, contemporary work in this field has little to say about the specific problem that has been assigned to us.[8] Furthermore, the older geopolitical tradition does not provide us with much help, and contemporary political scientists have for the most part ignored political geographers and have neglected to study geographical factors themselves.[9]

The Comparative Method

In laying out the design for this book, Professor Rosenau wanted to have each contributor attack the problem under consideration through the use of the comparative method. He suggested to us that in our treatment of insular polities we might compare the United Kingdom, Japan, and Ceylon. In exploring the question of whether the fact of insularity has any effect on the characteristics of the interface between the domestic polity and the international system, we must concentrate upon the characteristics of that intersection that are shared by the insular polities we are examining. Obviously the characteristics that are significantly different could not be affected by the common feature of insularity. But once we have discovered some common characteristics, we have only reached a halfway mark. As a next step we need to compare the insular polities with "noninsular" polities, because any characteristics that these two sets have in common could not be related to the factor of insularity. Unfortunately, this second—and the

[7] National Academy of Sciences, National Research Council, *The Science of Geography* (Washington, D.C.: Publication No. 1277, Report of the *Ad Hoc* Committee on Geography, Earth Sciences Division, 1965), p. 39. The comment is made about a special issue of *The Journal of Conflict Resolution*, IV, 1 (March, 1960), entitled "The Geography of Conflict."

[8] For a recent example of a political geographer's approach to international politics, see S. B. Cohen, *Geography and Politics in a Divided World* (New York: Random, 1963).

[9] For an example of how political scientists deal with geographic factors, see selected articles in "The Geography of Conflict," cited in footnote 7, above.

most crucial—step in the comparative analysis lies beyond the scope of this discussion. We can only hope that Professor Rosenau's original plan to have a treatment of "land-locked" polities can eventually be carried out. Until such a study is made, many of our findings cannot be tested with more refined measures.

THE EMPIRICAL FOCUS

The empirical data for this chapter have been gathered from an examination of three insular polities—Britain, Japan, and Ceylon—with some scattered references to a fourth polity, the Malagasy Republic. In selecting these four countries, we are focusing upon a particular type of insular polity, namely, those that lie directly off the shore of a continental land mass. We would expect these polities to differ in significant respects from a mid-oceanic insular polity like Iceland, while exhibiting some of the features of a "peninsular polity" like Denmark.

The United Kingdom is made up of one large island and a few small, neighboring islands, as well as the northern slice of Ireland. Great Britain is separated from the continent by the English Channel, which at its narrowest point is only 21 miles across. Today the population of the United Kingdom is over 50,000,000 people, which represents more than a ten-fold increase from the middle of the seventeenth century. The total land area is about 120,000 square miles.

The Japanese Archipelago consists of four main islands and several groups of smaller islands adjacent to them. The land area, which is less than 143,000 square miles, is inhabited by more than 97,000,000 people. The Korean peninsula is only a little more than 100 miles from the nearest Japanese island, but 210 miles from the closest main island. Mainland China is 450 miles away.

The main pear-shaped island of Ceylon, together with several groups of small islands off the northwest coast, embraces an area of slightly more than 25,300 square miles. The population, which is increasing at the rate of 2.8 per cent annually, is in the neighbourhood of 7,000,000 people. The northern tip of the island, the Jaffna Peninsula, is separated from the coastline of India by about 22 miles of shallow strait.

Madagascar is the fourth largest island in the world. Its 230,000 square miles are occupied by 4,000,000 people. Situated over 400 miles off the southeast coast of Africa in the Indian Ocean, it might not be considered by many to be an "off-continent" isle. Indeed, until very recently its contacts with the African mainland have not been as important in its development as contacts with peoples and states in other parts of the world.

It is from these four cases that we shall attempt to develop some preliminary generalizations about insular polities.

INPUTS FROM THE INTERNATIONAL SYSTEM TO THE INSULAR POLITY

Professor Karl Deutsch has presented a scheme for dealing with inputs from the international system which is compatible with the Rosenau framework, and which enables us to gain a bit more leverage in the treatment of our problem.[10] A primary concept in his formulation is that of the "linkage group." He defines it as a group in the domestic polity that has particular ties with the international environment. For example, it may be a group of businessmen who are active in foreign trade, a trade union that has close ties with an international labor association, or a collection of intellectuals who are acutely concerned with events in the international environment. These linkage groups are typically involved with a limited number of what Rosenau calls "issue-areas."[11]

From the illustrations presented by Deutsch on how linkage groups may operate, it is possible to compile a list of interrelated propositions which will be helpful to our analysis. The crucial variables in these propositions may be identified as follows: (1) the number of linkage groups; (2) the link between the group and certain events in the international environment; (3) the strength of the tie between the linkage group and the domestic system; (4) the inertia of the domestic system; and (5) the integration of the domestic system.

The following sets of propositions have been derived from Deutsch's examples:

Set No. I

1. If the impact of the international input on the linkage group is high, and
2. If the ties of the linkage group to the domestic system are strong, and
3. If the inertia of the domestic system is high, then
4. The linkage group will tend to shatter, and the input will have little effect on the domestic system.[12]

Set No. II

1. If the impact of the international input on the linkage group is high, and
2. If the ties of the linkage group to the domestic system are weak, and
3. If the inertia of the domestic system is high, then
4. The linkage group will tend toward greater alienation. (For example, its members may go into exile or become revolutionaries.)[13]

---

[10] "External Influences on the Internal Behavior of States," in Farrell (ed.), *op. cit.*, pp. 5–26.

[11] Rosenau, "Pre-theories and Theories," in Farrell (ed.), *op. cit.*, pp. 71–88.

[12] Deutsch, *op. cit.*, pp. 13–14.

[13] *Ibid.*, p. 14.

Set No. III

1. If the impact of the international input on the linkage group is high, and
2. If the ties of the linkage group to the domestic system are strong, and
3. If the inertia of the domestic system is low, then
4. The domestic system will tend to change in response to the international inputs.[14]

The basic question to which we must address ourselves is whether or not the magnitude of the variables listed in any of these propositions is affected by insular position. In the first place, we need to inquire whether the *number* of linkage groups is affected by the fact of insularity. This is important because, other things being equal, the greater the number of linkage groups, the greater will be the number and variety of international inputs.

Direct evidence on the number of linkage groups in a sample of polities can be obtained only after extensive research. It is our belief, however, that two pieces of indirect evidence may be used tentatively as rough indicators of the number of linkage groups: (1) foreign trade, and (2) foreign mail. One would anticipate that, *ceteris paribus*, the greater the amount of foreign trade, the greater will be the number of people who are responsive to events in the international environment, and the greater will be the salience of messages from other countries. The gross amount of foreign trade, of course, will be directly proportional to the size of the Gross National Product (GNP), and hence, for our purposes, the ratio of foreign trade to GNP is a more useful figure.

Professor Russett and his colleagues have gathered data on foreign trade as a percentage of GNP for 81 polities which embrace 92 per cent of the world's population. These data should be comparable and accurate to ±5 per cent. The mean—as well as the median—percentage is 38. Of the 17 insular polities in the sample, 10 have a ratio of foreign trade to GNP which is higher than the mean, 6 are below the mean, and one is at the mean. Four of the 8 polities in the first decile are insular, 3 of the 8 in the second decile are insular, and comparable figures for the tenth and ninth deciles are, respectively, 0 and 2.[15]

Russett and his associates also present data on items of foreign mail per capita for 74 polities, representing 55 per cent of the world's population. Of the 16 insular polities included in the sample, 10 are above the median and 6 are below. About 36 per cent of the cases above the mean are insular polities, while only 15 per cent of the cases below the mean are in this category.[16]

---

[14] *Ibid.*, pp. 14–15.

[15] Bruce M. Russett and Hayward R. Alker, Jr., Karl W. Deutsch, and Harold D. Lasswell, *World Handbook of Political and Social Indicators* (New Haven: Yale U.P., 1964), pp. 162–5.

[16] *Ibid.*, pp. 114–15.

While this analysis is suggestive, it should be followed up by more sophisticated statistical examination. Foreign mail per capita may be a reasonable index of linkage groups in a polity, but it is certainly influenced by such factors as literacy and GNP per capita. So long as few people can write, foreign mail per capita will remain a low figure. Higher GNP per capita will tend to be correlated with more commercial mail, and hence this factor must be controlled, for we are interested in the effect of insularity on the number of linkage groups if this variable were not affected by differences in GNP. A partial correlation between insularity and foreign mail per capita, holding literacy and GNP per capita constant, would seem to be an appropriate routine. But none of the latter three variables is distributed normally, and scattergrams indicate that the relationship is not linear. To make the appropriate transformations and to develop some non-linear measure of partial association would require a statistical treatise in its own right. While we firmly support the use of statistical routines for data analysis, we see little benefit in applying inappropriate routines and in reporting results that are both mathematically and theoretically uninterpretable.

We can only report this: our preliminary work, which normalized the distributions and experimented with various routines, none of which was completely appropriate, did indicate a slight positive relationship between foreign mail per capita and insularity.

This preliminary analysis suggests that insular polities have a slightly more active involvement with other countries, and that they are therefore likely to have a relatively larger number of linkage groups. To state the proposition more simply, the relative number of linkage groups in a polity— one of the variables that is important in accounting for the effect of international inputs—is likely to be greater in an insular polity than in a non-insular polity.

The second point that we need to consider in making use of Deutsch's linkage-group variables is somewhat more speculative. An important component in the Deutsch schema is the strength of the ties of the linkage group to the domestic system. We would argue that, other things being equal, the greater the cultural integration of the polity (or the greater its homogeneity), the greater will be the strength of the ties of the linkage groups with the domestic system. Thus, we raise the question: Do insular polities, *ceteris paribus*, exhibit greater cultural homogeneity than continental polities?

One hardly needs to remind the readers of this book of the cultural homogeneity of Great Britain and its influence upon government and politics. Virtually every treatment of British politics either begins or ends with a discussion of the high degree of cultural cohesion. Indeed, teachers in the classroom usually explain some of the differences between the evolution of democratic government in Britain, as compared with France and Germany, in terms of the higher level of consensus in the United Kingdom.

Although we accept this feature of the British polity as an obvious fact, it becomes more meaningful when viewed in historical perspective. At the end of the eleventh century, for example, there were five major groups, each speaking a different language, which had to be integrated into a national polity: Anglo-Saxon, Welsh, Scottish, Irish, and Norman-French. Moreover, these groups had significant social-structural and cultural differences, as well as distinctive legal systems. Yet over the centuries, these groups, with the exception of the Catholic sector of Ireland, were not only merged into a single polity, but into one that became noted for its high level of homogeneity and integration.

This pattern of development is in sharp contrast with that of the German-speaking areas of Western and Central Europe. Even with the advantage of a common language (albeit with regional variations in dialect), these territories have never been merged into a single society or polity. The distinctions between German society in the nineteenth and early twentieth centuries, as described by Robert Lowie,[17] and British society during the same time span are indeed striking.

But the question we must raise is not whether the British polity is more integrated than its continental neighbors; the answer to that query seems clear enough. The question of concern to us is whether the fact of insularity contributes significantly to the differences in polity cohesion. We do not have the necessary data to provide a positive affirmative answer. We can only suggest that perhaps the possibilities of coastal transportation and communication, together with physical separation from the continent, gave rise to the kinds of interactions that facilitated integration.

The Japanese case is more difficult to examine. The aboriginal inhabitants were the Ainu, who probably came from early Caucasoid stock. While the descendants of the aborigines now inhabit the northern island of Hokkaido, they were displaced in the other islands of the archipelago. In pre-historic times, there were probably waves of immigration from the mainland, largely through Korea, and perhaps even more from the islands to the south of China. In any case, by the first century B.C., when China and Japan had certainly entered into relationship, the population was, in Sansom's description, "heterogeneous," being composed of a "variety of ethnic elements, doubtless in different degrees of diffusion."[18] It seems likely that even after the beginning of the Christian era, immigration from the mainland continued. These were mostly Koreans and Chinese, perhaps refugees from the dynastic wars on the continent. Sansom claims that by the seventh century over one third of the noble families of Japan were of Chinese or Korean descent.[19]

Although some of the early patterns of immigration into Japan may

[17] Robert Lowie, *Towards Understanding Germany* (Chicago: U. of Chicago, 1954).
[18] George B. Sansom, *Japan: A Short Cultural History* (New York: Appleton, 1962), p. 43.
[19] *Ibid.*, p. 44.

have at least remote parallels with the early movements into England, the political history of the two polities during the modern era is very different. While the modern, centralized state system was emerging in Western Europe in the seventeenth century, the Shogunal form of feudalism was becoming more firmly entrenched in Japan under the Tokugawa clan. The Shoguns attempted, sometimes without much success, to govern the country from their capital at Edo, but many of the daimyo ruled their feudal domains with a minimum of interference from the central authorities. One might anticipate that this decentralized form of political organization, together with the topography of the islands and the difficulties of communication, would foster parochial tendencies and diminish the contacts among local and regional groups. One would also expect that this lack of inter-regional contact would encourage heterogeneity and would be antithetical to the development of a well-integrated, modern society. But these expectations seem not to apply to Japan. While scholars point out the regional diversification of the country, they do not call attention to any unusual heterogeneity in the culture. It is, of course, a difficult task to devise a measure of integration which could be applied to a long historical epoch and which logically could vary independently of political centralization. Data on the patterns and frequency of intercommunication among the various regions have not yet been gathered by the Japanologists.

There is, however, at least one piece of evidence that suggests a degree of integration and standardization of exchange and communication among the various regions. Early in Japanese history, perhaps by the middle of the ninth century, a fairly uniform system of weights and measures was developed. Later, at the time of Tokugawa rule, the central government set standards for dry and linear measures and managed to sustain them. After 1630, all scaling instruments were periodically inspected.[20]

From a modern perspective, this type of standardization might appear to be trivial. But when we discover that it not only exceeded the standardization that prevailed in China until recent decades and was much better than what France had until after the Revolution, the phenomenon takes on a bit more meaning. In Hangchow during the nineteenth century, for example, there were 17 different measures attached to the *catty* (a unit of weight). France during the *ancien regime* had no national standards that the central authorities could enforce; different units of measure were employed in different trades even in the same city. As powerful an administrator and economic rationalist as Colbert found it difficult to establish effective standardization in just the port cities.[21]

The fact that Japan was successful in standardizing weights and measures, even with a relatively weak central government and an unreliable

---

[20] See Robert T. Holt and John E. Turner, *The Political Basis of Economic Development: An Exploration in Comparative Political Analysis* (Princeton: Van Nostrand, 1966), pp. 200–1.

[21] *Ibid.*

enforcement mechanism, while France and China failed, suggests the possibility that the problem was easier for Japan owing to a higher level of integration and more active exchanges among regions. The existence of unit standards, in turn, probably contributed to greater regional interaction, and these contacts over the centuries may have helped to promote even more integration.[22]

The early history of Ceylon has some common elements with Japanese history. There were aboriginal inhabitants about whom almost nothing is known. According to legends, which might bear some resemblance to historical fact, migrations of Buddhists from northern India to Ceylon began in the sixth century, B.C., and continued for some time. The modern Sinhalese are the descendants of these immigrants. Later Hindus from southern India migrated to the northern parts of the island, and after the tenth century South Indian princes established their control over these areas. In more recent times, large groups of Tamils from South India were brought to Ceylon by the European colonists as plantation laborers, and these people now inhabit the Jaffna Peninsula in the northern part of the country.[23]

Ceylon in the twentieth century has had the basis for great conflict between Hindus and Buddhists, Tamils and Sinhalese, Northerners and Southerners. Since divisions of this sort tend to be mutually reinforcing, they could generate such ruptures in the social order as to endanger its existence. Despite these divergent groups, however, there appears to be an amazing degree of cohesion within the society. This is pointed out by Ryan:

> The social history of Ceylon indicates an early and surprisingly persistent unity. That political unity was, over considerable periods, lost in the isolation of the courts and the regional lords, is to be expected. The over-all historical view, however, indicates recurrent periods of national oneness and persisting cultural integration between the Sinhalese provinces.[24]

Indeed, when compared with India, Ceylon had a smooth journey from colonial status to independence.

The contrast between the caste systems of Ceylon and India draws attention to what may be evidence of a higher degree of integration in the former country. Two major differences are to be found. First, the notion

---

[22] It is interesting to observe that in the period before the French Revolution, England led France in the standardization of weights and measures. The rationalists who set up the metric system in France at the time of the Revolution looked to England as a model of standardization (cf. _ibid._).

[23] See Bruce Ryan, _Caste in Modern Ceylon: The Sinhalese System in Transition_ (New Brunswick, N.J.: Rutgers U.P., 1953), pp. 3–4; and E. F. C. Ludowyk, _The Story of Ceylon_ (London: Faber & Faber, 1962).

[24] Ryan, _op. cit._, p. 10.

210

of "untouchables," in the Hindu sense of the term, is absent in the Sinhalese stratification system, where the "out-caste untouchability" rests on a secular rather than a sacred tabu. According to Ryan, the absence of the Hindu concept "has rendered the Sinhalese caste system mild and humanitarian when judged by Indian standards."[25] Second, in the Sinhalese system the highest caste embraces the majority of the Sinhalese people. These differences support the view that the caste system in Ceylon is less schismatic and potentially less disruptive of the social order than its counterpart in India. Whether the less divisive nature of Ceylonese caste can be accounted for largely by the dominant Buddhist impact, we, of course, are not in a position to say. But it appears likely that the forces contributing to disintegration in Ceylon have been muted, comparatively speaking, just as they apparently have in Britain and Japan.

The ethnic diversity in Malagasy is probably even greater than in the other three cases we have discussed. Scholars disagree over the question of whether there was an aboriginal race of Pygmies—either Oceanic Negritos or African Twides—but even if they existed, they have been completely displaced. Today the ethnic composition of the population is a complex mixture of Negroid, Mongoloid, and Caucasoid. Malagasy culture has been characterized as "basically Malaysian (Mongolian) with a strong Arabic (Caucasian) overlay and a relatively weak Bantu (Negro) component."[26] The Malagasy language is most closely related to the Maanyan language of south-central Borneo.

Between eleven and eighteen major tribal groupings (depending upon which classification the student elects to accept) live on the island. But whichever figure is chosen, it is obvious that the potential for schism along tribal lines is very great. However, in spite of the ethnic complexity, the tribal groupings, and the topographical diversity, one observer points out that the Malagasy Republic displays considerable homogeneity in language and culture.[27] It would be difficult to mark out in Sub-Saharan Africa an area as large and as populous as Malagasy that has achieved a comparable degree of cohesion.

We are painfully aware that the evidence we have presented is scant, and certainly not conclusive. But the few shreds there are tempt us to advance the proposition that an insular polity may have a relatively larger number of linkage groups, and that these groups may have stronger ties to the domestic system. If this proves to be the case, then the insular polity should react more frequently, more quickly, and more strongly to inputs from the international system. We shall now consider a few examples which may fit into the Rosenau matrix.

---

[25] *Ibid.*, p. 17.
[26] George P. Murdock, *Africa: Its People and Their Cultural History* (New York: McGraw-Hill, 1959), p. 212.
[27] *Ibid.*, p. 214.

EFFECTS OF EXTERNAL EVENTS ON THE INSULAR POLITY

Inputs from the international environment have had a significant impact upon the cohesion of the political parties of the island countries under examination. It is to be expected, of course, that opposition parties, despite bipartisan agreements on foreign policy, would at least occasionally seize upon foreign policy issues to harass the government party or any coalition of parties. But, more important for our purposes, the policies designed by a government to meet developments on the mainland have often precipitated schism *within the political organizations themselves.*

In Britain, for example, as disciplined a unit as the Conservative Party has experienced important backbench dissidence since World War II over such issues as the American Loan (1945), the Bretton Woods Agreement, the Korean War, the evacuation of Suez (1954), the attack upon Egypt (1956), Cyprus (1956), Western European Union and closer economic ties with the continent, and support for the United Nations. While the rumblings of discontent in the Tory backbenches are usually louder and more frequent on domestic affairs, the schisms over foreign policy have impelled the rebels on a number of occasions to march into division lobbies against the instructions of their leaders or to willfully abstain from voting— actions that Conservative MPs undertake only under the most provocative conditions.

To record in detail the schisms which have rocked the British Labour Party on questions relating to continental foreign policy would require treatment in a full-length book. Partly as a result of the Party's traditional disdain for the use of military force and "power politics" and partly as a result of organizational procedures which deprive the dissidents of the kinds of channels open to the Conservatives, the Labour rebels have frequently revealed their displeasure in the division lobbies, and they have engaged their leaders on issues of defense and foreign policy more than have their Tory counterparts. A listing of serious disruptions within the Parliamentary Labour Party would include: American Loan (1945), Bretton Woods Agreement (1945), the demand for a truly "socialist" foreign policy (1946–47), the administration of conquered Germany (1947), military conscription (1947–48, 1950–51, 1953, 1955), Palestine (1948–49), the NATO alliance (1949), Korean War (1950–51), Tanks for Egypt (1950), rearmament (1951–52), Japanese Peace Treaty (1951), nuclear defense (1952–64), German rearmament (1954), closer economic and political ties with the continent (1962, 1967), and the war in Vietnam. Less serious disagreements within the Party occurred over the Evacuation of Suez (1954), the British attack upon Egypt (1956), and the dispatch of troops to Jordan (1958).

Where fractional groupings emerge within the British parties as a result of the issues arising from international inputs, they probably reflect, at least to some extent, the intricate patterns of pressures and cross-pressures which impinge upon them. To ferret out the salient pressures on each of

212

these issues requires a series of case studies in depth—a task that must be reserved for the future. However, a tentative glance at possible linkage groups may be taken in the case of the Common Market, which in important respects calls for a reversal of traditional British policy in the relationships between that country and its neighbors across the channel.

When the issue was coming to a head in 1960–61, the reaction of British industrial establishments was thoroughly mixed.[28] While many firms were convinced that their trading prospects would be improved by entry into the Market and they supported the Government's efforts, others anticipated competitive dangers of one form or another, and some exhibited little or no interest at all. Since a large proportion of Conservative MPs have intimate connections with the business community, the tides of business opinion were likely to sweep close to them. The people engaged in agriculture were particularly worried about the competitive position of that industry, and their anxieties could hardly be ignored by the Tory members who represented rural districts. Similarly, the trade unions of Britain, which are closely linked with the Labour Party, did not speak with a single voice on the Common Market, although the Trades Union Congress had been investigating the problem of continental relationships for some time. Many of the unions were sympathetic to Britain's entry into the Common Market on condition that certain safeguards be provided, while other unions, especially the craft organizations, evinced lukewarm, indifferent, or hostile attitudes. At the Labour Party Conference in 1962, Frank Cousins, the leader of the huge Transport and General Workers Union, pointed out that his organization had started off in support of the idea of economic cooperation in Europe but had shifted position when its leaders realized some of the implications:

> We are saying here as a Socialist group we want full employment, we want economic planning, we want the right to determine our own foreign policy, we want to protect our associations with the Commonwealth countries. . . . What are they [the Conservative Government] trying to do? Fix our wages and our conditions as low as they possibly can in relation to the least favorable of the European countries? . . . We will not have this.[29]

[28] See *The Times* (London), July 13, 1961. The Federation of British Industries had grown alarmed in 1958–59 by the deterioration of Britain's trading position on the continent and had urged the government to do something about it. The response of the government was to sponsor the establishment of the European Free Trade Area (EFTA) with those OEEC countries that were not members of the Common Market. Cf. Miriam Camps, *Britain and the European Community, 1955–1963* (Princeton: Princeton U.P., 1964), pp. 274–5. For earlier attitudes of the Federation of British Industries, see Hans J. Heisler, *British Policy with regard to the Unification Efforts on the European Continent* (Leyden: A. W. Sythoff, 1959), pp. 111–13.

[29] *Report of the Sixty-First Annual Conference of the Labour Party* (1962), p. 181. Other trade-union views were expressed during the course of this debate. When the question of Britain's entry was debated in the House of Commons in 1967, the Parliamentary Labour Party was split on the issue. The working-class members were conspicuous in their opposition.

On the other hand, the British press and the independent journalists, except for the Beaverbrook papers and the *Daily Worker*, were generally sympathetic with Britain's proposed role in continental affairs.   Thus, we can get some general notion of the patchwork of attitudes among some of the more active interest groups, and these represent linkage groups which have been divided among and within themselves as they have reacted in their domestic setting to inputs from the external environment.

In Japan, the inputs from the external environment have helped to dig a chasm between the strong Liberal Democratic Party (*Jiyu-Minshuto*) on the one hand, and the socialist groups (called the *Nihon Shakaito*, when they were united) on the other.   Whereas the conservative governing party has supported the United States-Japan Security Treaty, limited rearmament for defense purposes, and the normalization of relations with South Korea, and has officially stood for a policy of nonrecognition of Red China, at least for the time being, the Japanese Socialists have vigorously objected to the Liberal Democratic position on all of these questions.[30]   Under the strong influence of "anti-capitalism" dogma, the Socialists have called for a policy of "positive neutralism," under which the security pact would be scrapped, American military bases would be dismantled, and formal recognition would be extended to Peking.

But most of these burning issues have done more than merely draw a sharp line between the conservative and socialist groups.   As in the case of Britain, they have exacerbated the bitter factional rivalries within the parties themselves, which have always been characterized by "personalized politics."   At various times, for example, the ruling Liberal Democratic Party has been divided over the issue of the Security Treaty, the program of limited rearmament, and the question of recognizing the Peking government.[31]   The schism-inducing potential of foreign policy matters has been even more serious for the Socialists in Japan.   In October, 1951, the Party split into two separate organizations over the peace treaty and the military security pact with the United States, the right-wing group indicating reluctant acquiescence and the left-wing group remaining adamant in its opposition to these developments and in its support for neutralism.   Although the two factions papered over their differences and entered into uneasy union in October, 1955, they separated again early in 1960, with the right-wing Party attempting to develop a middle course between the left-wing organization and the Liberal Democrats over the issues of national security and relations with the continent.

As is true of the dissidence in British political parties, it is possible to detect potential linkage groups in the factional patterns of the Japanese parties, although the patterns are much more intricate and much more

---

[30] See Robert A. Scalapino and Junnosuke Masumi, *Parties and Politics in Contemporary Japan* (Berkeley: U. of California, 1962), pp. 105–7, 125–47.

[31] On the question of Chinese recognition, see R. G. Boyd, "China's Relations with Japan," *Australian Outlook*, XIV, 1 (April, 1961), 50–68.

difficult to research than is the case with Britain. Expanding the patterns established in prewar years, the Liberal Democratic Party has close ties with the business community, including the important financial circles, which pours large sums of money into the coffers of the organization.[32] Moreover, these business connections are interlaced with the factional groupings within the Party, each rival group having access to its own sources of revenue in the business world. Indeed, some commercial interests also contribute limited financial resources to the socialist cause so that they can have established connections on both ends of the political spectrum. To some businessmen who are eager to expand their markets, Communist China has for some years had a special attraction, and it is most likely that certain business groups have prodded the government into making limited trade agreements with Peking. Some groups, however, are so desirous of *expansion* of trade relations that they would be willing to grant at least *de facto* recognition to the Red regime.[33] The government, of course, with the support of some conservative factions, is reluctant to take such steps partly out of fear of antagonizing American opinion—an attitude that is likely to encourage potentially dissident conservative factions to look a bit harder at the nature of the alliance.

Although the right-wing Socialists have some business connections, probably from medium and small-scale establishments, and the business community is registered with one faction in the left-wing Socialist group, the Socialist organizations tend largely to be the political instruments of the trade unions.[34] The moderate federation of organized labor—the Japan Trade Union Congress (*Zenro*), which embraces about 950,000 members—is allied with the Socialist right-wing. But the largest federation—the General Council of Trade Unions (*Sohyo*), with more than 3,500,000 members—is affiliated with the leftist Socialists, and is militant in its opposition to the security treaty and in its support for normalized relations with the Communist countries, organizing numerous strikes and demonstrations to underline its position. More than half of the Socialist MPs have close ties with organized labor, especially on the left, and they are the beneficiaries of sizeable political contributions from the unions. The patterns of potential linkage groups is further complicated by the fact that the Japanese press is usually critical of the security pact, and that Liberal Democratic voters, while strongly supporting their leaders in the continuation of the American alliance, move away from their leaders as they express their opposition to American bases in Japan and Okinawa and their support for the recognition of Communist China.[35]

[32] On these interest groups in Japanese politics, see Scalapino and Masumi, *op. cit.*, pp. 63–72, 76–77, 88–89.

[33] See Floyd, *op. cit.*

[34] Scalapino and Masumi, *op. cit.*, pp. 66–77, 98–99.

[35] See Douglas H. Mendel, Jr., *The Japanese People and Foreign Policy: A Study of Public Opinion in Post-Treaty Japan* (Berkeley: U. of California, 1961), pp. 95–121, 234–44.

215

Like Britain and Japan, Ceylon has suffered ruptures within her party system as a result of the inputs from the external regional environment. Not only have the parties and coalitions experienced schisms akin to those in more advanced island polities, but Ceylon's recent acquisition of independence and the brittle nature of the party alliances, both on the government side and in the opposition benches, have added a deeper dimension to the problem. As might have been expected, one of the major points of difference between the ruling party and opposition groups in foreign policy matters was the question of the defense of the country.[36] When the new state was formed in 1948, the government fell under attack by leftist critics for allowing Britain to retain military bases on the island. Later, in 1954, when the Prime Minister, Sir John Kotelawala, exhibited some interest in the SEATO pact, most of the influential forces in the country registered vigorous objections to the whole idea. From 1951 until 1956, when Sir John's government was defeated in an election, the opposition grew in strength, demanding the revocation of the defense agreement with Britain and the adoption of a "neutralist" foreign policy. The trade unions were opposed to the military bases and to SEATO, and in 1955–56 Buddhist activists and the defenders of Sinhalese culture joined them in protesting against the defense arrangement, using this issue along with domestic grievances as a weapon against the Kotelawala Government. From 1948 to 1952, opposition groups, especially the leftist parties and the trade unions, urged closer links with Red China, but until the Government decided to enter into a trade agreement with Peking, it had been reluctant to enter into close relationships.

Issues of foreign policy, however, have also disturbed the uneasy equilibrium within the government coalitions and within the ranks of the opposition alliances, and a brief examination of these disturbances may provide a clue for potential linkage groups. Toward the end of the Kotelawala regime, for example, one of the cabinet ministers resigned his post partly as a result of his inability to convert his colleagues to a policy of more intimate trade relations with Communist China.[37] Some of Ceylon's political activists were also divided over the question of supporting Nehru's leadership in the diplomatic field, and on several occasions Sir John was attacked for his public arguments with the Indian leader which, it was felt, tended to generate friction between the two countries.[38] The Ceylonese Prime Minister came in for vigorous criticism for his anti-Communist statements at the Bandung Conference in 1955. When he returned to Colombo, a motion of no confidence was laid down by Mr. S. W. R. D. Bandaranaike, the leader of the Opposition, and, although the Prime Minister won a victory in the voting lobbies, a number of his party members were absent.[39]

[36] See W. Howard Wriggins, *Ceylon: Dilemmas of a New Nation* (Princeton: Princeton U.P., 1960), pp. 388–99.
[37] *Ibid.*, p. 112.
[38] *Ibid.*, p. 352.
[39] *Ibid.*, p. 449.

Perhaps the best issue for a fruitful search for linkage groups is the Chinese-Indian border dispute in 1962.[40] The Government, under the leadership of Mrs. Bandaranaike, maintained an official position of strict neutrality and sought to mediate the controversy. Even before the fighting broke out, however, the leaders of the political parties indicated their concern about China's precipitous actions. As the dispute grew more serious, elite groups began to express their fear that if China were to overcome India, their country would be the next victim on the Communist list. The press was solid in its support for Ceylon's neighbor to the north. Groups of Sinhalese nationalists, who only a few years earlier had engaged in a domestic struggle with the Indian minority, now united with them in volunteering to fight in support of India's cause. But although such political organizations as the United National Party (UNP), the People's United Front (MEP), and the Federal Party lined up behind India against the Chinese threat, one party—the Jatika Vimukti Peramuna (JVP), a group of extreme Sinhalese—branded India as the aggressor, and other organizations split on the issue. The Lanka Sama Samaja Party (LSSP), a Marxist organization, split into pro-Indian and neutralist factions. The same thing happened in the Sri Lanka Freedom Party (SLFP), with one group urging the abrogation of the trade agreement with Red China and the other demanding a posture of nonalignment.

In all three of these insular polities, we can see that international inputs have had a divisive impact upon political parties and coalitions, and that in many instances this has happened because interest groups having access to different segments of the parties have responded differently to the input. For some groups the response may be one of nationalism, generated by a desire to protect the homeland; in some cases the response is conditioned by ideological ties with parts of the external environment; and in many groups the response is influenced by the need to develop commercial linkages or to protect those that already exist. These organizations, we hasten to point out, are interest groups from the perspective of the domestic system, but are regarded as potential linkage groups in the analysis we are presenting in this chapter.

Whether a close examination of the reactions described above will reveal any patterns that are distinctive to an island polity is a question we are unable to answer until a research design is worked out to include non-insular polities. There is no doubt that inputs from the international system also affect political parties and coalitions in continental polities. We suspect, however, that (other things being equal) the immediate regional environment is of greater consequence to the continental powers. If the geographical distinctions that underlie our analysis represent a meaningful taxonomy, further work is needed to compare insular and continental polities. It is unfortunate that this volume does not include a companion piece on continental states, as originally planned.

[40] On this issue, see Urmila Phadnis, "Ceylon and the Sino-Indian Border Dispute," *Asian Survey*, III, 4 (April, 1963), especially 192–6.

POLITY OUTPUTS

Having glanced at prefatory evidence of potential common patterns among insular polities and of the reactions of some potential linkage groups to inputs from the international environment, it will be instructive to examine in a tentative way some of the polity outputs of these island countries that might be related to the fact of insularity. Here we shall have to rely upon a type of qualitative data, identifying certain foreign policy trends from the historical experiences of the insular powers under examination.

We can begin by making the obvious point that all polities are concerned about their immediate neighbors—that a "benign" regional environment is an objective of every country, whether a continental or an insular power. The question is: Does an island polity, in trying to cope with its regional environment, employ strategies (polity outputs) that are different from those employed by a continental polity? There are, of course, a number of strategies that any country might pursue as it attempts to create and maintain a regional environment that is congenial to its development.

1. Conquest and the creation of buffer areas on its own borders.

2. Regional alliances so as to maintain a stable regional balance of power.

3. "Splendid" isolation (holder of the balance of power).

4. Federative attachments (unification, customs unions, common markets, and so on).

5. Alliances with actors outside the regional system so as to strengthen the polity's regional position.

In considering the selection and use of particular strategies by island polities, we advance the following propositions for further consideration:

1. All (or most) countries attempt Strategy No. 1, but insular polities tend to be less successful in their use of it.

2. Insular polities are less likely than continental powers to pursue Strategy No. 2.

3. Insular polities are more likely to follow Strategy No. 3, provided that the regional environment conforms to the classical balance of power situation.

4. Insular polities are less likely to pursue Strategy No. 4.

5. Insular polities are more likely to pursue Strategy No. 5.

These statements are drawn in large part from the foreign policy trends of the island countries we have been examining. It will be useful at this point to sketch out the major lines of development for comparative purposes.

United Kingdom

From her early historical beginnings, when the Roman legions entered the country from Gaul, to be followed later by the Anglo-Saxons, the Danes, and the Normans, Britain has always been vulnerable to invasion by strong nations which dominated the approaches on the mainland. Even though no invasion has succeeded since 1066, the people of the isles have throughout their modern past suffered long intervals of anxiety as a result of threats from ambitious sovereigns who controlled the land across the channel—Louis XIV, Napoleon, and, more recently, Hitler. Thus, on security grounds alone, the British have had to be concerned with developments on the continent of Europe.

But, quite apart from the potential military threat to its insular position, Britain has always had an important commercial stake on the mainland. A country of limited natural resources, it has traditionally developed much of its strength by importing supplies of new materials, processing them, and exporting commodities for sale in European and colonial markets. As early as the fourteenth century, long before the industrial revolution, the British were exporting wool to the inhabitants of Flanders, and the two groups had grown economically interdependent. With the growth of industrialization in Britain, she became so economically linked with the continental powers that a diminution or stoppage of trade had a serious effect upon her industrial establishment. In more recent times, of course, Britain's trade with her colonies and the Commonwealth has constituted a significant part of her commercial activities. Nevertheless, in 1960, 29.5 per cent of her imports came from the nations of Western Europe, and she sold 30.4 per cent of her exports to those countries. (Her import-export figures from and to the members of the Common Market were 14.5 per cent in each category.)[41]

Given her insular position, which made Britain vulnerable to invasion and which helped to develop economic ties with continental countries, she gradually perceived a set of interests with respect to her mainland neighbors. These interests—perceived several centuries ago and still supported today— may be classified under two headings: (1) no great power or grouping of powers must be permitted to dominate the continent of Europe in such a way as to endanger Britain's security by controlling the channel ports; and (2) in order to compensate for her own limited resources and her narrow home market, Britain must be able to retain her continental markets against the sustained threat of a hostile power or a hostile grouping of powers in alliance against her.

In pursuing these interests, Britain has been forced to operate within a framework limited by certain "givens." In the first place, she had limited manpower resources, which made it difficult for her to put a large competitive army into the field for any length of time. Moreover, the British

[41] *Britain and the European Communities: Background to the Negotiations* (London: H.M. Stationery Office, 1962), p. 28.

people had a strong tendency to be anti-militaristic and were often inclined toward nonintervention in continental affairs so long as the security of the islands was not in jeopardy. Wars on the continent disturbed normal trade relations and impinged upon the interests of the merchant class, besides adding to their tax burdens. The "peace temper" which frequently swept over the islands placed restraints upon the use of military force to carry out foreign policy on the continent, for the British people had developed a set of political institutions through which they were sometimes able to thwart the monarch's military ventures. When the war against the Dutch in 1672 proved to be unpopular, for example, parliament refused to appropriate any more money for the venture in 1673, and in the following year the king was forced to withdraw.[42] Again, even though conditions on the mainland were still unsettled after the Peace of Ryswick with France (1697), the House of Commons managed to secure the reduction of the army to 10,000 men (and later to 7,000). The navy was also reduced from its wartime strength of 40,000 sailors to 8,000.[43] It was the small size and the inexperience of the British army that prompted political leaders like William Pitt to try to remedy the military deficiency by tapping the wealthy industrialists in order to subsidize Britain's allies.

Thus, a summary of the "givens" in the British case would include the following: (1) limited manpower resources for an effective land army (unless conscription were applied); (2) a popular antipathy toward militarism; (3) popular attitudes toward non-involvement on the continent, especially on the part of the merchants, unless British security was in danger; (4) political institutions through which politically relevant groups could make their will effective against the makers of foreign policy; and (5) limited resources and taxpayer resistance which eventually placed optimal limits upon naval strength and airpower, including modern methods of nuclear warfare. With these limitations, the leaders of Britain have had to supplement their available military strength with skillful diplomatic effort.

In light of these considerations, the outputs of the British polity have varied according to the requirements of the external regional environment and the changing situation within the polity. It is possible, however, to characterize the general nature of these outputs as follows: (1) a marked tendency toward aloofness from the political affairs of the continental powers as long as the forces on the mainland were in a relatively stable balance;[44] as Churchill once put it, "Each time we must choose between Europe and the

---

[42] See W. E. Lunt, *History of England* (New York: Harper, 1957), pp. 451–2. Mention should also be made of the difficulties experienced by James I and Charles I in trying to finance their continental military encounters.

[43] J. R. Green, *A Short History of the English People* (New York: Harper, 1897), pp. 677–8.

[44] It is not necessary for us in this paper to discuss the various types of "balance of power" or to deal with the question of whether the balance-of-power system thwarted or helped to precipitate the outbreak of war. We are concerned only with the balance of power as a *policy* of the country or countries under discussion.

open sea, we shall always choose the open sea"; (2) action to prevent any single power or group of powers from securing such a grip on the continent that they could threaten the invasion of Britain from the channel ports or to jeopardize permanently British trade with the mainland; (3) the avoidance of permanent commitments on the continent in order to be free to mediate the clash of interests when the equilibrium was disrupted, and to be flexible enough to improvise a collective arrangement (usually by joining the least threatening side) which would provide the resources and strength that she lacked and which would restore a favorable equilibrium among her potential enemies.

At the time of the Hundred Years' War (1337–1453), Britain was pursuing Strategy No. 1 by attempting to occupy a large slice of territory on the continent itself. A policy of this sort was possible at that time because the area was divided among rival principalities, the British had economic ties with Flanders, family linkages enabled some English monarchs to lay claim to the crown of France, and the British army—small and staffed mostly with paid soldiers—was reasonably successful in combat owing to innovative methods of warfare, as, for example, the use of the archers' longbows against the crossbows of the French. But after a century of intermittent struggle, the embryo forces of kinship, loyalty, and patriotism on the mainland made it difficult and costly for the British to hold on to their continental acquisitions, and by the end of the war they retained only Calais. After the loss of this district in 1558, the British abandoned the policy of claiming mainland territory when the fruits of military victory were being distributed, electing instead to take colonial areas and outposts of strategic importance.

After Britain gave up her attempts to hold territory on the mainland, she gradually established the main outlines of her balance of power strategy (No. 3), improvising temporary alliances to offset the strength of enemies who threatened to dominate the approaches to the British Isles. In the latter quarter of the seventeenth century, the main competitor was Spain, whose ruler held title to the Netherlands and was in a position to menace the security of England at a time when France was weakened by religious conflict. Queen Elizabeth followed the prudent course of building a counterweight against the Spanish enemy by supplying assistance to the Dutch rebels, by reaching a diplomatic understanding with France, and by helping to mobilize groups that were hostile to Phillip II.[45]

From the time of Louis XIV until the defeat of Napoleon in 1815, France was the heaviest weight on the balance, and she made an almost continuous bid for hegemony over the continent. England could not assent to having the Scheldt River under France's sole jurisdiction, and for many decades she fashioned whatever collective arrangements were necessary and possible to prevent her rival from becoming master of the mainland.

[45] See William R. Willcox, *Star of Empire: A Study of Britain as a World Power, 1485–1945* (New York: Knopf, 1950), pp. 12–14.

By the middle of the eighteenth century, Britain was using Prussia as one of her allies to checkmate her traditional enemy, especially when the French showed signs of moving into the low countries.

When her continental rivals were able to marshal huge land forces against her in the wars she fought, England found that her armies were not large enough to compete effectively, and, since parliament was often reluctant to increase her land strength, she was forced to devise other strategies. For these reasons, she tended increasingly to rely upon her naval arm, which also proved to be effective in enforcing blockades, and she depended upon her allies—appropriately financed through British subsidies—to do the land fighting on the continent, while employing the bulk of her own armies to attack the colonial possessions of her enemies.[46]

The biggest threat to British security and her continental trade occurred, of course, under Napoleon when he defeated or cowed the other components of the British alliance, closed the continental ports to Britain's commerce, ordered other nations to boycott her, and massed about 100,000 troops for an invasion of the islands. By 1808, Napoleon dominated virtually all of the mainland, and Britain stood alone against his power. British ingenuity in generating new coalitions and in supporting anti-French rebellions, as well as the effectiveness of her naval effort, helped to precipitate Napoleon's downfall and to end the threat of France as the single dominant force on the continent. The Treaty of Vienna (1815) designed a new map of Europe and established a more secure base in the low countries against potential inroads by the French. At the behest of England, France received reasonably generous treatment so that she could stand as one weight in the new balance of power, particularly against the growing strength of Prussia, which Britain had welcomed as long as France was her main rival. With the new balance established, Britain returned to her shores, refusing to intervene with the concert powers in the internal affairs of nations on the continent.

A new threat to the security of the low countries appeared in 1830, when the Belgians rebelled against Dutch rule. For Belgium to fall under the control of a major power would, in Britain's view, be the equivalent of having a "pistol pointed at her heart," and she attempted unsuccessfully to mediate the dispute. Since France was already supporting the demands of the Belgians, Britain decided to join her in driving out the Dutch. As a result of this episode, a treaty among the major powers in 1839 declared Belgium to be a perpetually neutral state, and England secured a firmer buffer zone against France and eventually became its guarantor.

By the latter part of the nineteenth century, changes in Britain's external environment began to require new changes in the nature of her polity outputs. The expansion of Austria and Russia and the rapidly growing strength of Germany posed difficult problems that could no longer be handled by traditional strategies. Her difficulties were compounded by

---

[46] See *Ibid.*, pp. 139–41.

the growth of Japan and the United States as competing naval powers, and before long Germany was to claim a place in that category. Confronted by these developments, it was no longer easy for Britain to improvise her collective arrangements for intervention on the continent *after* the crises had been generated; now she had to choose between a policy of long-term isolation and a policy of committing herself to relatively permanent alliances in advance.[47] Her chief competitor on the mainland was no longer Spain or France, but Germany; and Russia and Italy were scheduled to play new roles in virtually all of the political performances. The map that was drawn by the Congress of Vienna was now out of date.

Toward the end of the century, Britain found herself outside the arena of continental politics—isolated from the Triple Alliance (Germany, Austria-Hungary, and Italy) and the Dual Alliance (France and Russia). Since the latter tended to be anti-British in orientation, the British leaders made some overtures to the members of the Triple Alliance only to discover that the price of admission was too high—that their support might help Germany to gain the upper hand in continental affairs.[48] Thus Britain found herself without any powerful friends within the regional system at a time when strong rivals were ignoring her vital interests. Under these circumstances, Britain found it necessary to change her traditional strategy. She not only began a search for advance alliances, but she turned to a power outside of the regional system (Strategy No. 5), entering into a security agreement with Japan in 1902. The alliance was readjusted in 1911 to take account of Britain's amicable relations with the United States; under the terms of the treaty, Britain would not be obligated to fight the Americans.

With her position strengthened, especially in Asia, as a result of the Japanese agreement, Britain proceeded to load additional weights to the balance in order to counteract Germany's growing power. She resolved some of her disagreements with France, becoming a party to the *entente cordiale* in 1904, and she reached an understanding with Russia three years later. The imperatives of the regional environment now required more advance preparation than ever before. The military leaders of Britain and France began to coordinate their plans in case a war with Germany would break out, agreeing that Britain would land more than 150,000 troops on the other side of the channel within a fortnight and that the French fleet would be stationed in the Mediterranean so that the British naval forces could be concentrated in the North Sea.[49]

World War I, which came when Germany invaded Belgium in violation of the treaty of 1839, brought additional changes to the external environment. The struggle on the continent required that Britain commit a large land force which for the first time had to be mobilized through conscription. Moreover, air power made the islands vulnerable to attack and, along with

[47] *Ibid.*, pp. 269–74.
[48] *Ibid.*, pp. 300–1.
[49] Lunt, *op. cit.*, p. 774.

submarines, made the fleet a less reliable instrument of security. And, eventually, an ally from outside the European region—the United States— was called upon to help tip the balance in favor of Britain and her partners.

In the interwar years, Britain was hopeful that a new balance of power could be created on the continent and that she could once again operate as the balancer. Her leaders continued to be wary of treaties that would commit their country to automatic guarantees, nor were they prepared to underwrite large-scale commitments within the framework of the League of Nations. In line with her traditional strategy, Britain was in the process of trying to build up a counterweight against the German threat when the invasion of Poland set off World War II.

When Britain emerged from World War II with her own resources seriously depleted and much of the continent in ruins, she was quick to observe that the rudimentary balance of power of the interwar years had given way to a power vacuum, and that Western Europe was vulnerable to attack by an armed and expanding Russia. She was aware that her islands could never be secure under a policy of isolation, and that the small size of her population and land area and her limited command of energy resources would not permit her to act as an effective counter-weight against Soviet power on her own. Indeed, she was soon to discover that the new methods of nuclear warfare—so necessary to adequate defense in the postwar world— would place an enormous strain upon her resources, and that her precarious financial condition would dictate a substantial reduction in her international commitments.

Facing such serious problems, Britain tightened her links with the United States—a partnership of strategic interdependence which had come to be recognized in both world wars. Looking to the United States for military support and for financial assistance to rehabilitate the economy of Western Europe, Britain was prepared to negotiate the Atlantic Pact (1949) and to restore a measure of equilibrium in Europe by calling upon the power of an ally from outside the region. Here again Britain was pursuing a policy of relying upon collective regional arrangements rather than depending upon an international organization—like the League or the United Nations —to enforce the peace, preferring to use the international facilities as a forum for the diplomatic mediation of disputes. When the Korean War broke out and there was some fear that the defenses of Western Europe might be weakened as a result of American commitments in the Far East, the British began to examine the possibility of having Germany contribute to continental defense. Although resentment against Germany still ran high among the British people, the burdensome cost of rearmament and the need for a larger reservoir of manpower, as well as more ground area for military maneuver, prompted the leaders of the islands to support German participation in the defense arrangement.[50] To quiet the fears of the French,

[50] C. M. Woodhouse, *British Foreign Policy since the Second World War* (London: Hutchinson, 1961), pp. 104–7.

Britain pledged herself to retain forces of specified strength on the continent.

Despite the drastic changes in her external environment since 1945 and the modification of her policy outputs to deal with them, Britain has attempted to hang on to certain features of her traditional policy toward continental affairs. This has been especially noticeable in her attitude toward the integration of Western Europe.[51] Although she recognized the need to rehabilitate the nations of Western Europe economically and was interested in a degree of integration, especially functional arrangements, to thwart Russia's expansionist ambitions, she has been reluctant to enter into permanent commitments of a political nature which might diminish her sovereignty and deprive her of flexibility to maneuver. The British have felt that they could afford neither to remain isolated from these momentous developments on the continent, nor to become too deeply involved in them. For a viable Western Union to be formed and then to fall under the control of a single great power represents to many British policy-makers a nineteenth-century threat in twentieth-century form. On most of the projects which have been undertaken, Britain has conceded a willingness to be "associated" but has not been eager to enter into full membership status, and she has usually employed her diplomatic skills to try to develop loose, consultative, nonpolitical types of associations.[52]

Thus, in recent decades, when her traditional means of military security have grown outmoded and the cost of new military strategies has been more than her resources could stand, Britain has been forced to rely more heavily upon a strong ally outside of the geographic region. At the same time, however, she has taken pains to employ the full force of her diplomatic resources in an effort to exert significant influence in alliance decisions and to act as a restraint upon the dominant power in the alliance. In her approach to the unity of Western Europe, too, she has engaged in diplomatic maneuvers in order to influence the course of events in a fashionable direction. In nonmilitary affairs on the continent, Britain is still reluctant to make permanent commitments. She desires to retain freedom of action and to minimize the threat of any single power or group of powers dominating the mainland in a way that would jeopardize her interests.

Japan

During the earlier stages of her history, Japan was overshadowed by China whose cultural superiority awed the Japanese. Japan as a nation, however, did not become security conscious until the thirteenth century, when the Mongols subdued China and then set their sights upon the Japanese archipelago. In 1274, Kublai Khan dispatched an army of 27,000 from

[51] For excellent discussions of this problem, see F. S. Northedge, *British Foreign Policy* (London: Allen & Unwin, 1962), pp. 132–67; Heisler, *op. cit.*

[52] Britain's initial support of EFTA instead of the Common Market illustrates this policy.

Korea to Japan, but just as the invasion gave promise of success a severe storm destroyed many of the Mongol vessels, forcing the invaders to withdraw.[53] The Mongols attempted a second invasion from Korea seven years later, this time with an estimated 140,000 men and 4,000 ships. Defense preparations enabled the Japanese to put up stronger resistance, and their embryo fleet, aided by another well-timed storm, sent the Mongols on the way back to Korea. These victories have long been a source of historical pride to the Japanese, but the invasions underscored their vulnerable geographic position.

When the Ming dynasty established itself in China in 1368, the Chinese leaders attempted to include Japan among their tributary states.[54] For some time the Japanese resisted these attempts, but early in the fifteenth century the Shogun Yoshimitsu accepted vassal status, largely for economic reasons, and this relationship continued until the middle of the sixteenth century. At various times, however, the Japanese were concerned about developments in Korea and the role that China was playing in the affairs of that country. Thus, the historical experience of Japan with the continent laid the foundation for the later expression of Japan's strategic interests in that area—that Korea was "a dagger pointed at her heart."

As was the case with Britain, Japan also had significant commercial and industrial interests on the continent. She, too, is a country not abundantly endowed with natural resources, and has traditionally made a good part of her way by importing raw materials, processing them, and exporting large supplies of finished and semi-finished products to continental and Western markets. At the height of Japan's power in the interwar period, 20 per cent of her imports came from Korea, Formosa, and China, while 45 per cent of her exports were shipped to these areas.[55]

In light of her insular position and her need for sources of supply and export markets to help pay for her imports, it is hardly surprising that Japan, like Britain, perceived a set of interests with respect to her mainland neighbors. By the time that Japan emerged from isolation to make her position felt in the international scene, her policy makers began to define the country's interests in these ways: (1) in view of Japan's vulnerable location, she needed to develop a position of strength in Northeast Asia; Korea was the dagger at her heart, and the handle of the dagger was in South Manchuria; (2) she had to have access to raw materials, and she needed to keep open her lines of communication; (3) since China was being divided into spheres of interest by Western powers, it was necessary for Japan to counteract their growing influence, especially the nations (like Russia and Germany)

[53] Delmer M. Brown, _Nationalism in Japan: An Introductory Historical Analysis_ (Berkeley: U. of California, 1955), pp. 25–29.

[54] _Ibid._, pp. 32–35.

[55] Jerome B. Cohen, "International Aspects of Japan's Economic Situation," in Council on Foreign Relations, _Japan between East and West_ (New York: Harper, 1957), p. 137. It is important to note that the bulk of Japan's import-export trade with the areas mentioned was carried out in territories that were then under her political control.

that had strategic leaseholds close to the archipelago; and (4) if China were to shake herself loose from the foreigners' control, then it was important to Japan that a more independent China not become strong enough to develop an "anti-Japanese" posture—a "friendly China was desirable, but a strong China was unthinkable."[56]

In pursuing these interests, Japan, too, had certain "givens," some of which were advantageous to her program of expansion and some of which placed restraints upon her. Among the advantages she enjoyed was the fact that her elite was from the warrior class which espoused a dominant disciplinary ethic, and they were able, until after the beginning of the twentieth century, to develop a national conscript army and a large navy without the restraint of effective representative institutions through which non-military groups might express displeasure. Under these circumstances, Japan was in a position to use an army, a navy, and diplomacy in attempting to realize her objectives. A "given" that Japanese decision makers had to take into account was the condition of China; the fact that several Western states had made inroads through the threat or use of force and that Russia was already a perceived danger in Northeast Asia narrowed Japan's range of alternatives if she were to be effective in the region of greatest concern to her. Another limiting factor for Japan was her position of subordination to the West. She had had a series of treaties imposed upon her, and, vulnerable to further demands by the West, she had to be concerned about the reaction of Western nations to any policies she might contemplate. In other words, the existence of Western nations in the region was a part of her external environment, and for a long time it placed restraints upon her polity outputs. Thus, Japan was faced with the task of asserting her independence according to the international norms of the time, namely, by becoming a military power strong enough to compete effectively in the field.[57]

When Japan emerged in 1868 from her long isolationist slumber under the Tokugawa, she perceived the intrusion of Western powers on the mainland as a threat to her security, as well as to her economic interests. Of particular concern to the Japanese was the status of Korea, which, under the domination of an expansionist power, would endanger their islands. Hence, for more than four decades Japan's political leaders were preoccupied with the task of turning Korea into a buffer zone (Strategy No. 1). In 1894–95, the samurai decision makers took their country to war against China in a bold challenge to Chinese authority on the Korean peninsula. As a result of this episode, China was eliminated as an effective competitor for the domination of Korea, but Japan and Russia were now poised for conflict,

[56] See Marius B. Jansen, *The Japanese and Sun Yat-sen* (Cambridge: Harvard U.P., 1954), p. 130.
[57] For an excellent overview of Japan's foreign policy, see Robert A. Scalapino, "The Foreign Policy of Modern Japan," in Roy C. Macridis (ed.), *Foreign Policy in World Politics* (Englewood Cliffs, N.J.: Prentice-Hall, 1962), pp. 225–66.

especially since Russia had managed to win control of the Liaotung Peninsula in South Manchuria.

Not content to remain within the confines of Manchuria, Russia began to intrude herself in Korean affairs. Although Japan offered a plan to define their respective spheres of interest in Northeast Asia, the negotiations were unsuccessful, and the two countries vied for the hegemony of Korea until the outbreak of war in 1904.[58] Japan was hostile to the idea that an ambitious state like Russia should control the dagger as well as the handle. At the meeting of the Imperial conference in June, 1903, the Japanese leaders concluded that "under no circumstances must any other nation be permitted to establish control over Korea. Instead, Japan must obviate such a possibility by seeking control over it herself."[59] A few months later, Japan decided to use force against Russia in order to achieve her objective.

Before taking such a drastic step, however, the Japanese were careful to test the reaction of Western powers which were sensitive to the dangers of Russian expansion in Asia.[60] While this represents an attempt by the Japanese to strip Russia of her potential allies in Europe, the real effort by Japan to rely upon an actor outside the regional system to strengthen her regional position came with the Anglo-Japanese Alliance (1902)—an arrangement that had the support of the United States.[61]

By her military victory Japan won recognition of her "paramount political, military, and economic interests" in Korea, as well as the transfer to her of the Russian concessions in the Liaotung Peninsula and of the South Manchurian Railway. The Japanese then proceeded to absorb Korea, placing her in colonial status in 1910, and to use their new colony as a launching platform for further inroads into the region, first to the northeast and later to the south.

Japan's policy toward China after 1900 is a complicated story, and the relationships between the two sets of government leaders, as well as the interactions between secret societies on both sides, provides exciting research opportunities for the investigation of linkage groups. In his excellent monograph, Professor Jansen has pointed out that there was a diversity of views in Japan concerning an appropriate policy toward China, and that many of the shifts in the Japanese official position can be explained by the pressures of factional groups upon the government.[62] An important factor,

---

[58] See Yale C. Maxon, *Control of Japanese Foreign Policy: A Study of Civilian-Military Rivalry, 1930–1945* (Berkeley: U. of California, 1957), p. 67. See also John A. White, *The Diplomacy of the Russo-Japanese War* (Princeton: Princeton U.P., 1964), pp. 76–131.

[59] These words are Professor White's (*op. cit.*, p. 81).

[60] For the details, see Chitoshi Yanaga, *Japan since Perry* (New York: McGraw-Hill, 1949), pp. 290–315; White, *op. cit.*, pp. 76–94.

[61] The Japanese decision makers were divided over the question of allying themselves with Britain, some, especially Ito Hirobumi, preferring to reach an agreement with Russia. An examination of this issue may provide information about linkage groups.

[62] *Op. cit., passim.*

too, was the role of the Japanese military leaders on the continent, who operated without adequate civilian controls and who forced the government's hand on a number of occasions.

Although extremist elements in Japan, who were linked with dissident groups in China in an effort to rid China of the Western imperialists, found support among some Japanese officials for a time, as Jansen indicates, the attitudes of the government tended to shift after the turn of the century, when Japan decided to play the imperialist game with full vigor. Although her policy was not always consistent or explicitly expressed and her leaders changed their strategy from time to time, it seems apparent that Japan was not interested in a strong China; if the country was to become united, it must be under a government that was favorably inclined toward Japan and willing to concede to her economic interests on the mainland.

Whether the Japanese consciously promoted disunity in China may be an open question which scholars can ponder, but there is little doubt that her policies were conducive to disunity, and that on at least one important occasion (The Twenty-One Demands) she threatened to support revolutionary groups against the existing government unless her demands were granted.[63] This represented a crude form of balance of power strategy in which Japan would act as the balancer (Strategy No. 3). Japan's support of the ephemeral warlord governments in the 1920s was in some respects another manifestation of the same policy.

By 1931, important changes in Japan's regional environment had become noticeable, and these were accompanied by different polity outputs. To begin with, there were fewer international restraints upon her decision makers. The naval limitation agreements, although placing limits upon portions of the Japanese fleet, also restricted the sea power of the United States and other Western nations, thus giving Japan virtual control of her home and adjacent waters. Then, too, the Anglo-Japanese Alliance was no longer in force, and Britain was unable to act as much of a constraining force. Hence, under the aegis of army leaders, Japan embarked upon a series of military ventures in China (Strategy No. 2). These actions aroused the displeasure of what were to become the Allied Powers, and before long Japan found herself isolated diplomatically. This was an undesirable situation in the view of some of her leaders, who were alarmed by Soviet military pressure along the contiguous frontier. There was a need for a strong ally outside the region so that Japan's position within the region could be reinforced (Strategy No. 3). By this time, however, the list of potential allies was a short one. The first step was taken in 1936 when Japan and Germany were drawn together in the Anti-Comintern Pact, an agreement that was strongly opposed in Japan by many industrial leaders and some political figures who desired a quick end to the Chinese war.[64]

---

[63] *Op. cit.*, p. 166.
[64] See Frank W. Iklé, *German-Japanese Relations, 1936–1940* (New York: Bookman Associates, 1956), pp. 36–53.

Although this arrangement gave Japan a little protection, she was not receptive to Hitler's proposal in March 1939 that they enter into a general alliance against all potential enemies. The Japanese were favorably disposed toward a limited alliance, but they were unwilling to limit their flexibility by committing themselves to go to war automatically against such nations as Britain and the United States. Japan's position in the region received a serious jolt a few months later when Hitler and Stalin reached their "friendly understanding." The concluding phase of Strategy No. 3 occurred in September, 1940 when, in the wake of the German military victories, Japan agreed to become a signatory to the Tripartite Pact, and in April, 1941, when they entered into a neutrality agreement with the Soviet Union. The aim of the pact with the USSR was to provide Japan with a measure of stability in the northern part of the region while she prosecuted the war farther to the south.

World War II and its aftermath pointed up the failure of Japan's strategy of conquest on the mainland and wrought havoc in her regional environment. Military defeat forced her back on to the four main islands and certain small islands which the victors were free to designate. She was now cut off from the sources of supply and markets in Korea, Formosa, and China, which had been her mainstay in the interwar years. Moreover, with the Russian occupation of Sakhalin and the Kuriles and Russia's new position in South Manchuria, with mainland China falling under Communist control, and with the emergence of a Communist regime in North Korea and a government extremely hostile to her in the south, Japan was faced with an array of unfriendly neighbors—a situation she had always sought to avoid. In the immediate postwar years, the Communist regimes in adjacent states were taking a "hard line" in their blasts against Japan, and the Sino-Soviet Pact (1950) was aimed at her and "any state which directly or indirectly would unite in any way with Japan in acts of aggression." Thus, the dagger pointed at Japan's heart was for the first time in many decades entirely in the hands of unfriendly powers. For the Communists to bring Japan within their bloc would indeed have been an impressive gain for them. While the lineup of continental forces posed a security threat, just as frightening to many Japanese was the possibility that their homeland might become a battleground between the Communist and non-Communist blocs, without Japan having very much to say about it.[65]

Besides the shifting lineup of forces in the external environment there were significant changes in Japan's domestic setting. Their military machine was dismantled, and for a time the "renunciation of war" clause in the new constitution made it difficult for the Japanese to establish a defense force. Moreover, the restructuring of political institutions provided the masses with more effective channels of representation, and political

---

[65] For a discussion of Japan's postwar position, see William J. Jorden, "Japan's Diplomacy between East and West," in Council on Foreign Relations, *op. cit.*, pp. 240–97.

leaders, who increasingly depended upon popular support to remain in office, were forced to pay greater heed to public opinion than they ever had in the past. For a variety of reasons, many Japanese citizens were reluctant to support rearmament programs; "neutralist" attitudes among the people were strong, while opposition to foreign military bases was growing increasingly vocal.

In the light of these changes in both the external and domestic environments, it is hardly surprising to note a lack of consistency in polity outputs. In the first place, in order to offset the strength of the alignment against her, Japan has had to rely upon a strong ally outside the region (the United States) for military and economic assistance, and the structure of Japanese trade soon began to reflect this dependence. On the other hand, Japanese leaders, who are sensitive to nationalist urgings, have a strong desire to assert their independence and to begin to play a mediatory role in the bloc struggles, all of which makes a more neutralist posture seem attractive. Moreover, since Japan by herself lacks the power to compete militarily with her continental neighbors, the Japanese leaders recognize that diplomacy is likely to be their most effective weapon in the foreseeable future. Hence, many of them have urged the "normalization of relations" with other countries, including the Communist areas, so that Japan will not remain isolated from her continental neighbors, and by fostering good relations she will be in a better position to reap economic and political advantages.

Ceylon

When Ceylon won independence in 1948, her leaders recalled that many times during the course of the island's history she had been subject to invasions from India. They recognized that when the British withdrew from South Asia, a power vacuum was created in the Indian Ocean, and they perceived that this situation, combined with Ceylon's proximity to India, posed a threat to the security of the new nation. While Ceylon enjoys close cultural ties with her neighbor on the mainland, and the postwar governments have shown no imperialist designs, the Ceylonese nevertheless feel uneasy about India, for in their view there is always the possibility that an unfriendly regime may rise to power in the future. After all, India has a massive population, a sizeable army, and a growing navy, and in most respects overshadows the island only a short distance away. These latent fears may have been reinforced from time to time by a few of India's spokesmen on foreign policy. For example, K. M. Panikkar, a colleague of Nehru and one-time Ambassador to China, has pointed out the strategic importance of the Indian Ocean to India.[66] "The Indian Ocean," he suggests, "must therefore remain truly Indian."[67] Similarly, prominent writers like

[66] *India and the Indian Ocean: An Essay on the Influence of Sea Power on Indian History* (London: Allen & Unwin, 1951).
[67] *Ibid.*, p. 84.

Ramachandra Rao have indicated that Ceylon is at the "heart center" of Indian defense in the region.[68]

In unguarded moments, some Ceylonese leaders have voiced their concern about Ceylon's vulnerable position with respect to the power configurations on the mainland. Speaking before the House of Representatives on September 7, 1954, the Prime Minister justified the existence of British bases on the island on the ground that there was a hypothetical possibility of Indian intrusions into Ceylon, particularly because of her interest in the naval base at Trincomalee.[69] As recently as 1963, R. G. Senanayake, an independent member of parliament, condemned India for accumulating American weapons and warned that Ceylon was in potential danger of invasion from the north.[70] Further Ceylonese concern over India arises from the fact that the Tamils, who constitute more than 10 per cent of the population and reside for the most part in the northern part of the island, have close cultural links with the Tamils in Madras, and the latter occasionally advocate the establishment of a separate state in South India which would embrace their kinfolk in Ceylon.[71] That the Ceylonese sense the potential danger of an expanding power dominating the continent is illustrated by their reaction to China during the Indo-Chinese border disputes.

In considering their relations with the continent, however, the Ceylonese, like the British and the Japanese, have more than just security interests at stake. About 35 per cent of the GNP takes the form of imports, while the proportion of exports to GNP is around 40 per cent.[72] Ceylon trades extensively with other members of the Commonwealth, but India is one of her best customers.

In light of her environmental circumstances, the Ceylonese have developed a set of perceived interests with respect to the continent, which in embryo form resembles Britain's: (1) Ceylon must retain her independence; she must take every precaution to avoid being swallowed up by a power that controls the mainland; and (2) since she must live by exporting, it is necessary for her to foster good relations with her neighbors and to develop markets wherever she can.

As she seeks to achieve these objectives, Ceylon is seriously restricted by a number of "givens:" (1) She lacks military capability of virtually any sort; her military expenditures are only a slight fraction of her total budget; she lacks a navy; and her light infantry of 3,000–4,000 men is really too light to be effective in the modern world; (2) with her short tenure as an independent state, she tends to lack experience in diplomatic dealings; and (3) the ordinary citizens are just growing accustomed to the independent operation of political institutions, as evidenced by the 1956 election, and they

[68] Cited in Wriggins, *op. cit.*, p. 398.
[69] Cited in M. S. Rajan, *India in World Affairs, 1954–1956* (Bombay: Asia Publishing House, 1964), p. 385.
[70] *Dawn*, July 18, 1963.
[71] Wriggins, *op. cit.*, pp. 399–403.
[72] See Phadnis, *op. cit.*, p. 189.

may soon be able to use the channels of representation to place restraints upon their policy makers, who thus far have had to rule in coalition.

In trying to make up for these deficiencies, the Ceylonese leaders from 1948 to 1956 called upon Britain, a strong ally outside the regional environment, to help secure her position in the Indian Ocean (Strategy No. 3). Under the defense arrangement, she permitted Britain to base military forces on the island to be used when it was in their mutual interest. Britain was also employed to train Ceylon's native forces and to assist her in diplomatic representation abroad, in countries where she had not established missions of her own. This collective arrangement, negotiated by Ceylonese leaders who had long enjoyed cordial relations with the British, came at a time when the international situation was unsettled; the Soviet Union was intransigent, later blocking Ceylon's admission to the United Nations; India was in turmoil; and the Communists were getting the upper hand in China.

During this early period, however, Ceylon began to make good use of her diplomatic resources by participating in Commonwealth discussions and by trying to gain prestige among Asian nations at the periodical conferences held in that region. At some of these conclaves, the Ceylonese spokesmen exhibited reluctance at having India become the prime mover in any type of Asian association. In 1952–53, when commodity prices turned against her in the world market, Ceylon demonstrated her flexibility in diplomatic affairs by entering into trade relations with Communist China, especially in the export of rubber and the importation of rice, although at this juncture she did not develop strong ties with Peking.

As we have already indicated, the Ceylonese terminated their security alliance with Britain in 1956, when conditions in the Indian Ocean had grown more stable, and she proclaimed a policy of nonalignment, as "dynamic neutralism." This left her free to play a more flexible role in international affairs, and on occasion to act as a mediator, as she attempted to do in the Indo-Chinese dispute of 1962. Under this type of policy she attempts to maintain good relations with the competing power blocs and to receive economic assistance from both sides—a polity output that, in the words of one expert,[73] can best be described as a "balance of aid."

Generalizations about Polity Outputs

This review of the foreign policies of three insular polities, in two cases over long time-periods, suggests that the three powers are deeply concerned about being dominated by a strong state or group of states on the continent. The polity outputs designed to prevent this domination fall into three major strategies. In the first type, the insular polity attempts to occupy sections of the mainland, especially in those areas that can be launching grounds for invasions against the island. A second strategy is for the polity

[73] Wriggins, *op. cit.*, p. 415.

to try to maintain a balance of power among the mainland polities, usually supporting the weakest coalition. The object of this strategy is to prevent any power or combination of powers from dominating the adjacent continent. In the third strategy, the insular polity calls upon allies from outside the region to support its position vis-à-vis continental polities.

The first of these alternatives, pursued by Britain during her early history and by Japan from the time she struggled to gain control of Korea until the end of World War II, is, in our view, probably doomed to failure. The resources of a combination of continental powers will always exceed those of the insular polity, and their supply lines will be easier to maintain. In the long run, the island power is likely to be forced off the continent.

The second alternative strategy—playing the role of the holder of the balance—has the greatest probability of success for the insular polity. It can be a successful strategy, however, only if a classical balance of power system prevails on the continent. This means that there must be at least four major actors on the continent. When this kind of system obtained on the European continent, British foreign policy scored its greatest successes. Although her foreign policy in the eighteenth and nineteenth centuries is taken as the classic example of a polity acting as the balancer, it is interesting to observe that Ceylon in the pre-colonial period pursued a somewhat similar policy with respect to the states in South India, typically seeking alliances with states to the north of her immediate neighbors. Her policy failed when these alliances were used to support adventures on the mainland.

Japan, during most of her history, has existed in a regional environment in which a strong power or a group of powers controlled most of the continent adjacent to her, and it was difficult for her to hold the balance of power. But attention should be called to the fact that in the chaotic period following the Chinese Revolution, Japan tried to prevent the development of a strong, unified polity in China, and on several occasions was pursuing a type of holder-of-the-balance strategy. The regional environment, however, did not have the characteristics necessary for this policy to be successful, and Japan turned back to a policy of continental conquest.

The holder of the balance role is so attractive to insular polities that they may tend to pursue it under circumstances that are unfavorable to success. British attempts to follow this strategy after World War I and Japanese actions in China during 1915–24 period serve to illustrate this point.

The third alternative—seeking allies from outside the region—has been pursued by Britain, Japan, and Ceylon. The special relationship which the British sought with the United States after World War II is one example of this, as is the Anglo-Japanese Alliance after the turn of the century. When the regional environment does not permit the insular polity to occupy the balancer role, this third strategy seems the most likely to produce a successful outcome. But it is important to note that such a strategy may have unanticipated systemic consequences, the most important of which is the internationalization of regional balances of power.

234

We should mention that these three alternative strategies demand different instruments of statecraft. An attempt to dominate the mainland, for example, requires both a strong army and a strong navy. To successfully pursue a holder-of-the-balance role requires a strong navy, army reserves that can be mobilized, and astute diplomacy. The third alternative places greater reliance on diplomacy and much less on military power.

These generalizations, of course, are purely speculative. But while we speculate, we might as well move a bit further out on the limb. If the fact of insularity is a significant determinant of polity outputs, we would expect the foreign policies of Ceylon and Madagascar—as well as those of Indonesia and the Philippines—to differ in certain definable ways from the foreign policies of other developing ex-colonial states. We would anticipate, for example, that these island countries would be wary of entering into binding political and economic relationships with nearby continental powers. Compared with other powers, they might be less enthusiastic about common markets and organizations for collective political action. At the same time, we would expect them to be more willing to accept, if not to seek, alliances with states lying outside the region, including arrangements with former colonial powers.

CONCLUSIONS

In keeping with the spirit of this paper, we must again warn the reader that our conclusions are to be regarded as tentative and speculative—hypotheses for investigation rather than established propositions in a valid theory.

In an earlier section of this paper, we suggested that the insular polity may differ from the continental polity in the processing of inputs from the international environment because: (1) it is likely to have more linkage groups, and (2) linkage groups are likely to be more strongly tied to the domestic system. If these two characteristics accord with reality, we would expect the insular polity: (1) to be more responsive to events in the international environment, and (2) to have polity outputs in response to international inputs that are more autonomously determined.

With regard to polity outputs, it is our tentative conclusion that the regional environment, particularly the systemic characteristics of the regional environment, will impose fairly tight constraints upon the range of viable foreign policies that insular polities can pursue. Attempts to dominate the continent militarily are probably doomed to failure in the long run. When the regional environment conforms to the model of the classic balance of power, the insular polity can effectively play a "holder" role. When the environment does not conform to the classical model, the insular polity will have to seek allies from outside the region, or fall under the control of major continental powers.

While these conclusions may be viewed as crude hypotheses for further refinement and subsequent testing, we would like to inject a note of caution. There is nothing in this chapter to suggest that it would be wise to treat geographical factors like insularity as *independent variables* in a theory which tries to account for the behavior that lies in the interface between domestic polities and international systems. For example, we have suggested that the fact of insularity may be important because it leads to more linkage groups and to greater integration. But these two factors in themselves could be used as independent variables in useful theories which show that the number of linkage groups and the degree of integration account for significant variation. These theories, however, would not have to be concerned with the question of why some polities have more linkage groups or a greater degree of integration; of greater concern is the *effect* of these factors as independent variables. A first step in the development of theories concerning the relationship between the domestic polity and the international system is to establish clearly what factors can be most efficaciously conceived of as interdependent, intervening, and dependent variables.

CHAPTER NINE

Noncontiguity and Political Integration*

Richard L. Merritt

FEW political thinkers have paid attention to the theoretical implications of territorial divisions within polities. Classical philosophers generally noted the issue only in passing. Aristotle, for instance, in commenting upon the identity of the state, allowed the possibility that "the territory and population of a state may be divided into two (or more) sections, with some of the population residing in one block of territory, and some of it in another," but went on to consider only "the case in which the whole population of a state resides in a single territory."[1] Despite the fact that each of the five permanent members of the United Nations Security Council, as well as every one of the world's ten most populous or ten wealthiest polities, is internally noncontiguous in important respects, writers of recent textbooks on international relations almost invariably ignore the question of contiguity in their

* I am indebted to Arlene Saxonhouse for preparing a first draft of portions of the section on Classical Greece and for able research assistance on problems of Pakistani politics; to John F. Oates for his counsel on the Greek section; and to the Yale Political Data Program for its support of this project.

[1] Aristotle, *Politics* (tr. Ernest Barker) (New York: Oxford U.P., 1962), III, iii, § 3–4, p. 98.

examination of the geographical bases of state and behavior power. When they do raise the issue it is only to speak of the importance of a "compact territorial entity" or "territorial cohesion," without specifying why, or even what these concepts mean. Or, from their discussions of the Polish Corridor, the Berlin Blockade, and Pakistan, the student is left to draw the easy inference that noncontiguity somehow has a deleterious effect. Monographs on individual countries frequently touch upon the consequences of non-contiguity, to be sure, but nowhere has there appeared a systematic attempt to assess their relevance for theories of national and international political systems. Even those studies that approach the issue are careful to point out that their assumptions have not been subjected to rigorous testing.[2]

What accounts for this cavalier treatment of such a common attribute of polities? For one thing, the term "noncontiguity" may be applied to several types of geographic situations, each of which may produce different effects. Key variables in distinguishing among such situations are (a) the distinctiveness of the noncontiguous regions, (b) the nature of the inter-vening space, and (c) the distance between the major components. Using these criteria it is possible to identify at least seven varieties of noncontiguity:

Insular noncontiguity

1. Offshore islands (United States-Block Island; People's Republic of China-Quemoy; Australia-Tasmania)

2. Island groups, identifiable as distinct entities (Japan; Hawaii; New Zealand; England-Ireland; Corsica-Sardinia during the Middle Ages)

3. Extended island groups, not identifiable as distinct entities or separated by vast distances (the former West Indian Federation; the Caroline Islands)

Noncontiguity with intervening bodies of water

4. Land masses separated by straits (Turkey; Denmark; Michigan; Chile)

---

[2] Philip E. Jacob and Henry Teune, "The Integrative Process: Guidelines for Analysis of the Bases of Political Community," in Philip E. Jacob and James V. Tos-cano (eds.), *The Integration of Political Communities* (Philadelphia: Lippincott, 1964), pp. 16–18; and Amitai Etzioni, *Political Unification: A Comparative Study of Leaders and Forces* (New York: Holt, 1965), pp. 27–30. For other relevant discussions of political integration, see Karl W. Deutsch, Sidney A. Burrell, Robert A. Kann, Maurice Lee, Jr., Martin Lichterman, Raymond E. Lindgren, Francis L. Loewenheim, and Richard W. Van Wagenen, *Political Community and the North Atlantic Area: International Organization in the Light of Historical Experience* (Princeton: Princeton U.P., 1957), and Ernst B. Haas, *The Uniting of Europe: Political, Social, and Economic Forces, 1950–1957* (Stanford: Stanford U.P., 1958). For my own views on community-building, see Richard L. Merritt, *Symbols of American Community, 1735–1775* (New Haven: Yale U.P., 1966).

5. Land masses separated by open seas (Anglo-America to 1776; France-Algeria to 1962; Denmark-Greenland-Faroe Islands)

Noncontiguity with intervening land masses

6. Territories with mutual access by sea routes (United States-Alaska; Germany-East Prussia, 1919–39; United Arab Republic, 1958–61; Pakistan)

7. Territories mutually accessible only by land routes passing through intervening territory or by air routes (Prussia in the early nineteenth century; West Berlin-Federal Republic of Germany; West Berlin-Steinstücken; Israel-Mt. Scopus enclave to 1967).

The above are all examples of actual or attempted noncontiguous polities; and it would not be difficult to add to the list a number of potential noncontiguous polities, such as a united Europe, as well as a whole range of former empires.

For another thing, the effects of noncontiguity have sometimes been confused with those of other circumstances, such as distance. Amitai Etzioni, for instance, argues that noncontiguity impedes processes of political integration by hindering the transportation of goods and people.[3] This may be true in some instances, but counter-examples are too plentiful to permit the assertion to stand unchallenged. Ancient Greeks, if we may judge from the cost and rapidity of travel and transport, very frequently found it easier to journey from one island to another than to go overland to an adjoining city-state. At current rates it is cheaper for a resident of Seattle to fly to Anchorage or Honolulu than to New York City; sending a parcel post package to Anchorage costs less than, and to Honolulu just the same as, the cost of sending a similar package to Washington, D.C. Etzioni lists as another effect of noncontiguity the limitations it imposes upon the movement of military units. As an example he cites the case of the United Arab Republic: "Nasser might have suppressed the 1961 Syrian secession, or it might not have occurred, if the Egyptian army had been free to interfere from its home bases, unhindered by the interposed states of Jordan and Israel."[4] In this regard he fails to make a helpful distinction between the transportation capabilities of a country and problems due solely to its noncontiguity. It is doubtful, given the nature of Egypt's transportation facilities, that Nasser could have moved more quickly to put down a serious armed revolt within Egypt itself—at the Sudanese border, perhaps, or in the Sinai peninsula. And, as Etzioni himself later points out, Nasser

[3] Etzioni, *Political Unification*, p. 29.
[4] *Loc. cit.*

could have applied more military force than he did had he deemed the value of suppressing the Syrian revolt worth its cost in other terms.[5]

What is more important, both for explaining the lack of concern with the effects of territorial noncontiguity and for understanding some of the confusion that has arisen about these effects, is that noncontiguity is but one in a larger class of discontinuities within polities. Among these are topographical discontinuities: mountain ranges dividing the Swiss into valley communities, mountains and deserts between the east and west coasts of Australia as well as the United States, swamplands and virtually impenetrable forests separating important regions in Latin American and Southeast Asian countries. In some cases it is easier for citizens to travel to another land than to reach their own hinterlands. Second, there may be population discontinuities. Going from the center of one city to that of a second city, the traveler sees a decline and then an increase in population density. If the over-all population of the region is low, or if the cities are fairly far apart, then it is possible that he will pass through almost uninhabited stretches of countryside. Good examples are central Australia and the Soviet Union east of the Urals. Third, communication discontinuities are important in some polities. These may stem from a technological level too low to cope with hindrances to communication due to topography or distance. Or, more frequently, social differentiation along cultural, linguistic, ethnic, religious, political, or even national lines may hamper the development of habits of communication within the polity. Still another type of discontinuity is economic: the existence of separate but more or less self-sufficient economic regions with little interchange among them. Any of these internal boundaries, if significant enough for the polity or if several of them are coincidental, may suffice to tear apart its fabric of unity. To estimate the consequences of territorial discontinuity (that is, noncontiguity), then, requires a consideration of the presence and role of other internal boundaries. Unhappily enough, social scientists to date have not brought their full range of resources to bear upon the theoretical issues of within-nation differences on a cross-national basis.[6] Indeed, in some respects we have not progressed much beyond the type of proposition asserted by Aristotle in the middle of the fourth century B.C.:

> . . . every difference is apt to create a division. The greatest
> division is perhaps that between virtue and vice; then there is
> the division between wealth and poverty; and there are also
> other divisions, some greater and some smaller, arising from
> other differences. Among these last we may count the division
> caused by difference of territory.[7]

---

[5] *Ibid.*, pp. 120–1.

[6] For some beginnings, see Part III, "Cross-National Comparisons of Within-Nation Differences," in Richard L. Merritt and Stein Rokkan (eds.), *Comparing Nations: The Use of Quantitative Data in Cross-National Research* (New Haven: Yale U.P., 1966), pp. 191–372.

[7] Aristotle, *Politics*, V, iii, § 16, p. 211.

One of the purposes of this paper is to explore—even at the risk of slighting other, and possibly more important, intra-polity discontinuities—the relevance of noncontiguity for the systematic study of politics.

The focus of the paper, within the framework of the linkages between the international systems and national systems, is political integration. In this context I shall use the term "integration" to refer both to relationships (e.g., sense of community, common identity, common interests, effective division of labor, complementary habits of, and facilities for, communication) and to structural qualities (e.g., common political institutions). I shall also consider integration as both a characteristic (the state of being integrated) and a process (the act of integration). In looking at the consequences of territorial discontinuities for political integration, my concern is threefold: (a) the part played by noncontiguity in the polity's communication system; (b) the contribution that elite groupings make to political community in noncontiguous polities; and (c) the impact of the international environment upon both these aspects. The case studies that I shall look at—woefully few in view of the number and kind of noncontiguous polities—include Greece in the Golden Age, the Anglo-American community of the eighteenth century, Pakistan, and the relationship between West Berlin and the Federal Republic of Germany.

REALITY AND THOUGHT IN ANCIENT GREECE

The center of Hellas was the Aegean Sea. Around it, like ants or frogs round a pond, to borrow Plato's metaphor,[8] lived the Greeks. To the west was the Balkan peninsula, the area we know as modern Greece, populated by Ionians, Dorians, Aeolians, and others who had migrated from the north beginning about two thousand years before the birth of Christ. Still further to the west city-states flourished in southern Italy and Sicily. On the eastern shores of the Aegean Greek colonists had established settlements, none of them, however, penetrating very deeply into the Lydian hinterlands. Crete may be taken as the southern boundary of the ancient Greek world, although it is also true that substantial colonies existed in North Africa at Naucratis and Cyrene. And across the surface of the Aegean itself were scattered like rough diamonds hundreds of inhabited islands. One of these, Delos, was thought by ancient Greeks to be the hub of the universe.

The sea being at the focal point of Hellenic life, it is difficult to overestimate its influence on the inhabitants of that world. Perhaps Thucydides exaggerated somewhat when he wrote that, in the time of his forebears, "there was no commerce, and no safe communication either by land or sea," a condition that left the Greek states "weak in themselves and lacking in

[8] Plato, *Phaedo* (tr. Hugh Tredennick), in Edith Hamilton and Huntington Cairns (eds.), *The Collected Dialogues of Plato, Including the Letters*, Bollingen Series LXXI (New York: Pantheon, 1961), 109a, p. 90.

communications with one another," able to take "no kind of collective action."[9] But it is difficult to argue with his conclusion that only when the sea became the major thoroughfare did Greece begin to flourish. "As Hellas became more powerful," he continued, "and as the importance of acquiring money became more and more evident, tyrannies were established in nearly all the cities, revenues increased, ship-building flourished and ambition turned toward sea power."[10] It was sea power, not land armies, that carried Greek civilization to distant shores.

In fact, travel by sea proved in many instances to be more efficient and cheaper than overland transportation. "In a long day," wrote Herodotus, "a vessel generally accomplishes about 70,000 fathoms, in the night 60,000," a total distance of about 148 miles.[11] Xenophon notes that the distance from Byzantium to Heraclea, roughly 138 miles, "is as far as a trireme galley can row in the longest day."[12] The jagged inland terrain, by way of contrast, made overland travel as tedious by foot as it was hazardous by horse (particularly since stirrups and saddles were later inventions). Only the broad, lowland plains of Thessaly welcomed the man on horseback; and it is not without good reason that of all the Greek city-states only Thessaly developed a cavalry useful for military service. An example from the realm of commerce makes clear the relative merits of transportation by land and by sea: "In 329 B.C. the transport of 100 tiles overland from Laciadae to Eleusis, a distance of about twelve miles, cost forty drachmae, i.e., 40 per cent of their purchase-price, while it cost but 6 2/3 drachmae, to bring them by sea from Corinth, three times as far."[13] Where harbors were built, and ships stood ready to sail, communication by sea was vastly superior to that by land routes.

The thalassocentric universe of ancient Greece allowed states to exist though internally separated by an arm of the sea. Clazomenae and its island were one example; Rhodes and its territory carved out of the southern Anatolian peninsula another. Although they had to defeat the Megarians twice to gain ultimate control of the island, Athenians incorporated "lovely Salamis" into their political community.[14] Records that have survived the

[9] Thucydides, *The Peloponnesian War* (tr. Rex Warner) (Baltimore: Penguin, 1954), I, ii–iii, pp. 13–14.

[10] *Ibid.*, I, xii, p. 20.

[11] Herodotus, *The Persian Wars* (tr. George Rawlinson) (New York: Modern Library, 1942), IV, lxxxvi, p. 325.

[12] Xenophon, *The Expedition of Cyrus* [*Anabasis*] (tr. Edward Spelman, in *The Whole Works of Xenophon*) (London: Jones & Co., 1831), VI, iv, § 2, p. 313.

[13] Marcus N. Tod, "The Economic Background of the Fifth Century," in J. B. Bury, S. A. Cook, and F. E. Adcock (eds.), *The Cambridge Ancient History*, Vol. V: *Athens, 478–401 B.C.* (New York: Macmillan, 1927), p. 20. These conditions may not have changed very much during the course of the last two and a half millenia. In 1966, second-class railway fare in Greece costs about 2.24 cents (U.S.) per mile, whereas a ship voyage in tourist class from the Piraeus to Lesbos (approximately 206 miles) costs about 1.44 cents per mile and to Mykonos (113 miles) 1.81 cents per mile.

[14] The phrase is Solon's, and appears in his *Elegiac I*, entitled "Salamis," in which he laments the Athenian loss of the island. "Let us go to Salamis," the last of the frag-

ages indicate that inhabitants of both areas enjoyed full privileges as Athenian citizens. To the south, Laconia united to itself the island of Cythera. Less clear, however, is the precise nature of their constitutional relationship. Thucydides referred to Cytherans variously as provincials not enjoying full rights of Spartiates (περίοικοι or *perioikoi*) and as colonists (απoικοι or *apoikoi*), making it appear to later scholars that the island's legal position "was in an intermediate position between a colony and part of the Lacedaemonian state."[15] Summarizing a number of case studies of colonial relationships in ancient Hellas, A. J. Graham writes:

> . . . there was no unequivocal evidence for sympolity or iso-
> polity between Thasos and her mother city or Thasos and her
> colonies. Some evidence, however, . . . suggested at least
> relations close enough to approach such shared citizenship.
> Miletus certainly had isopolity with her colonies of Olbia and
> Cyzicus. . . . Colonies close to the mother city sometimes
> occupied an ill-defined position between separate communities
> and outlying parts of the founding state. Various arrange-
> ments for citizens of one community to transfer to the other
> are found early, and are signs that even in early times there
> was no rigid barrier against opening the citizenship of one
> community to citizens of the other. . . .[16]

In still another type of situation, the migration of the stronger Phocians into Locrian territory divided that unhappy state into two distinct sectors. From a period before recorded history down into the fifth century B.C. at least, the eastern and western portions of Locris maintained a measure of political community, before falling prey to drift and ultimate disintegration through the gradual emergence of independent governments.[17]

The most curious aspect of the Greek example for our study is the fact that, despite the omnipresence of territorially discontinuous polities, ancient political writers were singularly unconcerned with the issue of noncontiguity. More interested in the polis as a community of individuals working to fulfill and achieve their highest nature through the pursuit of virtue, these philo-sophers were generally oblivious to the territorial requirements of the state, except insofar as they related to defense and the cultivation of moral excellence. Indeed, Plato's Athenian Stranger, in response to the Cretan

---

ment reads, "that we may do battle for the lovely island, and fling off our bitter dis-grace." Kathleen Freeman, *The Work and Life of Solon, With a Translation of his Poems* (Cardiff: U. of Wales Press Board; and London: Humphrey Milford, 1926), p. 207.

[15] A. J. Graham, *Colony and Mother City in Ancient Greece* (New York: Barnes & Noble, 1964), p. 96. Graham also notes that "The fact that Sparta sent a yearly governor and kept a garrison on the island also differentiates it from Laconia proper." *Ibid.*, pp. 95–96, with references.

[16] *Ibid.*, p. 117.

[17] See M. Cary, "Northern and Central Greece," in J. B. Bury, S. A. Cook, and F. E.

Clinias and the Spartan Megillus who argue that the object of state institutions is military, even places virtue as a whole or goodness above purely martial objectives.[18] For his part, were he creating a polity, the Athenian would prefer a site away from the sea, away from the need for a mighty protector and lawgivers who can combat the corruptive influences of the sea. "It is agreeable enough," he says,

> to have the sea at one's door in daily life, but, for all that, it is, in very truth, a briny and bitter neighbor. It fills the city with wholesale traffic and retail huckstering, breeds shifty and distrustful habits of soul, and so makes a society distrustful and unfriendly within itself as well as toward mankind at large.[19]

In his plan for such a polity, with its elaborate system of plots and administrative divisions of territory extending starlike from the central capital, Plato takes for granted unity of territory. But nowhere does he make it an explicit demand. Rather, in the Republic, he writes, "So long as the Polis grows without losing its unity, let it grow—but no further."[20] Unity, for Plato, has more to do with qualities of citizens than with the territory they inhabit.

The more empirical Aristotle, as we saw earlier, recognized that cities in the real world could well be divided territorially. He even thought that his division could have deleterious effects—but certainly none so devastating as those due to other, social rather than geographic, discontinuities. W. L. Newman's comment on Aristotle's position is illuminating:

> As an instance of some inhabitants dwelling on one site and others on another, we may take the διοίκισις [dioikisis] of Mantineia by the Lacedaemonians. . . . The question then is—will a change of this kind have destroyed the identity of the πόλις [polis]? Aristotle's somewhat curt answer is that the word πόλις is used in many different senses, and that it is easy to solve the question if that is borne in mind. His meaning perhaps is that if we take πόλις in the sense of "an aggregate of human beings or citizens" the Mantineans after the διοίκισις will still constitute the same State as before, but if we take it in the sense of "an aggregate of human beings or citizens gathered on a given site," they will no longer do so.[21]

Adcock (eds.), *The Cambridge Ancient History*, Vol. III: *The Assyrian Empire* (Cambridge: U.P., 1925), pp. 611–15.

[18] Plato, *Laws* (tr. A. E. Taylor), in Hamilton and Cairns (eds.), *The Collected Dialogues of Plato*, 705d–705e, pp. 1297–8.

[19] *Ibid.*, 704a–704b, p. 1297.

[20] As quoted in Victor Ehrenberg, *The Greek State* (New York: Barnes & Noble, 1960), p. 28. The quotation is from the *Republic*, 423b.

[21] W. L. Newman, *The Politics of Aristotle, With an Introduction, Two Prefatory Essays and Notes Critical and Explanatory* (Oxford: Clarendon Press, 1887–1902), iii, 149.

Aristotle writes that walls do not make the city.[22] It is not the existence of a clearly delineated piece of land, but the unity of citizens engaged in an active political life, partaking in the offices and enjoying the benefits of the city, that determines whether or not a polis exists.

If territorial unity is not the key to Aristotle's idea of the polis, however, the city-state's role of protector and commercial center nonetheless bears some territorial implications. The ideal city, he writes, "should be, so far as circumstances permit, a common center, linked to the sea as well as the land, and equally linked to the whole of the territory." And, "for the purpose of military activities it should be easy of egress for its inhabitants, but difficult to approach or blockade for any enemies."[23] Unity of territory would doubtless facilitate the city's performance of its commercial and military role—but here, it must be stressed, Aristotle is discussing the *ideal* state. The ordinary state such as he saw around him in the Greek world might not satisfy all these requirements perfectly; it might not even form a territorial unit. Yet it will remain a state, provided its citizens participate communally in the government of whatever territory the state includes.

What accounts for the divergence between Hellenic realities and philosophical concerns? The answer seems simple enough: Noncontiguous polities functioned effectively. Factors other than noncontiguity could fragment political communities more easily. A key one in Aristotle's discussion of revolution was "heterogeneity of stock," meaning simply the presence of large numbers of inhabitants of different cities.[24] Plato's Athenian Stranger phrased this well: "It is not such an easy matter for a state to deal with a settlement when it is not formed, like a swarm of bees, by the emigration of a single stock from a single territory, with friendly feeling on both sides. . . ."[25] Pericles himself found this out in the mid-fifth century B.C. when he sought to establish at Thurii in southern Italy a truly panhellenic colony. What began as a model community, with streets laid out by Hippodamos and a constitution prepared in part by Protagoras in the best manner of the day, and with a sizable population from all Greece, did not end so happily. "Within a year or two the new citizen-body had divided itself into tribes, according to the previous nationality of its members," and, a year later, "Herodotus and other prominent upholders of the new principles retired ruefully to Athens, leaving the city in the hands of the

[22] Aristotle, *Politics*, III, iii, § 5, p. 98.

[23] *Ibid.*, VII, xi, §§ 1–3, p. 307. Aristotle also comments that "A territory which can be easily surveyed is also a territory which can be easily defended," but, judging by his earlier discussion of "the optimum standard of population" as "the greatest surveyable number required for achieving a life of self-sufficiency," it seems clear enough that territorial continuity is not of moment here. *Ibid.*, VII, v, §§ 3–4, p. 293; and VII, iv, § 14, p. 292. I can find no evidence in Aristotle's writings to support Ehrenberg's assertion that "When Aristotle wants to discover the essential qualities of a Polis, he mentions as the first: community of place." Cf. Ehrenberg, *The Greek State*, p. 28.

[24] Aristotle, *Politics*, V, iii, § 11, p. 210.

[25] Plato, *Laws*, 708b, pp. 1299–1300.

anti-Athenian majority."[26] Factionalism within city-states also proved disruptive, as Nathan Marsh Pusey has so clearly demonstrated. As a motivating factor in Greek politics, primary allegiance to political clubs, or even self-interest, frequently overrode a secondary loyalty to the city-state.[27] Nor should the role of topographical discontinuities be ignored. High mountains in the rugged interior, which had made the Greeks turn to the sea, also divided polities: A mountain range in Boeotia split Phocis, the northern sector connected with the south only by a pass across the southern spur of Mount Parnassus; in the Peloponnesus, the Thyrian territory of Argos was cut off from the city by high mountains, as was the Lepreate territory of Elis. In a culture where overland communication was more problematic than that by sea, distance across land was a factor separating individual city-states. This usually occurred in cities that, some distance from the sea themselves, had separate ports to service their commercial and military needs. We think immediately of conflicts between Athens and the Piraeus in this regard, or between Colophon and her port at Notium, but the list of examples could be extended considerably. In view of the ethnic, factional, topographical, and other differences causing division in city-states, it is small wonder that Aristotle could not get overly upset by mere territorial noncontiguity!

In all this it should not be forgotten that noncontiguity also served a positive function in the pre-Alexandrian international system. That system, if we may speak of it as such, was primarily intrahellenic in extent and scope: It was an arena for competition and cooperation among the Greek city-states themselves.[28] In such an arena, allies were important. If ties of blood or common citizenship bound the allies together, then so much the better, for the alliance might withstand greater strains upon it. The dispersal of parts of a single city-state, or even a colonial relationship between two or more colonies, who were expected to assist one another in event of war, could provide territorial checks against the likelihood that any single polity could establish its hegemony.[29] Even so, it may be added, the stability in the international system of the quarrelling Greeks that such

---

[26] Alfred Zimmern, *The Greek Commonwealth: Politics & Economics in Fifth-Century Athens* (Oxford: Clarendon Press, 1931), pp. 374–5.

[27] Nathan Marsh Pusey, "Alcibiades and τὸ Φιλόπολι," in *Harvard Studies in Classical Philology: LI* (Cambridge: Harvard U.P., 1940), pp. 215–31.

[28] There were to be sure the "barbarians," such as the Persians, of whom the Greeks were so contemptuous. But, particularly after their defeat in the mid-fifth century B.C., the Persians' role in the international system was narrowly circumscribed: The Greeks called upon them to arbitrate disputes that they themselves could not resolve; or, more frequently, individual city-states would seek alliances with them to improve their own position in the arena of Greek power politics. On aspects of the Hellenic international system, see Adda B. Bozeman, *Politics and Culture in International History* (Princeton: Princeton U.P., 1960), pp. 57–89.

[29] For a discussion of such military (as well as commercial) ties, and of Thucydides' shock that a colony could turn against its mother city, see Graham, *Colony and Mother City in Ancient Greece.*

noncontiguity helped to maintain ultimately contributed to the downfall of the Hellenic world.[30]

ANGLO-AMERICA IN THE EIGHTEENTH CENTURY

More clearly than any other case study, perhaps, the disintegration of the Anglo-American community shows the potentialities of interplay between national and international systems. "The achievement of American independence," Samuel Flagg Bemis writes with his characteristic force, "depended on European diplomacy and international politics," but also on the "perspicacity" of American diplomats who, "to clinch their own country's advantages and independence, . . . took advantage of Europe's rivalries and distresses."[31] How this came about is one of the more fascinating stories that history has to tell.[32]

Europe of the eighteenth century was a classic balance of power system. Of a large number of more or less independent actors—absolute monarchies, monarchies with constitutional limitations, confederations, republics, principalities, and even duchies—only a handful really counted for the politics of the day, and they were sufficiently well-matched and flexible in their alignment policies that no single one of them could gain hegemony. Colonies and other non-European areas were little more than pawns in the game of European politics. They were to be used to enhance the welfare, and particularly the power positions in European politics, of the Great Powers. To consult with colonial leaders about their policy preferences or about such matters as war, territorial exchanges, or even taxation probably did not occur to the minds of statesmen in the mother country; but, at the same time, connivance by one colonial power with dissident factions in the colonies of other states was, if not formally endorsed, at least practiced when the proper occasion arose.

At the beginning of this century of revolution the Anglo-American

---

[30] The nature of the Greek conflict system, panhellenism, and the unity of Greeks toward the outside world are topics that, though extremely relevant as well as interesting, cannot be explored here. See the unpublished paper by Arlene Saxonhouse, "Political Community in Ancient Greece" (New Haven: Yale University, typescript, 1966).

[31] Samuel Flagg Bemis, *The Diplomacy of the American Revolution: The Foundations of American Diplomacy, 1775–1823* (New York: Appleton, 1935), pp. vii–viii. My later discussion of French diplomacy during the Revolutionary years is based principally upon Professor Bemis' account.

[32] A more complete discussion of this topic, as well as relevant data and documentation, may be found in Richard L. Merritt, "Systems and the Disintegration of Empires," *General Systems: Yearbook of the Society for General Systems Research, 1963*, VIII (Ann Arbor: Society for General Systems Research, 1964), pp. 91–103; Richard L. Merritt, "Distance and Interaction among Political Communities," *General Systems: Yearbook of the Society for General Systems Research, 1964*, IX (Ann Arbor: Society for General Systems Research, 1965), pp. 255–63; and Merritt, *Symbols of American Community*.

community fit rather closely the dominance-submission paradigm of mercantile colonialism. The colonies, separated from one another in many cases by stretches of uninhabited wilderness and more generally by inadequate means of intercolonial transportation and communication, depended quite heavily upon the mother country for trade, financial assistance, and defense. The colonists, predominantly English in origin, looked to England for their rewards and models of social behavior. And the British Crown, for its part, provided an organizational basis for profitable interaction between colony and mother country.

This is not to say, however, that no seeds of separation were growing in American soil. One of the more important of these seeds was the colonial reaction to diffident British policy. With what they thought was a resolution of the colonial issue after the imperial reorganization of 1680, the British returned to their own political problems and court intrigues, and to the complications of the power struggle in the European state system. Colonial leaders, always eager to advance their own interests and those of their fellow colonists, took advantage of a drifting Royal policy to carve out patterns of local self-government that varied widely from imperial precepts. In a series of small but fiercely fought struggles with representatives of the Crown, colonial assemblies attained increasing power to make political decisions over an ever wider range of activities.

Meanwhile the ecology of the colonists' perceptions of themselves, the mother country, and the Anglo-American empire as a whole was undergoing gradual but vital changes. Throughout the first half of the eighteenth century, as Great Britain was becoming less important in the lives of the colonists, the number and scope of intercolonial communication transactions of all sorts were growing. Illustrative of these developments is the fact that intercolonial trade grew at a much more rapid rate than did trade with England. Moreover, the expanding American population began to fill the gaps separating the urban clusters scattered along the Atlantic seaboard, creating a fairly continuous line of settlement from Penobscot Bay in the north to Savannah in the south. With the expansion of the population came the construction of postroads, ferries, and other means to facilitate intercolonial travel and communication. Intercolonial mobility, in turn, made increasingly possible the exchange of ideas among the colonists: Religious organizations and movements (such as the "Great Awakening") spread throughout America; the newspapers increased in number, size, and scope of coverage, drawing to an ever greater extent upon intercolonial news sources; colonial printers, such as Benjamin Franklin, and other colonial merchants built up extensive familial and business connections in several colonies; and lawyers, doctors, and men of science often traveled to or corresponded with their colleagues in other parts of America. Thus by the early 1760s, such contrary factors as regional jealousies and the inadequacy of intercolonial credit facilities notwithstanding, a culture had emerged that was intercolonial in extent and sufficiently different from the

British model to be termed American. What the colonists lacked was a consciousness of their community.

And yet even this was beginning to appear. An examination of symbol usage in the colonial press reveals a number of interesting trends in this respect: a shift in attention from European wars and other events outside the Anglo-American empire toward an interest in American news, with fairly constant interest in the mother country; in America, less concern with purely local events and more with those affecting the colonies as a whole; and, beginning in 1763, a greatly enhanced willingness to view all the American colonies as a single territorial unit and all the colonists as a single group of people. Moreover, in their symbol usage and political expression alike, the colonists were beginning to divide their loyalties. To an increasing extent, on the one hand, they were redirecting their ties of allegiance, away from Great Britain alone and toward the British imperial system. There was to be continued recognition of the superior role of Britain in the imperial system, but the relationship that the colonists perceived was one of *primus inter pares*, and not one of dominance and submission. On the other hand, however, there was a growing group loyalty among the colonists themselves, pointing the way to identification with an exclusively American political system. Throughout the 1760s and early 1770s the colonists found it increasingly possible and fruitful to work together—in the Stamp Act Congress of 1765, in the committees of correspondence, and eventually in the Continental Congress—as well as to think of themselves as a community of fate.

If the British government had perceived the Anglo-American empire in the same light as did the colonists, the result might have been the emergence of a British Commonwealth in the eighteenth century. But, as it turned out, the British chose to persist in their image of a mercantile imperial system and set about to bring their colonial relationships into line with this image. The Townshend Acts of 1767 reorganized the customs service in the colonies, providing for more effective enforcement of existing regulations, and instituting new duties on colonial imports from Britain. The duties themselves were to be used to pay the salaries of colonial governors, thereby relieving them from their dependence upon the assemblies. Instructions to colonial customs officers in 1769 revamped existing trade regulations and sought to close some of the loopholes that had proved so advantageous to colonial merchants. The British response to the Boston Tea Party of 1773 was a policy of toughness: The Port of Boston was closed; extensive changes in Massachusetts' form of government were ordered; provision was made for transporting criminals to England for trial. But the policy of toughness backfired. Although it conceivably could have had some effect in maintaining the imperial system during an earlier era, it merely succeeded in pushing the colonists to greater extremes in the 1770s.

Nor were the Americans ready to retreat from their minimum demands for dynamic imperialism. Expressions of the idea of Anglo-American coequality in decision making under the aegis of the crown appeared regularly throughout the early 1770s. In what might be termed the last major colonial effort to save the Anglo-American empire from disintegration, Joseph Galloway of Pennsylvania sought to reconcile the differing British and American perceptions by institutionalizing the American idea of empire within the British framework. In September of 1774 Galloway boldly suggested to the delegates of the first Continental Congress "That a British and American Legislature, for regulating the administration of the general affairs of America, be proposed and established in America, including all the . . . colonies; within and under which government, each colony shall retain its own internal police in all cases whatsoever."[33] But his efforts went for naught. By a majority of one vote the colonies rejected Galloway's plan of union, and in its place they drafted a series of far-reaching resolutions petitioning King George III and the English population to heed the light of colonial reason and calling upon the colonists to refrain from trading with the mother country should the so-called "coercive acts" not be repealed.

By the end of 1774 the idea of complete independence from Great Britain seems to have taken hold of the colonists' thinking. Anglo-American coequality under an imperial monarch was no longer an acceptable solution for the Americans who wanted even greater freedom of action in policy making. By this time it was doubtless too late to prevent an open break and its resulting bloodshed. It was at this time, too, in late 1774, that news of the pending conflict reached Paris.

The young King Louis XVI's new Minister of Foreign Affairs, Count Charles Gravier de Vergennes, saw in the Anglo-American strife a major opportunity to pursue the long-standing French policy of humiliating the English. After careful exploration of the situation, and particularly the colonists' willingness to fight and their chances of success, he concluded that French military and financial assistance would serve three ends:

> First, it will diminish the power of England, and increase in proportion that of France. Second, it will cause irreparable loss to English trade, while it will considerably extend ours. Third, it presents to us as very probable the recovery of a part of the possessions which the English have taken from us in America, such as the fisheries of Newfoundland and of the Gulf of St. Lawrence, Isle Royale, etc. We do not speak of Canada.[34]

On 2 May, 1776, fully two months before the Americans declared their independence of Great Britain, the King acted on Vergennes' advice, sending

---

[33] *Journals of the Continental Congress* (Ford edition), vol. I, pp. 49–51; cited in Samuel Eliot Morison (ed.), *Sources and Documents Illustrating the American Revolution, 1764–1788, and the Formation of the Federal Constitution* (2nd ed.; Oxford: Clarendon Press, 1929), p. 117.

[34] Cited in Bemis, *Diplomacy of the American Revolution*, p. 24.

to the colonists munitions in the value of a million *livres* (about $181,500). By prior arrangement the King's ally, Charles III of Spain, matched this loan.   Together these two monarchs, interested not in the cause of American independence so much as in a weakened England, contributed nine million dollars in loans and subsidies to the American cause before the war was over.

A period of watchful waiting ensued.   Finally, in December, 1777, after news of the staggering American victory at Saratoga reached Vergennes' ears, and fearful that the British might offer acceptable terms to Washington and the Continental Congress, he decided to commit France to a full-scaled alliance with America, contingent only on the outbreak of war between France and Britain.   Two treaties, the first of amity and commerce and the second of "conditioned and defensive alliance," were signed in February of the following year.   In June, through circumstances that are still uncertain, war broke out between France and Britain.   And, before long, all Europe had become embroiled in some way in this struggle, a struggle that appeared to bind inextricably the fate of the new nation with Europe's ancient quarrels.   French support of the Americans throughout the war and even into the negotiations for peace made this tie seem still firmer.   That the American plenipotentiaries in Paris in 1783 ultimately proved able to extricate their country from continued involvement in European politics was a stroke at once masterful and vital for the future of an independent United States of America.

THE FRAGILE UNITY OF PAKISTAN

It is sobering to think that, of the problems facing newborn Pakistan in 1947, its division into two wings separated by a thousand miles of hostile India was not the most serious.   Social disorder stalked the countryside, and conflict with India over issues of partition weakened a government already beset by factionalism and financial chaos.   Even to survive seemed difficult enough.   That Pakistan would surmount its territorial division to form a united polity was more than most outside observers dared to hope.

Almost every possible differentiation that can separate communities exists in Pakistan, and each of them coincides with the boundary of territorial discontinuity.   To oversimplify somewhat, in both terrain and style of life East Pakistan is part of Southeast Asia whereas West Pakistan is closer to the Middle Eastern pattern.   The former is a subtropical alluvial plain, characterized by heavy rainfall, a long season of heat and humidity, and by monsoons and occasional cyclones.   It is particularly suited to the production of jute and rice.   The rivers Ganges, Brahmaputra, and Meghna, together with their tributaries, chop the countryside into pockets of virtual isolation, making river launches the most convenient means of transportation in many instances.   The people themselves are shorter in stature and browner in color than their countrymen to the west.   Prior to independence

251

they comprised part of a larger Bengali culture (a fact that had both social and economic ramifications when Bengal elected to divide itself between India and Pakistan in 1947). The 1961 census revealed that about fifty-one million East Pakistani (54 per cent of the total population) were crowded into an area of 55,126 square miles (fifteen per cent of the total)—a population density of 922 persons per square mile, greater than that of any member of the United Nations. Of these, only one in twenty (5.2 per cent) lived in urban areas, a few more than one-sixth (17.6 per cent) were literate and more than five in six (84.1 per cent) of those ten years or older worked in agriculture. By way of contrast, forty-three million Baluchi, Brachui, Pathans, Punjabi, Bahawalpuri, Sindhi, and others live in the mountainous and semi-arid plains of West Pakistan. An average rainfall of less than twenty inches per annum makes the area, only twenty per cent of which is cultivable, largely dependent upon irrigation waters from the Indus. That river also provides West Pakistani with their hydroelectricity. The population, considerably more urbanized (22.5 per cent) but less literate (11.7 per cent) than the East Bengali, is distributed rather unevenly: Population density ranges from 724 persons per square mile in Lahore Division to seven in Kalat Division (that is, Baluchistan, which comprises almost twenty-four per cent of the total land mass of West Pakistan), and averages 138 persons per square mile for the province as a whole. About three in four West Pakistani (74.3 per cent) work in agriculture, producing primarily wheat but also cotton and other crops. The census of manufacturing industries gives us another indication of territorial disparities: 1,851 West Pakistan establishments employ 208 thousand workers and produce goods and byproducts valued at 2.2 billion Rupees (1959–60); in East Pakistan, 907 firms employing 103 thousand workers have an output valued at 1.1 million Rupees.[35] Taken as a whole, all these data indicate that there is little to wonder at in the comments of East or West Pakistani who say that they feel more at home in some foreign countries than in the other wing of their own![36]

Amid this diversity were two main ties of unity, of which religion has doubtless been the more important. It was common faith that brought the Muslim League together in the later years of colonial rule in India. And, when its leaders announced that an "Islamic Republic" would be created in a

[35] Data in this paragraph are from Mohammad Iqbal Choudhry and Mushtaq Ahmed Khan, *Pakistani Society: A Sociological Analysis* (Peshawar and Lahore: Noorsons, 1964), pp. 22, 31, 34; and Government of Pakistan, Central Statistical Office, *Statistical Pocket-Book of Pakistan, 1963* (Karachi: Manager of Publications, 1963), pp. 44–45.

[36] See the comments recorded by Karl von Vorys, *Political Development in Pakistan* (Princeton: Princeton U.P., 1965), pp. 154–6. For an indication of governmental efforts to reduce such feelings, see comments like that attributed to President Ayub Khan after a recent visit to East Pakistan during a session of the National Assembly: He reported having come "into contact with people from different walks of life and he could say with confidence that 'the people of East Pakistan have unbounded love for their brethren in West Pakistan and they will not hesitate to lay down their lives for the stability of Pakistan.'" *Dawn* (Karachi, 2 April, 1966), 1.

252

partitioned India, it was in the name of that faith that literally millions of Muslims in Bombay and Bangalore, in Mysore and Madras, packed up what they could carry and began their trek to the northwest. To this, however, must be added the fact that the percentage of Muslims was lower in the East (76.8 per cent) than in the West Wing (97.1 per cent): Of East Bengal's non-Muslims, 9.2 million (22.0 per cent) were Hindus.[37] The second tie of unity was a common memory of British colonial rule, of minority treatment in India with its Hindu majority, of the slaughters that attended the migrations in the late 1940s, and of the subsequent Indian posture toward Pakistan. But even here there were regional variations. Unlike the blood baths of the Punjab partition that so embittered West Pakistani, the partition of Bengal had proceeded rather smoothly. East Bengali (only 1.7 per cent of whom, by the way, were refugees as opposed to 19.1 per cent in West Pakistan)[38] had in their collective consciousness a positive memory of the cultural ties and economic interdependence that had bound them to West Bengal; moreover, in that same collective consciousness was a stinging memory of the slight they had felt in 1912 when the British moved their ruling capital from Bengali Calcutta to Delhi in the south. Nor did the Kashmir quarrel arouse so much emotion in East Pakistan as it did among those West Pakistani who had suffered more or less directly by its loss.

The early years of independence did little to weld the two areas of Pakistan into a single nation. On the one hand, many West Pakistani suspected that their countrymen to the east were at heart autonomists whose politics were falling increasingly under the influence of pro-Indian Hindu minorities. The amount of noise made by those few East Bengali who were in fact seeking autonomy did not help to allay such suspicions. Many East Pakistani, on the other hand, began to fear that the Central Government, located at Karachi and then Rawalpindi in the West, was trying to impose a new form of alien rule upon them. And withal the inability of the new state to fulfil the expectations of its citizens only exacerbated existing strains between the two regions.

A particularly crucial issue was the language question. Pakistan's founders made early moves to adopt Urdu as the national language—despite the fact that only 1.1 per cent of East Pakistani and 15.0 per cent of West Pakistani spoke it as their native tongue.[39] Their reasoning was partly religious, partly nationalistic: Not only was Urdu the closest of the

[37] Data reported in Stanley Maron, *A Survey of Pakistan Society* (Berkeley: U. of California, Human Relations Area Files, South Asia Project, 1956), pp. 57–58. By 1961 the percentage of Hindus and Scheduled Castes in East Pakistan had dropped to 18.4 per cent, and the percentage of Muslims had risen to 80.4 per cent; see Choudhry and Khan, *Pakistani Society*, p. 29.

[38] Only 701,000 (9.7 per cent) of the total number of 7,150,000 refugees had moved to East Pakistan; see *ibid.*, p. 13.

[39] Data from 1951 census, as reported in Donald N. Wilbur et al., *Pakistan: Its People, Its Society, Its Culture* (New Haven: HRAF Press, 1964), p. 424. Wilbur estimates that more than 15 million persons (16 per cent of Pakistan's total population in 1961) understood the variety of Urdu-Hindi (that is, Hindustani) spoken in the bazaar. *Ibid.*, p. 76.

many Pakistani languages to that used in the Holy Qur'an, but it would also serve to distinguish Pakistan linguistically from Hindi-speaking India. Dissent from the east, where 98 per cent of the population spoke Bengali, led to a postponement of the issue until 1952, when Prime Minister Khwaja Nazimuddin, himself a Bengali, urged the constitution drafters to establish Urdu as the state language. Student riots broke out immediately in Dacca. In less than a day the provincial assembly of East Pakistan adopted a resolution calling upon the Central Government to make Bengali a state language as well. In the face of this opposition, enhanced by popular reaction to the savage police repression of the student riots, Karachi leaders abandoned their resolve and decided to bury the language issue as rapidly as possible. This is not to say that "linguistic imperialism" as a divisive factor in Pakistani politics has disappeared. Official governmental doctrine and assurances notwithstanding, the comments of an occasional West Pakistani politician or interpretations of Central Government attitudes by Dacca journalists periodically jog the sensitivities of East Pakistani.[40]

Another grievance of East Pakistani is economic discrimination. And it is true that, in the early years at least, the Central Government did slight the East Wing. From 1947 to 1955 the total amount of economic benefits it extended to West Pakistan was more than triple the amount that went to East Pakistan.[41] Moreover, the Central Government took a number of measures in the national interest that worked particular hardships upon East Pakistani: the continued hostility to India which damaged normal inter-Bengali trade and communication patterns; the failure to devalue the Pakistani Rupee after the Indians did so in 1949, which led to serious dislocations in the jute-exporting industry of East Pakistan; and important restrictions that made East Pakistani more dependent upon costlier sources of foodstuff and other vital goods from West Pakistan.[42] In the last decade,

[40] On the earlier phases of the language strife, see Keith Callard, *Pakistan: A Political Study* (New York: Macmillan, 1957), pp. 180–3. By now, universities have begun to implement plans to replace English as the language of instruction with Bengali in the East and Urdu in the West Wing. It may be added that not all is proceeding smoothly. In early January, 1966, the Central Ministry of Education issued a directive urging universities not to introduce these languages for the winter examinations. This directive was received after universities in the West had already held their examinations in Urdu, but before examinations in Bengali at the University of Dacca were scheduled. The article in the consistently autonomist *Pakistan Observer* discussing the directive clearly implied that this kind of duplicity was typical of the Central Government's attitude toward East Pakistan, and went on to applaud the decision of the Academic Council of Dacca University to use Bengali in the examinations anyway. *Pakistan Observer* (Dacca, 5 January, 1966), 1.

[41] Data from Richard D. Lambert, "Factors in Bengali Regionalism in Pakistan," *Far Eastern Survey*, XXVIII, 4 (April, 1959), 53.

[42] A related complaint was that hard currencies earned by East Pakistan's exports of jute were being used to improve the position of West Pakistani. For a general treatment of the trade question, see M. Akhlaqur Rahman, *Partition, Integration, Economic Growth, and Interregional Trade: A Study of Interwing Trade in Pakistan, 1948–1959* (Karachi: Institute of Development Economics, 1963). Other economic grievances are discussed in Lambert, "Factors in Bengali Regionalism in Pakistan," pp. 49–58.

however, the Central Government has sought to eliminate economic disparities between the two wings. The rate of growth both in national income and in per capita income was accelerated by the Second Five-Year Plan (1960–65) somewhat more rapidly in East than in West Pakistan; the Third Five-Year Plan (1965–70) foresees still greater investment in the East than in the West Wing.[43] And national leaders seem to take every opportunity to assure East Pakistani that they are taking further steps to reduce any economic disparities between the two provinces.[44] Per capita income in East Pakistan (273 Rs. = $57.33) in 1963–64 still ran about 25 per cent less than that in West Pakistan (363 Rs. = $76.23) and, at current growth rates of population and income, the East Pakistani's income in 1981 (498 Rs.) will still be considerably less than that of the West Pakistani (569 Rs.).[45] It will be some while, then, before the Central Government will be able to eradicate economic disparities completely.

East Pakistani have also felt that they have not been taken enough into the councils of government. The extent of disparities in the recruitment of elites is suggested in data published by the quasi-official newspaper *Dawn* in 1956 (Table 9.1). One response to complaints on this score was to step up recruitment in the East, sometimes through preferential treatment. For instance, in the selection of civil servants, the top 20 per cent are picked strictly according to merit (as indicated by examination scores), with the remaining 80 per cent chosen each year on a basis of parity between East and West Pakistan.[46] Then, too, the federal structure of the Central Government has built-in as well as tacit checks to ensure a measure of parity. Article 16 of the Principles of Policy in the 1962 Constitution explicitly

[43] Government of Pakistan, Planning Commission, *Outline of the Third Pive-Year Plan (1965–1970)* (Karachi, 1964), pp. 11 and 38. See also the Central Industries Minister's speech introducing the Comprehensive Industrial Investment Schedule for the Third Five-Year Plan, in "Positive Steps to End Disparity: Investment Opportunities Extended in E. Pakistan," *Dawn* (Karachi, 5 April, 1966), 1.

[44] See the report of Ayub's speech before the East Pakistan Muslim League Council in Dacca on 18 April, 1966, reported in several articles in *Dawn* (Karachi, 19 April, 1966), 1.

[45] Population data are from Choudhry and Khan, *Pakistani Society*, p. 19; income data from Government of Pakistan, Planning Commission, *Outline of the Third Five-Year Plan*, p. 11. Estimates for the 1981 population are based on growth rates from 1951 to 1961; those for national income on 1959–60 to 1963–64—a period of maximum growth for East Pakistan. Note that the projections of the 1981 population (74.1 million in East Pakistan and 69.7 million in West Pakistan) differ somewhat from those made by W. Parker Mauldin and Sultan Shah Hashmi, "Illustrative Estimates and Projections of the Population of Pakistan, 1951 to 1991," in M. L. Qureshi (ed.), *Population Growth and Economic Development, With Special Reference to Pakistan* (Karachi: Institute of Development Economics, 1960), pp. 83–84.

[46] On the Pakistani civil service, see Ralph Braibanti, "Public Bureaucracy and Judiciary in Pakistan," in Joseph LaPalombara (ed.), *Bureaucracy and Political Development* (Princeton: Princeton U.P., 1963), pp. 360–440; and Henry Frank Goodnow, *The Civil Service of Pakistan: Bureaucracy in a New Nation* (New Haven and London: Yale U.P., 1964). More recently an Indian publication noted: "In Pakistan's Foreign Service, 60 per cent of the jobs are held by Punjabis, about 30 per cent by Sindhis and the remaining 10 per cent are shared by Pathans, Baluchis and Bengalis." *Asian Recorder*, XI, 48 (26 November–2 December, 1965), 6798.

Table 9.1—Recruitment of Elites from East and West Pakistan, 1956

	From West Pakistan	From East Pakistan
A. Civil Service Elites		
Secretaries	19	0
Joint secretaries	38	3
Deputy secretaries	123	10
Under secretaries	510	38
TOTAL	690	51
B. Military Elites		
Lieutenant generals	3	0
Major generals	20	0
Brigadiers	34	1
Colonels	49	1
Lieutenant colonels	198	2
Majors	590	10
Air force personnel	640	60
Naval officers	593	7
TOTAL	2127	81

SOURCE: *Dawn* (Karachi), 18 January, 1956, p. 1; reported in Richard D. Lambert, "Factors in Bengali Regionalism in Pakistan," *Far Eastern Survey*, XXVIII, 4 (April, 1959), 54.

asserts that "parity between the Provinces in all spheres of the Central Government should, as nearly as is practicable, be achieved." The Constitution also specifies that Dacca will be "a second capital" and that the "principal seat of the National Assembly shall be at Dacca" (Articles 211.3, 211.5). Early in 1966 President Ayub Khan neatly summed up the gist of the constitutional arrangements when, according to a newspaper report, he pointed out that

> under the present Constitution the two provincial Governments had been given complete authority in all fields including judiciary, executive, industry, commerce, education and communications, so that both wings of the country could develop according to their own requirement. It was as a result of "meaningful and purposeful provincial autonomy" that both parts of the country had achieved an enviable progress.[47]

[47] *Dawn* (Karachi, 2 April, 1966), p. 1. The report continues: "He added only such advisory functions had been left with the Centre as were necessary to maintain national unity and strengthen the nation."

Not only do both East and West Pakistan have an equal number of representatives in the National Assembly,[48] but, by common agreement, the Speaker of the Assembly, who replaces the President both in the case of temporary absences and that of a permanent vacancy through death or removal, shall be from a different province than is the President. Added to all this is the extreme care that the Central Government has exercised in recent years to ensure that East Pakistani leaders are consulted (e.g., through inclusion in national cabinets) and to assure the population of its role in the nation.

A final item of major importance in the list of East Pakistani grievances is defense. Almost from the outset, when the army was engaged in struggles along the borders of West Pakistan, East Pakistani have expressed concern that their own province was not being properly defended. The most significant early manifestation of this fear came in the 1954 provincial elections in East Pakistan. The United Front, a temporary alliance in which the Awami League predominated, offered an electoral program of twenty-one points. The nineteenth of these read:

> East Bengal will get complete autonomy.... Our defense, currency and foreign policy will be joint subjects with the Center. Army headquarters will be in West Pakistan and naval headquarters are to be set up in East Pakistan, so that this wing can become strong enough to safeguard her freedom.[49]

That the United Front won a smashing victory gave considerable legitimacy to its program—and warning to the Central Government of the mood of East Pakistani.

The defense issue came to a head during the conflicts with India in 1965. At a time when there was a serious possibility of Indian incursions into East Pakistan, the army had but one division to defend the entire province. Although no invasion took place, the mere thought of its consequences for a virtually defenseless East Pakistan, surrounded as it is on three sides by India, sent shivers down the spine of many an East Pakistani politician.[50] Gamiruddin Pradhan, Senior Deputy Speaker of the Provincial Assembly and ranking member of the Government Party, voiced a sentiment "echoed again and again" by members of the Opposition and Government parties

[48] The question of representation was thorny in the early years. West Pakistani, on the basis of their greater territory, made claims for a majority of seats in any parliament; and the East Pakistani, with their larger population, wanted representation proportionate to the number of people residing in each wing. The first Constituent Assembly, representative of population units, had 44 East Pakistani (56 per cent) among its 79 members.

[49] Listed in Richard L. Park, "East Bengal: Pakistan's Troubled Province," *Far Eastern Survey*, XXIII, 5 (May, 1954), 72–73.

[50] An East Pakistani told a *New York Times* correspondent: "While West Pakistan was using its American tanks and American planes to fight India for the precious five million Kashmiris, 65 million Bengalis were left to fight with their bare hands if the Indians had attacked us." See Jacques Nevard, "Ayub's Rule is Combated by the East Pakistanis," *The New York Times* (21 April, 1966), 5.

alike: On the floor of the Assembly he argued that the seventeen-day war in September had taught the East Pakistani many lessons. "One of these," he said, is that "strategically East Pakistan is a separate region and that it must be made self-sufficient in defence."[51] Early spring of 1966 found the Awami League again coming out with a program of action, the sixth point of which demanded that "A militia or paramilitary force should be established in East Pakistan."[52] To all this the Central Government could only respond with statements of good intentions to improve the defenses of East Pakistan and, to date, with a few limited steps. Above all, the Government has sought to stress the fact that, in the words of President Ayub, "the country's defense is inseparable and can best be pursued through national unity."[53]

Varying reactions to the Tashkent agreement are also interesting in this regard. The agreement, reached by Ayub Khan and Lal Bahadur Shastri through mediation by Aleksei N. Kosygin, terminated the war on the basis of the status quo ante bellum and made various provisions to facilitate Indian-Pakistani discussions of their differences. In West Pakistan mobs, in some cases led by prominent politicians, rioted, urging the government to repudiate the pact since it did not resolve the Kashmir issue; and indeed Ayub himself soon let it be known that Tashkent did not mean that Pakistan was relinquishing either its claim to the territory or its hostility toward India. East Pakistani, however, were relieved that the immediate conflict was ended. Dissatisfaction arose only when it began to appear that the Central Government would not honor its pledge to improve trade and other relations with India, for this meant that the East Pakistani economy, already hard hit by the interruption of relations with West Bengal, would continue to suffer.[54]

[51] "Members Demand Self-Sufficiency in Defence for E. Wing," *The Pakistan Observer* (Dacca, 7 December, 1965), 1.

[52] Cited in Nevard, "Ayub's Rule is Combated by the East Pakistanis," p. 5. In a speech during the last week of March, 1966, Sheikh Mujibur Rahman, leader of the Awami League, declaimed: "The defence and security of East Pakistan could never depend either on West Pakistan or on a foreign country," Cited in *The Asian Recorder*, XII, 25 (18–24 June, 1966), 7145, with references to *The Statesman* and *The Times of India.*

[53] Cited in *Dawn* (Karachi, 20 April, 1966), 1. The same report also noted that two new ordnance factories would be set up in East Pakistan. More recently *The Times of India* (New Delhi) has been reporting, on the basis of "authoritative sources in Dacca," that China and Pakistan have agreed to make the defense of the East Wing the joint responsibility of both countries. See *The Asian Recorder*, XII, 25 (18–24 June, 1966), 7146; and XII, 27 (2–8 July, 1966), 7167–8. Foreign Minister Zulfikar Ali Bhutto denied these reports.

[54] Asked in the spring of 1963 what the most important problem facing Pakistan was, only 7 per cent of a sample of students at the University of Dacca responded "Pakistan-India relations" or "the Kashmir problem," whereas an average of 28 per cent of the students at the West Pakistani universities of Karachi (20 per cent), Lahore (25 per cent), and Peshawar (39 per cent) gave these answers. See United States Information Agency, Research and Reference Service, "Aspirations and Attitudes of University Students in Pakistan," Report R-218-63 (12 December, 1963), 14. On the East Pakistani attitude toward Tashkent and the resumption of trade, see "Storm Signals in East Pakistan," *The Times* (London, 9 June, 1966), 15.

The logical question at this point, given the concatenation of auto-nomist movements, mutual suspicions between the wings, disappointing levels of economic development, and a short but economically disastrous war with India, is: What holds Pakistan together? What keeps the East Pakistani from secession? On the one hand, disaffection in East Pakistan does not seem serious enough to support any intensive drive toward auto-nomy. The province's most prominent political leaders, with but few exceptions, have seen their rewards lying in a united Pakistan. Students at the University of Dacca see social and economic problems—not those of national unity—to be the most important facing Pakistan today.[55] And the voting population, as indicated by the Provincial Assembly elections in May, 1965, seems unwilling to support parties calling for autonomy.[56] This is not to say that any of these groups wholeheartedly supports the Central Government. Far from it! They have been among the first to bridle at real or imagined encroachments upon the "rights" of East Pakistani. But an active sense of what their own interests are, and how best to protect them, does not necessarily constitute sedition. On its part, as we have seen, the Central Government has made serious efforts to meet the legitimate demands of East Pakistani, thereby reducing the pockets of resentment that remain.

Such efforts have been particularly noticeable in the development of communications between the two wings. Before the partition of India, both areas were closer in their communication ties to neighboring areas in what remained India than to each other. Facilities for interwing com-munication were almost totally absent. Not until 29 December, 1962, was there a direct radio-telephone link between Dacca and Rawalpindi; ten months later the Executive Committee of the National Economic Council approved a radio-telegraph and radio-telephone link between the two wings via a relay station in Khatmandu in Nepal; and a submarine cable around India may provide additional facilities in the future.[57] Telephone

[55] United States Information Agency, Research and Reference Service, "Aspira-tions and Attitudes of University Students in Pakistan," p. 14. Of the sample at the University of Dacca, 39 per cent responded "Development of economic conditions" or "Food problem," 13 per cent said "Lack of education," and 7 per cent listed "Over-population"—a total of 59 per cent. Less than half that percentage fell under the rubrics "National integrity, interior political crises, lack of national character" (21 per cent) or "Civilization of different provinces and people, lack of coordination between West and East Pakistan, difference in culture" (7 per cent). By way of contrast, 49 per cent of West Pakistani students saw social and economic problems as the most important ones, and 25 per cent reported that national unity was most important.

[56] Of those who announced beforehand the party to which they would adhere, the Basic Democracies elected 69 Muslim League candidates, 20 from the Opposition Group (including six parties, among them the Awami League), and 58 "Independents." When the Provincial Assembly gathered, all but 17 of the Independents switched over to the Muslim League. The ultimate composition of the Assembly was 118 members of the Muslim League (76.1 per cent), 20 members of the Opposition Group (12.9 per cent), and 17 Independents (11.0 per cent).

[57] *The Asian Recorder*, IX, 2 (8–14 January, 1963), 4987; IX, 51 (17–23 December, 1963), 5570; IX, 29 (16–22 July, 1963), 5311. The cable was expected to cost $98 million.

calls between East and West Pakistan, averaging 450 per day in 1960–61, were expected to triple by the end of the Second Five-Year Plan in 1965.[58] Transportation has also proved a problem. It is possible to fly across India (a service that the tense months of 1965 and early 1966 interrupted): Sixteen flights per week leave Dacca for Karachi and vice-versa, twelve to and from Lahore. Despite government subsidies that reduce the price of such tickets by 41 per cent, one-way economy-class fare still costs an amount equivalent to 92 per cent of the average annual per capita income in East Pakistan.[59] Sailing from East to West around India is not popular, because of time and cost. In 1963–64, fifteen thousand persons undertook the week-long journey eastward, twenty thousand westward.[60] It is still possible, in principle at least, to take a train across India, but passport, visa, and customs complications make this all but impossible; agreements reached with India in 1963 to simplify these procedures came to naught.[61] Nor is east-west commerce a simple matter. At the time of independence, Pakistan possessed a total of three old ships with a gross tonnage of 18,000 tons. Through emphasis on constructing a shipping industry, no less than efforts to build up port facilities, the Central Government had developed by mid-1966 a fleet of 147 ships with a gross tonnage of 434,093 tons.[62] But the ratio of interwing to foreign trade has not risen commensurately. Total foreign trade (exports plus imports) rose from $727 million in 1953–54 to $1,407 million in 1963–64, and interwing trade (including reshipment of foreign merchandise) from $163 million to $294 million over the same period —but the ratio of interwing to foreign trade dropped from .22 to .21.[63] The Government has in effect subsidized this interwing trade, stepping in to reduce rates in both 1956 and 1964. In the latter year, "to assist in the maintenance of a reasonable freight level, incentives such as duty free fuel and increased rate of bonus earnings (30 per cent as against 20 per cent) were afforded."[64] Perhaps the Government has not done everything possible to facilitate interwing contacts but, in recent years at least, it has not been idle.

---

[58] *Ibid.*, VIII, 7 (12-18 February, 1963), 4425.

[59] The one-way economy fare from Dacca to Karachi is normally $89.50, but for purely domestic service it is reduced to $52.50. These flights, by the way, carry a maximum of 2,926 passengers per week each way if the planes are completely filled; I have no information, however, on the proportion of seats occupied by Pakistani. *Official Airline Guide: World Wide Timetable Edition*, XXVIII, 8 (May, 1967), part I, pp. B-90, C-913.

[60] *Pakistan—1963–64* (Karachi: Pakistan Publications, n.d.), p. 100.

[61] The Central Government attributes this to a failure by India to ratify the agreement, *ibid.*, p. 86.

[62] *Ibid.*, p. 99; holdings on 1 July, 1966, from *Lloyd's Register of Shipping Statistical Tables 1966* (London: Lloyd's, 1966), p. 3.

[63] Central Statistical Office, Economic Affairs Division, *Pakistan Statistical Yearbook, 1964* (Karachi: Government of Pakistan Press, 1966), pp. 171, 247. More generally, see Rahman, *Partition, Integration, Economic Growth, and Interregional Trade*, pp 99–100.

[64] *Pakistan—1963–64*, p. 100.

On the other hand, alternatives to a continuation of the status quo do not seem very attractive. Independence would leave a defenseless East Bengal in a hostile environment, with no recourse for protection to the army in the western province. Moreover, East Bengal's reliance upon a single crop for its economic well-being would leave the independent country at the mercy of fluctuations in world markets and prices (as well as the possibility that, someday, a substitute for jute products will be found that will ruin its economy entirely). Nor does Bengali regionalism seem to be more realistic. Even if the West Bengali were willing to break away from India, something that they were unwilling to do in 1947, there is no guarantee that India would sit idly by. Indian efforts to retain West Bengal might even result in its absorption of East Bengal as well. Well, what about union with India? There are probably few East Pakistani who would endorse this proposal. Whatever its disadvantages, union with West Pakistan on a basis of parity leaves the East Pakistani better off than they would be in a union with India. As a Muslim minority of fifty-one million in a Hindu country that can ill afford to feed its own population of 499 million,[65] the East Bengali could hardly expect to receive the consideration shown them by the Central Government in Rawalpindi.

These two facts, together with ties of Islam and common memory, have been sufficient to maintain Pakistan's unity for almost two decades. The future of this union seems less certain. "We are fed up with being treated as an occupied province," a Bengali politician recently told the *New York Times* correspondent in Dacca; "We were exploited for 200 years by the British before independence, and for the eighteen years since independence we've been exploited by West Pakistan."[66]

WEST BERLIN AND WEST GERMANY: NONCONTIGUITY IN A SPOTLIGHT OF ATTENTION

In the half decade after September of 1944, when the representatives of the Big Three met at Lancaster House in London to discuss the division of Germany and Berlin into zones of occupation, the community of Berlin experienced three successive waves of disruption and disintegration. The first of these stemmed from wartime destruction and postwar dismantling for reparations. Temporary in nature, it affected the whole of Berlin, and

---

[65] Mid-1966 estimate.

[66] Cited in Nevard, "Ayub's Rule is Combated by the East Pakistanis," p. 5. More recently, the Central Government has taken action to silence the opposition. An order dated 9 May, 1966, gave the Government power to stop the publication of newspapers under the Defence of Pakistan Rules; on 17 June the Government confiscated the printing press of the Awami League's newspaper *Ittefaq* (Dacca) and arrested its editor. See *The Asian Recorder*, XII, 26 (25 July–1 July, 1966), 7158; and *The New York Times* (19 June, 1966), 3.

subsided as the Occupying Powers sought to restore municipal services on a citywide basis. The second disruptive wave was the result of a conscious Allied policy designed to reduce the importance of the city's centralized government. Persistent agitation, sometimes subtle but often outspoken, by the Berliners themselves and, what was more important, growing friction between the Soviet Union and its Western Allies led to the abandonment of the idea of administrative decentralization—at least in the three western sectors of the city. It was this growing tension among the victorious Allies that led to the third wave of disintegration: the political division of Berlin, a process culminating in the creation of separate currency systems in East and West Berlin, the Soviet Blockade of West Berlin in June, 1948, and the establishment of separate governments in the two halves of the city in the fall of the same year. The next two decades have seen the steady deterioration of informal as well as formal communication between East and West Berlin, between East and West Berliners.[67]

As West Berlin has grown ever further away from neighboring East Berlin, it has grown increasingly close to the Federal Republic in spite of the one hundred miles separating the two areas. The leaders of West Berlin and West Germany have sought to bind the areas closer to one another whenever possible through legal, political, and economic means. West Berlin's constitution of 1950 gave the city the status of a Land in the federal system. When the Western Allies refused to accept this provision, preferring instead the maintenance of the Four-Power Agreements, the city remained West Germany's eleventh Land in everything but name. It has permanent, if nonvoting, representation in the Bundestag. West German laws become semi-automatically a part of West Berlin's legal system. West Berliners pay taxes to the federal government.

Of particular importance have been the economic and financial measures linking West Berlin to the Federal Republic. In part these measures have provided direct federal assistance to the city: subsidies to cover deficits in the municipal budget (averaging $220 million per year since 1951); subsidies and long-term, low-interest loans to finance such municipal projects as subway and housing construction; the relocation of some federal offices to West Berlin. Equally important has been federal assistance to the West Berlin economy: federal guarantees for the safety of goods transported through the German Democratic Republic (GDR) between West Berlin and West Germany, as well as subsidies to reduce transportation costs; special tax benefits for West Berliners, West Berlin firms, and West German firms who establish branch offices in the city or who deal with West Berlin firms; the provision of investment funds to expand the city's economy; and propaganda to encourage West German and foreign firms to buy West Berlin goods. One authority recently estimated that the total cost of the federal

---

[67] These trends are discussed, and data presented, in Richard L. Merritt, *Political Integration and Decay in Postwar Berlin* (forthcoming).

assistance program for the last fifteen years has been $9.7 billion, or almost two thirds of a billion dollars per year.[68]

That the social organization of the city—its political parties, labor unions, university and church groups, and so on—is merely an extension of the social organization of West Germany as a whole has also been an important factor bringing the two areas closer together. There is a community of information, with West Berliners and West Germans reading the same movies and newsreels, watching the same television programs, listening to the same radio commentators. There is free mobility of persons within West Berlin and the Federal Republic and, except for overland travel restrictions imposed by the East Zone officials, between the two areas: The singer performing in Hamburg tonight may sing at the Deutsche Oper in West Berlin tomorrow; and the director of a manufacturing plant on the Rhine River may also be on the board of directors of a firm located near the Spree.

Institutional arrangements and possibilities, however, often tell us little about the political processes that are important, such as the human links of communication between West Berliners and their fellow citizens in the Federal Republic. How have the events of the past two decades affected these ties of community? Public opinion data tell us that West Germans strongly support the Western position in Berlin, and would be willing to fight rather than to see the city switched to Soviet control.[69] We also know that the frequency of travel, the flow of mail, and the exchange of telephone calls and telegrams between West Berlin and West Germany have increased steadily since the Blockade. But what about the people themselves? Have the years of separation produced divergencies in the perspectives of the two populations? Or, despite vastly different experiences that they have undergone, have Berliners remained Germans after all?

One approach to answering such questions lies in large-scale public opinion surveying. Unfortunately, few studies of public opinion have specifically tried to contrast the attitudes and perceptions of West Berliners with those held by their West German contemporaries. From an examination of a variety of sources of data, however, it is possible to piece together

---

[68] Wolfram Pohl, "Berlin—die teure Stadt," *Die Zeit* (26 April, 1966), 17.

[69] In February, 1963, in response to the question, "If Soviet Russia increases its pressure on the Western Powers to get out of West Berlin, do you think we should use force if necessary to remain or should we withdraw our forces?" 59 per cent of West Germans favored the use of force as opposed to 19 per cent who would withdraw (with the remaining 22 per cent not responding). Of the 81 per cent responding "Use force to remain" or "Don't know" to the above question, 48 per cent continued to favor the use of force to remain even if it meant the likelihood of war with the Soviet Union and 14 per cent favored withdrawal in such a case (with the remaining 19 per cent responding "Don't know"). See Richard L. Merritt and Donald J. Puchala (eds.), *Western European Perspectives on International Affairs: Public Opinion Studies and Evaluations* (New York: Praeger, 1968), pp. 429–30.

the essential relationships into a consistent pattern.[70] For one thing, West Berliners do not seem to differ significantly from West German urbanites on nonpolitical topics. It is a maxim among West German market researchers that such differences are slight regarding their tastes in clothes, automobiles, household utensils, and other consumer goods; their attitudes toward work habits; their views about such matters as the extent to which the stars control man's fate. If we turn from nonpolitical to political topics, however, we get an entirely different picture. For one thing, West Berliners are more informed about events and are more likely to have opinions about them than is the case with West Germans. For another, when we come to such aspects of the political process as preferred form of government and views of recent German history, West Berliners seem somewhat more "liberal" than West Germans. Differences between the two populations are even more marked in their views of and attitudes toward the international situation. Generally speaking, West Berliners are much more inclined than city-dwellers in the Federal Republic to favor a pro-Western or even pro-American polity. They are more confident about Western defense measures as well: They attribute to NATO a greater part of the credit for maintaining peace in Europe during the crucial decade from 1949 to 1959; they have greater confidence in its effectiveness as a defense organization for Western Europe; and they are more inclined to feel that NATO will be of great assistance in maintaining German security in the future. Upon closer inspection the reason for such differences turns out not to be the one so frequently suggested—differential composition of the social structure in West Berlin and other urban centers in Germany. Rather it seems that they stem from the peculiar environment of West Berlin, an environment quite different from that of any other West German metropolis.

The combination of increasing contacts and convergent perspectives on nonpolitical affairs, which is indicative of a high degree of homogeneity in the urban culture of the two areas, together with diverging political perspectives have produced an interesting effect. If a modern state may be imagined to have a conscience, it is this function that West Berlin performs for West Germany. The voices of the city's leaders persistently warn the West to guard against complacency and smugness and against any tendency to ignore long-range political values in the pursuit of such short-range material goals as a higher standard of living. They have taken advantage of adverse circumstances to turn their city into a symbol of German unity—a symbol so important to West Germans that they are prepared to spend billions of marks every year to keep it alive. Moreover, these voices are a constant reminder of West Germany's commitment to the Western alliance.

[70] The discussion of differences in attitudes between West Berliners and West German residents of cities with more than 100,000 population is drawn from Richard L. Merritt, "West Berlin—Center or Periphery?" in Merritt and Rokkan (eds.), *Comparing Nations*, pp. 321–36; cf. Kurt L. Shell, *Bedrohung und Bewährung: Führung und Bevölkerung in der Berlin-Krise* (Köln und Opladen: Westdeutscher Verlag, 1965).

"We in Berlin," they seem to say, "know the Russians and the dangers of communism at first hand, and know full well that Germany cannot afford the luxury of 'neutral' attitudes." In this respect it is striking that the political attitudes of West Berliners cited earlier are more nearly reflected in official Bonn policy than are those images and opinions of the rest of the West German population.

West Berlin's function as a conscience also goes far beyond German borders. Time and again its leaders have reasserted the proposition that the city is a symbol of America's determination to protect its allies from communism. If West Berlin is given up or lost, they argue, then no longer will any nation be willing to entrust its fate to an American-backed defense system. It was this obligation that President Kennedy acknowledged in his trip in June, 1963, to West Berlin where, from the steps of the city hall, he delivered his deservedly famous "Ich bin ein Berliner" speech.

The central role of West Berlin in the consciousness of West Germans is in marked contrast to its peripheral role in the day-to-day life of West Germany. This paradoxical situation stems essentially from a high level of international tension, the tension of the East-West struggle for Europe and the repeated "Berlin crises." Were this tension to disappear—relieved, perhaps, by a Soviet-American détente, or by a system of treaties stabilizing and guaranteeing the status quo in Europe—West Berlin would doubtless become a peripheral island, no more the center of postwar West Germany than Danzig was of prewar Germany. Alternatively, the reunification of Germany would in all likelihood be followed by the relocation of the capital to Berlin, thus restoring the city to its central position in German politics if not (at least not immediately) in other aspects of German life.

The prospects, however, are for neither a stabilization of the status quo in central Europe nor the reunification of Germany. As long as international tension continues, West Berlin's center-periphery relationship with West Germany will fluctuate with the level of that tension. The ability of West Berlin to command a central position in the multicephalous political community that is West Germany depends upon the continuation of a fairly high level of friction between East and West. It is the recognition of this fact that has led many West Berliners to seek a new function—as an educational and cultural center, as a trade center between East and West—that will render their city more impervious to the vagaries of international politics. Until it attains such a goal, as one Berlin politician expressed it privately, the city's main export is tension. Without it, West Berlin runs the risk of becoming peripheral to the core of West German life.

THE EFFECTS OF NONCONTIGUITY

Their fewness and disparateness notwithstanding, these case studies suggest several points of general interest for the study of national and international linkages in noncontiguous polities. In presenting the points, however, I must stress the fact that they represent preliminary hypotheses, not empirical findings. The latter, as I noted at the outset, must await systematic, comparative treatment of the effects of noncontiguity upon polities.

Integration Within Noncontiguous Polities

The fact of noncontiguity is less important than its effects. And, in this regard, the most crucial effect is its impact on the establishment and maintenance of effective patterns of communication among the areas comprising the polity. To the extent that noncontiguity inhibits effective communication, it may create serious discontinuities in the lives and perspectives of the different populations—discontinuities that may in turn lead to disintegration.

The centrifugal effect that noncontiguity has within polities is stronger than distance alone. All other things being equal, George Kingsley Zipf has argued, communities tend to interact more with neighboring than with distant communities. And they have a higher rate of mutual interaction with more rather than less populous communities an equal distance away. Concern in the press of the eighteenth-century American colonies with news of Britain and America indicates that, although the relationships postulated by Zipf hold true in a rough sense, noncontiguity also plays a role. It is somewhat more likely that two noncontiguous portions of a polity will drift apart than that a pair of communities with territorial continuity will do so, even though the actual distances involved may be the same.[71]

Yet there is no reason why noncontiguity alone should disrupt communication within a polity. Given current technological means to overcome the communication problems inherent in noncontiguity, the very concept of "territorial noncontiguity" is relative. Nor was it much different in Greece during the Golden Age. The same arm of the sea that separated two parts of an ancient Hellenic polity became a broad highway between them after the development of sea power. And, for many decades, it was literally easier for the northern colonist to visit his brethren in London than his fellow colonists in the South. Modern means of transportation make island hopping and continent jumping still less problematic.

Territorial noncontiguity is only one among many types of discontinuities that may divide polities. It may well be one of the least important at that. Consider, for example, the traditional relationship of the parts of the polity. Noncontiguity is more inhibiting for groups of people without earlier ties than for those who had previously existed as a community of communication but then were separated through migration or the intrusion

---

[71] See George Kingsley Zipf, *Human Behavior and the Principle of Least Effort: An Introduction to Human Ecology* (Cambridge: Addison-Wesley, 1949); and Merritt, "Distance and Interaction among Political Communities."

of another state. Equally significant may be ethnic, linguistic, religious, political, or still other discontinuities. West Berlin is perhaps the clearest example of this fact. Its ties of community are closer with the West German Federal Republic, more than a hundred miles away from the city limits, than with either neighboring East Berlin or the German Democratic Republic. It frequently takes less time to fly from West Berlin to Hanover than to cross into East Berlin through the elaborate controls at Checkpoint Charlie. In an age when cargo planes can airlift supplies to a beleaguered city, or bridge scores of miles of enemy territory to rescue downed airmen, the mere fact of territorial noncontiguity is becoming still less important.

Leadership in Noncontiguous Polities

The centrifugal effects of noncontiguity are nonetheless serious enough that leadership cadres, if they wish to maintain national unity, must compensate for them. Georgian statesmen were unwilling to expend much effort to maintain the Anglo-American relationship until severe strains damaged it irreparably. Central Government officials in Karachi seemed to be following the same path prior to the military coup in 1958. If Ayub Khan's government has made greater efforts than previous ones to accommodate the legitimate interests of the East Pakistani, it remains true that tension continues to characterize the relations between the two wings. The German government in Bonn, in collaboration with American and West Berlin officials, has made massive efforts to prevent the ties of unity between West Berliners and West Germans from deteriorating. Arresting drift after it has begun appears to be considerably more difficult than preventing it from occurring in the first place. But either is expensive in time, effort, and money.

The more important central government leaders perceive the noncontiguous territory to be to them, the more likely they are to make the effort required to maintain unity. What makes this obvious statement problematic is the fact that criteria of importance vary widely. For many eighteenth-century British leaders, America was important only as an instrument to be used in the continuing British struggle against France. That the colonists had fought bravely and suffered severely when they captured Louisburg from the French in 1745 mattered not a whit when these statesmen came to the bargaining table. Indeed, surprise was the response in the mother country when New Englanders grumbled about peace terms that returned the port to France. In the Revolutionary War itself the British were more willing to suffer the loss of the colonies than to risk weakening their position vis-à-vis France by sending too many troops to the New World. At a later stage in their history, the British were to fight doggedly to maintain a foothold in colonies that were of far less strategic importance to them than was America.

A noncontiguous polity trying to maintain its national unity may deliberately create particular patterns for the recruitment of elites. The

Central Government in Pakistan, for instance, has leaned over backwards in recent years to bring a fair share of East Bengali into elite positions. The net effect of such efforts may be to lower the overall level of efficiency of the civil service and other organizations in the short run but, in the long run, to train East Pakistani for leadership positions while at the same time stilling some of their demands for parity. Such a procedure is not, of course, peculiar to noncontiguous polities. Preferential treatment of certain groups or classes of citizens may occur whenever the government is trying to reduce the impact of discontinuities in a society. Witness, for example, the elaborate efforts of political parties in New England states and elsewhere to "balance" electoral tickets along ethnic lines; or college admission procedures (such as at the United States Military Academy) designed to achieve a regional balance among entering students; or the tacit agreement in some countries to choose a president of a religious faith different from that of the prime minister.

The Noncontiguous Polity in the International System

Roughly the same is true of the noncontiguous polity's relationship to its international environment: Generalizations applicable to territorially contiguous polities apply to noncontiguous ones as well. Any state, for instance, is sensitive to its immediate environment. It prefers friendly to hostile neighbors; and many a war has been fought by major powers to surround themselves with friendly or at least neutral buffer zones. If the environment is intolerable, states can build barriers (high tariff walls, export restrictions, limitations on travel and on the flow of capital, censorship, and even armed guards along the borders to prevent human contacts or the flight of refugees) to shut out some of its impact. Figuratively speaking, the Soviet Union, finding in the early 1920s that it could not change its environment, rejected it, drew very much in toward itself, and concentrated on building "socialism in one country." And Switzerland remained an island of democracy surrounded by totalitarianism during World War II. To withdraw from the environment does not preclude territorially continuous states from maintaining their habits and patterns of communication. To the contrary, emphasis upon the stranger at the gates is frequently a device to strengthen that national unity.

Where noncontiguous polities differ from other states is in their dependence upon that external environment for maintaining communication ties among their various parts. To take the extreme example, West Germans and West Berliners alike are well aware that the hundred miles separating them comprise hostile territory. They may speak of legal rights accruing from Four-Power agreements. They may refuse to recognize the legality of the government controlling East Germany. They may even rest confident that any GDR tampering with access rights to Berlin will meet Allied opposition. But all of this hardly alters the fact that the bulk of West Berliners' food and other stores pass in trucks, trains, and barges through East German territory. When East German chief Walter Ulbricht said, "he who lives on an island should not make enemies with the sea," they understood what he was talking about.

It is not surprising, then, that noncontiguous polities are extremely sensitive to shifts in the environment that could affect their lines of communication. In the case of polities separated internally by bodies of water, they frequently have sought general recognition of claims to special rights in these seas or straits. Indeed, conflicting interpretations of internal waters, territorial seas, contiguous zones, and high seas lie at the heart of modern concepts of international law. The case of mid-ocean archipelagoes is typical:

> Both the Philippines and Indonesia have claimed to delimit the territorial sea from the outer islands of their respective archipelagoes, transforming the waters separating the islands into internal waters. The opposing claim is the same as that for other island groups, namely that the territorial sea should be separately delimited for each island.[72]

Polities separated internally by land masses, too, have upon occasion been preoccupied with control over their communication channels. The possibility of another Blockade is something that West Berliners cannot forget, even if they have learned to live with it in the years since 1949.[73] And Pakistani leaders continue to bridle at the Indian refusal to facilitate transport from East to West Pakistan across Indian territory.

By the same token, the fact of noncontiguity gives states in the environment possibilities to make their influence felt. By filling intervening waters with their warships or by blockading access routes by land, they can at the very least cause mischief and, in the long run, even determine to a large extent the nature of communication patterns between the parts of a noncontiguous polity. Such tactics may, of course, backfire. The most noticeable instance of this in recent times was the Soviet-imposed Berlin Blockade of 1948–49. Although in other respects its consequences were more ambiguous, the Blockade failed to force the Western Allies to give up their sectors of the city. Indeed, if anything, it even hardened the will of West Berliners to resist enticements and encroachments from the East.

[72] The stakes of such conflicts have been security, international prestige, wealth (resources such as fishing and, more recently, oil), and even health in the sense of preventing passing ships from befouling the coastline. The best recent treatment of these issues is Myres S. McDougal and William T. Burke, *The Public Order of the Oceans: A Contemporary International Law of the Sea* (New Haven: Yale U.P., 1962).

[73] In his press conference of 15 June, 1961, in which Ulbricht first raised formally the possibility of a Berlin Wall by denying any intention to build one, he also spoke of possible restrictions on air travel in the interests of "air safety" to be imposed after the conclusion of a separate Soviet-GDR peace treaty. It was on the latter point that the Western press dwelled, in some cases even ignoring the former!

There is also a danger that the temptation to cause mischief by harassing noncontiguous polities—possibly a blockade in retaliation for some restrictive trade measure—could escalate into a fullscale conflict. The exposed channels of communication nonetheless give states with real or imagined grievances a peculiar set of opportunities to exert a kind of pressure upon noncontiguous polities that would not be possible vis-à-vis states without territorial discontinuities.

The implications of drift between the parts of a noncontiguous polity compounds the opportunities for outside pressures. In the absence of high rates of communication, and in the presence of disaffection among local leaders in an outlying territory, the propensity for autonomist sentiments is high. The outside power that would like to see the polity weakened through dismemberment, or that has designs of its own upon the outlying territory, confronts the temptation of giving covert or overt support to the disaffected. The French in 1776 saw assistance to the Americans as a means to weaken Great Britain and its empire. And West Berliners, fearful of a takeover from the East, sometimes see even legitimate opposition to standard operating procedures as communist-inspired attempts to subvert and destroy these procedures. The same possibility exists, of course, regarding contiguous polities. In this case, however, the outside state can exert less control over internal lines of communication. The central government can move more quickly to reduce the disaffection—without having to worry about permission from the outside to do so.

On its part, in seeking to reduce disaffection, the central government runs the risk of attributing too much to the effects of external agitation. Misunderstandings of this sort simply exacerbate the usual communication difficulties. Pakistani leaders, for instance, paint the Indian menace in bold colors. But with recent changes in the country's foreign policy has come an interesting shift in the identification of domestic villains and patterns of disruption. A decade ago it was presumed that Communist agents were helping Indian sympathizers and infiltrators to fan the flames of separatist sentiment. The resurgence of autonomist demands in East Pakistan after the 1965 conflicts with India, in which the Central Government found its chief source of support to be China, posed a tricky problem. The first tack chosen by Ayub was to damn the agitators as fanatics. But, as the crowds supporting them grew in number and began to incorporate some of the more conservative elements of East Pakistani society, the official line reverted to the theme of foreign plotters (the Indians)—but now they are said to be supported and financed, not by Communists, but by the United States! Such propaganda may be useful for domestic consumption but, unless it is accompanied by concrete steps to meet what East Pakistani leaders consider to be their legitimate demands, it is unlikely to be of much use in reducing internal dissension.

Another tactic could be to seek ways to increase the likelihood of communication across the distances separating parts of the noncontiguous polity. In ancient Greece special privileges of common citizenship in a city-state were supposed to serve this function. In the world of the eighteenth century, such means as credit facilities, banking, and commercial arrangements pursued the same end. Improvements in communications have facilitated this task for the modern world. Both the German and the Pakistani governments have expended large sums to build up facilities for communication between their separated portions. Both have sought to encourage complementary habits of communication through subsidization of transportation, tax benefits to those engaged in commerce between the separated portions, and outright bonuses (for example, the "jitters premium" paid to West Berliners shortly after the construction in 1961 of the Wall, ostensibly to finance vacations in West Germany).

As in other respects, however, both responses to disaffection are not unique to, although they may appear in exaggerated form in, noncontiguous polities. I stressed earlier the fact that territorial noncontiguity is only one form of communication discontinuity. To the extent that it contributes to a breakdown in habits of and facilities for intrapolity communication, or to the extent that it prevents the development of such habits and facilities, it is important for maintaining the unity of the polity and presents outside states with opportunities to intervene in varying degrees for various reasons. But there is nothing inherent in noncontiguity saying that this must be so. Given the technological means at the disposal of modern states, they have the capabilities to resolve the internal problems that do arise. Where they are limited is in their ability to control the behavior of states in the environment.

One other possibility should be noted, although none of the case studies included in this paper illustrates the point. Outside pressure may contribute to the political unification of a noncontiguous territory. British influence, for instance, was instrumental in the formation of the West Indian Federation. In fact, the omnipresence of the former mother country may even account in part for the early demise of this union. The history of Western imperialism is replete with instances where the colonizing power has lumped groups of rather different tribes or territories together into a single administrative network—a network that may later have become the basis of one of today's emerging nations.

That noncontiguity is a relevant variable for the study of political systems, as well as linkages between national polities and their international environment, seems clear enough. Less in focus is the question of how the effects of this variable may best be analyzed. The case-study method is useful, for it provides some of the rich detail that enables us to balance the consequences of noncontiguity against those of other intrapolity discontinuities and variations, and it gives us a few hypotheses from which we may proceed. Before we can learn much about the impact of this variable, however, it will be necessary to examine in a systematic manner a large number of noncontiguous polities, both those in the world of today and in times past. This in turn implies the need for an extensive data bank and for tools adequate for sorting out or indicating those effects due primarily to noncontiguity. Given the wealth of noncontiguous polities, past and present, the task is a feasible one. And, from the viewpoint of theory in the study of national and international politics, and particularly the theory of political integration, it is a task worth doing.

Part V

Transitional Structures

CHAPTER TEN

The Communist Polities of Eastern Europe

R. V. Burks

The Communist polities of Eastern Europe operate in all the environments defined by Professor Rosenau in Chapter 3, except the racial. But for these polities the crucial environments has been that created by the cold war of which, indeed, they were the very creatures. From the moment of their emergence the West was sharply hostile to them; at the same time they were reflections of the new power and authority of the East. They formed part and parcel of a prospective new world order and they were marked by the distinctive features of this order.

The linkages obtaining among the Communist polities of Eastern Europe have been close and reciprocal. They are, to borrow another term from Professor Rosenau, fused. This results in part from the totalitarian nature of the system and in part from the preponderance of Soviet Russia within the system. The three linkages which seem to the present writer especially worthy of examination in the Rosenau context are leadership selection, policy formulation and implementation, and ideological community. These three provide the structural framework of what has been variously called the Soviet Bloc, the Socialist Camp and Communist Eastern Europe.

These linkages are much less tightly knit today than they were at the time of Stalin's death. The Communist system in Eastern Europe has since then undergone an historically rapid evolution, so much so that it would probably be advisable, when speaking of the system as a whole, to talk of two substantially different sets of linkages. One of these sets would obtain most clearly, say, in 1952, roughly the last year of Stalin's life. This set may be characterized with the adjective "satellite." The second set is still in process of becoming, but some of its broad outlines are already visible and for want of a better term the system may be described as "national Communist"; for the sake of convenience we will counterpose to 1952 the year 1968. Thus our three linkages must be looked at twice, once in terms of a satellite model, and a second time in a national Communist framework.[1]

THE FIRST LINKAGE: LEADERSHIP SELECTION, 1952

At the time of the Soviet military occupation of Eastern Europe two types of Communist leader were available to the Soviet authorities. There were those who had spent the war years in the comparative safety of Moscow and returned to their native lands in the Soviet baggage train. In the popular parlance these were known as "Moscovites." And there were those who had spent the war years underground, or in guerrilla operations, or in prison, or in concentration camps, but at any rate in the homeland; these men had a local following, however small. This second group of leaders we may refer to as "nativist." With the exceptions of the Yugoslav and Albanian parties, the early Communist leaderships were made up of both elements. Thus in Poland W. Gomulka had led the underground while J. Berman had spent the war years as a functionary in Moscow. For East Germany we may contrast the names of W. Zaisser and W. Ulbricht; for Czechoslovakia, L. Novomeský and R. Slánský; for Hungary, L. Rajk and M. Rákosi; for Romania, G. Gheorghiu-Dej and A. Pauker; for Bulgaria, S. Trnski and G. Dimitrov.

The Yugoslav and Albanian leaderships, being overwhelmingly "indigenous," constituted an exception to the general rule. The Yugoslav

---

[1] For the structure of the satellite polities at the earlier date see Hugh Seton-Watson, *The East European Revolution* (New York: Praeger, 1951); Robert Lee Wolff, *The Balkans in Our Time* (Cambridge: Harvard U.P., 1956); Francois Fejtö, *Histoire des Democraties Populaires* (Paris: Editions du Seuil, 1952). For the contemporary situation see Zbigniew Brzezinski, *The Soviet Bloc: Unity and Conflict* (revised edition; New York: Praeger, 1961); Stephen Fischer-Galati (ed.), *Eastern Europe in the 'Sixties* (New York: Praeger, 1963); J. F. Brown, *The New Eastern Europe; The Khrushchev Era and After* (New York: Praeger, 1966); H. Gordon Skilling, *The Governments of Communist East Europe* (New York: T. Y. Crowell, 1966). A good documentary collection is Paul E. Zinner (ed.), *National Communism and Popular Revolt in Eastern Europe; a Selection of Documents on Events in Poland and Hungary, February–November, 1956* (New York: Columbia U.P., 1956). See also Alexander Dallin, Jonathan Harris, and Grey Hodnett, *Diversity in International Communism. A Documentary Record, 1961–63* (New York: Columbia U.P., 1963).

party leaders were in the country at the time of the German invasion. They did not escape to the relative safety of the Soviet Union but instead took to the hills and organized a successful guerrilla operation. When the first Soviet divisions reached Yugoslavia, these guerrillas were already in control of the country, and the Soviet forces were soon withdrawn. There was no exogenous leadership element in Albania either. Indeed, there had been no Albanian Communist Party prior to the war. The Albanian party was organized by the Yugoslavs and the Albanian Communist guerrilla force was supported, insofar as it had outside support, by Yugoslav advisers and Yugoslav arms. The purely indigenous character of the Yugoslav and Albanian leaderships is related to the deviational character which these regimes later assumed, and the subsequent shift to the second system of linkages.[2]

Of the two leadership elements, Soviet authorities naturally preferred the Moscovites. Frequently the Moscovites had acquired Soviet citizenship; sometimes they held commissions in the Soviet armed forces; now and again they had married Soviet wives.[3] Such men could be presumed to understand what Moscow wanted and to do their best to supply it. As a rule the Moscovites were assigned to the key positions in the government of the newly conquered countries, reported directly to the Kremlin and maintained important contacts in Moscow. The nativists were not entirely trusted by the Soviet authorities, who feared the patriotism of these colleagues and therefore gave them prominent but secondary positions in the new regimes.

Both leaderships, the nativist as well as the Moscovite, included sizeable minority elements, but the Moscovites were more heavily minoritarian and, in some countries (e.g., Hungary and Romania), overwhelmingly so. The minority character of the key leaders was an additional reason for popular dissatisfaction and led to many bitter witticisms. It was a standing joke in Budapest that the politburo contained a single gentile in order that there might be someone available to sign decrees on Saturday. Indeed, the masses of the population tended to regard their minority leaders as foreigners in the service of a foreign power.[4]

To everyone it was evident that in this early period the leaders of all East European parties were appointed and removed by the Kremlin. The visit of a key Soviet leader, a Mikoyan or a Malenkov, would give rise to rumors that this or that satellite leader was about to be removed. Striking

---

[2] For the origins of the Yugoslav regime, see particularly Stephen Clissold, *Whirlwind; an Account of Marshal Tito's Rise to Power* (New York: Philosophical Library, 1949) and Ernst Halperin, *Der Siegreiche Ketzer. Titos Kampf gegen Stalin* (Köln: Verlag für Politik und Wirtschaft, 1957). For Albania see Stavro Skendi, "Albania within the Slavic Orbit: Advent to Power of the Communist Party," *Political Science Quarterly*, LXIII (June, 1948), 257–74 and Skendi and others (eds.), *Albania* (New York: Praeger, 1956).

[3] Ferenc Nagy, *The Struggle Behind the Iron Curtain. Translated from the Hungarian by Stephen K. Swift* (New York: Macmillan, 1948), p. 83; Wolff, p. 278.

[4] R. V. Burks, *The Dynamics of Communism in Eastern Europe* (Princeton: Princeton U.P., 1961), pp. 165–70; Ithiel de Sola Pool (ed.), *Satellite Generals. A Study of Military Elites in the Soviet Sphere* (Stanford: Stanford U.P., 1955).

proof of Moscow's control was provided by the great purge which shook the East European parties in the wake of the breach in the Cominform. The trials themselves, whatever the country affected, were apparently arranged for and staged from Moscow to begin with. It is said that, at least in some instances, the fallen satellite leaders were arrested and interrogated by the Soviet security police operating for this purpose on foreign soil.[5] In any case, the trials themselves displayed highly comparable patterns of accusation, confession, and testimony and were followed by the shooting of the principal Yiddish writers in the Soviet Union and the arrest of the Kremlin physicians (most of them Jewish). The Kremlin doctors were accused of having murdered, among others, A. Zhdanov, principal formulator of the new Soviet anti-Semitism, which masqueraded as the expurgation of capitalist cosmopolitanism. We note in passing that the declaration of the Cominform (28 June, 1948) which placed the Yugoslav party under ban of excommunication also contained an undisguised plea to the Yugoslav cadres to overthrow the "clique" of Tito, Ranković, and Kardelj. Apparently Stalin harbored the illusion that such an appeal would bring about the removal of this obstreperous leadership at the hands of "reliable" pro-Cominform elements.[6]

The purge of Titoists which is the central theme of the political history of Communist Eastern Europe in the years 1949–52 was more complex than its name implies. In part the leaders who were liquidated were nativists whom Moscow feared might one day or another, by reason of their local popularity, be tempted to imitate the defection of the Yugoslavs. In this category belong L. Rajk in Hungary and W. Gomulka in Poland. For another part the victims of the purge were those who had apparently associated themselves with Tito and the Soviet leader Zhdanov in their effort to push aggressively forward with the world revolution. Tito and Zhdanov had apparently been the moving force in the formation of the Cominform, which they wished to exercise a much wider jurisdiction than was actually given it. Tito and the Yugoslav party were at the same time involved in an effort to create a federation of Balkan states and, on this account, had become involved in supporting the Greek Communist guerrillas of 1946–49. In this Zhdanovite-Titoist classification we would place G. Dimitrov, who was involved in the federation project, and R. Slánský, who had led the group within the Czechoslovak Communist party favoring an immediate seizure of power in Prague in 1945. In the third place, the purge brought down an especially large number of Communist leaders of Jewish origin, who were probably sacrificed partly because the foundation of the state of Israel gave rise in the Kremlin to doubts concerning the loyalty

---

[5] Dana Adams Schmidt, *Anatomy of a Satellite* (Boston: Little, 1952), pp. 469–70, 481.

[6] For the breach in the Cominform see Adam B. Ulam, *Titoism and the Cominform* (Cambridge, 1952); Eugenio Reale, *Avec Jacques Duclos au Banc des Accusés à la Réunion Constitutive du Kominform à Szklarska Poreba* (22–27 Septembre, 1947); Halperin, pp. 86–96. Cf. also n. 18.

of Jewish cadres and partly as a peace offering to wide-spread popular discontent caused by forcible collectivization and rapid industrialization. This group also includes Slánský, of course, but as well A. Pauker in Romania and literally hundreds of others who never appeared for public trial. Finally, many were liquidated because they had close contacts with the West and were therefore regarded as potentially deviationist. This group includes the "Spaniards," who had fought in Spain, and the Hungarian emigré group which spent the war years in Switzerland.[7]

As of 1952 the satellite leaders were appointed and removed by the Kremlin much in the fashion of party cadres in the Soviet Union proper. This pattern assuredly did not apply to Yugoslavia, and probably not to Albania (for reasons we shall see). Satellite personnel policy was determined by Bloc wide considerations as the Soviet leadership understood them. If need arose, personnel policy was implemented by the Soviet security police. The removal of "Spanish," Jewish, "Titoist," and other cadres was not an effort to replace one linkage with another but was instead an attempt to maintain an existing linkage by replacing personnel believed unreliable with others believed more reliable. It makes little difference to this analysis that the Kremlin's judgment in both cases was wrong, disastrously so in the case of Romania, where A. Pauker was replaced with G. Gheorghiu-Dej.

LEADERSHIP SELECTION, 1968

In 1968, the leadership linkage is very different. Except for the "German Democratic Republic" (GDR) and possibly Bulgaria, Moscow no longer appoints and Moscow no longer removes. We are not likely again to observe the persistence of a paralyzing division of authority between an Hungarian first party secretary and an Hungarian prime minister because each was supported by a different faction in the Kremlin. Indeed, the struggle between First Secretary Mátyás Rákosi and Prime Minister Imre Nagy was the central theme of Hungarian political history from 1953 to 1956 and led directly to the uprising of October, 1956. Nor will we again witness the precipitous flight of Soviet hierarchs to Warsaw in an effort (vain as it turned out) to prevent the return to power of a leader whom they had imprisoned as a national deviationist and therefore did not trust. (In due course, the rehabilitated first secretary, W. Gomulka, proved that far-reaching domestic autonomy could be combined with strong support of most Soviet foreign policy positions). With the exceptions noted, i.e., the

---

[7] A perceptive general though early account of the purges is to be found in Fejtö, pp. 217–78. See also Zbigniew Brzezinski, "The Pattern of Political Purges," in Henry L. Roberts (ed.), *The Satellites in Eastern Europe. The Annals of the American Academy of Political and Social Science*, CCCXVII (1958), pp. 79–96; Burks, pp. 165–70 provides an analysis of the Jewish aspect of the purges.

GDR and Bulgaria, there is no longer an operational connection between leadership in the Soviet Union and leadership in Eastern Europe.

Probably the last instance in which Moscow effected a change of satellite leaders occurred in Bulgaria. This was the replacement of V. Chervenkov by T. Zhivkov, a touchy process which covered the years 1956–61 and involved innumerable visits to Bulgaria by ranking Soviet officials. Chervenkov was an able leader, much admired by his party, connected by family tie with the great Dimitrov, and above all an unrepentant Stalinist. It was for this last reason, evidently, that Khrushchev decided to remove him. Chervenkov's replacement, on the other hand, was known as a weak administrator and, in respect of the Soviets, a "yes man" of distinction; he faithfully, if cautiously, introduced Khrushchev-type de-stalinization policies.[8]

It is also to be recorded, however, that as of April, 1965, there had developed a conspiracy in the Bulgarian army aimed at the overthrow of Zhivkov and the establishment of a regime on the Romanian and Yugoslav models, i.e., one showing greater concern for Bulgarian national interests and less desire to please the Kremlin. The conspiracy was crushed, and there were rumors to the effect that it had been uncovered by Soviet officials living in Bulgaria.[9] Nonetheless, the conspiracy had taken form; it was, furthermore, the first of its kind in the history of Communism in power.

In evaluating the Bulgarian case we must keep another fact in mind. Soviet influence in Sofia has remained greater than Soviet influence in any other East European capital, except Pankow. One very noteworthy reason is the fact that the unfinished industrial complex at Kremikovtsi is heavily dependent on Soviet subsidies and Soviet engineers for its completion. The Bulgarian-Russian tie has long been close, moreover, and the Bulgarians have had to look to Russia for support against their traditional enemies the Turks, the Greeks, and the Serbs; against all these peoples Bulgaria has in the past raised territorial claims.

Except for Chervenkov, Soviet efforts to remove undesirable East European leaders have, since 1956, come gloriously a cropper. There is some evidence to suggest that Khrushchev attempted in 1959–61 to replace A. Novotný, First Secretary of the Czechoslovak party, with R. Barák, Minister of Interior, again on grounds of refusal to conform to the Soviet policy of de-Stalinization. This evidence has been marshalled by Professor Michael Montias of Yale.[10] Certainly it is clear that the December,

---

[8] Brown, pp. 6–15, 87–94; R. V. Burks, "Die Auswirkungen des sowjetisch-chinesischen Konflikts auf die kommunistischen Parteien in Südosteuropa," *Osteuropa,* XV (Stuttgart, 1965), 393–408.

[9] Brown, p. 19; J. F. Brown, "The Bulgarian Plot," *The World Today,* XXI (London, 1965), 261–8.

[10] John Michael Montias, "Uniformity and Diversity in the East European Future: Speculations on the Economic and Political Problems of a Polycentric Empire," an unpublished MS. which the author kindly lent the present writer. The material on Barák is to be found on pp. 24–30. Cf. also the comment by Gordon Skilling on pp. 29, 98–99 of his *Communism National and International. Eastern Europe after Stalin* (Toronto: U. of Toronto, 1964).

1967, visit of Soviet First Party Secretary Leonid Brezhnev did not prevent the overthrow of Novotný by Czech and Slovak revisionists. There have been, furthermore, rumors suggesting that Khrushchev attempted to unseat Gheorghiu-Dej, the boss of the Romanian regime. This is indeed a possibility, in view of what we now know of the serious conflict between the two leaders over the issue of industrialization.

It is probable, moreover, that Khrushchev attempted to overthrow the Albanian leader, E. Hoxha, and again for nonconformity with Soviet policy. In August, 1960, the Soviet submarine base at Valona was the center and source of an attempted *coup d'état*. In the spring of 1961 an Albanian admiral and several other prominent figures were tried and executed for attempting to depose the Albanian first secretary. At the trial the plot was alleged to have been inspired by that great source of Balkan conspiracy, the United States Seventh Fleet (in conjunction of course with the Italians, the Greeks, the Yugoslavs, and other nefarious plotters).[11] It was a curious fact that, alone of Soviet Bloc newspapers, a Bulgarian journal (*Trud*) reported this trial with words of approval. The editors of *Trud* were afterward cashiered for this performance, no doubt on grounds of impudence.[12]

The current relationship between the Soviet and East European leaderships was probably summed up by the Romanian Central Committee in its famous declaration of 22 April, 1964. The Romanian party, asserted this declaration, recognized in no party the right to depose or select the leadership of any other party.[13] This assertion is demonstrably true for the Romanian, Albanian, Czechoslovak and Yugoslav parties, probably true for the Hungarians and Polish parties, perhaps true for the Bulgarian party, and untrue only for the East German party.

On the other hand, it probably remains true that except for Yugoslavia, Albania, and Romania, the rise or fall of this or that leader, or group of leaders, in an East European country is much more heavily influenced by the views and concerns of Moscow than would be the case in a grouping of nontotalitarian dependent states, that is to say, in an alliance system instead of an ideological bloc. The likely Soviet reaction to a key appointment would carry far greater weight in Budapest or Warsaw than would the U.S. reaction in Mexico City or Bogotá. This is partly a reflection of the overweening dependency of most East European Communist countries on Soviet raw materials. It is sometimes a function of parallel security interests, as in the case of Polish and Soviet concern, both real and feigned, over the revival of German military power. It is more generally the awareness of a common faith and a common cause whose world prospects affect each regime's own future. It therefore seems reasonable to believe that,

---

[11] Burks, *loc. cit.*; William E. Griffith, *Albania and the Sino-Soviet Rift* (Cambridge: M.I.T. Press, 1963), pp. 47–48, 80–81.

[12] "Situation Report," *RFE Research: Bulgaria* (Munich, 18 July, 1963).

[13] Central Committee Declaration of 22 April, 1964, *Scînteia* (Bucharest, 26 April, 1964).

except in the case of Yugoslavia, Albania, and Romania, the Soviet Union could in normal circumstances still today exercise a quiet veto power in the matter of leadership selection.

Normally, this veto would work automatically. A man known to be disliked or distrusted by the Soviet authorities, would simply not be named to high office unless, indeed, it were the intention of the local leadership to make a gesture of independence. Should the Soviet attitude be unknown, an unlikely event in a system where consultation with the metropole is regular and frequent, and where most ranking officials have had long periods of residence or training in the USSR, the prospective candidate would be included in a delegation to a Soviet party congress, or otherwise put on display, and the Soviet reaction observed. It could also happen that Soviet authorities, fearing a misunderstanding, would informally make clearer their views about a given individual. We are, of course, probably discussing appointments to the secretariat and the politburo, but not to the central committee, and to the positions of head of security police and chief of the general staff, but not to the ministries generally. This Soviet veto power is an important one and probably constitutes a linkage peculiar to the Communist polities.

In 1968 Moscow no longer appoints and removes, except in the GDR; probably she exercises only a quiet veto right in four of the remaining seven regimes; in these four the local authorities will not normally advance any one to key position who is *persona non grata* in the Kremlin. The East European leadership is now self-opting and thoroughly indigenous. The Moscovites have virtually disappeared. Time alone, recurrent purges and, in particular, the increasing autonomy of the regimes account for this development.

THE SECOND LINKAGE: POLICY FORMULATION AND POLICY IMPLEMENTATION, 1952

With the obvious exception of the Yugoslav regime, which had been hurled into ideological outer darkness in 1948, policy for the Eastern Europe of 1952 was formulated for the most part in Moscow. This or that satellite could plead on tactical grounds for the right of delay in the implementation of one or the other policy. But policy itself was scarcely distinguishable from doctrine; it was an organic whole carrying very nearly the force of divine revelation; and its pundit and pronouncer was the great Stalin himself.

Official doctrine held that there existed but a single road to Socialism and this road had already been travelled by the USSR. Every satellite, regardless of its resources or its location, was to follow the Soviet example in setting up a command economy and in concentrating on the development of heavy industry, a policy symbolized by the construction in each country of a huge iron and steel complex (based on ores and fuels imported from the Soviet Union.) There was the Black Pump in East Germany, Nowa Huta in Poland, Dunaujváros in Hungary, the East Slovak Iron Works in Czechoslovakia and, of more recent date, Kremikovtsi in Bulgaria and Galați in Romania. Albania alone provided an exception to the general rule.[14]

Second, each satellite undertook to collectivize its peasantry along Soviet lines. The Polish regime demurred out of pure weakness and, by 1956, only some 25 per cent of Polish agriculture fell in the socialized sector. The Bulgarian and Romanian regimes invented a variety of intermediate steps, unknown to the Soviet past, but this was only an effort to make the end product more palatable.[15] As far as the industrialization of the Soviet Union was concerned, some economic justification could be alleged for the cruelties of forcible collectivization, since it was only through the exploitation of the peasantry that the Soviets could derive from domestic sources the huge quantities of investment capital required. But in the case of the satellites there were other sources, Soviet loans for example, and in Czechoslovakia, East Germany and to some extent Poland an already developed industry and an advanced technology which could supply capital. Nonetheless, each satellite was willy-nilly bound to collectivize. Each satellite, furthermore, assumed the political form of a people's democracy, with its official retention of traditional legislatures and rump non-Communist parties, and its reality of proletarian dictatorship.

Not only were the generalities of policy, as revealed for one thing by their identity from satellite to satellite, determined in Moscow, but as well the particularities. Thus all the satellites continued to raise the heavy industry goals of their five-year plans as the Korean war dragged on. All the regimes took identical anti-American positions in negotiations at the United Nations. All the regimes banned jazz music as a weapon of Western capitalist culture for the subversion of Eastern youth. With the expulsion of Yugoslavia, all the regimes loyally purged their Titoists—actual, potential, or imaginary—along with assorted Jews, Spaniards, and other elements regarded as undesirable by the Kremlin.

Satellite implementation of the policy formulated in Moscow was guaranteed by a network of arrangements and pressures. In four of the seven countries (East Germany, Poland, Hungary, and Romania) there was the imponderable of the physical presence of Soviet divisions. In all

[14] For the forced industrialization of Eastern Europe see Nicholas Spulber, *The Economies of Communist Eastern Europe* (New York: Wiley, jointly with the Technology Press of M.I.T., 1957); John Michael Montias, *Central Planning in Poland* (New Haven: Yale U.P., 1962); and Gregory Grossman (ed.), *Value and Plan: Economic Calculation and Organization in Eastern Europe* (Berkeley: U. of California, 1960).

[15] The figures on Polish collectivization are to be found in Richard F. Starr, *Poland 1944–1962. The Sovietization of a Captive People* (Baton Rouge: Louisiana State U.P., 1962), pp. 87–93. For the specific Romanian road to collectivization see Wolff, pp. 498–504, for the Bulgarian L. A. D. Dellin (ed.), *Bulgaria. Published for the Mid-European Studies Center of the Free Europe Committee, Inc.* (New York: Praeger, 1957), pp. 292–3.

countries was felt the prestige of that great revolutionary, Stalin, and of a Soviet Union which had not only turned back the Nazi German onslaught but had emerged from the holocaust as one of the two great superstates now locked in the world-wide combat of the Cold War. In all East European countries there were Soviet embassies with greatly inflated staffs. In many there were the so-called joint companies, formed with Satellite capital resources and Soviet management for the common exploitation of, for example, Romanian oil, Hungarian river shipping, Yugoslav air transport.[16] In all key fields—major industry, the armed forces, the security police— there were resident Soviet advisers who saw to it that Moscow's wishes were carried out. As in the Soviet Union it was control of the security police which was the key to Stalin's domination of the state and party apparatus, so in the Satellites it was the Soviet advisers to the local security police, and the administration of terror in large and repeated doses, which was the ultimate Soviet control.[17]

Prior to 1948 there was emerging in the Balkans a second center of policy

[16] For the Romanian case cf. Wolff, pp. 344–6.

[17] For Soviet advisers to the security police see "The Swiatlo Story," *News From Behind the Iron Curtain*, IV, 3 (1955), 3–36. See also Flora Lewis, *Case History of Hope: The Story of Poland's Peaceful Revolutions* (New York: Doubleday, 1958). According to a Western source, W. Gomulka spoke to a select group of Polish newspaper editors on 29 October, 1956, as follows: ". . . the comrades have been raising the problem of the dismissal of advisers. With respect to this matter we have probably said everything that could have been said. Everything depends on us. We can dismiss them any time; the practical situation is such that we can call today a meeting of the bureau or the government and say that we are dismissing all the advisers, who can leave tomorrow after a parting celebration and the granting of decorations and that's that. They will go; they will go away without a word of protest or the slightest opposition. But again there is no reason for doing these things in such a way. This should be done reasonably, with common sense. We have to see who is where, who can be replaced and who still cannot be replaced (such a policy has been implemented for many, many years. In many cases we have still not educated military cadres which could fully cope with the tasks facing the armed forces.) With respect to tendencies, there is a tendency among us to dismiss the advisers and the instructors rather early, without waiting for the complete termination of the training of our cadres. Where figures are concerned this problem is not so very important. This is a matter of several tens of persons, who do not have Polish citizenship. Well, I do not know and I cannot say how we shall have to consult our comrades from the forces and examine the situation. We shall do this gradually and carry out the dismissals. This does not mean that we want to delay the matter for a longer period. On the contrary starting probably from yesterday or today, we shall today make concrete decisions. In given posts changes will take place.

"Therefore, these matters will be settled as far as possible but, as I say, without excitement and calmly.

"Where the security apparatus is concerned, we already do not see any need for a settlement. As agreed upon, the advisers have probably already left. A few days ago I received a letter from Comrade Khrushchev, addressed to me already, in which he says: 'Send back all the people you do not need without consulting us and making arrangements, because in these matters you decide.' Comrades, this procedure has to be implemented gradually; one cannot make violent moves and we shall not make them. . . ." *Sześć Lat Temu . . . (Kulisy Polskiego Października)* (Paris: Instytut Literacki, 1962), pp. 72–74. Translation by RFE Polish Research with minor corrections by this writer.

formulation and implementation provided by Tito, the second most re-
nowned revolutionary in the whole area of European Communism, and his
partisan-based party and regime. The Yugoslav leader had in mind the
formation of a Balkan federation with Belgrade as its capital. Preparations for the incorporation of Albania as a seventh Yugoslav republic were
already far advanced, negotiations for the union of Yugoslavia and Bulgaria
had taken place at intervals, and the Greek civil war was being waged under
Tito's sponsorship so as to permit the unification of the three parts of
Macedonia and their admission to the projected federation as a single state.
This grandiose scheme was increasingly opposed by Stalin who had his own
ideas about the value of Balkan federation, and this was a major factor in
the schism which followed. But there were other elements, such as Yugoslav
reluctance to accept joint companies and above all Belgrade's refusal to
have Soviet advisers stationed with the Yugoslav security police. This
refusal led, after 1945, to a curious kind of underground war, with the Soviet
police mission attempting to subvert Yugoslav party members and the
Yugoslav UDBA hot on the trail of the Soviet agents.[18]

Ultimately, Stalin decided to eject the Yugoslavs from the Communist
comity. This put an end to Yugoslav influence especially in Albania,
Bulgaria, and Romania, and it hastened the Greek guerrilla war to its
well-known conclusion. As we have said, Stalin had believed that the
blast of Cominform excommunication would topple the Tito-Ranković-
Kardelj "clique," and the ultimate re-admission of the badly-shaken Yugoslavs on Stalin's terms. The Georgian terrorist well understood that re-
admission on any other terms would tend to loosen the bonds of his whole
East European structure. It was no accident that after the expulsion of
the Yugoslavs, Soviet control of the satellites reached its apex, in part as a
consequence of the anti-Titoist purges; this is why we have chosen the year
before Stalin's death as the most revealing and characteristic for the satellite
system of linkages.

The 1952 system of linkages was characterized by the centralization
of policy making in Moscow. This was achieved through the near identification of policy and doctrine and through control over satellite implementation
by means of a system of Soviet advisers. The key role was played by police
advisers since political terror was the essential glue holding the entire
structure together. When the Yugoslav leaders (who could afford to do
so because they possessed an army of their own) refused to accept this kind
of control, and began to emerge as a secondary center of power and authority, their expulsion was inevitable, unless Stalin had been willing to re-
structure the whole Bloc along the lines of autonomy.

[18] For the issues leading to the schism in the Cominform see Burks, pp. 97–101;
Halperin, pp. 71–85; and note 6 of the present paper.

POLICY FORMULATION AND
POLICY IMPLEMENTATION, 1968

In 1968 policy formulation (not to speak of implementation) is national. There are now many roads to Socialism, some of which the great Soviet Union clearly has not traveled. The multiplicity of roads was publicly admitted in June, 1955, when Khrushchev and other Soviet leaders traveled to Belgrade to apologize to the Yugoslavs and seek reconciliation. In the years of its enforced isolation from the Bloc the Yugoslav regime developed along lines quite heretical from a Stalinist point of view. A collectivized agriculture had been decollectivized, and everyone knew the change was permanent, regime protest to the contrary notwithstanding. Central planning gave way to a mixed economy for which the Western economist developed the adjective "semi-market"; that is to say, there was an effort to combine government ownership with the play of market forces. Yugoslavia had consistently received economic, not to speak of military aid from that arch-capitalist country the USA. And the Yugoslav citizen enjoyed a personal freedom and security which was to be found in no other Communist country.[19] Thus when Khrushchev insisted, in the struggle with his domestic opponents, that Yugoslavia was "building Socialism" he greatly enlarged the area of policy maneuver available to Communist leaderships.

Equally important, however, was the fact of Yugoslavia's re-association with the Bloc. This was accomplished—insofar as it was accomplished at all—on Yugoslav terms. Belgrade recognized the existence of a special affinity between its own system of government and society and that of the other Communist countries of Eastern Europe. It wished to profit from this affinity by obtaining substantial economic assistance. The Soviets proposed to grant large credits for the construction of a hydro-electric and aluminium works in Montenegro which would be the Yugoslav equivalent of the Bulgarian Kremikovsti. Belgrade also hoped to find in the East a market for some of the manufactured goods which only with the greatest difficulty could compete in the capitalist market places of the West. In the field of foreign policy the Yugoslavs believed there were basic common interests and stood ready to cooperate in their achievement.

But at the same time the Yugoslavs were quite unwilling to give up the aid they received from or the trade which they now carried on with the non-Communist world (70 per cent, roughly, of total Yugoslav foreign trade) and they were adamant on the subject of their own independence. They refused to reassume the obligations of international party discipline in any shape or form. Thus, in addition to broadening the long road to

[19] The best general discussion is George W. Hoffman and Fred Warner Neal, *Yugoslavia and the New Communism* (New York: Twentieth Century Fund, 1962). Cf. also R. V. Burks, "Yugoslavia: Has Tito Gone Bourgeois?" *East Europe* (August, 1965), 2–14.

Socialism, Yugoslavia's reassociation with the Bloc, however casual and tenuous, also served as a solvent of satellite ties.[20]

Khrushchev sought to make a virtue of necessity. He was not only influenced in his approach by the effects which the Yugoslav reconciliation was having on the satellite system. He was also moved by the imperatives of Soviet domestic politics, which had in part led him to the Yugoslav reconciliation in the first place. He was struggling with the Stalinists for supreme power; he based himself on the party apparatus whose primacy he was bound to restore; and he believed that Stalin's system of permanent purge had become counterproductive from the viewpoint both of Soviet and of Communist interests. On the analogy of the British Commonwealth of Nations, Khrushchev proposed to replace the Stalinist set of linkages with something he grandly called *sotsialisticheskoe sodruzhestvo*, the Socialist Commonwealth.[21]

Under the aegis of this slogan, the joint companies were abolished, Soviet garrisons either withdrawn or reduced, and the Soviet advisers quietly called home. The withdrawal of the security police advisers was no doubt hastened by Radio Free Europe, which put on the air a defected official of the Polish security service, Joseph Świato, who described the system of police advisers in the Polish case in some detail, naming names, places, and dates, to the great embarrassment of the regime.[22] The Cominform, which had been set up in 1947 by Zhdanov and Tito as an agency of political coordination, was formally abolished in April, 1956; its newspaper, with the curious name *For a Lasting Peace, for a People's Democracy*, ceased publication.

In the place of joint companies, the staff advisers and the Cominform newspaper came a new set of ambassadors drawn from the Soviet party apparatus and (after considerable delay) a new journal, published in Prague with the more reasonable title of *Problems of Peace and Socialism*. Policy was no longer to be determined in Moscow but was to be coordinated among a set of fully equal regimes. The instrumentality of coordination was to be the Communist party; that is to say, the party apparatus. Just as in the Soviet Union the party had been returned by Khrushchev to its "rightful" place at the apex of the political pyramid, and the hitherto ubiquitous security police downgraded, so in the East European regimes, in

---

[20] For a substantially different view, see Viktor Meier, "Yugoslav Communism," in William E. Griffith (ed.), *Communism in Europe. Continuity, Change, and the Sino-Soviet Dispute* (Cambridge: M.I.T. Press, 1964), pp. 19–84.

[21] Wolfgang Leonhard, *Kreml ohne Stalin* (Köln: Kiepenheuer und Witsch, 1959), *passim*; Ernst Halperin, "Is Russia Going Titoist," *Problems of Communism*, V, 5 (1966), pp. 9–15; Richard Lowenthal, *World Communism. The Disintegration of a Secular Faith* (New York: Oxford U.P., 1964), pp. 3–22.

[22] "The Świato Story," *loc. cit.* The Soviet divisions were withdrawn from Austria after the state treaty of 15 May, 1955, which provided for Austrian neutrality. The Soviet garrison in Poland was substantially reduced in size after the events of October, 1956. All Soviet troops were withdrawn from Romania in 1958. The number of divisions in the GDR has been gradually reduced from 22 to 20.

Khrushchev's conception, the party would be restored to its normal primacy. In the future the real channel of communication would run via the embassies, and not from a Moscow ministry to a set of Soviet advisers *in situ*. Being apparatchiki of long experience, the ambassadors would be able to talk to the local party in the understandable language of comrades. *Problems of Peace and Socialism*, though under Soviet editorship, would appear in the various national languages and would serve as a channel for the exchange of ideas and the coordination of policy among party big-wigs. On the economic side, the Comecon would be revitalized so as to serve as a forum for the economic ministers and the technical experts. In regularly scheduled sessions they could negotiate out an international Socialist division of labor which would gradually overcome the wasteful duplication of effort which was a necessary by-product of Stalinist autarky.[23] Ultimately, these negotiations were intended to lead to the establishment of a central planning organ for all the members of the Comecon. Since in Socialist countries central planning affects virtually every aspect of the national life, such an organ would return to the USSR via economic channels much of the control it had lost in the political and ideological spheres.

The formulation of this new policy of *sotsialisticheskoe sodruzhestvo* involved a number of assumptions. Khrushchev believed that if the regimes were granted internal autonomy the type of problem symbolized by Yugoslavia, i.e., the national deviation, would not arise. It was Stalin's constant interference in the domestic affairs of the ruling parties which accounted for the stresses and strains which had built up within the East European comity. Khrushchev also assumed that, once the regimes were granted autonomy, the coordination of foreign policy would be more or less automatic. The regimes all shared the same basic aims, if only because they upheld the same *Weltanschauung* and accepted the same Marxist-Leninist canon. Finally, Khrushchev assumed that, within the formal framework of equality, the Soviet Union would exercise a natural preponderance, because of its size, its military strength, its raw material deliveries and its Socialist pioneering. The regimes while each seeking Socialism in their own, autonomous way, would instinctively gather around the Soviet hegemon. This was to be the system of linkage as Khrushchev conceived it.

We should perhaps make clear at this point that what Khrushchev proposed was not, either in his mind or in reality, a return to the standard diplomacy of a traditional alliance. There was to be extensive and conscious coordination of the foreign policy of the member states. In the domestic field there was to be autonomy, i.e., each regime would achieve Socialism in its own way, taking into account the national peculiarities, and at its own pace. But the separate national versions of the Socialism achieved would be very similar indeed, and the emergence of a Socialist

[23] Michael Kaser, *Integration Problems of the Planned Economies* (London: Oxford U.P., 1965), pp. 83–107; Skilling, pp. 212–17, 219–23.

288

division of labor and a common planning organ would bring the Communist polities to function as a single entity in all essential matters. The difference between Khrushchev and Stalin was that the peasant from Kalinovka proposed to achieve Soviet imperial objectives through a voluntary co-operation which was to be motivated by mutual interdependence in the economic field and by common political interests as defined by a shared ideology. All would behave, both nationally and internationally, as good Socialists should, not out of fear of the security police, but because they wished to do so.

But for all the apparent reasonableness of the proposed system, and for all Khrushchev's efforts in its behalf, *sotsialisticheskoe sodruzhestvo* failed to function properly. In 1961 the Albanian party openly defined the Moscovite papacy and became a satellite of the Peking sun. This suggested that with two Romes and two popes, the international Communist movement was breaking up and international Communist discipline was breaking down. The more perceptive students of the great ideological schism began to come up with the notion that Communist doctrine, so far from replacing national interests, only served to reflect them while the encasement of these interests in an ideological cellophane only tended to make them more difficult to handle, since every difference of interest tended to escalate itself into a difference of dogma.[24]

In 1963 the fact that the Romanian party was deviant in a national sense came out in the open and struck the world, if not the Bloc, as a clap of thunder. In the face of a flat prohibition from the Soviet leaders, who sought to promote an economic division of labor among the Communist polities of Europe, the Romanians proceeded with the rapid build-up of heavy industry, using Western equipment and employing Western engineers. The national interests of the USSR and of Romania were in direct conflict. The Romanian defiance was not only successful, indicating once again how badly the Bloc had been shaken by the Great Schism, but the Romanians capped it off with a public declaration (22 April, 1964) of ideological independence.

What must have been an especially bitter pill for the Russians was the fact that the Romanian defiance made it very difficult to proceed with the economic integration of Soviet Russia and Eastern Europe. This integration had been proposed by the Russians in part in the interests of efficiency, in part as a substitute for a political coordination which was fraying at the edges, and in part as a counter to the Common Market which unhappily, from the Soviet point of view, was an enormous success. Since the economies of Eastern Europe were of the planned rather than the market variety, Comecon integration meant, not the gradual merger of markets, but the gradual coordination of national plans. The Romanians, however, flat-footedly refused to coordinate. They declared (22 April, 1964) that any

---

[24] Lowenthal provides a penetrating analysis of the breakdown of party and state relations between Peking and Moscow (*op. cit.*, pp. 139–231).

alienation of the planning function to a supranational body was an intolerable surrender of national sovereignty.

The repercussions of the shift away from the old linkages were not always easy to foresee. Czechoslovak industry, as perhaps the most advanced in the Communist world, had been geared to supplying the agrarian and semi-agrarian states of that world with complex machinery. In return, the Czechs were to receive raw materials. But the Great Schism left Czechoslovakia with whole fields of rusting tractors built to Chinese specifications, undeliverable in China and almost unusable elsewhere. The determination of Romania to industrialize across-the-board resulted in a drastic reduction of Romanian machinery imports from Czechoslovakia. Imports from Czechoslovakia dropped from 50 per cent of total Romanian imports to ten. The Soviet Union itself rejected deliveries of Czechoslovak machinery on the grounds that it was not up to standard and began to argue that Soviet raw materials cost more to produce than world prices allowed and that the selling prices of these materials within the Bloc would have to be raised substantially or, alternatively, the East Europeans would have to contribute investment funds to help expand the Soviet raw materials base. Thus, Czechoslovakia was faced with a foreign trade problem; she must reverse the process of the Stalinist era and increase her exchanges with the West where competition was severe while decreasing those with the East where competition scarcely existed. Such a shift could not remain without its political consequences.[25]

One other development also proved the Khrushchevian assumption to be wrong, or at least to be in need of a wide-ranging reformulation. This was an unexpected decline of Soviet prestige. Aside from such jolts as the Great Schism, the Albanian defection and the Romanian deviation, Soviet prestige suffered also from the shocks of de-Stalinization, the Cuban confrontation, and the removal of Khrushchev himself. De-Stalinization had shaken the claim of the Soviet regime to Socialist righteousness; it was a necessary but overpowering confession of error and sin. The removal of the Soviet first party secretary from office was without precedent and clearly reflected the long succession of Soviet defeats as well as the institutional evolution of the Soviet system. But the confrontation over Cuba made clear to all, but especially to the East European Communists, that the

[25] For the Romanian national deviation and its consequences, see R. V. Burks, "The Rumanian National Deviation: An Accounting," in Kurt London (ed.), *Eastern Europe in Transition* (Baltimore: Johns Hopkins Press, 1966), pp. 93–116; John Michael Montias, "Background and Origins of the Rumanian Dispute with Comecon," *Soviet Studies*, XVI (Glasgow, 1964), 125–51; J. F. Brown, "Rumania Steps Out of Line," *Survey* (London, October, 1963), 19–34; John Michael Montias, "Economic Nationalism in Eastern Europe: The Last Forty Years," in London (ed.), pp. 173–206. For the change in the Soviet position on raw material prices see Richard Rockingham Gill, "USSR Exploited by Comecon?—II," *RFE Research: Communist Area* (13 July, 1966), 4 pp.; Richard Rockingham Gill, "USSR Exploited by Comecon?" *ibid.* (2 June, 1966), 5 pp.; I. Dudinskii, "Toplivno-Syrevaia Problem Stran SEV i Puti ee Resheniia," *Voprosy Ekonomiki* (Moscow, April, 1966), pp. 84–94.

balance of military power was not shifting to the Socialist camp and would not likely shift to the camp for the foreseeable future. Therefore further territorial acquisitions by the camp, and especially the control or neutralization of West Berlin, were unlikely.[26] It is one thing for a regime to belong to a Bloc which is in forward movement, so that credit and strength may be borrowed from the future. It is quite another thing for a regime to realize that it must make do with what it has, and face up to its present weakness.

Thus none of Khrushchev's assumptions as to the linkages among the European Communist polities proved valid in practice. Autonomous regimes were also prey to national deviation; Stalin's interference in their domestic affairs was not the sole, nor even the prime, reason for their malfeasance. The Socialist division of labor developed only slowly, if at all, and central planning for the Comecon had been rejected outright. Nor did autonomy mean an automatic, or virtually automatic, coordination of foreign policies. The common ideology seemed to make more, rather than less, difficult the resolution of conflicts of national interest. While the physical preponderance of the USSR remained, as a basic fact of geography, population strength, and gross national product, the prestige and world influence of the USSR declined noticeably, and this fact affected adversely its position in Eastern Europe. For the enforcement of the Soviet will in Communist Eastern Europe it seemed very difficult to find an effective substitute for political terror.

Sotstialisticheskoe sodruzhestvo thus proved to be only a phase in the evolution of the linkage system away from the Stalinist model. As of 1968 the pattern for policy formulation is highly diverse, to say the least. In matters of foreign policy the regimes (except, of course, Albania and, depending on the issue, Yugoslavia and Romania) tend to follow the Soviet lead in all matters which do not affect them directly. This is not so much a matter of subservience as it is of self-interest. Accretions to Soviet power and prestige in the international area generally reflect favorably on the kindred Communist polities of Eastern Europe (e.g., the entrance of Cuba into the ranks of the Communist powers). (This is the converse of the proposition that the decline of Soviet prestige contributed to the erosion of Khrushchev's linkage system.) But let the issue affect the particular interests of the regimes adversely, as in the proposed excommunication of the Chinese by a great and formal conclave, with all its implications for international party discipline, and the Communist polities (except East Germany and Bulgaria) adopt attitudes ranging from stubborn opposition to sulky reluctance. There is little doubt, however, that in a foreign policy pinch Soviet influence is great. In the event of a major crisis in Soviet-American relations, for example, one threatening a nuclear exchange, the regimes, or most of them, would rally to the Soviet side. They would fear that either a Soviet diplomatic retreat of catastrophic proportions, or the

---

[26] Richard Lowenthal, "The End of an Illusion," *Problems of Communism*, XII, 1 (1963), pp. 1–9.

physical destruction of much of the Soviet Union in a nuclear war, would endanger their own existence. At the same time the regimes would probably use such influence as they possessed both in Moscow and in Washington to persuade the contending parties to compromise.

In respect of domestic policy, the area of maneuverability enjoyed by the regimes is considerably larger. Moscow probably no longer presumes to give advice. Khrushchev struggled long and manfully to re-establish a watered-down version of *For a Lasting Peace, for a People's Democracy*. Even so, the articles in *Problems of Peace and Socialism* do not appear to have a binding character. They represent divergent viewpoints and Bucharest blithely omits from the Romanian language version pieces which are not to its liking.

The degree to which policy coordination is lacking in 1968 may be illustrated by the extent to which the different regimes follow divergent domestic policies. At the two extremes are Albania and Yugoslavia, two neighbors which share the harsh environment of the Dinaric Alps. Tirana continues the government management of industry, whereas Belgrade is developing a semi-market economy. Tirana has a collectivized agriculture, but Belgrade has returned to private agriculture. Tirana relies heavily on security police and political terror, living as a city under seige, while Belgrade has downgraded and purged the police and its citizens enjoy a significant quantum of personal liberty and security. Tirana openly and stridently supports the extremist Chinese in their quarrel with the Soviet Communists now grown cautious, while Belgrade supports the Soviet side but would not go so far as to participate in a general excommunication of the Chinese. Between these two extremes are all manner of variation. On the question of economic reform, to mention another example, Czechoslovakia and Hungary propose to go very far, much further than the Soviet Union, whereas Romania and Albania virtually ignore the issue while East Germany, Poland and Bulgaria take moderate steps in the direction of reform.

Even though Moscow has little to say these days in the formulation of policy, not to mention its implementation, we would suppose that in this field also she retains a veto right (not applying, of course, to either Yugoslavia or Albania). She could, for example, probably forbid the adoption of a policy, such as decollectivization, which she regarded as harmful or dangerous. Thus decollectivization in Czechoslovakia, where the Soviet agricultural system has been closely imitated and doctrinally proclaimed by an industrialized state, might constitute a severe blow to the stability of the Soviet regime itself. The human cost of collectivization in the USSR was extremely high; the regime has a major moral investment in the system, and has constantly treated it as a great social achievement, a pillar of the good society to come. Decollectivization in Communist Czechoslovakia, assuming the process were not undertaken gradually and under camouflage, could raise in the Soviet Union grave doubts about the entire social system, doubts with which the regime might have difficulty in coping. In forbidding, e.g., decollectivization in Czechoslovakia, the Soviet Union would likely have the support of other regimes, whose own agricultural arrangements and whose own stability could be threatened by such defection. The combined pressure of several regimes would probably suffice, unless the deviant was bent upon decommunization as well as decollectivization.

At the present time, furthermore, the Soviet leaders could probably exercise a right of armed intervention, with the open or tacit support of the other Communist capitals, if one regime or the other should formally withdraw from the Warsaw Pact or prepare to hold free elections. Since Albania does not participate in Warsaw Pact activities, and since Yugoslavia is not a member, the question of intervention would probably not arise. What the Russians would do in case Yugoslavia prepared to hold free elections is not clear.

THE THIRD LINKAGE: IDEOLOGY

A third set of linkages, supplementing and reinforcing those involving leadership selection and policy formulation-implementation is the ideological. Curiously enough, the ideological linkage was relatively unimportant in the 1952 arrangement, when the public emphasis on doctrine and on conformity to it was greatest. The Stalinist system of controls was so far-reaching and so effective that ideology and ideological pronouncements served primarily as a signal and announcement system for the initiated. There was, of course, only a single center of doctrine. There were in addition a limited number of East European epigones who were entitled to offer local glosses of central pronouncements. M. Rákosi in Hungary was one of these. Prior to 1948, Tito was another. As we have seen, the Yugoslav leader sought to make of Belgrade a second, if subordinate, center of world Communism. It was for this reason, as well as for many others, that a ban of excommunication was laid upon him and his associates. In view of what happened in Hungary and in Poland in 1956, shortly after the Soviet leaders attempted to achieve a reconciliation with the Yugoslavs, and in the light of the ideological diversity and conflict of 1968, it is clear that Stalin's decision to expel Tito was not purely arbitrary or personal. The great anti-Titoist purges of 1949–52 served also as an instrument for the preservation of ideological purity and for the exclusion of alien doctrinal influences. Ideologically, the purges were a necessary part of the Stalinist system.

In 1968, ideology is of greater importance in holding the East European Communist system together, even though its pronouncement is no longer punctuated by the beating of drums. The current veto power of the USSR is in part rooted in the commonly held official ideology, precisely because the disappearance of one regime would endanger the existence of the others, particularly if this renunciation were demonstrably voluntary. The victory of Communism on a world-wide scale being inevitable, it follows that no population which has ever known the "benefits" of Socialism would relinquish these of its own free will. The contrary case would constitute a heavy blow to the world prospects of the movement, the future of which depends, for one part, on the naive belief of millions of simple, hungry people that Communist society is the brave new world and, for another part, on the conviction of elite groups that certain doctrines are practical instruments of rule. This situation was true in 1952, but in 1968 the role of ideology is accentuated because the other linkages have become attenuated.

It is characteristic of 1968 that it is necessary to define the geographic boundaries of the ideological realm of European Marxism-Leninism in order to say what it includes and what it excludes. The realm excludes, to be sure, the capitalist states and their institutional set-up as both decadent and hostile. But it also excludes Communist China and Albania. Although these states are recognized as "building Socialism," this recognition is due as much as anything to tactical considerations. These two states being separated from the main body by a great ideological chasm, they and their ways are (except for Romania) anathema. Even the friendly regimes and parties of the non-European continents do not play much of a role in the European realm of Marxism-Leninism, partly because the regimes are client states, and partly because the problems of these continents are not altogether pertinent. Included in the European realm of Communism are, besides the Soviet Union itself, the satellite GDR regime, the Bulgarian half satellite, the semi-independent regimes of Poland, Czechoslovakia, and Hungary, the independent Communist countries of Romania and Yugoslavia, and the Communist parties of France and Italy. Although not in power, and with little prospect of coming to power in the foreseeable future, the two West European parties are relatively so strong in their following, and so strategic in their location, that they count as regime equivalents.

The realm thus defined is characterized by the existence of more than one ideological capital. In addition to Moscow, there are Belgrade, Bucharest, and even Milan. To state the same proposition in a perhaps more accurate form, there are no ideological capitals any more, but only centers of ideological influence. The Romanian CC declaration of 22 April, 1964 only described the state of affairs prevailing for most parties when it declared that the Romanian party recognized in none of its fellows the right to issue binding doctrine. The ideological confusion created by this situation is magnified by the existence of the Great Schism, and by the competition of inimical and contending Communist parties in such countries as Spain, Belgium, India, and Japan.

Another feature of the European Marxist-Leninist realm of 1968 is the remarkable extent to which ideology is influenced by considerations of national interest. The Romanian deviation is the most prominent example of this tendency; in this case, the Stalinist doctrine of the primacy of heavy industry provided a convenient cover for Romanian opposition to a newly proclaimed "Socialist division of labor" under the terms of which Romanian industrialization would have been limited to petrochemicals, synthetic fertilizer, and food processing.   But neither are Soviet policy makers exempt from the proclivity of seeking a closer correlation between doctrine and national interest.   As already mentioned, Soviet economists are beginning to point out that the USSR cannot sell its raw materials (coal, iron ore, cotton, and so on) in Eastern Europe at world market prices without accepting sizeable losses.   Owing to its great distances, relatively sparse population, and unfavorable climate, production costs in the Soviet Union are substantially higher than those of other European powers.   This being the case, the European Communist regimes ought, in the Soviet view, either to be willing to pay higher prices for the materials or to assist investment-wise in the development of those Soviet material resources in which the associated regime has an interest.   Continuation of the present inequitable price system, the Soviet writers point out, would in effect lower the living standards of the Soviet people (obviously an intolerable thought!).[27]   Fraternal Socialist solidarity must evidently adapt itself to production costs and national interests.   (The Soviets did not recognize the higher cost of their raw material extraction until after they abandoned the Marxist notion that interest payments were exclusively a device of capitalist exploitation.   The idea that capital was not a free good, even under conditions of state ownership of industry, was something of a shock to the whole system.)

The growing consonance of Communist ideology and national interest has come to express itself in the post-Stalinist period in the form of ideological pairings.   The contrast between the revisionist regime in Yugoslavia and the Stalinist one in Albania has already been mentioned.   There are good reasons for this contrast.   The Albanians not only fear absorption by Yugoslavia but they have a territorial claim to the autonomous Yugoslav district of Kossovo-Metohija, which is inhabited in great majority by Albanians.   These factors operate in addition to the natural tendency of Communist regimes in developing areas to take extreme left positions (a tendency which manifests itself within the Yugoslav federation in the form of conflict over investment policy between the northern and the southern republics).[28]   But Bulgaria also fits into this pattern, having clung throughout the Khrushchevian period to Stalinist doctrines and practices even in the face of steady Soviet pressure for a revisionist turn.   Not only do Bulgaria and Yugoslavia compete for Soviet favor and for the position of principal Soviet sentinel in the Balkans but they are divided by a long-standing quarrel over the territory of Slavic Macedonia.   Thus revisionist Yugoslavia faces on the south Stalinist Albania and semi-Stalinist Bulgaria.

Hungary and Romania also tend to pair off.   Romania has been strongly Stalinist in its ideological outlook, including a continuing high

---

[27] See note 25.

[28] R. V. Burks, "Die Auswirkungen des sowjetisch-chinesischen Konflikts auf die kommunistischen Parteien in Südosteuropa," *loc. cit.*

priority for heavy industry, the final collectivization of agriculture as late as the spring of 1962, and heavy reliance on the security police.   The latter feature of the regime has undergone substantial change, the government in Bucharest having largely replaced police pressure with nationalist appeals. Romania has adopted an openly independent attitude toward the Soviet Union; it down plays the German danger, entertains increasingly close relations with the Federal Republic and, in January, 1967, went so far as to exchange ambassadors with the government in Bonn.   The relationship between Bucharest and Pankow is usually strained.

Hungary, on the other hand, is a revisionist regime whose citizens are vouchsafed a degree of personal liberty probably surpassed only in Yugoslavia; the security police have long been tethered on a leash.   There is greater emphasis on living standards in Hungary, and Hungarian collectivization has been attenuated by the employment of a variety of material incentives, including a version of share-cropping.   The Hungarians regularly emphasize their loyalty to the Soviet Union; they accept the official Moscovite version of the German danger, they cultivate friendly relations with the leftist GDR, and so far have refused to recognize Bonn.   In addition to their differing levels of development, and their traditional enmity, the Romanians and the Hungarians are divided over the situation of the sizeable Hungarian minority in the Romanian province of Transylvania.   One feature of the Romanian nationalist deviation has been strong assimilationist pressure against this minority.[29]

In the so-called northern tier, this ideological pairing is obscured by the Polish and Czech interest in the continued existence of the GDR, i.e., in the continuing partition of Germany.   The GDR publicly accepts its frontier with Poland along the Oder-Neisse as definitive.   Nonetheless, the Polish regime has been revisionist since 1956, in contrast with the conservatism of the GDR, and by 1968 Czechoslovakia had placed both feet in the revisionist camp.   Czech Communist intellectuals carried out the rehabilitation of Franz Kafka in 1963; to the visible embarrassment of Pankow, all other European regimes followed suit, and issued their first translations of the works of this seminal writer.   Kafka's works, the original language of which was German, remained unavailable in East Germany until very recently.[30]   The establishment of a West German *Handelsmission* in Prague in August, 1967, was even more embarrassing.   The most important case of this combination of conflict of national interests, differing internal requirements, and ideological contrast is, of course, that of the revisionist Soviet Union and dogmatic Communist China, but this is external to the area of our interest.

Apart from the existence of several centers of ideological influence and an increased correlation between national interests and ideological doctrine,

---

[29] For the situation in Transylvania see R. V. Burks in London (ed.), *op. cit.*

[30] For a summary of the recent internal evolution see particularly Edward Taborsky, "Where is Czechoslovakia Going," *East Europe* (February, 1967), 2–12.

a prominent feature of the European realm of Marxism-Leninism in 1968 is a tendency to ideological innovation. The regimes find themselves very much in a where-do-we-go-from-here situation. They have either abandoned police terror as a regular instrument of government or have reduced it to a modicum, and they are attempting to secure the positive cooperation of their dissident populations with repeated doses of material incentives. With this "goulash" approach they are having some success; but there is a serious question whether in the longer run material incentives will be enough or, rather perhaps, whether even in the short run there are enough resources to provide the necessary minimum of incentive. Will not the regimes be forced over the longer term to resort to "spiritual" incentives, with scarcely foreseeable consequences? The Romanian regime has already thrown over the rudder hard and bases its appeal for cooperation on the national issue, i.e., on pressure on the Hungarian minority for assimilation, on defiance of Soviet Russia on the issue of across-the-board industrialization, on bringing out into the open the territorial issue of Bessarabia.

A principal source of in-system ideological innovation is Titoist Yugoslavia. For nearly twenty years this regime has faced in very stark form the problems of self-reliance which the others (except, of course, the USSR, the GDR, and, in part, Bulgaria) are now beginning to face. In its efforts to work out practical solutions in the absence of Soviet credits, raw material deliveries and markets, the Yugoslavs sought to combine state ownership of the means of production with increasing reliance on market forces, in the hope of developing a reasonably efficient economy, of competing in the Western market and of attracting Western capital. All regimes, except the Romanian and Albanian, are currently engaged in introducing, as we have already noted, economic reforms which move in the same direction as the Yugoslav, although none of them are as radical.[31] The Yugoslavs are also experimenting with some form of greater public participation in the political process, an experimentation they refer to as "direct democracy." So far they have made of parliament a forum for the discussion of national issues, formally if not in fact placed the nomination of all candidates in the hands of the electorate, and introduced contested elections at the level of local government, the institutions of which now possess real power. So far the regimes, except for Czechoslovakia and possibly Hungary, have not manifested much interest in "direct democracy." But if material incentives prove inadequate, the regimes may show a greater interest in "direct democracy."[32]

[31] For a recent survey, see John Michael Montias, "Economic Reform in Perspective," *Survey* (April, 1966), 58–60 and Gregory Grossman, "Economic Reforms: a Balance Sheet," *Problems of Communism* (November–December, 1966), 43–55.

[32] For the revival of parliament see Vincent C. Chrypinski, "Legislative Committees in Polish Law-Making," *Slavic Review*, XXV (1966), 247–58, as well as Chrypinski's forthcoming "The Revival of East European Parliaments" (*Parliamentary Affairs* [London]). Cf. also R. V. Burks and S. A. Stanković, "Jugoslawien auf dem Weg zu halbfreien Wahlen?" *Osteuropa*, XVII (1967), 131–46.

Another center of revisionist innovation and, indeed, of revisionist pressure is the Italian Communist party. The CPI, with approximately one quarter of the Italian electorate behind it, is seeking to increase its voting strength so as to make impossible the formation of an Italian government without Communist participation. The CPI therefore seeks to reassure those who vote Socialist as well as the left wing of the Christian Democratic Party that the CPI, everything to the contrary notwithstanding, is an ordinary, democratic party whose participation in the government involves no serious risk of a revolutionary overturn. Thus the Italian Catholics are told that there is nothing in Communism which is incompatible with the Catholic faith; at the same time the Italian Communist leadership puts pressure on the Polish regime to moderate its conflict with Cardinal Wyszynski and the Polish hierarchy. Italian intellectuals are assured by the CPI of its innate respect for the creative process and its support of experimentation in the field of art. The CPI also intervenes with the authorities in Moscow, Prague and Budapest to prevent the punishment of literati whose boldness has incurred the wrath of the regimes. Finally, the CPI publicly takes the stand that, even in the event of its coming to power with a majority of its own, there will be no danger to the multi-party system. Elections will continue free and the opposition parties will be treated as loyal critics of the government in office.[33] The content of the Italian Communist press is generally known in Eastern Europe, through the broadcasts of RFE, through the circulation of Italian Communist periodicals in Eastern Europe and, in Poland, through the extensive reproduction in the Warsaw press of key Italian articles and editorials.

In contrast to these centers of innovation are the conservative pressures emanating above all from the USSR and the GDR. Even apart from ideological considerations, the USSR possesses an enormous natural weight in the European Communist system. Its population is nearly twice as numerous as that governed by all the other European regimes combined; it is one of two superpowers in the world and the only one to border directly on the area; it supplies Eastern Europe with critical raw materials and it provides, except in the case of Yugoslavia and Albania, the single most important market for the regimes. This great Soviet influence is sometimes used for the promotion of reform (as when the GDR and Bulgaria transfer the management of industry from central ministries to a series of trusts in the interests of

---

[33] Giorgio Galli, "Italian Communism," in William E. Griffith, *Communism in Europe. Continuity, Change and the Sino-Soviet Dispute. Volume I* (Cambridge: M.I.T. Press, 1968), pp. 301–83; see also the series by William McLaughlin in *RFE Research: Free World*, i.e., "The PCI and the XI Congress" (2 November, 1965), 5 pp; "The XI PCI Congress: Towards a New Party?" (24 January, 1966), 5 pp.; "Marxism and Freedom at the XI PCI Congress" (25 January, 1966), 5 pp.; "XI PCI Congress: The International Aspects" (31 January, 1966), 6 pp.; "The XI PCI Congress: An Evaluation" (1 February, 1966), 6 pp. Cf. also the essay by Kevin Devlin, "The Prospects for West European Communism," in R. V. Burks et al., *The Future of Communism in Europe* (Detroit: Wayne State U.P., 1968).

greater efficiency) but it has been mainly used to slow down the rate of change and differentiation and to promote coordination of policy and the restoration of international discipline.

These latter motives played a major role in the effort, begun already in 1960, to transform the Comecon into an agency for coordinating the Five Year Plans of the members and to persuade them to shift from a policy of industrial self-sufficiency to an acceptance of the Socialist division of labor. The Comecon effort was spoiled by the intransigence of Romania. No doubt these same motives were to be found in the repeated efforts of the Soviet leadership to assemble a world conference of Communist parties and solemnly to excommunicate the Chinese. This effort was opposed, not only by the Romanians, but by the Italians and the Poles as well, who thoroughly understood the disciplinary implications *for them* of such an excommunication. In 1966, the Soviet Union attempted to strengthen, in some specific way not made clear to the outside world, the Warsaw Pact as a means of improving coordination and discipline among the regimes of Eastern Europe. The Romanians reacted by first denouncing all pacts as a violation of national sovereignty, then proposing to reform the Warsaw Pact in the opposite direction (e.g., the post of commanding officer to rotate among the member nations and not to be reserved to the Soviet Union), and finally settling, happily enough, for the *status quo ante*.[34] Despite such failures, the USSR will continue to exert its very great influence to keep reform and ferment within acceptable limits and will almost certainly exercise its veto power if one or the other regime gets too far out of line.

The GDR also exerts a conservative influence, and since this regime represents a very important and perhaps a vital Soviet interest, Pankow can usually get Soviet backing for its major objectives. The GDR is inherently anti-revisionist and opposed to national, that is to say, anti-Soviet, deviation. This inherent conservatism is rooted in weakness. A revisionist policy might sweep the regime away in a flood of Social Democratism, which is probably the dominant preference both within the party and in the population as a whole. A national Communist solution is not likely since there is no such thing as an East German nation. Union with West Germany (roughly two thirds of the nation by population and three fourths by national product) is clearly the preferred alternative of the great bulk of the East German population; it is prevented primarily by the presence of twenty Soviet divisions. Thus Pankow continues to hold the East German intellectuals on a tight leash and normally will not permit the visit of Polish intellectuals lest they contaminate their East German colleagues. Cultural exchange with the West and tourism are also limited. East Germans under 65 years of age are not allowed to visit the West for fear they will defect. The visit of West Berliners to East Berlin, even for

[34] For the Romanian effort to prevent an upgrading of the Warsaw Pact see J. F. Brown, "Chou's Visit to Romania," *RFE Research: East Europe* (22 June, 1966), 4 pp.

compassionate purposes, is subjected to continuous haggling and long periods of interruption.[35]

Despite its best efforts, however, the GDR appears to be fighting a losing battle in its efforts to prevent the restoration of normal relations between West Germany and the Communist regimes. There are now West German *Handelsmissionen* in all the East European capitals except Tirana. Since the *Handelsmissionen* can supply both long-term credits and advanced types of machinery, both of which are scarce in Eastern Europe, these missions have tended to undermine Pankow's prestige and influence. The agreement of Bucharest and Bonn to exchange ambassadors, reached in January, 1967, was a grievous blow. A wave of recognition of West Germany by Eastern capitals was only prevented by the intervention of the USSR, which engineered a renewed propaganda barrage against the "Nazi war-mongering republic" and arranged a special series of bilateral treaties of mutual support among East Germany, Poland, Czechoslovakia, and Hungary, thus creating a northern tier of Communist regimes. The exchange of ambassadors between Bonn and Belgrade in January, 1968, also hurt.

If we attempt to synthesize all these observations concerning the ideological linkage we may say that Marxism-Leninism provides the East European regimes with a variety of services. It offers a means of discourse, enabling the regimes to discuss the problems peculiar to them and to formulate possible solutions. Because of the emergence of a variety of ideological centers, and especially of Belgrade, the ideological linkage provides a source of policy innovation. This is much needed since the basic problem is how to find, in the circumstances of 1968, an institutional arrangement that will work with reasonable efficiency without, at the same time, impairing the viability of the regimes themselves. The existence of a European realm of Marxism-Leninism sharply sets off its member regimes from their West European competitors and simultaneously provides a bond with Soviet power of great and even vital significance. Finally, the ideological linkage also permits increasingly the protection and promotion of national interests against other Communist regimes, on occasion serving as a shield even against the Soviet Union itself.

SUMMARY AND CONCLUSIONS

The notion of linkages is not entirely new. As far back as the middle years of the nineteenth century the Prussian historian Leopold von Ranke

---

[35] For the standard view of the GDR see Carola Stern (*pseud.*), "East Germany," in William E. Griffith (ed.), *Communism in Europe. Continuity, Change, and the Sino-Soviet Dispute. Volume Two*, (Cambridge: M.I.T. Press, 1966), pp. 43–142, and Ernst Richert, *Macht ohne Mandat. Der Staatsapparat in der Sowjetischen Besatzungzone Deutschlands* (Köln: Westdeutschen Verlag, 1958). For the minority view that the East German regime is coming to govern a new nation see Welles Hangen, *Muted Revolution. East Germany's Challenge to Russia and the West* (New York: Knopf, 1966).

conceived of developments in England as both affecting events in Europe as a whole, and being influenced by contemporary changes in Europe. Take, for example, this paragraph from the preface of his *Englische Geschichte*, in which he attempts to explain his general approach.

> In the sixteenth century England took part in the work of emancipation from the rule of the occidental hierarchy to an extent which brought with it decisive consequences both for her own constitution and for the development of ecclesiastical deviation in Europe. In England the royal power assumed a peculiarly self-conscious relationship to this innovation; while the royal power favored the change for its own reasons, it was able nonetheless to preserve the traditional institutions in large measure: in no other country were the practices of the middle ages so well preserved and in no other country did the spiritual unite with the secular power so closely. In England's case, the conflicts over dogma, which found their classical site elsewhere, were not so important: in England the principal interest lay in the political reorganization which, amidst the most varied shifts in opinion, trends and events, was finally accomplished in a struggle involving the whole national existence. For it was precisely against England that the hierarchical reaction ran most strongly. In order to resist this reaction, the country was obliged to draw close to the related elements on the continent; that England was able to resist was for these elements the greatest help. In order to bring this reciprocal relationship into view, it would not be advisable to place emphasis on each passing relationship to the outside world, or on each move of domestic administration, and to investigate their personal motivation: a shorter treatment would be best suited to bringing into full view the outstanding characteristics and the basic content of this development.[36]

Ranke goes on to argue that the triumph of Protestantism in England was closely associated with the coming of the supremacy of parliament, whereas the victory of royal absolutism in France was related to the accomplishments of the Counter Reformation. The titanic duel between the two states which got under way toward the end of the seventeenth century represented for Ranke a transference to the European scene of the issues fought out in the English civil war.

As the paragraph from Leopold von Ranke suggests, linkages are a universal phenomenon. The domestic life of any country is affected to a greater or lesser degree by the circumstances which prevail in the outside world and the converse of this proposition is also true. There are, furthermore, a set of institutional arrangements through which these reciprocal

---

[36] Leopold von Ranke, *Englische Geschichte. Herausgegeben von Professor Dr. Willy Andreas*, I (Berlin: Emil Vollmer Verlag, 1957), pp. 1–2. Translation by the present writer.

forces are normally channelled. The diplomatic service of the sovereign powers is one such institution; the frontiers between states, with their various functionaries, another; the regularized exchange of goods and persons, or the sharing between two microcosms of a macrocosmic religious or political doctrine, still others. Linkages exist at all times, but because of the standard division of labor among social scientists, e.g., as between those who specialize in comparative politics and those who follow international relations, we do not as a rule deal with linkages in their own right.

In the present chapter we have focussed our attention on the linkages prevailing among the Communist regimes of Eastern Europe over the last twenty years. We have observed that these linkages have been unusually important and effective, and have been embedded in special institutional arrangements. We express the fact that the linkages binding together the internal regimes of the Communist polities with the East European Communist system as a whole are unusual or abnormal by referring to this group of polities as a Bloc or a camp, as distinct from an alliance of states, or a regional grouping.

If we were to contrast normal linkages with the exceptional linkages of, say, Stalin's Eastern Europe, we would note that while the satellite states continued to exchange ambassadors with the Soviet Union and with one another, the functions of these envoys tended to be largely ceremonial. The diplomatists were in fact replaced by the Soviet advisers assigned to the military, police and planning establishments of the satellite regimes. It was also true that between the regimes and the West, as between themselves, frontiers existed as before. But the frontiers were so difficult to cross, whether for persons or goods or ideas, that we speak of an iron curtain sealing off these populations from outside influences, or at least from those outside influences which their ruling parties did not wish to admit. While goods were exchanged among the Communist polities, this was accomplished on a barter basis, and not with the normal means of convertible currencies, international banking, and the like, and the whole was subject to regulation by a supernational body called the Comecon. The character of this trade reflected the character of the planned, or command, economies of these states. And while the Communist polities evidently shared in the common doctrine of Marxism-Leninism, just as the West European states for the most part held in common some variant of the democratic faith, in Eastern Europe the common ideology took under Stalin political form in the recognition of Moscow as the proper center both of doctrine and of policy and in submission to a common discipline reflected in such organs as the Cominform.

As has become abundantly clear in the course of this chapter there have been, in Communist Eastern Europe, two sets of special linkages in a twenty year period. The second set is still in rapid evolution. The development of two different sets of special linkages in such an historically short time in turn suggests a high degree of political instability. The first set, that which we chose to describe as of 1952, amounted to a camouflaged incorporation of

Eastern Europe by the Soviet Union. The main difference between a Socialist Soviet Republic and an East European People's Democracy was that the latter remained formally independent and sovereign, with separate armies, bureaucracies and parties of their own. Theoretically, the 1952 system of linkages could have served indefinitely as a substitute for annexation. But the peoples of Eastern Europe remained irreconcilably hostile, while Moscow found it necessary, for its own good internal reasons, to abandon the police terror which was the cement holding the system together. This Stalinist set of linkages was peculiar not only to Communist Eastern Europe but also to a given period in the history of that system.

The new set of linkages now evolving must in its finished form reflect the fact that not much more than normal use can be made of the police power and that, consequently, the regimes must secure a modicum of positive cooperation from their populations by such devices as material incentives. The regimes themselves are still in search of a post-Stalin political equilibrium which they much prefer to discover without losing either their identity as Communist states or their hold on power. This makes the one remaining special linkage common to them all, that of ideology, of growing value. Now that the advisers are gone, the leadership self-opting and the whole set of polities shaken by destalinization and rendered by schism, the ruling parties are increasingly sovereign. In this situation, ideology is not only a field of discourse and, because of its multi-centered character, a source of policy innovation, but it is also vital to the self-identity of the regime and their coordination. If in order to survive over the longer run the regimes, or some of them, evolve away from Marxism-Leninism, then we will no longer be able to speak of a special set of linkages. There may remain profound institutional similarities, such as state ownership of the means of production, or one-party governments, but these similarities will not be interrelated from state to state by special institutional ties. Eastern Europe will in that case have returned to normal linkages.

CHAPTER ELEVEN

Postwar Democratic Polities: National-International Linkages in the Defense Policy of the Defeated States

Lloyd Jensen

THE making of national security policy involves an intricate web of inter-acting internal and external environments. Armament and alliance policy, though heavily influenced by the foreign policy of other states, is also subject to numerous internal restraints and opportunities. These range from ideological foundations, elite attitudes, and decision-making structures to such things as pressure group politics and public opinion. The internal and external environments are closely linked in the foreign policy process as each affects the other and in turn influences the decisions made with respect to national security policy.

By using national security policy, or in Professor Rosenau's terms "the polity output,"[1] as the dependent variable, some attempt will be made in the present chapter to probe more deeply the effects of both external environmental outputs, e.g., the foreign policy of other states, and polity inputs upon the efforts of the three defeated states of World War II to provide for their common defense. In using foreign policy, or perhaps more

[1] See Chapter 3.

accurately a state's national security policy, as the dependent variable, the linkages between national and international politics are certainly not exhausted. One might also view the effects of the external environment upon the internal political situation, and such may or may not have foreign policy implications. Conversely, happenings within a state which are not part of the foreign policy of the state may constitute the external environment of another state and thus affect the latter's foreign policy decisions. A prime example of the second case is that of race relations within the United States.

No attempt is made in the present chapter to test hypotheses concerning national-international linkages as the linkages relate to states on the way to becoming democracies or even to democracies as such. To do this would require an examination of a larger number of polities, including nondemocratic polities. The chapter does suggest hypotheses relating to certain democratic attributes such as party structure and public opinion which might be tested in a broader context. For the present the objective is merely to reflect upon some of the differences and similarities in the linkages of the three states.

Germany, Italy, and Japan are of special interest not because they are the best prototypes of democracies, but rather because they offer the social scientist a rudimentary base for control. Each had an authoritarian background, emerged from the war as a defeated and disarmed state, and was confronted with the problem of eventually rejoining the family of nations as equal partners. Their efforts at providing for their national security since World War II, however, have diverged with varying degrees of enthusiasm for rearmament and alliance. Italy has experienced the fewest problems in the area of rearmament and has been the most willing ally of the United States, while Japan has encountered severe difficulties on both scores.

In compliance with the other papers in this series, the effects of the Cold War upon national security policy will be contrasted with those inputs deriving from a regional or contiguous context. Internally the focus will be upon competitive elite structures and attitudes and the role of public opinion, all of which are essential attributes for the state with democratic aspirations. Finally, an effort will be made to measure the relative importance of the various internal and external factors as demonstrated by specific foreign policy decisions.

The research is based primarily upon secondary source material in an effort to tie together some of the existing knowledge. Such a procedure has many shortcomings, for frequently the data necessary to answer the prescribed questions are either not available or cannot be located. The researcher becomes dependent upon the work of his predecessors as well as newspaper reportage. The result is that there are bound to be gaps, and judgments must be based upon varying amounts of evidence. For example, in the case of Italy's foreign policy the data are scant when compared with that for Germany and Japan.

EFFECTS OF THE EXTERNAL ENVIRONMENT UPON
NATIONAL SECURITY POLICY

Germany, Italy, and Japan have been subjected to considerable restraint in foreign policy-making by both the Cold War environment and their respective regional environments. One would expect the external environment to have a considerable impact upon the foreign policy of a state defeated in war, particularly if disarmament and occupation are made a part of the peace settlement. Choices must frequently be made in accordance with the occupying power as opposed to internal political considerations. Professors Deutsch and Edinger have concluded that the main influence over German foreign policy during the period 1949 to May, 1955 was exercised from abroad by the United States and the Western allies with minimal spontaneous domestic support for the policies that emerged.[2] Another estimate has suggested that Japanese policy "must operate within the framework provided more by world conditions than by developments within her own boundaries."[3]

In this section the main question to be examined is whether the three states have formulated their national security policies more in terms of their immediate regional and contiguous environment or have reacted more to events in the Cold War.[4] One way of tapping the question is by looking at changes in military expenditures in an effort to ascertain whether increments relate more to events in the contiguous or regional environment or to Cold War events.

As might be expected, the crucial determinant affecting arms expenditures appears not to have been whether the issue was one of Cold War or regional origin, but rather how directly the issue affected the state involved. Germany increased its military expenditures by 62 per cent in 1959 in reaction to the Berlin crisis and Japan increased its by 54 per cent between 1964 and 1965 in reaction to Chinese progress on atomic development and the Sino-Indian conflict.[5] The former is quite properly a part of the Cold War, the latter is a regional issue. In checking other changes in defense expenditure, no clear pattern evolved between Cold War events and military

---

[2] Karl W. Deutsch and Lewis J. Edinger, *Germany Rejoins the Powers* (Stanford: Stanford U.P., 1959), p. 199.

[3] Chitoshi Yanaga, *Japanese People and Politics* (New York: Wiley, 1956), p. 368.

[4] The Cold War environment is defined broadly to encompass both systemic characteristics of United States-Soviet interaction such as tension and conflict and the foreign policy outputs of the two super powers, the United States and the Soviet Union. The regional and contiguous environment refers to relations within a single Bloc and with neighboring states *outside* the confines of the Cold War.

[5] Changes in military expenditures for Italy and Germany are based upon data located in Timothy W. Stanley, *NATO in Transition* (New York: Praeger, 1965), p. 325. Japanese expenditures are taken from the *United Nations Statistical Yearbook*, using in each instance the latest estimate available since the figures vary occasionally from *Yearbook* to *Yearbook* given later re-evaluations. The expenditures were not adjusted for inflationary effects, but data concerning changes in the wholesale price index for the three countries usually showed only a one or two point change from year

expenditures. Germany, instead of reacting toward Sputnik with an increase in armaments, actually decreased its armaments in 1958 by 24 per cent. Italy's arms expenditures fluctuated little except for early increases that might be expected of a state beginning to rearm, with more recent increases related in part to inflation.

The three states were somewhat slower in rearming than the United States would have liked to have seen. It was 1965 before Germany reached the goal set in 1954 for twelve NATO divisions. Defense expenditures of Italy and Germany ranged between 3 and 6 per cent of their GNP, and Japan proved the slowest of all with one of the lowest defense expenditures in the world, hovering as it did between 1 and 2 per cent. These figures contrast with military expenditures by the United States amounting to around 10 per cent of its GNP and about 20 per cent for the Soviet Union.

The hypothesis that states increase their support for armaments as Cold War tension mounts is contradicted by poll data in the defeated states, suggesting that incentives for arms build-up have actually increased as Cold War tensions have been reduced. A possible explanation may be found in the suggestion made by one writer to the effect that although relaxation in tension may lead to a decrease in the concern for rearmament, the population may believe that it is safer to rearm under relaxed conditions.[6] Interest in rearmament increased in Germany following the death of Stalin despite the fact that Cold War tensions were decreasing. In 1950, just one year after the Berlin blockade, fewer than one half of the German respondents in national opinion polls favored rearmament, whereas by 1956 with the Spirit of Geneva and progress in disarmament negotiations affecting the level of tension nearly all of the respondents thought rearmament necessary.[7] It might be argued that there is a tendency on the part of the mass public to accept and support whatever the status quo might be at any given time. By 1956 German rearmament had become a reality. A similar increase was found over the years in support of stationing allied troops in Germany, as polls taken by the West German affiliate of the American Institute of Public Opinion between 1952 and 1960 showed the proportion viewing allied troops as a necessity or welcome protection increased gradually from 48 per cent to 77 per cent of the respondents.[8] National polls have also

---

to year. Germany between 1955 and 1964 never exceeded two points, Italy never more than five, and Japan, with the exception of a five and seven point change in 1956 and 1958, fluctuated only a point or two in the remaining years. Consequently, it was concluded that inflation did not account for much of the variance.

[6] James R. Thayer, "The Contribution of Public Opinion Polls to the Understanding of the 1953 Election in Italy, West Germany, and Japan," *Public Opinion Quarterly*, XIX (Fall, 1955), 278.

[7] W. Phillips Davidson, "Trends in West German Public Opinion, 1946–1956," in Hans Speier and W. Phillips Davison (eds.), *West German Leadership and Foreign Policy* (New York: Harper, 1957), p. 294.

[8] Hazel G. Erskine, "The Polls: Defense, Peace, and Space," *Public Opinion Quarterly*, XXV (Fall, 1961), 478–89.

indicated that as many as 25 per cent fewer respondents in Germany in October, 1958, were willing to side with the United States during war than were willing to side with the West at that time.[9]

Professors Lloyd A. Free and Renzo Sereno in looking at national poll data for Italy concluded that "affirmative neutralist sentiments reached their lowest proportions immediately after the meeting at the Summit— and again in the spring of 1956—when belief in the likelihood of war was at very low levels."[10] This was indeed a curious time for a more militant public posture.

Further evidence of the inverse relationship between Cold War tension and sentiment for rearmament is suggested by a Japanese scholar who asserts that the increasing opposition to rearmament during 1952 and 1953 was due to the rise in the fear of nuclear war which is closely related to the United States-Soviet tension level.[11]

If a threat is perceived as one to the nation itself as opposed to a general Cold War threat, the reaction is likely to be one of increased support for armaments. For example, one finds in Japan relatively high support for rearmament during the early part of the Korean War with a decline in such support as evidenced in regional and national surveys during the period 1953 to 1957.[12] Similarly, Italian interest in alliance with the West was stimulated by the Czechoslovakian coup in 1948, particularly in view of the high Communist vote in Italy and the subsequent fear that an internal coup might be executed in that state.

Changes in arms expenditure have perhaps even been less related to events in the contiguous and regional environments, yet it would be an exaggeration to say that these environments have not affected the national security policies of the defeated states. Much of the delay in German rearmament can be directly linked to French recalcitrance over the European Defense Community. Efforts at bringing Germany into the Western alliance system through EDC collapsed with the French rejection, and a new formula had to be developed with Germany joining the Western European Union and NATO.

Although recent bellicosity on the part of Communist China might have increased Japanese anxiety, the Japanese have not seen the Chinese as overly aggressive. Interviews conducted with some one hundred parliamentarians in 1958 showed that 61 per cent of the respondents, when asked the question whether China was "sincerely working to promote peace and the relaxation of international tensions at the present time," indicated

[9] Karl W. Deutsch et al., *France, Germany, and the Western Alliance* (New York: Schribner's, 1967), p. 270.

[10] *Italy: Dependent Ally or Independent Partner* (Princeton: Institute for International Social Research, 1956), p. 88.

[11] Akira Takahashi, "Development of Democratic Consciousness Among the Japanese People," *International Social Science Journal*, XIII (1961), 87.

[12] Douglas H. Mendel, *The Japanese People and Foreign Policy* (Berkeley: U. of California Press, 1961), pp. 69–70.

"a great deal" or "somewhat," with only 31 per cent choosing the categories "not very much" or "not at all."[13] If Japan has armed in response to its regional environment, such rearmament would more likely have been a reaction to South Korea, but even these relations were smoothed in 1965 with the signing of a treaty between the two states.

The most extensive regional conflict confronting Italy during the postwar period was the issue of Trieste which was resolved in 1954. This conflict may have had something to do with the early increases in military expenditures, but just as important during the late 40s was the internal threat of the Communists against whom the government might sometime have need to use military force.

In addition to being influenced by the general course of events in the regional and Cold War environments, the defeated powers have been confronted with a variety of informal and formal attempts to influence their policy. Most of these pressures upon the defeated states have emanated from the super powers who, given their superior status, have a more powerful arsenal of influence.

The power to reward with foreign aid and trade was an important factor during the early postwar period when such aid was so vitally needed. All three states have been cognizant of their benefactor, and one can find innumerable statements of the various elites to the effect that the United States should be supported in order not to risk losing American aid.

In Germany, the United States had a strong supporter of rearmament and alliance policy, for Chancellor Adenauer saw such a plan as a way of speeding German independence and sovereignty. As a result, United States pressures were exerted toward helping him stay in power through various electoral supports. This is not to say that Adenauer had become a puppet of the United States in its rearmament plans for Germany, for the Chancellor was able to extract a number of concessions from the United States relating to German policy. After yielding once again to Adenauer, John J. McCloy, the United States High Commissioner, was reported to have remarked: "All right, then. This is now the 122nd concession the Allies have made to the Germans."[14] The statement was made, in 1952, three years before German rearmament became a reality.

Prime Minister De Gasperi of Italy (1947–54) also followed the US lead on national security policy in an effort to bolster his political position in Italy. Confronted with a high Communist vote and widespread poverty, American economic aid had become a virtual necessity. As a result, De Gasperi sold the nation on the North Atlantic Treaty Organization on the basis that continued economic aid from the United States was essential.[15]

United States pressures for Japanese rearmament were heightened

---

[13] Lloyd A. Free, *Six Allies and a Neutral* (New York: Free Press, 1959), p. 38.
[14] Reported in Hans Speier, "Introduction: The German Political Scene," in Speier and Davison, *op. cit.*, p. 2.
[15] Norman Kogan, *The Government of Italy* (New York: T. Y. Crowell, 1962), p. 167.

309

during the Korean War, but Japan proved to be the most reticent of the three to commit itself to a position of rapid rearmament. Prime Minister Yoshida won considerable electoral support in 1952 by campaigning on the basis of highly restricted rearmament despite American pressures. He urged that the arms build-up be limited until Japan became a member of the United Nations and that rearmament not interfere with Japanese economic well-being. The reluctance of Japan to join the American alliance system was underscored the following year when Yoshida was forced into retirement on the premise that he was too pro-American. It has been argued that the ability of Japan to limit its armament effort to less than 2 per cent of its annual GNP, one of the lowest expenditures in the world, has been due to the United States underwriting approximately one third of the Japanese military effort and the American bases located there.[16]

The Soviet Union in reacting to the defeated powers has tended to emphasize punishment rather than reward. In an effort to stem the tide toward rearmament, the Soviets have threatened "dire consequences" and have offered nonaggression pacts. It has been argued, at least in the case of Germany, that these pressures have only had the effect of increasing armament and alliance cohesion. According to Brzezinski, the Berlin and Korean crises increased United States interests and pressures toward German rearmament; the second Berlin crisis intensified the demands for nuclear sharing; and Soviet opposition to MLF may increase the prospects for the creation of a national force.[17]

Just as important as the threat of punishment in the Soviet arsenal of influence is that of the power to deny certain rewards. For example, the Soviet Union holds the trump card with respect to the reunification of Germany and the return of the Oder-Neisse territories. As such, Germany, as long as desires for reunification continue, is highly dependent upon Soviet decisions in the area. The Soviet Union also controls the Kuriles and the islands of Habomai and Shikotan, the latter of which it has promised to return to Japan as soon as a peace treaty between the two states is signed. In 1960 the Soviets threatened to renege on the promise unless the Japanese rejected the revised mutual security pact with the United States. Apparently the threat was not sufficient to counter American pressures for continued alliance.

The Soviet Union has not confined itself to external pressure in its attempts to influence other states, for with the international communist movement it can frequently penetrate and influence internal structures and decisions. Such is particularly true of Italy where the party receives about one quarter of the popular vote. The Communist Party is negligible in Germany, and in Japan it frequently shows loyalty to the Chinese Communist Party, as shown in the vote on the 1963 nuclear-test ban treaty which the Japanese Communist Party opposed.

[16] *Deadline Data on World Affairs* (July 18, 1961), p. 56.
[17] Zbigniew Brzezinski, *Alternative to Partition* (New York: McGraw-Hill, 1965), p. 85.

In addition to instruments of reward and punishment, ideological and institutional compatibility are important linkage factors enhancing influence. It might be hypothesized that a state will be most heavily influenced by those states with whom it shares similar ideological orientations. To the extent that the defeated states share democratic norms with the United States and other democracies, one might expect a greater exchange of influence. Similarly, other things being equal, a state will be more influenced by other members within an organization with which it identifies than by outsiders. Cold War alignment constantly risks being superceded by more contiguous or regional alignments.

How a state links itself with the external environment depends upon what it believes will maximize its power and provide adequately for state security. A state, in attempting to maximize its power and to minimize the power of others over it, has the option of joining and emphasizing collective security arrangements such as the United Nations, alignment with a super power such as in NATO, or membership in a more restricted regional organization such as the Common Market and Euratom. In general, a weaker power is more likely to favor a broader organization, for such an arrangement enhances the prospects for playing the various powers in the organization against each other and thereby reducing the risk of domination. Such an example may be found in the Japanese insistence upon emphasizing the United Nations over alignment with the United States in 1952. Similarly, Italy rejected De Gaulle's proposed Mediterranean Pact in 1958, favoring instead an emphasis upon the NATO alliance. However, it was safer for Germany to sign a Franco-German collaboration agreement in 1963 in view of the relative equality of German-French power capabilities.

Regional alignments, excluding the US and USSR, are motivated by the desire of a state to decrease its subservience to the super powers as well as to increase its power within an organization. Thus Japan has sought alignment with other Asian states, Italy has courted countries in North Africa for a Mediterranean alliance, and Germany has sought European integration.

While nations seek regional organization, they are also concerned with maximizing their power within the Cold War alliance system. For example, in 1958 De Gaulle was interested in the establishment of a NATO directorate composed of the United States, the United Kingdom, and France. Both Germany and Italy were tempted to support the MLF proposal in order to obtain a more important voice in the Atlantic Alliance, and both states have benefited by the gradual French withdrawal from NATO as they seek to fill the European power vacuum.

It might be expected that as Cold War tensions are alleviated the regional and contiguous context will become more important in affecting the policy of a state, for there are certain trade and cultural advantages accruing to the contiguous and immediate regional environments. As states become more dependent upon one another through common market arrangements,

311

they also become more likely to influence the behavior of other members in the organization, for the costs of disrupting these interdependent relationships may be very great. The future of linkages from the external environment is consequently dependent upon the progress of regional and universal political, military, and economic integration. The greater the progress made in regional arrangements excluding the super powers, the less the state will be influenced by pressures emanating from the Cold War. This has been a factor in the desire of some for the creation of a third force in Europe.

INTERNAL DETERMINANTS OF NATIONAL SECURITY POLICY

Before attempting to assess the relative contribution of internal and external factors to the making of national security policy in the defeated states, an effort will be made to suggest in general terms the role of such internal characteristics as the stability of the top leadership, the competition of the elite through party and pressure group structures, and the relationship of the elite to mass opinion in the making of national security policy.

The stability of the political leadership has a decided effect upon the foreign policy output. It might be hypothesized that a less stable government will tend to be more subject to external pressures than a stable one. This may be accounted for by the fact that the super powers are concerned that a weak government not fall into the camp of the opposition. The extreme lengths to which a super power will go to discourage the establishment of an undesirable government is illustrated by United States action in the 1948 Italian election, threatened as it was by a heavy Communist vote. Among the measures taken were threats of withdrawal of aid, the use of propaganda, including the encouragement of American citizens to write to relatives in Italy, and attempts to bolster the existing government by announcing diplomatic support on Trieste on the eve of the election. Internal stability also creates incentives for the state to align more closely with an outside power, and this alignment in turn affects the state's ability to prevent infringement of its sovereignty.

Government instability tends to resist the role a state plays in international affairs, for such a situation requires that constant attention be given by the elite to domestic issues. A highly active foreign policy is a luxury to be enjoyed by the stable government. Italy in particular has been hampered in the role it plays in NATO because of internal difficulties.[18]

A weak government threatened by internal difficulties may make a determined effort to obtain concessions from its super power allies in order to bolster its support at home. If the state is important to the Cold War

---

[18] Timothy W. Stanley, *NATO in Transition* (New York: Praeger, 1965), p. 325.

balance of power, success might be achieved as in the case of the limited concessions which Prime Minister Kishi received following his 1957 visit to the United States. In a sense a position of weakness becomes an element of strength, for the weak state has little to lose and the super power is forced to pay more attention to the weak state or risk losing it. At the same time, this attention might begin to infringe on the sovereignty of the weak state.

Even stable governments have on occasion emphasized potential internal threats in an effort to extract political concessions from a super power ally. Chancellor Adenauer was quick to emphasize the foreign policy differences between the Christian Democrats and the Social Democratic Party (SPD) and the threat the latter presented for the continued viability of the Adenauer government. The use of the SPD for external political purposes was a major factor in the failure of the two parties to join a coalition government for many years. In this particular instance a strong opposition party served as an important political asset for Germany in obtaining leverage over the control of its own national security policy.

The degree of stability of a government also has an effect upon the stability of a state's national security policy. For example, defense policy has been most consistent in Germany where the Christian Democratic Party has dominated the policy process. There has been no "opening to the Left" with the attending creation of certain pressures toward policies favored by the Left as in Italy. If anything, the Social Democrats have accepted the Christian Democratic position on foreign policy. Even prior to the coalition with the CDU/CSU, Willie Brandt, who now serves as Vice Chancellor and Foreign Minister, supported NATO, conscription, and/or indicated a willingness to accept the atomic bomb for Germany.[19] While the Nenni Socialists in Italy had to modify their foreign policy position in order to join the 1963 coalition, the Christian Democrats in Italy have also had to make certain concessions. The removal of missile bases was perhaps as much due to opposition by the Italian Socialists as it was to United States recognition that "soft" missile bases were provocative.[20]

The situation in Japan with its so-called one-and-one-half party system is more closely related to that of Adenauer's Germany as the majority Liberal Democrats have paid scant attention to the position of the Socialists on foreign policy issues. This neglect is exemplified by the vote on the 1960 security treaty with the United States during which time the Socialists were boycotting the Diet. The electoral patterns in Germany and Japan have been such that coalition with the Socialists has, for the most part, not been necessary for the creation of parliamentary government. Adenauer was sometimes able to get leverage over his frequent coalition partner, the Free Democratic Party, by threatening to join a coalition with the Social

[19] Uwe Kitzinger, *Britain, Europe, and Beyond* (Leyden: A. W. Sythoff, 1964), p. 76.
[20] See H. Stuart Hughes, *The United States and Italy* (Cambridge: Harvard U.P., 1965), p. 255.

Democrats. However, it remained for the post-Adenauer period to establish a coalition of the two parties.

The desire for political power has certainly been a factor in the movement of the Social Democrats in Germany toward the position on national security issues taken by the Christian Democrats. The same might be said of the Nenni Socialists in Italy. On the other hand, the Left Wing Socialist Party in Japan has derived much of its electoral support from its continued opposition to rearmament and alliance with the United States, although it has frequently seen the majority party co-opt some of its policies as in the case of Prime Minister Kishi's demands for a revision of the United States-Japanese security treaty as well as pressures for improved relations with Communist China.[21]

Another important internal determinant affecting the posture of national security policy is the nature of the elite cluster which plays a dominant role in the decision-making process. While in the three states included in the present study the bureaucracy has traditionally been an important factor in the decision-making structure, defeat at the end of the Second World War had the effect of decreasing the prestige of the military bureaucracy. Such has particularly been the case in Japan where interest in military service has been minimal. With the recent growth of the military in the three states, it might be expected that the prestige will again increase.

In the three states the business elite aligned primarily with the conservative political forces, while the labor leaders have thrown their support to the Left. Such is particularly the case in Japan where the cleavage on basic issues of national security between labor and socialist opinion, on the one hand, and business and government, on the other, is quite extreme. On the question of rearmament, a 1954 poll including approximately 50 respondents for each group indicated that some 87 per cent of the business executives and 51 per cent of the government officials favored rearmament in contrast with 10 per cent of the labor elite.[22] Votes on national security bills as well as interviews conducted with 100 Japanese parliamentarians in 1958[23] illustrate the almost unanimous socialist opposition to arms expansion and preference for neutrality.

The relationship between the elite and mass opinion is a vital one in democratic society, for democracy implies a government elite responsive and responsible to the public mood. If responsiveness is an appropriate measure of democracy, it would seem that Japan has fared least well of the three defeated powers. Professor Mendel concludes that "rearmament has earned only minimal and grudging support from most Japanese voters.

---

[21] Royama Masamichi, "The Japanese Approach to World Affairs," *Japan Quarterly*, X (April–June, 1963), 165.

[22] Lloyd A. Free, *The Dynamics of Influence in Today's Japan* (Princeton: The Research Council, 1954), p. 62.

[23] Free, *Six Allies and a Neutral*, pp. 33–56.

Two-thirds admit the need for some native defense forces but far fewer approve constitutional revision, conscription, or full rearmament."[24]

The Italian situation differs from that found in Japan, for in Italy mass opinion is largely apathetic on political issues. The a-political character of the Italian voter has been effectively documented in *The Civic Culture* in which questions tapping such information as exposure to political communications, the tendency to discuss politics, and interest in local affairs and elections revealed lower positive responses than were obtained in any of the other countries included in the study—United States, Great Britain, Mexico, and Germany.[25]

Professors Deutsch and Edinger conclude their analysis of the relationship between elite and mass opinion with the observation that the "German elites have not only unusually wide leeway for decision, but also the likelihood of unusual effectiveness in execution, so far as mass compliance is concerned."[26] Such a relationship not only permits the enactment of policies not fully supported, but it also enhances the rapidity with which decisions can be made and put into effect.

In sum it would seem that all three states have certain weaknesses in their democratic fabric. In Japan public opinion is highly fractionated, in Germany it is subservient, and in Italy the mass public is apathetic. Thus public moods are not the best predictors of national security policy.

THE BALANCE BETWEEN EXTERNAL AND INTERNAL FACTORS

While it is easy to speculate on the role played by internal and external factors in the development of foreign policy, measuring the relative impact of these factors is at best a delicate operation. Following the Lasswellian formula, it is possible to ascertain which groups are able to obtain decisions compatible with their policy preferences. Although not conclusive, such a measure provides some evidence of the determinants of specified policy decisions. The basic structure for such an approach has been developed by Deutsch and Edinger in their work on Germany.[27] The procedure consisted of taking several policy decisions and evaluating the relative satisfaction of various internal and external political groups under the assumption that those groups having their preferences incorporated in policy decisions most frequently have the greatest political power, or perhaps more accurately, those groups usually on the losing side have little power,

---

[24] Mendel, *The Japanese People and Foreign Policy*, p. 92.
[25] Gabriel A. Almond and Sidney Verba, *The Civic Culture* (Boston: Little, Brown, 1965), pp. 189–329, 332.
[26] Deutsch and Edinger, *Germany Rejoins the Powers*, p. 193.
[27] *Ibid.*, pp. 195–216.

Table 11.1—German Satisfaction Score Ex Post Facto Reactions of Internal and External Components

Issue	EDC (1953)	Paris Agreement (1955)	Diplomatic Relations USSR (1955)	One Year Conscription (1955)	Slow Arms (1956)	Reject Rapacki (1958)	Atomic Arms (1958)	Missile Bases (1958)	MLF (1965)	Average
Elites										
Cabinet	3	3	1	1	2	3	3	1	2	2.1
CDU	3	3	1	2	2	3	2	1	2	2.1
SPD	−3	−3	3	2	2	−3	−3	−3	−1	−0.1
Civil service	2	2	1	0	0	2	0	1		1.0
Diplomats	2	3	1	0	0	2	3	1		1.5
Military	−1	3	1	−2	−2	00	3	2	−1	0.3
Business	−1	2	2	2	0	2	1	1		1.1
Labor	−3	−3	3	2	2	−2	−3	−3		−0.9
Catholic church	2	0	−1	0	0	2	1	0		0.5
Evangelical church	−2	−2	3	0	0	−2	−2	−2		−0.9
Press	00	1	2	2	2	00	−1	−2		0.5
Average elite	0.18	0.82	1.55	0.82	0.73	0.64	0.36	−0.27	5	0.63
Mass opinion	−2	2	2	2	3	2	−3	−2	1	0.6
External factor[a]										
United States	3	3	−2	−3	−3	3	3	3	3	1.1
United Kingdom	3	3	−2	−3	−3	3	1	3	−1	0.4
France	3	1	−2	−3	−1	3	1	2	−2	0.2
USSR	−3	−3	3	3	3	−3	−3	−3	−3	−1.0

Key: 3, very favorable; 2, mostly favorable; 1, mildly favorable; 0, indifferent; 00, divided; −1, mildly opposed; −2, opposed; −3, strongly opposed.

a—Official Reaction of government.

SOURCES: adapted from Karl W. Deutsch and Lewis J. Edinger, *Germany Rejoins the Powers*, pp. 208–11. Additional data on MLF from Deutsch et al., France, Germany, and the Western Alliances.

since compatability of position might be more indicative of followership rather than leadership.

Tables 11.1 through 11.3 provide a summary concerning the relative satisfaction on various national security policy issues of certain groups and interests in Germany, Italy, and Japan. Rankings range from +3 for very favorable to −3 for strongly opposed.

In those cases in which a cell has not been filled, it was believed that the available data were inadequate for making an estimate. A further qualification should be noted. As a result of the averaging procedure, some distortion in the figures is likely to develop. Because of the frequency of data gaps for Italy not all averages have been computed.

The pieces of information leading to these weightings are widely scattered. An attempt was made to look at a vast amount of primary and secondary literature, some of which has been discussed in earlier sections. In general, it was easier to ascertain the position of political parties since votes were taken in the respective parliaments on most issues. Although roll call votes are not always used, journalistic reporting generally emphasizes the positions taken by political parties. Similarly the official position of the external actors is usually well-documented in newspapers and chronologies. Particularly useful in this regard was *Deadline Data on World Affairs* and *The New York Times*.

Evaluations of mass and elite opinion were more difficult to ascertain, particularly in view of the fact that polling techniques utilized in these states are not as sophisticated as those employed by prestigious American polling organizations such as the Survey Research Center and the National Opinion Research Center. The bulk of opinion data cited for Japan, for example, is based upon polls conducted by the *Mainichi* and *Ashai* newspapers. Consequently, rather than accept these polls at face value, corroberative sorts of evidence were sought such as evaluations of political observers and writers.

The chart for Germany with the exception of the MLF issue is based entirely upon evaluations by Deutsch and Edinger and is supported by their massive collection of relevant data.[28] Evaluations for Italy and Japan, on the other hand, were based upon somewhat more scattered sources. Perhaps the best analysis in terms of Italian attitudes on national security issues is that of Free and Sereno[29] and the several books by Norman Kogan.[30] The many blank cells in Table 11.2 attest to the fact that poll data and educated guesses concerning the attitudes of Italian elites on the various issues were not available. Surveys of attitudes among the Japanese elite conducted by Professor Free[31] provided some basis for evaluating Japanese

---

[28] *Ibid.*

[29] *Italy: Dependent Ally or Independent Partner.*

[30] *Italy and the Allies* (Cambridge: Harvard U.P., 1956); *The Government of Italy* (New York: T. Y. Crowell, 1962); and *The Politics of Italian Foreign Policy* (New York: Praeger, 1963).

[31] Lloyd A. Free, *The Dynamics of Influence in Today's Japan.*

Table 11.2—Italian Satisfaction Score Ex Post Facto Reactions of Internal and External Components

Issue	Peace Treaty (1947)	NATO (1949)	Trieste (1954)	EDC (1954)	WEU (1955)	MLF	Average
Elites							
Christian democrats	1	3	2	2	2	2	2.0
Socialist democrats	−3	0	1	2	2	1	0.5
Socialist (Nenni)	−3	−3	−3	−3	−3	00	−2.5
Communist		−3	−1	−3	−3	−3	−2.6
Liberal		3	2	2	2	2	2.2
Republican		3	2	2	2	2	2.2
Average party elite	−1.67	0.50	0.50	0.33	0.33	0.67	0.11
Civil service	1				2	2	
Military	−2				2		
Business	−2				2		
Labor	−2						
Press	−2						
Intellectuals	−2						
Mass opinion	−2	1	00	1	1		0.2
External factor[a]							
United States	3	3	2	3	3	3	2.8
France	3	3	2	−2	3	−2	1.2
United Kingdom	3	3	2	2	3	−1	2.0
USSR	3	−3	2	−3	−3	−3	1.2

Key: 3, very favorable; 2, mostly favorable; 1, mildly favorable; 0, indifferent; 00, opposed; −1, mildly opposed; −2, opposed; −3, strongly opposed.

[a]—Official Reaction of government.

SOURCES: Lloyd A. Free and Renzo Sereno, *Italy, Dependent Ally or Independent Partner* and Norman Kogan, *The Politics of Italian Foreign Policy.*

Table 11.3—Japanese Satisfaction Score Ex Post Facto Reactions of Internal and External Components

Issue	Peace Treaty (1951)	Security Treaty (1951)	Rearmament (1951–1955)	Non-recognized China (1952)	Defense Bill (1954)	Treaty Rev. (1960)	Japan-Korea (1965)	Average
Elites								
Liberal Party[a]	2	2	2	−1	3	2	2	1.7
Democrat	2	2	3	−1	3	2	2	1.9
Right Socialist	2	−2	1	−3	−3	−2		−1.2
Left Socialist	−2	−3	−2	−3	−3	−3	−3	−2.7
Civil service		2	3	−2	3	2		1.6
Military		2	3		3	2		2.5
Business		2	3	−2	3	2	2	1.7
Labor		−2	−2	−3	−2	−3	−2	−2.3
Press	2	−2				−2		−0.7
Intellectuals		−2	−2	−3	−2	−3		−2.4
Average elite	1.20	−0.10	1.00	−2.25	0.56	−0.30	0.20	0.04
Mass opinion		−1	1	−3		−2		−1.3
External factor[b]								
United States	3	3	3	3	3	3	3	3.0
Red China	−3	−3	−3	−3	−3	−3	−3	−3.0
USSR	−3	−3	−3	−3	−3	−3	−3	−3.0

Key: 3, very favorable; 2, mostly favorable; 1, mildly favorable; 0, indifferent; 00, divided; −1, mildly opposed; −2, opposed; −3, strongly opposed.

a—Since 1955 the Liberal-Democratic Party has been united and the Socialist combination has been on and off.

b—Official Reaction of government.

Sources: Douglas H. Mendel, Jr., *The Japanese People and Foreign Policy* and Lloyd A. Free, *The Dynamics of Influence in Todays Japan.*

positions on the issues, but by and large elite data for Japan is based upon scattered evaluations of political commentators. The various mass opinion data as well as some elite data have been carefully compiled by Professor Mendel in his work on Japanese foreign policy attitudes.[32] The most complete assessment of positions taken on the 1960 revision of the security treaty with the United States, however, is found in a recent study by George R. Packard.[33]

Despite the incompleteness of the data, certain patterns appear. For example, the external component seems to have been more important in the making of the early decisions. In the case of Germany, Deutsch and Edinger note that since mid-1955 there has been a marked shift of influence from the external to the internal factors.[34] While it is not that simple to date the shift for the other states because of the relatively small number of issues surveyed, it is clear that in the case of Italy there has been no "diktat" of the type received when confronted with the peace treaty. Although the United States showed satisfaction on all seven issues rated for Italy, the ruling Christian Democrats also favored the moves, a tendency which led Professor Free to categorize Italy as the "constant ally" in contrast with Japan as the "semi-ally" and Germany, the "divided ally."[35]

The data fail to provide an adequate notion of the effect of the opening to the Left in Italy upon the external-internal balance. It is clear, however, that the Nenni Socialists now support policies closer to those favored by the United States. Nenni was even reported to have been in favor of MLF if Britain would support it.[36]

A peace treaty, rearmament, and United States bases were imposed upon Japan despite widespread elite and public opposition. Japan has now reduced the burden of United States military bases and obtained a number of concessions under the 1960 treaty. Such changes would seem to suggest that internal forces are becoming more important in the policy process.

If influence is measured by satisfaction with the results, it is clear that the United States has been the most significant external actor in the policy process of the defeated states. As noted in Tables 11.1 and 11.2, within the regional environment the United Kingdom has been more successful in influencing policy than has France. A major factor in explaining this situation is French fears of German rearmament as well as the rise to power of De Gaulle and the concomitant disinterest in certain NATO policies. Communist China, on the other hand, has had little effect in influencing policy decisions vis-à-vis Japan.

Cleavages among the groups appear most pronounced in Japan, particularly in view of the movement toward the left in Italian politics. Germany,

---

[32] Douglas H. Mendel, *The Japanese People and Foreign Policy*.
[33] *Protest in Tokyo* (Princeton: Princeton U.P., 1966).
[34] Deutsch and Edinger, *Germany Rejoins the Powers*.
[35] Free, *Six Allies and a Neutral*.
[36] *The New York Times* (March 4, 1964).

on the other hand, is moving toward the consensual society. The average satisfaction score is positive for most of the groups included in the analysis. Even the SPD appears not to have been greatly dissatisfied with the outcome of the nine national security issues for it scored an average of only −1. The two parties are even closer today as they have joined together in a governmental coalition.

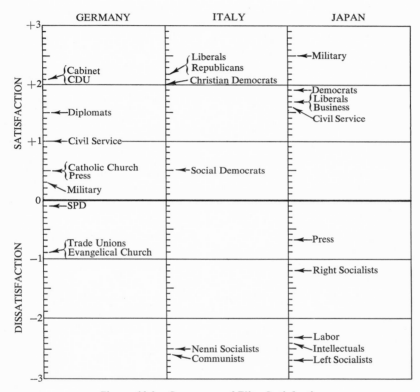

Figure 11.1. Summary of Elite Satisfaction

Figure 11.1 provides a summary of the relative satisfaction of the various elite groups ranging from the most satisfied to those who have not been satisfied with the policy output in the area of national security policy. While the scores are close, the Liberals and Republicans in Italy rated one-tenth of a point higher than the Christian Democratic Party. This suggests the caveat that satisfaction is not a completely valid measure of power. However, wide disparity in satisfaction scores among the groups is indicative of the relative power positions. In terms of the making of national security policy, there is little doubt as to the power of the left and moderate wings of the political continuum in the three states. The role of the military in Japan is somewhat distorted in the results, perhaps because adequate cognizance has not been taken of issues indicating a slow down in armaments. Instead, the computations are based upon the broad issues rather than the annual military budget in which dissatisfaction with amount is more likely to be expressed.

The data as summarized in the tables and figure provide greater substance for the point made above that Japanese public opinion has opposed a number of national issues adopted by the government. Opinion in both Italy and Germany, on the other hand, demonstrate considerable acquiescence, if not enthusiastic support, for the course chartered by their governments.

CONCLUSIONS

The purpose of this paper has been to summarize in descriptive fashion the external and internal linkages in the making of national security policy in postwar Germany, Italy, and Japan. Given their status as defeated states, the external environment was found to be critical in influencing foreign policy decisions. It was because of the rise of the Cold War that pressures were placed by the United States and some of its allies upon the defeated states to rearm. Yet Cold War events, unless of immediate threat to the state, appear to have had minimal effect in boosting enthusiasm for rearmament. Cold War tensions instead seemed to induce caution for fear that the state might be brought into a war not of its choosing.

The regional and contiguous environments appear not to have been major factors affecting national security policy despite various traditional rivalries within the area. However, as the Cold War recedes and as the regional environment integrates more extensively economically, politically, and militarily, one might expect the super powers to play a less significant role as far as influence is concerned. The motivation for the establishment of regional third forces in order to escape dependence upon the super powers is high.

Efforts to contrast linkages from the external and internal environments suggest that over the years the latter environment has become more important in the policy process. During periods of internal political instability, however, there becomes an increased chance for external political pressure to be effective.

Although, as pointed out earlier, the three defeated states are not the best prototypes of democracies, they at least enjoy free elections and competitive political parties. Rearmament might have been more rapid in all three states had public opinion been more in favor of it. Perhaps the greatest disregard of public opinion on national security issues is found in Japan where large segments of the population opposed many governmental rearmament policies. Such neglect of popular opinion appears possible only by virtue of the overwhelming parliamentary majority of the ruling Liberal-Democratic Party, a position the party enjoys more because of its domestic policies than its position on national security issues.

Whether similar patterns exist with respect to other policy issues or in other democratic states is difficult to say. It has been impossible to make generalizations concerning how democracies as such are linked to their internal and external environments. To do so would require an analysis of more democracies as well as nondemocracies. Whether having democratic status would make much difference in the national security policies a state selects may be dubious. A state reacts to other states in the international system in terms of basic power relationships in an effort to increase its own power over others and to reduce power over itself. Democracies have been found to be neither more peaceful nor more warlike than autocratic states.[37]

This does not mean, however, that democratic ideology is unimportant, for this is indeed an age of ideological conflict. The democratic aspirations of the defeated powers make them more compatible alliance partners for the United States, though alliance with Portugal suggests that democracy is not a prerequisite of alignment. As long as the defeated states did not swing to the communist side, they probably had little choice in whether or not to rearm on the side of the West. As they become less dependent upon the United States, one may begin to expect greater divergence, including pressures for independent nuclear forces or a European nuclear force, but this has little to do with democratic features.

[37] See the findings of Ivor Thomas, "War and its Causes, 1815–1914," in *War and Democracy* ed. by E. F. M. Durbin and George Catlin (London: Kegan Paul, 1938); Lewis F. Richardson, *Statistics of Deadly Quarrels* (Chicago: Quadrangle Books, 1960), p. 176; and Quincy Wright, *A Study of War* (Chicago: U. of Chicago, 1942), p. 221.

CHAPTER TWELVE

Linkages between Domestic and International
Politics in Underdeveloped Nations

Michael O'Leary

THE underdeveloped nations provide a promising, yet frustrating, testing ground for the linkage concept. We can be reasonably confident that national and international phenomena are indeed connected in the movement and change which we observe in these countries. At the same time, however, we cannot avoid noting the diversity of these nations, and the intricacy and complexity of their national-international linkages. We face, therefore, immense problems in making sensible statements about these linkages. This essay will attack this difficult problem by first setting forth some propositions about the international system, then by turning to the evolving role of the underdeveloped nations in the system, and finally by considering how the pattern of national-international linkages may affect their future roles in the system. As it will become quite clear, the hypotheses advanced are quite tentative and primitive. They are occasionally buttressed with examples of state behavior, logical deductive argument, and rather broadly based empirical evidence. But in no instance can these hypotheses be said to have been subjected to any kind of rigorous testing. The only claim on their behalf is that they are susceptible to testing and that as they are treated they provide some possibility for enlarging our under-standing of the underdeveloped world.

One common thread which runs through the diversity of the developing states is outrage which their leaders feel about the injustices of the world in which they must live. As their leaders see it, the new states have been born in chains, and everywhere struggle to be free. The removal of colonial domination has often only highlighted the multitude of forces impinging upon the choices available to leaders and citizens in the developing nations. Peoples of the underdeveloped world are constantly aware of the continued foreign influences in their economic and political lives. As the Latin Americans, the first generation of new nations, have already discovered, the influence may at times seem almost to negate the formal perquisites of inde-pendence. Unhappiness with the status quo is summed up in the phrase "neo-colonialism," encompassing the predominance of international economic involvement, the substantial residues of foreign personnel in governmental, economic, and social structures, and the persistence of both blatant and clandestine external intervention.

But in some ways the most obvious of the restrictions upon these states are the least troublesome. The varieties of economic subordination, the imperfect national control over domestic politics and administration, and the shock-waves emanating from big-power rivalry all offer at least the hope of mitigation with the passage of time. At minimum, these problems are soluble in principle, they lend themselves to diagnoses which recommend plausible steps toward reform, and they provide an agenda for discussions with those states which have the capacity to help alter the unpleasant condition of the developing states. Even when these problems are not susceptible to actual reform they allow for what in political life is often an adequate substitute—talk about reform.

These encumbrances are also limited in the sense that their impact may be ameliorated through marginal changes in the existing international system. Indeed, the most prominent reforms advocated—repatterning foreign aid and trade, prohibiting external interference, up-grading the impact of international organizations, and the like—are designed to enhance the existing international system's capacity for absorbing new strains and demands.

But we must also consider the extent to which leaders are intentionally or unintentionally pursuing objectives which cannot be obtained by changes at the margin of the established international order. Leaders in the third world may well be motivated not only by complaints about specific national injuries, but also by a malaise which cannot be satisfied without radical transformations of the whole international system. To the degree that leaders do in fact act on the basis of these feelings, they represent the most serious challenge to the status quo.

One proposition which helps explain this style behavior may be briefly stated as follows: Although the underdeveloped nations have been given membership in a generally unintegrated international system, the inclinations of their leaders, their international status, and, most importantly, the interplay of domestic and international politics all induce them to work within this system largely to undermine it in favor of a more highly integrated system both in their immediate geographical regions and throughout the world.

In the present discussion we are defining integration solely in terms of the style of relationship among the primary units of a system—in this case, nation states. If the units interact with one another in such a way that their discreteness and integrity is generally maintained, we may say the system is largely unintegrated. To the degree that units interact in such a way as to bring about a good deal of mutual penetration of boundaries, then we may say the system is rather highly integrated.

From the perspective of the developing nations, the system in which they are currently expected to operate is most noteworthy for the degree to which it represents an extension of the competitive nation-state system, a system which is in our terms rather unintegrated. This is a system which has characterized not only European international relations since the Renaissance, but also, as some studies indicate, some pre-modern non-Western international relations as well.[1]

From the viewpoint of the underdeveloped nations, especially the newer ones, what is important about the present system is this continuation of patterns from the past. The most basic continuing element is the fact that the primary actors of the system are territorially based nation states.

It is the preeminence of these nation states which gives the system a certain continuity over time, and which renders to the system a quality which we have termed lacking integration. Put in another way, a system is considered integrated to the degree that the role of individuals is not predetermined by their membership in one single unit or grouping within the system. Whatever else may characterize a relatively integrated system, it must be one in which individuals may act through alternative units within the system.

This concept of integration is, unhappily, different from—although not directly antithetical to—the term as used by many other writers.[2] But it is consistent with at least one systematic analysis of international relations, that of Morton Kaplan. In his elaboration of six international systems—or, more accurately, as he says, "six states of equilibrium of one ultrastable international system"—he suggests a scale as to the system's degree of

[1] See, for example, some of the pre-Machiavelli *Realpolitik* doctrines reprinted in Joel Larus (ed.), *Comparative World Politics* (1964), pp. 117–22; and George Modelski, "Kautilya: Foreign Policy and International System in the Ancient Hindu World." *American Political Science Review*, LVIII (September, 1964), 549–60.

[2] See Amitai Etzioni, *Political Unification* (1965), pp. 5–6; Karl W. Deutsch et al., *Political Community and the North Atlantic Area* (1957), pp. 5–7, 31; Ernst B. Haas and Philippe C. Schmitter, "Economics and Differential Patterns of Political Integration: Projections about Unity in Latin America," in *International Political Communities* (1966), pp. 259–99; and Philip E. Jacob and William L. C. Wheaton (eds.), *The Integration of Political Communities* (1964), pp. 3–45.

integration.[3]   The unit veto system, in which each state is completely on its own in a potential war of all against all, without friend or ally, is held to be the least integrated.[4]   The universal and hierarchical international systems, especially the latter, are judged to be the most integrated.   They are both characterized by possible alliances of national actors with other members of the international political subsystem.   In the hierarchical system, the most integrated of Kaplan's systems, there is large opportunity for alliance across national boundaries on the basis of economic, functional, or other similarities.[5]   According to Kaplan, "while these 'interest group-ings' may have some degree of territorial organization, the functional lines across territorial divisions will be more communicative than channels linking diverse functional activities within a given territory."[6]

The near monopoly of political communication among groups, no matter how diverse, within territorial boundaries, describes the condition of low integration of the international system; it also conceptually links the current international system with earlier patterns of international relations.

This basic underlying continuity is also, we shall argue, associated with several other important persistent characteristics of the international system.   At this point, however, we should point out that certain behavioral patterns often considered a part of integration are not part of the concept as it is here employed.   Frequent usage of the concept makes assumption about the relationship between levels of integration and the degree of solidarity, stability and harmony within a system.   "Political integration," in one suggestion of a consensus definition, " . . . is characterized by a sense of community on the part of those within a territory, coupled with ex-pectations of peaceful change and means for achieving it."[7]

It may be, as a matter of empirical observation, that the majority of integrated systems (as the concept is defined in this Chapter) will, on the whole, tend to demonstrate these characteristics.   But it is argued, for reasons elaborated later, that stability and community feelings are not a necessary part of the concept.   Integrated systems may be harmonious and stable, or they may be extremely divisive and unstable.   And the same may be said for unintegrated systems.   The degree of integration may be an important variable for both the likelihood and the kinds of cooperation and conflict, but it does not assure any particular state of the system in these respects.   It also follows from this concept that members of some units may be integrated within a larger system against their wishes.[8]

[3] Morton Kaplan, *System and Process in International Politics* (1957), p. 21.
[4] *Ibid.*
[5] *Ibid.*, pp. 45–50.
[6] *Ibid.*, p. 49.
[7] Michael Barkun, "Integration, Organization, and Values," in Robert W. Gregg and Michael Barkun (eds.), *The United Nations System and Its Functions* (1968), p. 451.
[8] Referring to its "moral neutrality" Barkun concludes that political integration does not "exhibit any necessary affinity for what we may choose to regard as social pro-gress." (*Ibid.*, p. 459.)

327

The dynamics of an unintegrated international system may best be exposed by reviewing Kaplan's general formulation of the balance of power system and its necessary rules.[9] Units of the system—nation states—are induced to engage in constant jockeying for political advantage to increase their bases of power and to improve access to new sources of power. When it is advantageous to do so, a state may engage in war to defend or improve its position. But war is conducted for explicit, relatively limited purposes. The relationship between costs and benefits usually induces states to stop fighting rather than eliminate or enfeeble another national actor. Indeed, victors are frequently eager to restore a defeated power to the system in order to promote stability surrounding the new status quo. Most importantly, defeated nations should be so treated that they may in the future become allies against other members of the system.

This system resembles the classical model of the uncontrolled free economic market. "Like Adam Smith's 'unseen hand' of competition, the international system is policed informally by self-interest. . . ."[10] But it also contains some regularities of behavior which may be termed institutions, or structures. One of the most important is alliances. Whenever members of a system feel themselves threatened by opposing members they will form defensive alliances to maintain the status quo. This is especially important when a member of the system comes to be motivated by supranational goals. The existence of alliances is relatively permanent; they are, in Thomas Schelling's phrase "prominent solutions" to certain international problems.[11] But membership in alliances will change rather rapidly. Neither friendship nor enmity is permanent; acceptable partners are determined by the shifting exigencies of the situation.

Other institutional forms may develop as part of an unintegrated international system. These generally fall into one of two categories. There may arise, first of all, those institutions which permit the conduct of relatively neutral activities such as humanitarian affairs, the sharing of technical knowledge and provision for postal, telegraphic, and other forms of exchange. Second, there may develop organizations which provide a central forum for the conduct of diplomatic communication and competition. In an unintegrated system organizations produce weak feedback of their own to alter the behavior of system members acting through them.

Nevertheless, the existence of such organizations may be important, especially for weaker members of an international system. Weaker members will tend to keep a watchful eye out for new partners and allies. Weak states will, therefore, generally prefer to have issues considered in the widest forum available. The wider the forum, the more likely they are to find states which will take their side in opposition to the stronger system members.

[9] Kaplan, *op. cit.*, pp. 22–36.
[10] Morton Kaplan, "Some Problems of International Systems Research," in *International Political Communities* (1966), p. 478.
[11] Thomas Schelling, *The Strategy of Conflict* (1960), pp. 57 ff.

Conversely, the stronger national actors will seek decisions in the most limited forum, where their predominance is less likely to be challenged effectively. Bilateral relations will be preferred over multilateral, and limited, regional actions will be preferred over system-wide action.

As was suggested earlier, decision making within an unintegrated system may demonstrate many combinations of cooperation and competitiveness. It will generally be true, however, that the amount and kind of cooperation will be circumscribed by the lack of integration. When states deal with one another, they may do so in quite friendly and cooperative fashion. But even in such cases, agreement proceeds from a mutual acceptance of quite limited shared substantive goals. The mores of such a system generally provide for negotiation which is either of a short-run instrumental nature, or for quite limited long-run purposes. Military alliances are examples of the first type; treaties of friendship, commerce, and navigation are examples of the second. Insofar as political leaders operate within the framework of the unintegrated state system, they expect no more than this from partners in an international agreement.

The international system has of course undergone many changes. Yet the foregoing consequences of the lack of integration within the system seem to be of continuing importance. Bipolarity (in various degrees of looseness and tightness)[12] and balance of power are separate conditions of the international system which are in some ways similar, and in some ways different from one another. It is fashionable these days to speak of moving beyond power, the balance of power, and the whole structure of international relations characterized by competitive power politics. Much of this argumentation, however, is based on a conception of power and power politics which is wedded to the use of force. But as Hans Morgenthau has himself argued, political power and force are not synonymous.[13] If we take some notion of power such as that of Dahl's or Singer's, it is quite easy to see in the world today countless attempts of one or more nation states trying to alter the behavior of others.[14] The inhibitions upon the use of force as a sanction (which are clearly not absolute themselves) do not seem to have removed competition and the attempt to influence. Even some views of a radically changed future international system, as Roger Masters has shown, can include at least partial workings of Kaplan's rules for the balance of power system.[15] The independent nation state, however much it has been "objectively" undermined, remains a significant unit of action for decision

---

[12] See Kaplan's *System and Process*, pp. 36–45; and his "Some Problems of International Systems Research," pp. 479–94.

[13] Hans J. Morgenthau, *Politics Among Nations* (1963), pp. 28–29.

[14] See Robert Dahl, "The Concept of Power," *Behavioral Science*, II (July, 1957), 201–15; and J. David Singer, "Inter-Nation Influence: A Formal Model," *American Political Science Review*, LVII (June, 1963), 420–30. For a most perceptive discussion of power in international theory, see Charles A. McClelland *Theory and the International System* (1966), pp. 61–89.

[15] Roger D. Masters, "A Multi-Bloc Model of the International System," *American Political Science Review*, LV (December, 1961), 780–98.

makers. A good deal of their concerns continue to be devising means of applying some traditional moves of power politics under new conditions.

DOMESTIC POLITICS AND THE INTERNATIONAL SYSTEM

The low level of integration within the international system, the relative impermeability of the nation state, and the expectation that all system members will follow the same set of rules have tended to produce the so-called "billiard ball" approach to international politics. Whether derived from general historical analysis (as in Morgenthau's writings) or from more formal deduction (as represented by Kaplan), the image is that of holistic, independent nation states striking and rebounding against one another according to patterns which may be more or less clearly analyzed and predicted. Often this image has been only implicit. Occasionally it may be more explicitly stated:

> International politics . . . is the arena in which ultimately authoritative states, almost like Leibnizian monads, have to come into contact with each other and settle their conflicts without the supravention of any external political authority or master monad.[16]

In linkage terms this view holds that all significant transactions are channeled through, or controlled by, governments. This approach has necessarily led writers to pay highly selective attention to domestic political processes. This is not to say that these topics are completely ignored. Indeed, the major writers of the "billiard ball" school make frequent reference to public opinion, national morale, the quality of government, and the like. Yet, almost without exception, such references are in the context of assessing the strength of nations through capability analysis. As Harold Sprout has noted, they are not concerned so much with how domestic politics will influence what nations *will try to do*—the individual and the systemic goals they will pursue and the alternative means which will be favored as they try to reach their goals. They are concerned instead with what nations *will be able to accomplish* in international relations.[17] Motivations seem to be treated in one of two ways: either by assuming that any differences between state motivations are unimportant, or by assuming that the prime sources of motivation are to be found in the international, rather than national environment.

Concepts such as the struggle for power, an automatic balance of power system, and imperialism stemming from an international power vacuum are examples of this style of analysis. Morgenthau, in particular,

[16] Morton Kaplan, "Is International Relations a Discipline?" *Journal of Politics* 44 (August, 1961), 470.

[17] Harold and Margaret Sprout, "Environmental Factors in the Study of International Politics," *Journal of Conflict Resolution*, 1 (December, 1957), 309 ff.

has expressed these ideas. He has also stressed the legal dimension of this concept: a view of national sovereignty which holds that the state participates in international relations as a monolithic actor whose integrity and unity cannot be modified or compromised.[18] Other writers have proceeded somewhat differently, while still relying on similar concepts in constructing models of the international system which stress universal rules and requirements binding on all states. Kaplan's contributions, as we shall argue below, are not limited to the "billiard ball" approach, but the bulk of his analysis has been addressed to alternative sets of system-wide rules. Arthur Lee Burns, to cite one more example, has focused on the levels of technological military capabilities in the construction of international systems models.[19]

At minimum, relying on system-wide rules and events requires adoption of a convenient fiction. Technological change, decision making, and other phenomena do not occur within a system as such, but rather within the individual nation states. Simultaneous events within states, or common reactions to international situations can of course profitably be regarded as representing system-wide phenomena. There is no denying the great analytical contributions made by Kaplan and others proceeding from a system-wide viewpoint.

But international systems analysis has simplified the view of domestic processes in another way which leads to more serious problems. In their concern with the international system writers have seemingly underplayed the critical role which domestic politics of the member states may play in determining the rules and operations of the system.

This important relationship obtains in at least two levels of analysis, the historical and the theoretical. This dual relationship can be clearly seen with reference to the classical balance of power system in Europe. As a matter of historical fact, during the highpoint of the balance of power the nature of European regimes was vital in affecting the way in which balance of power policies were carried out. From the beginning of the state system in Europe to the end of the nineteenth century the major European governments and leaders, with the partial exception of the French, were united by the principle of legitimacy of monarchical rule. Furthermore, they were often tied together by the complex system of intermarriage among ruling families in differing nations. These communal bonds eventually proved to be weak and imperfect foundations for a stable international system. But they help point out an important principle in analyzing international relations of the period. Because of common values and family ties the European system was partially integrated in important respects. This limited integration was critical in helping the system persist as long as it did.

---

[18] Morgenthau, *op. cit.*, pp. 312–31.

[19] Arthur Lee Burns, "From Balance to Deterrence," *World Politics*, IX (July, 1957), 494–529.

It is equally important to note that descriptions of the model derived from this experience generally ignore or depreciate such integration which did exist. Those analyses evaluate the balance of power as essentially an unintegrated system. One historical study of the European system, for example, argues that the existence and persistence of the independent state system was the *sine qua non* of the balance of power. The fact of an integrative homogeneity was a facilitating but not vital condition. One could envision the preservation of equilibrium, albeit with difficulty, among nonhomogeneous states:

> The absence of homogeneity would not be destructive of the balance of power in the same way that the absence of . . . the state system itself would be. If you took away the state system, you would simply have no possibility of a balance of power among states; it would be like depriving the omelet of eggs.[20]

In somewhat different fashion, Kaplan makes the same point. His six essential rules of the balance of power system are clearly related to the actions of units whose internal differences are considered irrelevant.[21] State motivations are considered as simple (and in their own way quite as useful) as the maximizing man of economic analysis.

For a number of reasons it seems advisable to consider the possibility of a much more complex connection between domestic and international political systems. Kaplan himself provides the opening wedge for such consideration. He points out the need for sensitivity to the existence of "coupled" social systems, when the output of one (say domestic political system) is input for another (the international political system), and vice-versa.[22] Later, he refers to the fact that the composition of national actors— as to their government's degree of central control and the amount of political democracy—will influence their behavior in any of the six systems he out-lines. Yet one is given to infer that the impact of differing national actors upon the international system is at best marginal. The primary difference among them seems to be the degree to which one kind of actor or another will be able to conform to the "givens" of a particular international system.[23]

These suggestions are a helpful step away from the pure "billiard ball" approach to international politics. But is it a big enough step? To put the question directly, should we not consider adding a new rule to the requirements for balance of power system (and possibly the "very loose" bipolar and other similar systems) which would read something as follows: "National actors must be composed of stable subsystem-dominant (strongly centralized) political systems which rely in part upon professional staffs for making and implementing policy."

[20] Edward Gulick, *Europe's Classical Balance of Power* (1955), p. 24.
[21] Kaplan, *op. cit., System and Process*, p. 23.
[22] *Ibid.*, pp. 5–6.
[23] *Ibid.*, pp. 54–74.

Once again, Kaplan provides some support for this requirement. In discussing national actors and their role in the balance of power, he says:

> The directive [nondemocratic], subsystem dominant [centralized] actors will extend its primary attention to external consideration and will be able sufficiently to manipulate public opinion to carry out a diverse and rapidly changing policy. . . . The nondirective [democratic], subsystem dominant actor will find it somewhat easier to manipulate public support and may also find this manipulation less necessary. Under some conditions the public may be prepared to support changes in policy without being manipulated. This is the case in some subsystem dominant, nondirective systems [such as Great Britain] in which there is a tradition that external affairs are primarily the concern of the executive.[24]

On the other hand, says Kaplan:

> The nondirective system dominant [decentralized] actor will pay primary attention to internal considerations in the formulation of external policy. If the attempt is made to manipulate public opinion, it may succeed in a specific instance if strong statements concerning external dangers are made. In this case, however, *it may prove exceptionally difficult to reverse policy should that later prove desirable.*[25]

Since it is almost always desirable, because it is necessary, to reverse policy in competitive international politics, and since it is necessary to give primary attention to external affairs, these statements of Kaplan seem to support the additional rule proposed above.

We can derive some expected patterns of behavior from the foregoing model of the balance of power or similar unintegrated international systems. National leaders are likely to be concerned with demands and opportunities derived from the external system. Foreign policy makers will tend to be more sensitive to international politics than to the internal politics of the domestic systems over which they preside.

Determination of the "national interest" is likely to be dominated by external considerations—maintenance of alliances, access to important resources, and the like—to the relative lack of concern with satisfying domestic political and material demands. Policies leading to improvement of the total domestic system may be followed, but policies specifically designed to provide differential benefits for internal groups will frequently be resisted and rejected when possible, and explained away when necessary.

Strong, independent governments, and a stable unintegrated international system tend to reinforce one another. This supportive relationship suggests that the leaders of a strong and stable domestic political

---

[24] *Ibid.*, p. 60. For an historical-theoretical study which makes the same point, see Richard Rosecrance, *Action and Reaction in World Politics* (1963), pp. 281–3.

[25] Kaplan, *op. cit.*, *System and Process*, p. 60.

system (in Kaplan's terms, a system dominated by a subsystem) may have a special affinity for an unintegrated, competitive international system. Such an international system is likely to intensify the characteristics of those governments which participate in it. The leaders of a strong state, with adequate resources at their command, and flexible control over these resources, gain in two ways in an unintegrated system: they will generally improve their position over other states which do not have such strong power base at home; and they will increase their domestic political control by appealing for support in the face of constant international crisis and un-certainty. (The obverse of this generalization, which we will consider shortly, is that governments beginning with a weak power base will have that weakness intensified through participating in an unintegrated system.)

There is another important linkage between domestic politics and inter-national political systems which is relevant for our present concerns. Active participation in international relations requires the establishment of an effective cadre of officials charged with successful management of their nation's foreign relations. In recent times the tendency has been to bureau-cratize this staff, to organize their jobs into a career service and to protect them as much as possible from the vicissitudes of internal politics. The creation of similarly organized foreign office bureaucracies is clearly an example of the potency of international inputs into the domestic polity. For every manner of active nation state, no matter how democratic or dictatorial, no matter what philosophy or ideology has motivated it, has had to establish a professional bureaucracy to support its international activities.

In the unintegrated international system, skilled diplomats are essential. Representation among system members normally takes place among these national agents selected for their skill at international representation, reporting, and negotiating. They are essential in the reciprocal communica-tion of which much international interaction is composed.

We can hypothesize here the existence of what Rosenau terms a "fused" linkage relationship.[26] The institutions organized in response to international inputs may create, in turn, pressure upon their national governments for conducting policy along certain lines. They can influence, in other words, the nature of the output from the polity to the international environment. Some of the pressure created by professional diplomatic services upon their governments may coincide with the tendencies of strong government leaders to play an active role in an unintegrated international system. Both bureaucrats and policy-leaders will feel most sanguine about pursuing a vision of the national interest which is derived from the contours of the external environment rather than domestic values and pressures. More specifically, professional diplomatic staffs will tend to favor a policy which is characterized by deliberateness of conduct, consistency, and general pre-

[26] See Chapter 3.

dictability once a course of action is determined. This is not to deny the diplomat's sympathy with the catch-as-catch-can style of international competition. It merely refers to the prescription that once a strategy for a particular subgame has been determined, it should be followed through despite any deviating pressures from domestic political or other sources. The professional diplomat will feel most sanguine about dealing with his counterparts in other nations; his influence upon policy will, therefore, be in the direction of encouraging as much activity as possible through traditional diplomatic channels and techniques.

Diplomacy will be viewed as a continuous enterprise; precedent will rank high as a guideline for action. And the preferred diplomatic style will include a willingness to avoid firm and final decisions in international dealings. Diplomats, more than others, will tend to view any given international confrontation within a field of action possessing both temporal and spatial dimensions; that is, each problem must be considered in terms of its history and future, and in terms of other simultaneous diplomatic engagements. As much as possible the diplomat will tend to isolate himself from the domestic politics of both his own nation and the nations with which he deals. Diplomats will tend to be desirous of extending their own nation's power and influence, but rarely its internal values. International considerations such as the policies of allies and problems of military strategy are likely to rank higher as guides to action than the satisfaction of demands by economic, ideological, and other domestic interest groups.[27]

DEVELOPING NATIONS AND THE INTERNATIONAL SYSTEM

This rather lengthy introduction has been constructed to provide an outline of the international environment in terms most relevant to the developing nations. The process of decolonization, begun in the Western Hemisphere in the nineteenth century, and proceeding at headlong pace since World War II, may be considered a conservative, or (in game theory jargon) a kind of minimax response by the major powers to a series of international problems. The major European states were faced with protests and disturbances in their colonies which generally became too costly to continue repressing. Their reaction was to take the minimum steps necessary to see that the maximum amount of the old order could be maintained. This response was to grant to the protesting peoples formal membership in the traditional nation state system.

This system itself was undergoing change of course. The primary power centers were becoming polarized to the East and West of Europe,

[27] These assertions are in large measure derived from an attempt to link typical bureaucratic and other governmental behavior with the problems of foreign policy making. For a related attempt at this task, see Ernst Haas, "The Balance of Power as a Guide to Policy-Making," *The Journal of Politics* (August, 1953).

their former locale; new military and other technology was transforming old concepts of strategy; new doctrines were activating peoples in Europe and elsewhere; and new experiments in international organization were being undertaken. But for all this newness, the primary actions taken, in creating the United Nations and other moves, had the effect of bolstering, to the maximum feasible degree, the old, unintegrated, nation state system. As Herz has written, the notion of collective security, hailed as a milestone of progress between the two World Wars, was nothing but a new technique for protecting the territorial state.[28] A good deal of contemporary international law—such as the formal equality of states, and prohibitions on domestic intervention—is also carried over from an early period when it described more accurately than today the operative norms of the system.

The new states have been given more than formal membership in the world-wide international system; former colonial rulers have moved to structure the nature of domestic politics in these states so as to make them compatible with participation in the old system. As far as one can tell this was not done deliberately for the purpose of maintaining the old international system (in consonance with the hypothetical rule previously suggested); but whatever the reasons, to the extent that the Westernization process has been successful, one of its consequences would seem to be a strengthening of the traditional nation-state system. The attempt to maintain Western influence has taken many well-known forms. Western style parliamentary constitutions have been used as the basis for organizing newly-independent governments. Colonial economic relationships have been turned into trade and investment patterns. University training has been provided for potential leaders. Nationals of the former colonial power remain in the developing country to administer many of its private and government enterprises. To formal diplomatic relations are added, in most cases, extensive economic assistance and propaganda activities.

THE PULL OF THE OLD ORDER

For a number of reasons, the behavior of the developing states has in part conformed to the pattern of the traditional international system. Some of the participation in the game of power politics has been through circumstances not of their own choosing. Many of the underdeveloped countries contain within their boundaries critical raw materials; many are strategically located for military or transportation purposes; others have had attention centered on them as "showcases" in which, the Western countries hope, it can be demonstrated that non-Communist governmental systems have a future in the underdeveloped world. In global Cold War politics, not to mention the host of international subgames which have sprung up, the

---

[28] John Herz, *International Politics in the Atomic Age* (1959), pp. 76–95.

main participants have developed an eagerness for their position to be vindicated and supported by as many nations as possible. Thus, any nation, no matter how small or insignificant, becomes a potential voting supporter in the United Nations General Assembly. The quest for favorable votes has motivated much of the relations between the developed and developing nations. President John F. Kennedy was promising a substantial policy change indeed when he said in his inaugural address that the United States would offer assistance to the underdeveloped "not because we seek their votes."

Beyond gaining what limited advantages they may from their status as objects in major power competition, some states have actively essayed a role in the manner of traditional diplomacy. The first new nations— United States and the Latin Americans—rather early demonstrated this course of action. In their early years they strove for philosophical as well as political independence from Europe. This led to a search for new forms of international relations to replace those of Europe, which were seen as immoral in substance and ludicrously frivolous in outward forms and rituals.[29]

But this hoped for autonomy proved illusory as the political demands of international life soon worked their influence. From the very beginning of relations among North and South American states, political dialogue was conducted in a vocabulary of union and community; but actual policy was based on the normally discredited but still influential politics of international power.[30]

As time went on the forms and concepts employed in Western Hemisphere state-craft came to resemble more closely the model of traditional European diplomacy. The American states, in fact, took many of the traditions and rules of the European system and applied them with remarkable vigor and thoroughness. Diplomatic exchange has always been used by states to accord one another status and prestige. Through most of the nineteenth century the highest diplomatic rank, ambassador, was rarely used. Most diplomatic relations were conducted by envoys, ministers, and lower ranking officials. As American states embarked on diplomatic relations with one another, however, they frequently exchanged ambassadors in order to symbolize their high mutual esteem and respect. This practice, viewed by traditionalists as an undesirable inflation of diplomacy's symbolic currency, has spread throughout the world so that nearly all diplomatic exchanges are conducted at the ambassadorial level.[31]

The passage of time saw other elements of the traditional nation-state system carried to what seemed logical conclusions. The principle of non-

---

[29] See Warren Frederick Ilchman, *Professional Diplomacy in the United States 1779–1939* (1961), pp. 18–40.

[30] See J. Lloyd Mecham, *The United States and Inter-American Security, 1889–1960* (1961), pp. 33 ff.

[31] Harold Nicolson, *Diplomacy* (1964), pp. 100–1.

intervention, "discovered" in Latin America, was quite consistent with traditional concepts of international law which legitimized the territorial sovereignty on which the state system was based. The Drago Doctrine, one Latin American contribution to international legal thinking, was essentially an extension of the principle of territorial integrity; it held that force could not be used by foreign governments to collect public debts. Another Latin American principle is the Calvo Clause, a commercial contract provision by which foreigners must renounce the protection of their own government in dealing with the host government. Some writers have considered this a dubious legal doctrine, since it attempts to require a citizen to relinquish a right which belongs not to him, but to his own government.[32]

Some few other states around the world today are attempting to play the diplomatic game on a world-wide scale. One prominent indicator of the attention paid to traditional diplomacy is the number of diplomats which a country sends abroad. Much of the sending and receiving of information involved in diplomacy can be accomplished only through established foreign representatives. Furthermore, the size of a nation's diplomatic establishment is an indication of the amount of influence which the diplomatic style of policy making will have within the counsels of government. As can be seen in Table 12.1 below, there is a strong relationship between the level of a country's development and the size of its overseas diplomatic establishment. The less developed a country, the fewer diplomats it will tend to have. In crude terms, a country must have a sufficient Gross National Product to be able to "buy" diplomats. Pearson's correlation coefficient between GNP and size of diplomatic staff is .89. Some countries, however, have unexpectedly large diplomatic staffs. In the listing of countries with the most numerous diplomatic establishments abroad, two underdeveloped countries, the United Arab Republic and India, are found among the top ten.[33] These two states probably are among the most active of the underdeveloped in attempting to play a major diplomatic role in their own regions as well as on a world-wide basis. All underdeveloped countries, even when not as active as the UAR or India, maintain at least some secondary interest in the traditional system. For it provides formal equality; and it offers the conceptual basis for protests against real or alleged undesirable interventions in their domestic affairs.

We might also add that on occasion circumstances permit one of the less developed nations to play a far from trivial role in world affairs even from the most traditional viewpoint. India's confrontation with China; Egypt's seizure of the Suez Canal; Panama's imbroglio with the United States— these are a few recent examples in which underdeveloped nations have caused concern and frustration in even the mightiest chanceries. Given the

[32] See the discussion in J. L. Brierly (Sir Humphrey Waldock, ed.), *The Law of Nations* (1963), pp. 287–9.
[33] Steven J. Brams, "Diplomatic Exchanges, Trade, and Common Memberships in Intergovernmental Organizations: Statistics and Tables" (June, 1965 processed), p. 6.

right ingredients, which usually include hypersensitivity by the large powers, a critical resource attached to the underdeveloped nation and, either a risk taking government or an inflamed population, even the smallest international actor can steal the scene from the major players at least for a short while. Consequently it is not necessary to construct, as some have done, a nonpolitical, or powerless analysis of the role of the underdeveloped states in world politics.[34] Their activities as communicators, mediators, and general third-party safety valves may be important as well, but this does not encompass the full extent of their role in contemporary international affairs.

ASPIRATIONS OF THE DEVELOPING STATES: NEW WINE IN NEW BOTTLES

But these considerations should not detract from our previously stated hypothesis. We are concerned with the extent to which the evolving international style of the developing nations differs from that of the older nations—which is essentially to repair and reform the traditional system to help it endure under radically changed conditions. Under this hypothesis we can expect the developing states to act within the rules of traditional power politics only out of necessity and, if their objectives are to be fulfilled, only as a temporary expedient. Their vision for the future may be quite different from either their former colonial masters or the two superpower bloc leaders. Their stated goals for changes in the international system, under the model suggested here, would not be, like those of the more established powers, mere rhetoric to pacify the more extreme reformers within their own territories, or to serve as a cover for conserving the old system. If they are in fact diverging from elite behavior in the developed world, the leaders in the underdeveloped world are nevertheless showing parallel behavior in one sense. They would be adopting those domestic and international political strategies which minimize the risks of leadership and maximize the conditions which consolidate the government and provide it with the widest number of alternative courses of action.

It is possible to adduce several sets of evidence in support of this hypothesis of a nontraditional evolution of international behavior by the underdeveloped states. In the first place almost any alternative to the traditional nation state system would probably be looked at with favor by leaders in the developing nations. The old system represents to them the process of their national enslavement, their exploitation as pawns in the European power struggle and the vehicle by which their people were often drained economically and brutally treated. Furthermore, their reading of Western history has led them to conclude that the traditional system has

[34] See, for example, J. W. Burton, *International Relations, A General Theory* (1965).

little to recommend it in terms of stability or justice, especially as far as small states are concerned.

Beyond this negative feeling is the desire of peoples throughout the Third World to reassert cultural patterns which have often been repressed by outside forces. One can spend long hours arguing about the existence of a "Latin American Spirit," "African personality," or similar alleged cultural distinctions. And one could argue just as long over what implications any of these characteristics have for unique styles of politics and foreign policy. But an "objective" analysis is hardly significant as long as the peoples themselves believe in these differences, since the belief leads to a desire to experiment and assert independence of action. Anything new and different has a headstart over the received tradition from foreign sources.

The course which the new leaders are attempting to chart for themselves is also influenced by the reciprocal linkages between their domestic politics and the international system which envelopes them. Let us state directly a further hypothesis which was implied earlier in the discussion of the relationship between domestic politics and the international system: the more that domestic leaders do not preside over a strong and stable political system (the more that the in system is not dominated by a subsystem), the more that the leaders will seek alternatives to an unintegrated international system. In the terminology of linkage analysis, we can say that the conditions in the developing nations induce leaders to move away from a system in which the great bulk of national-international linkages are funneled through the formal institutions of government.[35]

In most of the developing nations the linkages between domestic and international politics create policy tendencies quite different from those in the stronger nations. The general foreign policy goals of these states may be viewed as an attempt to replace the formal and informal rules of the prevailing unintegrated international system with a stable and tolerable integrated system which eliminates the preeminence of the territorial state as well as the style of representation, bargaining, and competition which accompanies that preeminence.

In large measure the search for an integrated international system is simply an attempt to make the best of a *fait accompli* which history has rendered to the underdeveloped nations. In ways already alluded to, the concept of a unitary state interacting with other similar states cannot be as fruitfully applied to the underdeveloped nations as it has been in studying the international relations of Western, industrialized societies.

Much has been made of this set of foreign policy motivations. The leaders of underdeveloped nations have been termed greatly concerned, if not obsessed, with international inputs which circumvent governmental control. Indeed, leaders have been accused of using foreign intervention as a scapegoat for every unmanageable problem which their countries

[35] See Chapter 3.

face.[36] These accusations may have some validity. But aside from their accuracy as normative judgments about leaders, they raise a question about the likely persistence of current foreign policy attitudes. The implication of such analysis is that present attitudes are but a "stage"—like a child's lisping or talking back to parents—which will be left behind when and if time brings about an approximation of the modernized, stable societies in the developing world. Political leaders will then, so the argument implies, revise their viewpoints and play the game of international politics like the older states. It should be clear that the hypothesis we have advanced is in direct contrast to this view of conventional evolution of the developing states.

It seems at least possible that the trends of national development will create permanent differences in the approach of these nations toward international relations. Dissent against the present system is more than a mere excuse for unfulfilled promises and more than an attempt by leaders to glorify themselves and take the minds of the followers off problems at home. Their behavior stems, in part at least, from the most basic political decisions and outlooks of the leaders of the present and, in all likelihood, the future.

To begin with, there are both positive and negative consequences of a linkage framework in which outputs and inputs are exchanged broadly through the political system (rather than through the formal institutions, as is the case in an unintegrated system). In fact, the total net result of the diffused linkage pattern which obtains in the underdeveloped nations today may be decidedly favorable. Much of the hard-core problem solving and physical construction necessary to maintain a momentum of development is accomplished only through intricate coalitions between the host government and foreign national, international, and nongovernmental personnel and resources. In virtually all the developing states foreign and local personnel cooperate to build roads and other public works, promote health and sanitation, provide technical assistance and training, and a wide scale of other related activities. Many internal institutions, even those such as education, traditionally a key element in the syndrome of exclusive national self-consciousness, are "multinational" in the sense that the original organization and sustaining resources are derived at least as much from outside the territory as within it.[37]

Furthermore, the process by which many leaders attain and attempt to hold on to political power is dependent upon a wide range of unconventional international activities. Through their personal skills and their ability to discern and exploit sympathetic factions in the developed nations,

---

[36] Robert C. Good, "State-Building as a Determinant of Foreign Policy in the New States," in Laurence W. Martin (ed.), *Neutralism and Nonalignment* (1962), pp. 3–12.

[37] For the use of the phrase "multinational" and many of the ideas in this section, I am indebted to Professor Julian R. Friedman's unpublished paper, "East African Diplomacy."

the new political leaders have frequently acquired international experience and prestige long before they took charge of their own governments. Nehru, Kenyatta, Mboya, Nyerere, and others are just a few of the leaders whose international activities preceded, and helped facilitate their rise to national power. Nor does this style of behavior cease with national independence. The familiar practice by which American political aspirants play the diplomat in order to gain influence at home is but child's play compared to much of the political infighting in underdeveloped nations. Individuals are constantly on the look out for open or covert foreign allies in their struggles for personal and partisan advantage in the new nations.[38]

The relationship between leaders and publics in the underdeveloped countries adds further reason for seeking alternatives to the competition of standard international politics. A tendency toward what Kaplan terms system-dominant political systems is a major characteristic of politics in the developing states. The net result of internal (as well as international) politics has generally resulted in a policy of neutralism, or nonalignment for these states. (Although factions within the states might be very much aligned.) Nonalignment has important implications for the international system, of course. Nonalignment can be viewed as an updated version of the role of holder of the balance, or it may be seen as a communication function.

But it also has implications concerning internal conditions of these nations. The instability, the competition among counter-elites, the defensive claims for cultural and philosophical uniqueness vis-à-vis the developed societies, and the monumental tasks of development all contribute to a style of policy making which differs markedly from the characteristics of the more developed states outlined above.

This tendency is enhanced by the lack of foreign policy bureaucracies which in the older states contribute their special perspective on the making of foreign policy (see Table 12.1). In the newer states a diplomatic service was the one administrative structure to which the colonial powers devoted least attention in the preparations for statehood. Foreign relations remained the prerogative of Whitehall or the Quai d'Orsay right down to the moment of independence, even after many domestic functions had already been turned over to the future government. Foreign offices have, consequently, been built almost from scratch. Typically, they have remained small, suffering in the competition for personnel and resources with government activities more directly related to the problems of development. They have frequently been manned by young officials with limited experience in the intricacies of diplomacy. They have likewise possessed uncertain influence in the counsels of their own governments.

The training that has been received, from the former colonial power or from private organizations such as the Carnegie Endowment for Inter-

---

[38] Especially noteworthy is the domestic infighting among such African political leaders as Oginga Odinga, Tom Mboya, and Julius Nyerere, *ibid.*, pp. 12–13.

national Peace, has tended to provide instruction in emulating Western diplomatic forms. This has not necessarily produced diplomats with special skills and orientations most relevant to the particular needs of their own nations.[39]

Table 12.1—The Lower a Country's Level of Development, the Smaller the Size of the Diplomatic Staff

Size of Diplomatic Staff	LEVEL OF DEVELOPMENT			
	Very Underdeveloped	Underdeveloped	Intermediate	High
0–49	.41	.12	.18	.05
50–99	.38	.18	.00	.05
100–199	.16	.41	.29	.16
200–399	.06	.24	.48	.36
400 and above	.02	.06	.06	.37
TOTALS	1.00	1.00	1.00	1.00
(N)	(19)	(17)	(17)	(56)

$X^2 = 67.37$ Kendall's Tau $= .50$

SOURCES: Levels of Development, Arthur S. Banks and Robert S. Textor, *A Cross-Polity Survey* (1963); Diplomatic staff size, Steven J. Brams, "Diplomatic Exchanges, Trade, and Common Memberships in Intergovernmental Organization: Statistics and Tables."

Furthermore, even the small staffs which do exist must frequently compete with other domestic ministries and officials who are likely to have extensive international concerns themselves. Just as the conduct of domestic policy has become "internationalized" in these nations, the conduct of foreign policy has in many respects become "domesticized."

Policy making tends to follow a mirror-image of the bureaucratic style outlined above: the focus of attentions and the choice of international friends and enemies is more changeable and more unpredictable than the traditional style. Policy is more likely to be directed toward seeking solutions and final answers to problems. Policy is more likely to concentrate on isolated events and individual problems which happen to be salient from one time to another. Judgments about other states tend to be made largely in terms of their forms of government or other internal criteria as well as in terms of their international behavior. Policy is motivated by a desire to share and extend the nation's own values to an extent bordering on cultural, if not political, imperialism. And domestic factors, such as the satisfaction of group demands and provision for development resources, will rank at least equally high with external criteria in conceiving the national interests.

[39] *Ibid.*, pp. 16–17.

RESTRUCTURING THE INTERNATIONAL SYSTEM

What Rosenau has termed "the organizational environment"[40] takes on special importance in the national-international linkages of the developing polities. The UN in particular stands as a telling symbol of the ambiguous position in which the developing nations find themselves. On the one hand it represents the arrival of the weaker nations into membership with formal equality in the traditional system. It affords the developing nations their easiest and least risky opportunity to participate in the major diplomatic issues of the day. It also allows them their most efficient means of gathering and sending information concerning the world about them. The under-developed nations have far more government-to-government contacts through the UN and other international organizations than through bi-lateral diplomatic establishments.[41] The less developed states have low international organization membership, as well as small diplomatic staffs. But the ratio obtained when we divide the number of countries dealt with through organization by the number dealt with bilaterally is much higher for the underdeveloped states. The lower a country's GNP, for example, the relatively more organizational rather than bilateral contacts it will have (See Table 12.2). The UN has been a central forum for agitation to

Table 12.2—Countries with Low GNP Deal with Other Governments through International Organization more than through Bilateral Diplomacy

RATIO OF ORGANIZATIONAL TO DIPLOMATIC CONTACTS	GROSS NATIONAL PRODUCT			
	Very low	Low	Medium	High
High	.41	.12	.12	0.0
Medium	.40	.56	.20	0.0
Low	.08	.20	.48	.16
Very Low	.11	.12	.20	.84
TOTAL	1.00	1.00	1.00	1.00
(N)	(24)	(24)	(25)	(24)

$X^2 = 63.56$ Kendall's Tau $= -.56$

SOURCES: Gross National Product, Bruce Russett et al., *World Handbook of Political and Social Indicators* (1964); Organizational and Diplomatic contacts, Brams, *op. cit.*

substitute the nation state system in place of the remnants of the colonial system. At the same time, however, the UN represents the goals of a new world of a more highly integrated system implied in the Charter's opening words, "We the *peoples* of the United Nations."

[40] See Chapter 3.
[41] Brams, *op. cit.*, pp. 6–11.

Insofar as the UN can evolve into the center of decision making for world-wide international problems, the developing nations will be able to participate in these decisions on terms most favorable to them. The power of numbers, as in the General Assembly, is more notable in the UN than elsewhere. The battles over words and symbols may be peripheral to many of the great international struggles, but they are not totally irrelevant. And it is in this realm that the developing nations, especially as they can act as a bloc to advance their purposes, are able to hold greatest sway.

The UN also serves as the potential vehicle for transforming the world arena into a more community minded cooperative system. The cultural, technical, and economic assistance conducted through the UN serves as double function. The resources obtained add a desirable increment of assistance in development. Organizational assistance also provides, according to the functionalist analysis of the leaders in the developing nations, the framework for more extensive integrative cooperations in the future.

The desire to bring about an institutionalized reordering of the international environment has helped direct attention to local as well as global problems. It may be, in fact, that regional organization is the more actively growing sector of system transformation. Although the motives differ from one area to another, most of the developing nations are concerned with building institutions among neighboring states for political, social, and economic purposes. Regional development affords several advantages for the underdeveloped states. Even the most globally minded of the newer states have the most extensive diplomatic, economic, and functional transactions with neighboring or near-by states.[42]

The belief in a Latin American, African, Asian, or Arab "special personality" or unique style of operation finds expression in geographically exclusive organizations. At the functional level, regional groupings can help make maximum use of the scarce local talents and resources available for development purposes. In some cases regional institutions may serve as an effective conduit for external aid which insulates the recipients from demands often accompanying bilateral assistance. The Asian Development Bank and the Inter-American Development Bank seem likely candidates for this role. In the political-security field regional institutions seem equally attractive. They simultaneously perform two functions: they bring together, in considering a dispute, nations which are most closely involved with the issue and are therefore less likely to engage in the unproductive moralizing which so often marked UN debates; and insofar as they are successful they can help insulate the local region from competitive intervention by the major powers.

The Organization of American States, the Organization of African Unity, and the Arab League—the three leading regional institutions containing underdeveloped nations—are currently prey to a formidable array

[42] *Ibid.*, pp. 15–27.

of problems. The OAS suffers from the internal struggle over whether to be a genuine collective organization or merely a cover for United States adventures south of the border. The OAU and the Arab League are stymied from achievement of shared goals by a host of individual and collective divergencies and hesitations among their members. But to say that regionalism is weak today is not, in the eyes of the underdeveloped nations, to say that it should be weak tomorrow. Considerable energies continue to be directed toward activities in this field.

PROSPECTS FOR CHANGE

In closing it may be wise to recall the critical distinction between the intentions and capabilities of states. For this distinction is just as relevant in our present discussion as it is in the analysis of traditional nation-state behavior. We have argued the proposition that the linkage pattern between domestic politics and international system is leading the underdeveloped states to seek a quite radically revised international order.

Even if this is true, it is no assurance that their desires will be served. The states we have been discussing are still, after all, on the outside looking in as far as the major decisions concerning the shape of future international events are concerned. They can petition, dissent, and protest, but there is relatively little they can do, in the short run at least, to make others move toward the goals they favor. And it must be recognized that part of their weakness is a common tendency to be much more active in encouraging other states to lessen their independence and sovereign rights than they are in surrendering their own.

On the other hand, however, they are not completely hypocritical, nor are they without allies in the developed world. It must be recognized that they have actually taken a variety of steps to share problem solving across national boundaries and to permit (occasionally even encourage) external influence and comment upon domestic matters. These steps range from the rather limited and concrete to the broad and symbolic. Witness, for example, the fact that several African nations have provided in their constitutions the possibility of submerging their sovereignty into a genuine African political union.

Finally, if their vision of the future is not shared by the policy makers and diplomats of the developed world today, it is shared by many subgovernmental groups in the industrialized states. For better or worse, the logic of the developing states is supported by the scientists, technicians, economic managers and others who have been, in their own diverse fashions, also undermining the theory and practice of the traditional state system. In any event the linkage patterns of the underdeveloped nations are generating pressures and opportunities for the rich and poor nations to create new forms for the future international system.

INDEX

BOOKS PUBLISHED FOR THE
CENTER OF INTERNATIONAL STUDIES

Published by Princeton University Press, Princeton, N.J.

The Appeals of Communism, Gabriel A. Almond (1954).
Military Policy and National Security, William W. Kaufmann, ed. (1956).
The War Potential of Nations, Klaus Knorr (1956).
Guerrilla Communism in Malaya, Lucian W. Pye (1956).
The Political Process and Foreign Policy: The Making of the Japanese Peace Settlement, Bernard C. Cohen (1957).
Theory and Reality in Public International Law, Charles de Visscher, trans. by P. E. Corbett (1957).
Party Politics in India: The Development of a Multi-Party System, Myron Weiner (1957).
Law in Diplomacy, Percy E. Corbett (1959).
NATO and American Security, Klaus Knorr, ed. (1959).
Economic Integration: Theoretical Assumption and Consequences of European Integration, Rolf Sannwald and Jacques Stohler, trans. by Herman Karreman, Foreword by Klaus Knorr (1959).
The Politics of the Developing Areas, Gabriel A. Almond and James Coleman, eds. (1960).
On Thermonuclear War, Herman Kahn (1960).
Tojo and the Coming of the War, Robert J. C. Butow (1961).
The International System: Theoretical Essays, Klaus Knorr and Sidney Verba, eds. (1961).
Deterrence and Defense: Toward a Theory of National Security, Glenn H. Snyder (1961).
Small Groups and Political Behavior: A Study of Leadership, Sidney Verba (1961).
The Civic Culture: Political Attitudes and Democracy in Five Nations, Gabriel A. Almond and Sidney Verba (1963).
The Press and Foreign Policy, Bernard C. Cohen (1963).

Peace-Making and the Settlement with Japan, Frederick S. Dunn (1963).
National Leadership and Foreign Policy: A Case Study in the Mobilization of Public Support, James N. Rosenau (1963).
Nigerian Political Parties: Power in an Emergent African Nation, Richard L. Sklar (1963).
Communism and Revolution: The Strategic Uses of Political Violence, Cyril E. Black and Thomas P. Thornton, eds. (1964).
Britain and the European Community 1955–1963, Miriam Camps (1964).
International Aspects of Civil Strife, James N. Rosenau, ed. (1964).
The Third World in Soviet Prospective: Studies by Soviet Writers on the Developing Areas, Thomas P. Thornton, ed. (1964).
Security and Disarmament, Richard A. Falk and Richard J. Barnet, eds. (1965).
Conflict and Decision-Making in Soviet Russia: A Case Study of Agricultural Policy, 1953–1963, Sidney L. Ploss (1965).
The Ecological Perspective on Human Affairs, Harold and Margaret Sprout (1965).
Political Development in Pakistan, Karl von Vorys (1965).
On the Uses of Military Power in the Nuclear Age, Klaus Knorr (1966).
Division and Cohesion in Democracy: A Study of Norway, Harry Eckstein (1966).
Southeast Asian Tribes: Minorities and Nations, Peter Kunstadter, ed. (1967).
The Revolutionary Personality: Lenin, Trotsky, Gandhi, E. Victor Wolfenstein (1967).
The Intermediaries: Third Parties in International Crises, Oran R. Young (1967).
Affluence and the French Worker in the Fourth Republic, Richard F. Hamilton (1967).
World Order and Local Disorder: The United Nations and Internal Conflict, Linda Miller (1967).
Tanzania: Party Transformation and Economic Development, Henry Bienen (1967).
Britain and the Russian Civil War: Anglo-Soviet Relations, 1917–1921, Volume II, Richard H. Ullman (1968).
France in the Age of the Scientific State, Robert Gilpin, Jr. (1968).

Published by Frederick A. Praeger, Inc., New York

Limited Strategic War, Klaus Knorr and Thornton Read, eds. (1962).
A Theory of Strategic War, George Modelski (1962).
Guerrillas in the 1960s, Peter Paret and John W. Shy (1962).
Peace-Keeping by United Nations Forces: From Suez Through the Congo, Arthur L. Burns and Nina Heathcote (1963).
Law, Morality, and War in the Contemporary World, Richard A. Falk (1963).
French Revolutionary Warfare from Indochina to Algeria: The Analysis of a Political and Military Doctrine, Peter Paret (1964).

Published by The Free Press, New York

Internal War, Harry Eckstein, ed. (1964).
Domestic Sources of Foreign Policy, James N. Rosenau, ed. (1967).

Published by Harper & Row, New York

The Dynamics of Modernization: A Study in Comparative History, Cyril E. Black (1966).

Published by Columbia University Press, New York

The UN Secretary-General and the Maintenance of Peace, Leon Gordenker (1967).